POETRY

FOCUS

2016

LEAVING CERTIFICATE POEMS & NOTES FOR ENGLISH HIGHER LEVEL

MARTIN KIERAN & FRANCES ROCKS

Gill & Macmillan

Gill & Macmillan
Hume Avenue
Park West
Dublin 12
with associated companies throughout the world
www.gillmacmillan.ie

© Martin Kieran and Frances Rocks 2014
978 0717 1 5955 0

Design by Tanya M Ross, Elementinc.ie

The paper used in this book is made from the wood pulp of managed forests. For every tree
felled, at least one tree is planted, thereby renewing natural resources.

Any links to external websites should not be construed as an endorsement by Gill & Macmillan
of the content or view of the linked material. Furthermore it cannot be guaranteed that all
external links will be live.

For permission to reproduce photographs, the authors and publisher gratefully acknowledge the
following:

© Alamy: 24, 43, 49, 83, 116, 121, 135, 193, 200, 274, 284, 319, 326, 354, 396, 409, 449,
459, 470, 475, 484, 489, 494, 515, 532, 548, 561; © The Art Archive: 503; © Bridgeman Art
Library: 87, 140, 268, 391, 433; © Collins Agency: 415; © Corbis: 12, 445; © Francine Scialom
Greenblatt: 165; © Getty Images: 5, 18, 30, 55, 63, 78, 111, 131, 152, 178, 215, 229, 246, 300, 306,
312, 343, 349, 369, 376, 381, 386, 402, 421, 427, 454, 480, 511, 527, 544, 566; © Imagefile: 92,
96, 101 ,106 ,465, 506, 539; © Irish Times: 222; © The Josef and Yaye Breitenbach Charitable
Foundation, New York: 1; © Mary Evans Picture Library: 75, 260, 333; © PD Smith: 557; © Press
Association: 37; © RTÉ Stills Library: 338, 365; © Saint Patrick's Cathedral: 553; © Shutterstock:
146, 157, 208, 236, 252, 279; © Sportsfile: 186; © TopFoto: 297, 520.

The authors and publisher have made every effort to trace all copyright holders, but if any has
been inadvertently overlooked we would be pleased to make the necessary arrangement at the
first opportunity.

CONTENTS

Introduction

Poetry Focus is a new, modern poetry textbook for Leaving Certificate Higher Level English. It includes all the prescribed poems for 2016 as well as succinct commentaries on each one. In addition, there are sample student paragraphs on each poem, sample question plans and full graded sample essays. Well-organised and easily accessible study notes provide all the necessary information to allow students to explore the poems and to develop their own individual responses.

- **Explorations** (a series of short questions) follow the text of each poem. These allow students to make initial responses before any in-depth study or analysis. Exploration questions provide a good opportunity for written and/or oral exercises.
- **Study notes** highlight the main features of the poet's subject matter and style. These discussion notes will enhance the student's own critical appreciation through focused group work and/or written exercises. Analytical skills are developed in a coherent, practical way to give students confidence in articulating their own personal responses to the poems and poets.
- **Graded sample paragraphs** aid students in fluently structuring and developing valid points and in using relevant quotations and reference in support.
- **Key quotes** encourage students to select their own individual combination of references from a poem and to write brief commentaries on specific quotations.
- **Sample essay plans** on each poet's work illustrate how to interpret a question and recognise the particular nuances of key words in examination questions. Evaluation of these essay plans increases student confidence in working out clear responses for themselves.
- **There is no single 'correct' approach** to answering the poetry question. Candidates are free to respond in any appropriate way that shows good knowledge of and engagement with the prescribed poems.
- **Full sample Leaving Certificate essays**, graded and accompanied by experienced examiners' comments, show the student exactly what is required to achieve a successful A grade in the Leaving Cert exam and to develop a real enthusiasm for English poetry. This is essential in identifying the task as required by the PCLM marking scheme.

HOW IS THE PRESCRIBED POETRY QUESTION MARKED?

Marking is done (ex. 50 marks) by reference to the PCLM criteria for assessment:

- Clarity of purpose (P): 30% of the total (15 marks).
- Coherence of delivery (C): 30% of the total (15 marks).
- Efficiency of language use (L): 30% of the total (15 marks).
- Accuracy of mechanics (M): 10% of the total (5 marks).

Each answer will be in the form of a response to a specific task requiring candidates to:

- Display a clear and purposeful engagement with the set task. (P)
- Sustain the response in an appropriate manner over the entire answer. (C)
- Manage and control language appropriate to the task. (L)
- Display levels of accuracy in spelling and grammar appropriate to the required/ chosen register. (M)

GENERAL

'Students at Higher Level will be required to study a representative selection from the work of eight poets: a representative selection would seek to reflect the range of a poet's themes and interests and exhibit his/her characteristic style and viewpoint. Normally the study of at least six poems by each poet would be expected.' (DES English Syllabus, 6.3)

The marking scheme guidelines from the State Examinations Commission state that in the case of each poet, the candidates have **freedom of choice** in relation to the poems studied. In addition, there is **not a finite list of any 'poet's themes and interests'**.

Note that in responding to the question set on any given poet, the candidates must refer to the poem(s) they have studied but are not required to refer to any specific **poem(s), nor are they expected to discuss or refer to all the poems they have chosen to study**.

In each of the questions in **Prescribed Poetry**, the underlying nature of the task is the invitation to the candidates to **engage with the poems themselves**.

EXAM ADVICE

- You are not expected to write about any **set number of poems** in the examination. You might decide to focus in detail on a small number of poems, or you could choose to write in a more general way on several poems.
- Most candidates write one or two well-developed **paragraphs** on each of the poems they have chosen for discussion. In other cases, a paragraph will focus on one specific aspect of the poet's work. When discussing recurring themes or features of style, appropriate cross-references to other poems may also be useful.
- Reflect on central **themes** and viewpoints in the poems you discuss. Comment also on the use of language and the poet's distinctive **style**. Examine imagery, tone, structure, rhythm and rhyme. Be careful not to simply list aspects of style, such as alliteration or

repetition. There's little point in mentioning that a poet uses sound effects or metaphors without discussing the effectiveness of such characteristics.

- Focus on **the task** you have been given in the poetry question. Identify the key terms in the wording of the question and think of similar words for these terms. This will help you develop a relevant and coherent personal response in keeping with the PCLM marking scheme criteria.

- Always root your answers in the text of the poems. Support the points you make with **relevant reference and quotation**. Make sure your own expression is fresh and lively. Avoid awkward expressions, such as 'It says in the poem that...'. Look for alternatives: 'There is a sense of...', 'The tone seems to suggest...', 'It's evident that...', etc.

- Neat, **legible handwriting** will help to make a positive impression on examiners. Corrections should be made by simply drawing a line through the mistake. Scored-out words distract attention from the content of your work.

- Keep the emphasis on why particular poets **appeal to you**. Consider the continuing relevance or significance of a poet's work. Perhaps you have shared some of the feelings or experiences expressed in the poems. Avoid starting answers with prepared biographical sketches. Details of a poet's life are better used when discussing how the poems themselves were shaped by such experiences.

- Remember that the examination encourages **individual engagement** with the prescribed poems. Poetry can make us think and feel and imagine. It opens our minds to the wonderful possibilities of language and ideas. Your interaction with the poems is what matters most. Study notes and critical interpretations are all there to be challenged. Read the poems carefully and have confidence in expressing your own personal response.

ELIZABETH BISHOP

1911-79

'The armored cars of dreams, continued to let us do so many dangerous things.'

Elizabeth Bishop was born in Worcester, Massachusetts, in 1911. During her early life she experienced a series of family tragedies. She spent part of her childhood with her Canadian grandparents following her father's death and mother's hospitalisation. She then lived with various relatives who, according to Bishop, took care of her because they felt sorry for her. These unsettling events, along with the memories of her youth, inspired her to read poetry – and eventually to write it. Like many poets and artists, Bishop was a great observer with a vivid sense of place. After studying English at university, she travelled extensively and lived in New York, Florida and, for 17 years, Brazil. She also taught at several American colleges. Throughout her life she suffered from ill health and depression. As a poet, she wrote sparingly, publishing only five slim volumes in 35 years. However, her work received high acclaim. 'I think geography comes first in my work,' she told an interviewer, 'and then animals. But I like people, too. I've written a few poems about people.' Recurring themes in her refreshing and thought-provoking poetry include childhood experiences, travel, the natural world, loneliness, detachment and the art of writing itself. Bishop died suddenly in her Boston apartment on 6 October 1979. She was 68 years old. Her poetry continues to gain widespread recognition and study.

Prescribed Poems   HIGHER LEVEL

1   THE FISH

I caught a tremendous fish
and held him beside the boat
half out of water, with my hook
fast in a corner of his mouth.
He didn't fight.   5
He hadn't fought at all.
He hung a grunting weight,
battered and venerable
and homely. Here and there
his brown skin hung in strips   10
like ancient wallpaper,
and its pattern of darker brown
was like wallpaper:
shapes like full-blown roses
stained and lost through age.   15
He was speckled with barnacles,
fine rosettes of lime,
and infested
with tiny white sea-lice,
and underneath two or three   20
rags of green weed hung down.
While his gills were breathing in
the terrible oxygen
– the frightening gills,
fresh and crisp with blood,   25
that can cut so badly –
I thought of the coarse white flesh
packed in like feathers,
the big bones and the little bones,
the dramatic reds and blacks   30
of his shiny entrails,
and the pink swim-bladder
like a big peony.
I looked into his eyes
which were far larger than mine   35
but shallower, and yellowed,
the irises backed and packed
with tarnished tinfoil

seen though the lenses
of old scratched isinglass.   40
They shifted a little, but not
to return my stare.
– It was more like the tipping
of an object toward the light.
I admired his sullen face,   45
the mechanism of his jaw,
and then I saw
that from his lower lip
– if you could call it a lip –
grim, wet, and weaponlike,   50
hung five old pieces of fish-line,
or four and a wire leader
with the swivel still attached,
with all their five big hooks
grown firmly in his mouth.   55
A green line, frayed at the end
where he broke it, two heavier lines,
and a fine black thread
still crimped from the strain and snap
when it broke and he got away.   60
Like medals with their ribbons
frayed and wavering,
a five-haired beard of wisdom
trailing from his aching jaw.
I stared and stared   65
and victory filled up
the little rented boat,
from the pool of bilge
where oil had spread a rainbow
around the rusted engine   70
to the bailer rusted orange,
the sun-cracked thwarts,
the oarlocks on their strings,
the gunnels – until everything
was rainbow, rainbow, rainbow!   75
And I let the fish go.

'He hung a grunting weight'

GLOSSARY

1   *tremendous*: huge, startling, fearsome.
8   *venerable*: ancient, worthy of respect.
9   *homely*: comfortable, easy-going, unpretentious, plain.
17 *rosettes*: rose-shaped decorations made of ribbon, often awarded as prizes.
19 *sea-lice*: small parasites that live on the skin of fish.
24 *gills*: breathing organs of fish.
31 *entrails*: internal organs.
33 *peony*: large, flamboyant flower, usually pink.
37 *irises*: coloured parts of an eye.
40 *isinglass*: gelatine-like substance obtained from the bodies of fish, opaque.

45 *sullen*: bad-tempered, sulky.
46 *mechanism*: workings.
52 *leader*: wire connecting fishhook and line.
59 *crimped*: pressed into ridges.
62 *frayed*: unravelled, worn.
68 *bilge*: dirty water that collects in the bottom of a boat.
71 *bailer*: bucket that scoops water out of a boat.
72 *thwarts*: rowers' benches.
73 *oarlocks*: metal devices for holding oars.
74 *gunnels*: upper edges of the side of a boat.

EXPLORATIONS

1. List two details that appealed to you in the description of the fish in lines 1–15. Why did they impact on you? Were they unusual or did they appeal to your senses? Support your response with quotation from the poem.

2. What is the poet's attitude towards the fish? Where does it change as the poem progresses? Give a reason for this change. Refer closely to the poem in your response.

3. Who had the 'victory' in this situation – the fish or Bishop? Why did you come to this conclusion? Support your discussion with clear references from the poem.

STUDY NOTES

'The Fish' is from Elizabeth Bishop's first published collection, North and South *(1946).
She lived in Florida during the 1930s and the poem is based on her experience of
catching a large jewfish at Key West. Bishop once said, 'I like painting probably better
than I like poetry' and 'The Fish' is certainly a very visual poem. Bishop uses the fish as
a way of exploring a 'green' awareness, the respect for nature and all living things.*

The poem's **opening line** is direct and forceful ('I caught a tremendous fish').
Bishop's use of the personal pronoun 'I' gives a sense of immediacy and intimacy.
The adjective 'tremendous' reflects the **poet's breathless excitement and awe
at this magnificent specimen of fish**. The act of catching the fish is described
in a personal, down-to-earth way. Bishop once said, 'I always tell the truth in my
poems ... that's exactly how it happened.' The fish is 'half out of water', no longer in
its natural habitat.

In **line 5,** the focus shifts from the person who caught the fish to the fish itself. **It
is now given a personality**: 'He didn't fight.' The onomatopoeic 'grunting' allows
us to be part of this scene, as we hear the distressed noises from the gasping, ugly
('homely'), exhausted ('battered') fish. Then another facet of the fish is presented
to us: it is 'venerable', ancient and worthy of reverence. Bishop the participant
is giving way to Bishop the observer. While in college, Bishop met Marianne
Moore, a famous American poet whose focus was on the accurate description of
a particular thing. This poetic movement was known as imagism. We can see the
similarity of style between the two poets in Bishop's description of the fish: 'Here
and there/his brown skin hung in strips/like ancient wallpaper'.

The surface **detail is painstakingly and imaginatively described** ('like full-
blown roses'). There seems to be an attempt to domesticate the creature, but the
sordid reality of the blotches on the skin is also noted ('stained and lost through
age'). The texture of the fish is described graphically, as if we were examining the
skin under a microscope: 'speckled', 'infested', 'rags'. Colours ('lime', 'white' and
'green') help convey this vivid picture. The wildness of the creature is caught in the
detailed phrasing 'frightening gills,/fresh and crisp with blood' **(line 24)**. Its interior
is also imagined ('pink swim-bladder/like a big peony'). These original and striking
images appeal to both our visual and tactile senses.

Bishop's delight in catching this fine specimen soon gives way to an **emotional
involvement with the fish** and his struggle for survival **(line 34)**. She compares

his eyes to her own ('far larger'). She notes the wear and tear from a long, hard life ('yellowed'). The irises are 'backed and packed/with tarnished tinfoil'. Here, assonance and alliteration give emphasis to the image. However, the fish's eyes are unresponsive, so there seems to be no interplay between creature and poet. This suggests both the independence and the vulnerability of the fish.

Progression in the poem is shown in the verbs: 'I caught', 'I thought', 'I looked' and, in **line 45**, 'I admired'. The **poet admires the resolute nature of the fish** ('his sullen face'). This fish has survived previous battles ('five big hooks/grown firmly in his mouth'). Precise detail emphasises the severity of these battles ('A green line, frayed at the end/where he broke it'). Military language highlights the effort the fish has made to survive: 'weaponlike', 'medals'. Bishop's sympathy is clear as she notes the fish's 'aching jaw'. For the fish, it is clear that the pain of battle remains.

Line 65 shows the poet transfixed ('I stared and stared'). Now the scene expands from a single fisher in a 'little rented boat' to something of **universal significance** ('victory' fills up the boat). Ordinary details (the 'bilge', the 'thwarts' and the 'gunnels') are transformed. The oil has 'spread a rainbow'. Everything is coloured and Bishop's relationship with the fish changes. She exercises mercy. A moment of epiphany occurs and she lets 'the fish go'. The tension in the poem is finally released. The underlying drama contained between the opening line ('I caught a tremendous fish') and the closing line ('And I let the fish go.') has been resolved. **Victory belongs to both the poet and the fish**. The fish is free; the poet has seen and understood.

This poem is a long narrative with a clear beginning, middle and end. Bishop has chosen a suitably unrhymed form. The metre is appropriate for the speaking voice: dimeter (two stresses) and trimeter (three stresses). Short run-on lines suggest the poet excitedly examining her catch and the recurring use of dashes indicates her thought process as she moves from delight to wonder, empathy and, finally, comprehension. The concluding rhyming couplet brings a definite and satisfying resolution to the dramatic tension.

ANALYSIS

Elizabeth Bishop has been praised for her 'painterly eye'. Discuss this aspect of her style in 'The Fish'. Support your views with close reference to the poem.

Sample Paragraph

An artist looks, then sees, orders, recreates and leads both themselves and their viewers to a new insight. I think Elizabeth Bishop accomplishes all this in her poem 'The Fish'. The poet looks at the event ('I caught a tremendous fish') and then moves to describe the fish, using striking images ('brown skin hung in strips/like ancient wallpaper'). Like a camera, she pans this way and that, making us see also 'its pattern of darker brown' with 'shapes like full-blown roses'. She leads us to imagine the exotic interior of the fish, its 'coarse white flesh/packed in like feathers'. We see the order and symmetry, the 'dramatic reds and blacks'. If Bishop were painting this fish, I could imagine it in glistening oil colours. In her poem, she paints with words: 'the pink swim-bladder/like a peony'. She engages with her subject and has an emotional response to it: 'I looked into his eyes'. She acknowledges this veteran survivor, as she notes his 'medals', the 'five big hooks/ grown firmly in his mouth'. They have been there so long that the skin has grown over them and she draws our attention to the fish's 'aching jaw'. Just like a painter leads us to see what they see, Bishop orders her picture so that we can see the 'five-haired beard of wisdom/trailing' from the fish. The poem concludes with a burst of colour ('rainbow, rainbow, rainbow!'). The rainbow from the oil-soaked, dirty bilge water has transformed the poet's relationship with the fish. Like Bishop, we now see the proper relationship between people and nature – one of respect. So the 'painterly eye' of Bishop has led us to see the drama of the occasion, the fish and what it really was, and finally our correct response to the earth and its creatures.

Examiner's Comment

A mature and interesting interpretation of the question. The response is very well focused and there is a sustained personal perspective throughout. Judicious use of quotations rounds off the answer. With the exception of the last sentence, expression is generally fluent and assured. Grade A.

CLASS/HOMEWORK EXERCISES

1. Bishop often structures her poems like a mini-drama. Examine the poem 'The Fish' and comment on how a dramatic effect is achieved. Consider setting, characterisation, conflict, the interior debate, tension building to climax, and resolution. Refer closely to the text of the poem in your response.

2. Copy the table below into your own notes and fill in critical comments about the last two quotations.

Key Quotes

He hadn't fought at all	The poet's surprise at the fish's lack of engagement in its struggle for life is caught in this colloquial statement.
the frightening gills,/fresh and crisp with blood	An awesome sight is conveyed by the use of the adjective 'frightening'. The onomatopoeic 'crisp' vividly suggests the drying blood on the dangerous, sharp gills.
grim, wet, and weaponlike	Three adjectives describe the fearsome lower lip of the fish as it is pierced. The fish is likened to a veteran soldier.
and victory filled up/the little rented boat	
And I let the fish go	

❷ THE BIGHT

(*On my birthday*)

At low tide like this how sheer the water is.
White, crumbling ribs of marl protrude and glare
and the boats are dry, the pilings dry as matches.
Absorbing, rather than being absorbed,
the water in the bight doesn't wet anything,   5
the color of the gas flame turned as low as possible.
One can smell it turning to gas; if one were Baudelaire
one could probably hear it turning to marimba music.
The little ocher dredge at work off the end of the dock
already plays the dry perfectly off-beat claves.   10
The birds are outsize. Pelicans crash
into this peculiar gas unnecessarily hard,
it seem to me, like pickaxes,
rarely coming up with anything to show for it,
and going off with humorous elbowings.   15
Black-and-white man-of-war birds soar
on impalpable drafts
and open their tails like scissors on the curves
or tense them like wishbones, till they tremble.
The frowsy sponge boats keep coming in   20
with the obliging air of retrievers,
bristling with jackstraw gaffs and hooks
and decorated with bobbles of sponges.
There is a fence of chicken wire along the dock
where, glinting like little plowshares,   25
the blue-gray shark tails are hung up to dry
for the Chinese-restaurant trade.
Some of the little white boats are still piled up
against each other, or lie on their sides, stove in,
and not yet salvaged, if they ever will be, from the last bad storm,   30
like torn-open, unanswered letters.
The bight is littered with old correspondences.
Click. Click. Goes the dredge,
and brings up a dripping jawful of marl.
All the untidy activity continues,   35
awful but cheerful.

'and the boats are dry'

EXPLORATIONS

1. Using close reference to the text, describe the atmosphere in the first six lines of the poem.

2. Choose one simile that you think is particularly effective in the poem. Briefly explain your choice.

3. Although the poem is not directly personal, what does it suggest to you about Elizabeth Bishop herself? Refer to the text in your answer.

'The Bight' showcases Elizabeth Bishop's aesthetic appreciation of the world around her. The setting for this poem is Garrison Bight in Florida. In describing the small, untidy harbour, Bishop displays a characteristically keen eye for observation and an expert use of metaphor. The subtitle, '(On my birthday)', suggests a special occasion and, per- haps, a time for reflection and reappraisal of life.

The poem begins with an introduction to the bight at 'low tide' and gradually constructs **a vivid picture of an uninviting place**: 'White, crumbling ribs of marl protrude and glare'. Grim personification and a sharp 'r' sound effect emphasise the unsettling atmosphere. There is a sense of unreality about sea water that 'doesn't wet anything'. The description in these **opening lines** is typically detailed, sensual and precise – all carefully shaped by the poet's own personal vision of the world. References to 'the pilings dry as matches' and the 'gas flame' water are rather disturbing, suggesting that something dangerous might be about to happen.

Bishop's mention of the French poet Charles Baudelaire (**line 7**) would suggest that she shares his belief in expressing human experience through objects and places around us. The poet imagines Baudelaire being able to 'hear' the water 'turning to marimba music'. She also finds an unexpected jazz rhythm ('perfectly off-beat claves') coming from the machine that is dredging 'off the end of the dock'. In lines **11–19**, Bishop depicts the 'outsize' birds through a series of vigorous images. They seem awkward and out of place in this busy, built-up location. **Figurative language illustrates their mechanical movements**: pelicans 'crash' into the sea 'like pickaxes', while man-of-war birds 'open their tails like scissors'. An underlying sense of disquiet can be detected in the detailed observations of these 'tense' birds as they 'tremble' in flight.

The poet's portrayal of the bight is quite realistic: 'frowsy sponge boats keep coming in' to harbour. With wry humour, she acknowledges their unlikely beauty, 'bristling with jackstraw gaffs' and 'decorated with bobbles of sponges'. The cluttered dockside is a busy working environment where 'blue-gray shark tails are hung up to dry' (**line 26**). The 'little white boats' are a reminder of the local fishing community and its dependence on the sea. Bishop compares the small fishing boats to 'torn-open, unanswered letters'. The bight suddenly reminds her of a cluttered writing-desk – her own, presumably – 'littered with old correspondences'.

This metaphor is developed in lines **33–36**. Bishop returns to sharp sounds: the 'Click. Click.' noise of the dredger (compared to an animal unearthing the wet clay) as it 'brings up a dripping jawful of marl'. The ending is highly symbolic of the poet's own impulse to dig deep into her memories. Drawing a close comparison between her own life and the 'untidy activity' of the bight, she concludes that both are 'awful but cheerful'. **The matter-of-fact tone of these closing lines is derisive but good humoured.** It reflects her realistic approach to the highs and lows of human experience – and the kinds of thoughts that are likely to have crossed her mind as she celebrated yet another birthday.

ANALYSIS

'Closely observed description and vivid imagery are striking features of Elizabeth Bishop's poems.' Discuss this statement in relation to 'The Bight'. Refer to the poem in support of your views.

Sample Paragraph

I think 'The Bight' is a good example of how Elizabeth Bishop slowly builds up a picture of a fairly inhospitable place, layer upon layer. At first, she describes the 'sheer' water and the 'crumbling ribs of marl', personifying the loose soil as an emaciated body. This is a vivid and disturbing image that suggests that the bay is bleak and unattractive. We get a sense of the sounds she hears – the 'dredge at work' pounding away in the background. Bishop uses dramatic imagery to bring the birds to life – particularly the vicious man-of-war birds whose tails are 'like scissors' and 'tense' as wishbones. We also see the poet's eye for precise detail in her imaginative description of the damaged fishing boats that lie on the shore 'like torn-open, unanswered letters'. Bishop uses colour imagery very effectively – 'blue-gray shark tails' are hanging out to dry for the local restaurant trade. But she is not restricted to visual effects. Her descriptions appeal to other senses, particularly sound. The poem ends with the rasping sound of the dredger – 'Click. Click' digging up 'a dripping jawful of marl'. This remarkable image suggests to me how the bight keeps bringing back memories to the poet, both pleasant and unpleasant. It is an impressive way of rounding off the poem, as she associates the untidy harbour with her own varied life – 'awful but cheerful'.

Examiner's Comment

A very well-focused response, making excellent use of numerous accurate quotations. The various elements of the question are addressed and there is evidence of good personal engagement with the text. Expression throughout is also fluent and controlled. Grade A.

CLASS/HOMEWORK EXERCISES

1. 'Elizabeth Bishop's poetry is both sensuous and reflective.' To what extent is this true of 'The Bight'? Support the points you make with suitable reference to the text of the poem.

2. Copy the table below into your own notes and fill in critical comments about the last two quotations.

Key Quotes

the boats are dry, the pilings dry as matches	The hesitant rhythm and repetition of 'dry' suggest an underlying sense of danger.
open their tails like scissors	This simile is a typically dynamic image, one of many comparisons used to convey the birds' mechanical movements.
The bight is littered with old correspondences	The clutter and disorder of the small harbour reminds Bishop of her own experiences and former relationships.
bristling with jackstraw gaffs and hooks	
Click. Click. Goes the dredge,/ and brings up a dripping jaw-ful of marl	

❸ AT THE FISHHOUSES

Although it is a cold evening,
down by one of the fishhouses
an old man sits netting,
his net, in the gloaming almost invisible,
a dark purple-brown,   5
and his shuttle worn and polished.
The air smells so strong of codfish
it makes one's nose run and one's eyes water.
The five fishhouses have steeply peaked roofs
and narrow, cleated gangplanks slant up   10
to storerooms in the gables
for the wheelbarrows to be pushed up and down on.
All is silver: the heavy surface of the sea,
swelling slowly as if considering spilling over,
is opaque, but the silver of the benches,   15
the lobster pots, and masts, scattered
among the wild jagged rocks,
is of an apparent translucence
like the small old buildings with an emerald moss
growing on their shoreward walls.   20
The big fish tubs are completely lined
with layers of beautiful herring scales
and the wheelbarrows are similarly plastered
with creamy iridescent coats of mail,
with small iridescent flies crawling on them.   25
Up on the little slope behind the houses,
set in the sparse bright sprinkle of grass,
is an ancient wooden capstan,
cracked, with two long bleached handles
and some melancholy stains, like dried blood,   30
where the ironwork has rusted.
The old man accepts a Lucky Strike.
He was a friend of my grandfather.
We talk of the decline in the population
and of codfish and herring   35
while he waits for a herring boat to come in.
There are sequins on his vest and on his thumb.
He has scraped the scales, the principal beauty,

from unnumbered fish with that black old knife,
the blade of which is almost worn away.   40

Down at the water's edge, at the place
where they haul up the boats, up the long ramp
descending into the water, thin silver
tree trunks are laid horizontally
across the gray stones, down and down   45
at intervals of four or five feet.

Cold dark deep and absolutely clear,
element bearable to no mortal,
to fish and seals . . . One seal particularly
I have seen here evening after evening.   50
He was curious about me. He was interested in music;
like me a believer in total immersion,
so I used to sing him Baptist hymns.
I also sang 'A Mighty Fortress Is Our God.'
He stood up in the water and regarded me   55
steadily, moving his head a little.
Then he would disappear, then suddenly emerge
almost in the same spot, with a sort of shrug
as if it were against his better judgment.
Cold dark deep and absolutely clear,   60
the clear gray icy water . . . Back, behind us,
the dignified tall firs begin.
Bluish, associating with their shadows,
a million Christmas trees stand
waiting for Christmas. The water seems suspended   65
above the rounded gray and blue-gray stones.
I have seen it over and over, the same sea, the same,
slightly, indifferently swinging above the stones,
icily free above the stones,
above the stones and then the world.   70
If you should dip your hand in,
your wrist would ache immediately,
your bones would begin to ache and your hand would burn
as if the water were a transmutation of fire
that feeds on stones and burns with a dark gray flame.   75
If you tasted it, it would first taste bitter,

then briny, then surely burn your tongue.
It is like what we imagine knowledge to be:
dark, salt, clear, moving, utterly free,
drawn from the cold hard mouth   80
of the world, derived from the rocky breasts
forever, flowing and drawn, and since
our knowledge is historical, flowing, and flown.

'In the gloaming'

GLOSSARY

4   *gloaming*: twilight, evening.
6   *shuttle*: tool used for weaving and mending fishing nets.
10   *cleated*: wooden projections nailed to a ladder to prevent slipping.
10   *gangplanks*: removable ramps used for boarding or leaving boats.
15   *opaque*: murky, dark, difficult to see through.
18   *translucence*: semi-transparent, light shining partially through.
24   *iridescent*: glittering, changing colours.

24   *coats of mail*: armour made of metal rings.
28   *capstan*: round machine used for winding or hauling rope.
32   *Lucky Strike*: American cigarette.
37   *sequins*: small, shiny discs used for decorating clothes.
52   *total immersion*: completely covered in liquid; a form of baptism.
63   *associating*: linking.
74   *transmutation*: changing shape.
77   *briny*: very salty.

EXPLORATIONS

1. In your opinion, what role has the old fisherman in the poem? Is he a link with the past, a person in harmony with his environment or something else? Refer closely to the text in your response.

2. Bishop uses a chilling maternal image at the conclusion of the poem. What effect has this startling metaphor on the poem's tone? Support your discussion with clear references from the text.

3. Did you find 'At the Fishhouses' thought provoking? What questions did the poem raise about the poet and her attitudes? Refer to the text in your answer.

STUDY NOTES

'At the Fishhouses' comes from Elizabeth Bishop's award-winning second collection, A Cold Spring (1965). What Bishop sees is never quite what the rest of us see. She challenges us to look again. She gives us poetry as 'normal as sight ... as artificial as a glass eye'. An ordinary sight of an old fisherman 'in the gloaming' mending nets in Nova Scotia becomes a strange, exact hallucination examining the essence of knowledge. Bishop saw; now we see. She changes the view.

The poem's opening section (**lines 1-40**) gives us a **detailed, sensuous description** of a scene from Nova Scotia. Bishop has an unerring sense of place. The fishhouses are described so vividly that we can almost smell the fish ('it makes one's nose run and one's eyes water'), see the fish tubs ('completely lined/with layers of beautiful herring scales') and hear the sea ('swelling slowly as if considering spilling over'). The poet draws us right into the scene with microscopic detail, making us pore over the surface of 'benches', 'lobsterpots' and 'masts'. We experience the 'apparent translucence' of the weathered, silvered wood, which matches the cold, opaque, silver sea. Musical language lends beauty to this timeless scene. The long 'o' sound in 'Although' is echoed in 'cold', 'old' and 'gloaming'. All is harmony. The colours of the fisherman's net, 'dark purple-brown', become 'almost invisible'. Nothing jars. The rhythmic work is conveyed in the pulsating phrase 'for the wheelbarrows to be pushed up and down on'. Physical effort is suggested by the assonance of 'u' and 'o'. In **lines 23-25**, the wheelbarrows are described in minute detail ('plastered/with creamy iridescent coats of mail'). The small, circular fish scales are like the metal rings on a medieval knight's coat of armour. Bishop moves in closer to show us similarly coloured little flies, also 'iridescent', moving on the scales.

The poet's eye focuses on 'the little slope behind the houses' and an 'ancient wooden capstan'. Here is a **forlorn reminder of the tough physical work** of the past. The discarded cylinder is 'cracked' and has 'melancholy stains, like dried blood'; the ironwork has also 'rusted'. In **line 32**, a human connection is made when the 'old man accepts a Lucky Strike' cigarette. The personal detail ('a friend of my grandfather') gives a surface intimacy to this chill poem. But there are hidden depths. The man is described as having 'sequins on his vest and on his thumb'. This decorative detail is more usually associated with glamorous ball gowns than an old fisherman's jersey. Does the image of the man's black knife, 'almost worn away', suggest an ebbing life?

In the poem's short second section (**lines 41-46**), we are at the water's edge and the repetition of 'down' draws us nearer the element of water as we note the 'long ramp/descending'. **The movement seems symbolic of Bishop's own descent into her subconscious mind.** As before, the graceful fish scales have transformed the wooden ramp into 'thin silver/tree trunks'.

The third section (**lines 47-83**) **changes the view**. We are now not merely looking, but seeing. We are **entering the interior**. We journey with Bishop to examine an element that is 'bearable to no mortal', yet is home 'to fish and to seals'. No human can survive in the icy waters of the North Atlantic Sea: 'Cold dark deep and absolutely clear'. Another figure, a seal, appears in this bleak, surreal sequence. In this compelling episode, seal and poet are linked by a shared belief in 'total immersion'. For the seal, this is into water. Is it some form of baptism for Bishop? The poet, however, finds no comfort in religion, despite singing hymns for the seal ('A Mighty Fortress Is Our God'). Religion, like the distant fir trees, is behind her, waiting to be cut down.

The sea now takes on a nightmarish aspect as Bishop describes it 'indifferently swinging above the stones' (**line 68**). It is becoming a sea of knowledge. The poet warns us against it, telling us that we will be hurt if we delve in: wrists 'would ache immediately' and hands 'would burn'. Just as in the Garden of Eden, knowledge came with a terrible price. Knowledge gleaned from the world is hard earned. Mother Nature is depicted with a 'cold hard mouth' and 'rocky breasts'. Here is no warm, comforting, maternal presence. Instead, Bishop's own dark life is suggested. These final lines – filled with harsh sea imagery – are insightful. Place has receded and insight is present. We, together with the poet, realise that knowledge is like water ('flowing'). It is also 'drawn', like waves are moved by the power of the moon. As we recognise that the mysterious waves pass into the past, so we realise that knowledge is 'historical' and ends up 'flown'. **All are part of the flux of nature.** In the end, Bishop seems to accept that the vast ocean – like life itself – defies understanding.

ANALYSIS

'Bishop gives us facts and minute details, sinking or sliding giddily off into the unknown.' Discuss this statement with reference to the poem 'At the Fishhouses'. Support your views with close reference to the text.

Sample Paragraph

I certainly agree that Elizabeth Bishop give us 'facts and minute details'. The 'five fishhouses' are clearly described for the reader to see, with their characteristic 'steeply peaked roofs' and their walkways, 'narrow, cleated' to enable the wheelbarrows to move smoothly. The exchange between the poet and the old man ('a friend of my grandfather') is realistically shown, with even the brand of cigarette identified ('Lucky Strike'). We not only see the fish scales, 'sequins', 'coats of mail', but we also note the 'crawling' flies on the scale-splattered wheelbarrows. Then the poem turns from this detailed scrutiny of the actual to an abstract meditation. Here, the poet is 'sliding giddily off into the unknown'. From contemplating the icy North Atlantic Sea ('Cold dark deep and absolutely clear'), Bishop starts to explore the essence of knowledge – and even of life itself. Knowing hurts, it makes you 'ache', just as the icy water 'burns'. Knowledge is not comfortable; the world is not a nice place, with its 'cold hard mouth'. Experience and knowledge come with an expensive price tag. The last two lines, for me, are dreamlike and surreal. I imagine a sea of knowledge that has been gained in the past ('historical'). This knowledge is always changing and 'flowing' as new discoveries are made. Elizabeth Bishop has brought us from a minute exploration of place to a meditation on an abstract concept.

Examiner's Comment

A precise discussion that deals directly with both aspects of the statement: 'facts and minute details' and 'sliding ... into the unknown'. Some good personal engagement and a clear understanding of the poem are evident. There is also effective use of apt quotation. Grade A.

CLASS/HOMEWORK EXERCISES

1. How does Bishop's style contribute to the communication of her themes? Refer to two literary techniques used by the poet in 'At the Fishhouses' and comment on their effectiveness in each case. Refer closely to the text in your response.

2. Copy the table below into your own notes and fill in critical comments about the last two quotations.

Key Quotes

the heavy surface of the sea,/ swelling slowly as if considering spilling over,/is opaque	The sluggish movement of the sea is expertly caught by the combined use of alliteration ('s') and broad vowels ('a', 'o', 'u').
The old man accepts a Lucky Strike	By naming a popular brand of American cigarette, Bishop adds a touch of authenticity to this moment of human interaction.
He has scraped the scales	The harsh, grating noise that the old, black knife makes is conveyed by the alliterative 's' sound and the onomatopoeic verb 'scraped'.
Cold dark deep and absolutely clear	
It is like what we imagine knowledge to be	

❹ THE PRODIGAL

The brown enormous odor he lived by
was too close, with its breathing and thick hair,
for him to judge. The floor was rotten; the sty
was plastered halfway up with glass-smooth dung.
Light-lashed, self-righteous, above moving snouts,   5
the pigs' eyes followed him, a cheerful stare –
even to the sow that always ate her young –
till, sickening, he leaned to scratch her head.
But sometimes mornings after drinking bouts
(he hid the pints behind a two-by-four),   10
the sunrise glazed the barnyard mud with red;
the burning puddles seemed to reassure.
And then he thought he almost might endure
his exile yet another year or more.

But evenings the first star came to warn.   15
The farmer whom he worked for came at dark
to shut the cows and horses in the barn
beneath their overhanging clouds of hay,
with pitchforks, faint forked lightnings, catching light,
safe and companionable as in the Ark.   20
The pigs stuck out their little feet and snored.
The lantern – like the sun, going away –
laid on the mud a pacing aureole.
Carrying a bucket along a slimy board,
he felt the bats' uncertain staggering flight,   25
his shuddering insights, beyond his control,
touching him. But it took him a long time
finally to make his mind up to go home.

'the pigs' eyes followed him'

GLOSSARY

Title: The title comes from the biblical parable of the Prodigal Son, a young man who wasted his inheritance on drunkenness and ended up working as a swineherd. The word 'prodigal' refers to a spendthrift or wastrel.

1   *odor:* odour, smell.

3   *sty:* pig-shed.

5   *snouts:* pigs' noses.

9   *bouts:* sessions.

20 *companionable:* comfortable.

20 *the Ark:* Noah's Ark. In the Bible story, Noah built a boat to save animals from a great flood.

23 *aureole:* circle of light.

EXPLORATIONS

1. In your opinion, is Elizabeth Bishop sympathetic to the central character in this poem? Give reasons for your answer, using close reference to the text.

2. Choose two images that you found particularly memorable in the poem. Comment briefly on the effectiveness of each.

3. Write your personal response to the poem, referring to the text in your answer.

STUDY NOTES

In 'The Prodigal', published in 1951, Elizabeth Bishop returns to the well-known Bible parable of the Prodigal Son. She imagines the squalor and degradation this wayward youth endured when he was forced to live among the pigs he looked after. The poet herself had experienced depression and alcoholism in her own life and could identify with the poem's marginalised central figure. Bishop uses a double-sonnet form to trace the prodigal's struggle from wretchedness to eventual recovery.

The poem's **opening lines** present the repugnant living conditions of the exiled prodigal's everyday life: 'The brown enormous odor' engulfs him. The abhorrent stench and filth of the pig-sty is the only life he knows. Immersed in this animal-like state, he has lost all sense of judgement. Even the odour, 'with its breathing and thick hair', is beyond his notice. Bishop's graphic imagery is typically precise, describing the foul-smelling sty's shiny walls as 'plastered halfway up with glass-smooth dung'.

In **lines 5–8**, the 'Light-lashed' pigs are given human traits ('self-righteous', 'a cheerful stare'). The poet conveys a disturbing sense of the young man's confused and drunken grasp on reality. In his sub-human state, overwhelmed by nausea and isolation, he now seems almost at home among the pigs. Although he is 'sickening', he can still show odd gestures of affection towards them – 'even to the sow that always ate her young'.

Bishop delves deeper into the alcoholic's secretive world in **lines 9–14**. Ironically, the morning hangovers are not entirely without their compensations: 'burning puddles seemed to reassure'. Despite the ugliness and deprivation of his diminished existence, he can occasionally recognise unexpected beauty in nature, such as when 'the sunrise glazed the barnyard mud with red'. It is enough to give him hope: 'then he thought he almost might endure/his exile'. Emphatic broad vowel sounds add a further dimension of pathos to this line.

The poem's **second section** begins on a more startling note: 'But evenings the first star came to warn' (**line 15**). There is a suggestion that the prodigal is finally confronting his personal demons. For the first time, he seems to realise that he is out of place among the orderly routine of farm life that is going on around him. Unlike the sleeping animals ('safe and companionable as in the Ark'), the unfortunate young man is now intensely aware of his dismal alienation. He is poised on the brink of coming to his senses.

For the frustrated prodigal, a defining moment occurs when he finally disassociates himself from the snoring pigs. Yet ironically, it seems as though he almost envies their simple comfort and security 'beneath their overhanging clouds of hay'. Vivid images of routine farm life, such as 'The lantern – like the sun, going away' (**line 22**), take on a new symbolic significance for the unhappy exile. Is he finally considering the transience of life? Is there still a possibility of regaining his humanity? For an instant, the young man seems to find a vague kind of hope in the beautiful 'pacing aureole' of lamplight reflected on the mud.

A renewed vigour and purpose mark the poem's **final lines**. Bishop identifies exactly when the prodigal experiences 'shuddering insights'. This defining instant is symbolised by his acute awareness of 'the bats' uncertain staggering flight'. Taking his cue from nature, he slowly accepts responsibility for his own destiny: 'But it took him a long time/finally to make his mind up to go home'. This crucial decision to return from exile is a powerful illustration of human resilience. The poem's affirmative ending is emphasised by the importance placed on 'home' (the only unrhymed end word in the poem). Bishop's reworking of the well-known biblical tale carries a universal message of hope, offering the prospect of recovery not just from alcoholism, but from any form of human debasement.

ANALYSIS

'Elizabeth Bishop's mood can vary greatly – from deep depression to quiet optimism.' Discuss this statement, with particular reference to 'The Prodigal'.

Sample Paragraph

Bishop's poem, 'The Prodigal', is extremely grim. The early mood, describing the 'brown enormous odor' (American spelling) is clearly meant to capture the terrible living conditions of the young alcoholic son who had left his home, partied non-stop and fallen on hard times. The description of the outhouse is extremely repulsive. Bishop's tone is one of despair. The prodigal has fallen as low as any person, living among the pigs he looks after. The images are negative – 'rotten', 'sickening', 'barnyard mud'. The stench makes him queasy. But the mood changes when the alcoholic becomes more aware of himself and dares to hope that he will get it together and return to a decent life. Images of light and beauty suggest this – 'catching light', 'a pacing aureole'. The turning point is when the prodigal stumbles on 'shuddering insights' – which refers to his belief that he can regain his dignity and humanity if he really wants to. Although this is extremely difficult and 'took him a long time', he succeeds in the end. The last line emphasises his optimistic mood – as he decides to 'make his mind up to go home'.

Examiner's Comment

A well-focused response, in the main, that addresses the question. Effective use of accurate quotation throughout. The answer would have benefitted from some discussion on the restrained ('quiet') nature of the final optimism. Expression is weakened by slang and over-use of the word 'extremely'. Grade B.

CLASS/HOMEWORK EXERCISES

1. 'Bishop's poetry often goes beyond description to reveal valuable insights about people's courage and resilience.' Discuss this statement with particular reference to 'The Prodigal'. Refer to the poem in your response.

2. Copy the table below into your own notes and fill in critical comments about the last two quotations.

Key Quotes

The brown enormous odor he lived by	The overpowering, filthy condition of the pig-sty is a startling metaphor for human degradation.
he hid the pints behind a two-by-four	Shame and deception are characteristics of Bishop's realistic portrayal of the alcoholic's behaviour.
pitchforks, faint forked light-nings	This striking comparison suggests the clarity, disorientation and paranoia that can accompany alcoholism.
the sunrise glazed the barn-yard mud with red	
shuddering insights, beyond his control, /touching him	

❺ QUESTIONS OF TRAVEL

There are too many waterfalls here; the crowded streams
hurry too rapidly down to the sea,
and the pressure of so many clouds on the mountaintops
makes them spill over the sides in soft slow-motion,
turning to waterfalls under our very eyes.   5
– For if those streaks, those mile-long, shiny, tearstains,
aren't waterfalls yet,
in a quick age or so, as ages go here,
they probably will be.
But if the streams and clouds keep travelling, travelling,   10
the mountains look like the hulls of capsized ships,
slime-hung and barnacled.

Think of the long trip home.
Should we have stayed at home and thought of here?
Where should we be today?   15
Is it right to be watching strangers in a play
in this strangest of theatres?
What childishness is it that while there's a breath of life
in our bodies, we are determined to rush
to see the sun the other way around?   20
The tiniest green hummingbird in the world?
To stare at some inexplicable old stonework,
inexplicable and impenetrable,
at any view,
instantly seen and always, always delightful?   25
Oh, must we dream our dreams
and have them, too?
And have we room
for one more folded sunset, still quite warm?

But surely it would have been a pity   30
not to have seen the trees along this road,
really exaggerated in their beauty,
not to have seen them gesturing
like noble pantomimists, robed in pink.
– Not to have had to stop for gas and heard   35
the sad, two-noted, wooden tune

of disparate wooden clogs
carelessly clacking over
a grease-stained filling-station floor.
(In another country the clogs would all be tested.   40
Each pair there would have identical pitch.)
– A pity not to have heard
the other, less primitive music of the fat brown bird
who sings above the broken gasoline pump
in a bamboo church of Jesuit baroque: 45
three towers, five silver crosses.
– Yes, a pity not to have pondered,
blurr'dly and inconclusively,
on what connection can exist for centuries
between the crudest wooden footwear   50
and, careful and finicky,
the whittled fantasies of wooden cages.
– Never to have studied history in
the weak calligraphy of songbirds' cages.
– And never to have had to listen to rain   55
so much like politicians' speeches:
two hours of unrelenting oratory
and then a golden silence
in which the traveller takes a notebook, writes:

'Is it lack of imagination that makes us come   60
to imagined places, not just stay at home?
Or could Pascal have been not entirely right
about just sitting quietly in one's room?

Continent, city, country, society:
the choice is never wide and never free.   65
And here, or there ... No. Should we have stayed at home,
wherever that may be?'

'the pressure of so many clouds on the mountaintops'

GLOSSARY

1   *here*: Brazil.
11 *hulls*: main sections of ships.
11 *capsized*: overturned in the water.
12 *barnacled*: covered with small shellfish.
20 *the sun the other way around*: the view of the sun in the southern hemisphere.
22 *inexplicable*: incomprehensible, mysterious.
34 *pantomimists*: people taking part in a pantomime, a slapstick comedy.
37 *disparate*: very different, separate.
45 *church of Jesuit baroque*: ornately decorated 17th-century churches, often found in Brazil.

51 *finicky*: excessively detailed, elaborate.
52 *whittled*: carved.
52 *fantasies*: amazing creations.
54 *calligraphy*: decorative handwriting (in this case, the swirling design of the carved birdcages).
57 *unrelenting*: never stopping, endless.
62 *Pascal*: Blaise Pascal, a 17th-century mathematician and philosopher who wrote that 'man's misfortunes spring from the single cause that he is unable to stay quietly in his room'.

EXPLORATIONS

1. From your reading of lines 1–12, describe Bishop's reaction to the landscape spread before her. How does she feel about this abundance of nature? Is she delighted, unhappy, awestruck? Support your response with quotation from the text.

2. Choose two examples of repetition in the poem. Briefly explain what each example contributes to Bishop's treatment of the poem's theme.

3. Would you consider the ending of the poem conclusive or inconclusive? How does Bishop really feel about travel? Refer closely to the text in your response.

This is the title poem of Elizabeth Bishop's 1965 collection, Questions of Travel. *Bishop herself was a great traveller, aided by an inheritance from her father. In this poem, she questions the need for travel and the desire that people have to see the world for themselves. The poet provokes the reader by posing a series of questions about the ethics of travel. She places her original observations of Brazil before us and wonders whether it would be better if we simply imagined these places while sitting at home. Finally, she challenges us to consider where our 'home' is.*

The poem's **opening line** is an **irritable complaint** about Brazil: 'There are too many waterfalls here'. In the first section (**lines 1–12**), Bishop observes the luxuriant, fertile landscape spread out before her. She finds fault with the 'crowded streams' that 'hurry too rapidly' and the 'pressure of so many clouds'. The richness of the misty equatorial landscape is caught in a series of soft sibilant 's' sounds ('spill', 'sides', 'soft slow-motion'). Clouds melt into the 'mile-long, shiny, tearstains'. Everything is on the move, changing position and shape. Both Bishop and the water are 'travelling, travelling'. **Repetition emphasises this restless movement.** The circular motion suggests that neither traveller nor clouds have any real purpose or direction. An original and striking image of a mountain range ('like the hulls of capsized ships') catches our attention. The vegetation is 'slime-hung'; the outcrops of rocks are like the crustaceans of shellfish ('barnacled'). As always, the poet's interest lies in the shape and texture of the words.

A more **reflective mood is found in the poem's second section (lines 13–29)**. Bishop presents readers with a **series of challenging questions** for consideration. In all, eight 'questions of travel' are posed. Should we remain 'at home' and imagine 'here'? Bishop is uneasy at the prying scrutiny of tourists 'watching strangers in a play'. She is aware that this is how people live; it is not a performance for public consumption. The emphasis here is on the 'childishness' of the tourists as they rush around, greedily consuming sights, viewing the sun from its other side in southern countries, such as Brazil. But as far as Bishop is concerned, historic ruins and 'old stonework' do not speak to the visitor. The repetition of 'inexplicable' stresses the inaccessibility of foreign cultures. The bland, unknowing response of tourists is captured in the conversational phrase 'always delightful'. Their selfish desire for more and more experiences is vividly shown in the image of the traveller nonchalantly packing views, as if they were clothes or souvenirs being placed in a bag at the end of a trip: 'And have we room/for one more folded sunset, still quite warm?' Perhaps Bishop is asking whether any famous sight ever actually touched the traveller, or was it skimmed over in a frenzy to pack in as much as possible?

Justification for travel is the dominant theme of the third section (lines 30–59): 'But surely it would have been a pity/not to have seen'; '– A pity not to have heard'; 'a pity not to have pondered'; '– Never to have studied'; 'never to have had to listen'. The repetition of 'pity' beats out a tense rhythm as the poet seeks to condone travel. Bishop's well-known 'painterly eye' provides the evidence, as she presents a series of fresh, first-hand vignettes, e.g. the trees 'gesturing/like noble pantomimists, robed in pink'. The flowing movement of the trees, their flamboyant colour and their suggestion of Brazil's mime plays would be hard to imagine if not really experienced. The sound of this easy-going, carefree society is captured in the hard 'c' sound of 'carelessly clacking', which evokes the slovenly walk of local peasants. The Brazilian love of music is evident in 'clacking', a sound usually associated with the rhythmic castanets. The difference in cultures is wryly noted: 'In another country the clogs would all be tested./Each pair there would have identical pitch.' Elsewhere, all would be sanitised uniformity.

Are these the experiences the traveller would miss by not being in another country? The locals' cavalier attitude to functionality is shown in the contrasting images of the 'broken gasoline pump' and the intricate construction of a 'bamboo church' with 'three towers, five silver crosses'. **The spirit of the people soars in 'Jesuit baroque'.** A similar contrast is seen in wooden carving – the 'crudest wooden footwear' does not have the same importance for these free-spirited people as the 'careful and finicky ... fantasies of wooden cages' (**line 51**). Another unstoppable force, that of equatorial rainstorms, is likened to the endless rant of a politician bellowing out his 'unrelenting oratory'. Could any of this be imagined from afar?

Lines 58–67 begin in 'golden silence', as Bishop attempts to clarify her own thinking on the value of travel. In the final lines, she **wonders if we travel because we lack the imagination to visualise these places**. However, in the previous section, the poet has graphically shown that nothing can surpass a person **actually hearing and seeing** a place and its people. A reference is made to the 17th-century philosopher Blaise Pascal, who preferred to remain at home. The poet feels that he was not 'entirely right' about this, and by sharing her whimsical images of Brazil with us, she has led us to agree with her. Another interesting question is posed:

How free are we to go where we wish? Bishop states that the choices are 'never wide and never free'; there are always constraints on the traveller. But an emphatic 'No' tells us that this does not take away from the authenticity of the experience.

In the poem's **concluding lines**, Bishop returns to the question of whether or not people should stay at home. She then teases the reader with the follow-up, 'wherever that may be?' (**line 67**). This is a much deeper, philosophical reflection, which reverberates in our minds. **Home is a place of belonging**, from which travellers set out and to which they return. The visited countries are not secure bases; the tourist does not belong there, but is merely a visitor en route to somewhere else. In short, the traveller's role is one of an outsider – observing, but not participating. Bishop's own life experience is revealed here. Perhaps she travelled so extensively because she never felt truly at home in any single place.

ANALYSIS

'Elizabeth Bishop's poems are not only delightful observations, but are also considered meditations on human issues.' Discuss this statement with reference to the poem 'Questions of Travel'. Support your views with close reference to the text.

Sample Paragraph

Elizabeth Bishop was a tireless traveller and in the poem 'Questions of Travel', she presents the reader with evocative images from the lush, misty equatorial landscape of Brazil, where clouds 'spill over the sides' of mountains 'in soft slow-motion'. The giant mountain ranges are imaginatively conjured up before our eyes as upturned ships, and their vegetation and rocky sections are likened to the 'slime-hung and barnacled' appearance of the bottoms of these ships. The sounds of the people intrude upon our consciousness – disparate clogs 'carelessly clacking'. The harsh alliteration mimics the sound of wood hitting floor. No detail is too minute to escape her famous 'eye': 'the broken gasoline pump', 'the whittled fantasies of wooden cages', the 'three towers' and 'five silver crosses' of the small bamboo church. These are Bishop's delightful observations. But the poet also addresses ethical questions surrounding travel, particularly relevant in our times. The reader is asked to ponder 'Questions of Travel'. What right have we to watch people's private lives, as if they were performing in public? Why should we consume experiences and squeeze them up like clothes in a suitcase ('have we room for one more folded sunset ...?'). Why are we rushing around, 'travelling, travelling'? Why do we not 'just stay at home'? These issues have a modern resonance, as we are aware nowadays of the effect of our carbon footprint on the environment when we travel. The poem concludes with a curious question on the meaning of 'home'. Bishop asks us to consider where it is ('home,/wherever that may be'). Suddenly an accepted certainty becomes as hard to define as the disintegrating clouds at the start of the poem.

Examiner's Comment

A careful examination of both parts of the statement – the poet's 'delightful observations' and her treatment of issues – is presented by the candidate. The thoughtful approach is referenced accurately with pertinent quotations from the poem. Grade A.

CLASS/HOMEWORK EXERCISES

1. Comment on the different tones in 'Questions of Travel'. Refer closely to the text in your response.

2. Copy the table below into your own notes and fill in critical comments about the last two quotations.

Key Quotes

the crowded streams/hurry too rapidly down to the sea	There is a tone of complaint from the jaded traveller in this run-on line.
Oh, must we dream our dreams/and have them, too?	The poet uses questions throughout this poem to invite the reader to consider accepted ideas in society. Do we have to experience directly as well as imagine?
blurr'dly and inconclusively	The awkward word 'blurr'dly' is made even clumsier by the poet's removal of the vowel 'e'. Bishop's lack of connection with foreign sights is cleverly shown.
weak calligraphy of song-birds' cages	
at home,/wherever that may be?	

Handwritten annotations at top:

Set in Brazil

Theme - festival, survival and instinct.

Tone - delightful, turning sour and admiration. conversational tone. easy language.

6 THE ARMADILLO

For Robert Lowell

A This is the time of year
B when almost every night
A the frail, illegal fire balloons appear.
B Climbing the mountain height,

Margin notes: person-ification; illegal as of fire hazard.

Handwritten: Describes the balloon offerings and traces their movements as they go skywards. They are offerings & prayer drifting towards heaven. She doesn't dwell on the religious source just beauty.

rising toward a saint
still honored in these parts,
the paper chambers flush and fill with light
that comes and goes, like hearts.

Margin notes: Alliteration not her native home. Simile

Handwritten: she is an observer, not to participate. detailed description of balloons, their delicacy is captured, responds to their charm and suggests they are expressions of love.

Once up against the sky it's hard
to tell them from the stars –
planets, that is – the tinted ones:
Venus going down, or Mars,

Handwritten: Beauty further captured. Tone is still admiration as she views the floating fire balloons as stars / planets. 10

or the pale green one. With a wind,
they flare and falter, wobble and toss;
but if it's still they steer between
the kite sticks of the Southern Cross,

Handwritten: each verb signifies the different movements of the wind. On a still night, they seem to be part of the Southern Cross - Constellation. 15

receding, dwindling, solemnly
and steadily forsaking us,
or, in the downdraft from a peak,
suddenly turning dangerous.

Handwritten: verbs describe their movements. gives us a sense of our earthbound selves + watching them float away & we can't be with them. tone changes to danger as they are in a downward wind. 20

Margin notes: onomatopeia; simile

Last night another big one fell.
It splattered like an egg of fire
against the cliff behind the house.
The flame ran down. We saw the pair

Handwritten: Negative side. Human + natural world are being affected. Describes one falling against a cliff and the effects of the flame. we later find out it is an owls nest.

of owls who nest there flying up
and up, their whirling black-and-white

Margin note: Metaphor

stained bright pink underneath, until
they shrieked up out of sight.

Handwritten: The repetition of up suggests the owls urgency to get away. But they get caught up in the fireball 25

Handwritten at bottom: Last line suggests pain + terror.

The ancient owls' nest must have burned. *Reiterating the owls suffering:*
Hastily, all alone, *we find out they are not the only animals alone.*
that suffer.   30
a glistening armadillo left the scene, *we meet the armadillo, he can protect*
rose-flecked, head down, tail down, *himself from any situation but not*
fire. The last two lines gives us a vivid sense
(from flames) of animals fighting for survival.

and then a baby rabbit jumped out, *The suffering rabbit is the most horrifying*
short-eared, to our surprise. *and moving image. The vulnerability of the rabbit*
it captured. he is now ash (unsubstantial)
So soft! – a handful of intangible ash *May suggest me35 cant understand*
with fixed, ignited eyes. *why this has happened – this poor defenseless*
rabbit.

Too pretty, dreamlike mimicry! *Language highly emotive depicting the*
O falling fire and piercing cry *effects of the balloons one innocent animals.*
Expresses her feelings. Italics for emphasis
and panic, and a weak mailed fist *and force. Its not clear to whom she*
clenched ignorant against the sky! *is referring to.*   40

She may be referring to the sailors   as being deceptive by pretty
as she herself described them in the 2nd two lines she reveals
them for what they really are or perhaps she is addressing
herself as a poet- criticizing her .... of the scene as too
beautiful through similes, metaphors, alliteration, rhyme.
When in reality it represents panic + pain

Mailed Fist : Metaphor signified both the
armadillos defiance and vulnerability. It cant understand or
protect itself from the menacing fire. The armadillo symbolises all those people
'the paper chambers flush and fill with light' *+ animals who fall victim to violence that they cant*
apprehend
and are
which
they
have
no
control

GLOSSARY

Dedication: Elizabeth Bishop dedicated 'The Armadillo' to her friend and fellow poet, Robert Lowell. An armadillo is a nocturnal burrowing creature found mainly in South America. It rolls up into a ball to protect itself from danger.

1   *time of year:* St John's Day (24 June).

3   *fire balloons:* helium-filled balloons carrying colourful paper boxes.

5   *a saint:* St John.

6   *these parts:* Rio de Janeiro, Brazil.

7   *chambers:* hollow boxes.

11   *tinted:* shaded.

13   *the pale green one:* probably the planet Uranus.

16   *kite sticks of the Southern Cross:* cross-shaped constellation of stars.

35   *intangible:* flimsy, insubstantial.

36   *ignited:* lit up.

37   *mimicry:* imitation

39   *weak mailed fist:* the animal's bony armour (defenceless against fire).

EXPLORATIONS

1. Based on your reading of the first four stanzas, how does the poet present the fire balloons? Are they mysterious, beautiful, threatening? Refer to the text in your answer.

2. Comment on Bishop's use of interesting verbs in the poem.

3. In your view, is this an optimistic or pessimistic poem? Give reasons for your response.

STUDY NOTES

'The Armadillo' describes St John's Day (24 June) in Brazil, where Elizabeth Bishop lived for more than 15 years. On this annual feast day, local people would celebrate by lighting fire balloons and releasing them into the night sky. Although this custom was illegal – because of the fire hazard – it still occurred widely.

The **opening lines** introduce us to an exotic, night-time scene. The sense of drama and excitement is palpable as Bishop observes these 'illegal' balloons 'rising toward a saint'. They are also presented as fragile ('frail') but beautiful: 'the paper chambers flush and fill with light'. There is something magical and majestic about their ascent towards the heavens. **The language is simple and conversational**, reflecting the religious faith of the local people. Bishop compares the flickering light of the 'paper chambers' to 'hearts', perhaps suggesting the unpredictability of human feelings and even life itself.

Lines 9–20 associate the drifting balloons with distant planets, adding to their romantic air of mystery. The unsteady rhythm and alliterative description ('With a wind,/they flare and falter') suggest an irregular, buoyant movement. The poet is **increasingly intrigued by the fire balloons** as they 'wobble' out of sight. She notes that they sometimes 'steer between' the stars. Although she appears to be disappointed that the balloons are 'steadily forsaking us', she also worries about them 'suddenly turning dangerous' as a result of downdrafts buffeting and igniting them.

The tone changes dramatically in **line 21**, as Bishop recalls the destructive force of one exploding balloon that fell to earth near her house: 'It splattered like an egg of fire'. This characteristically stirring simile and the onomatopoeic verb highlight the sense of unexpected destruction. The shock is immediately felt by humans and animals alike. Terrified owls – desperate to escape the descending flames – 'shrieked up out of sight' (**line 28**). Contrasting **colour images emphasise the garish confusion**: the 'whirling black-and-white' bodies of the owls are 'stained bright pink underneath'.

The poet suddenly notices 'a glistening armadillo', isolated and alarmed. Determined to escape the fire, it scurries away: 'rose-flecked, head down, tail down' (**line 32**). Amid the chaos, a baby rabbit 'jumped out', its urgent movement reflecting the lethal atmosphere. Bishop expresses her intense shock at seeing its burnt ears: 'So soft! – a handful of intangible ash'. **This graphic metaphor emphasises the animal's weakness and suffering.** Its 'fixed, ignited eyes' reflect the fire falling from the sky.

Bishop's emotive voice emerges forcefully in the poem's **closing lines**. She rejects her earlier description of the elegant fire balloons as being 'Too pretty'. Having witnessed the horrifying reality of the tormented animals, she castigates all her earlier romantic notions about the colourful festivities. Such thoughts are suddenly seen as 'dreamlike mimicry'. **The final image of the trapped armadillo is highly dramatic.** Its 'piercing cry' is harrowing. Bishop imagines the terrified creature in human terms ('a weak mailed fist'). Although the armadillo's helpless body is 'clenched ignorant against the sky', it is unlikely that its coat of armour will save it from fire. The irony of this small creature's last futile act is pitiful. Despite its brave defiance, the armadillo is doomed.

Some critics have commented on the **symbolism** in the poem, seeing the victimised creatures as symbols for powerless and marginalised people everywhere. It has been said that the careless fire balloons signify warfare, mindless violence and ignorant destruction. Is Bishop indicating that people's fate is beyond their control? It has also been suggested that the fire balloons symbolise love ('that comes and goes, like hearts') or even the creative impulse itself – beautiful, elusive and sometimes tragic. As with all poems, readers must decide for themselves.

ANALYSIS

Describe the tone in 'The Armadillo'. Does it change during the course of the poem? Refer to the text in your answer.

Sample Paragraph

The opening section of 'The Armadillo' is dramatic and filled with anticipation. Bishop sets the night-time scene during the noisy Brazilian festival to honour St John. 'This is the time of year' suggests a special occasion. The tone is celebratory and excited as the local community release countless 'illegal fire balloons' which light up the skies. The poet seems in awe of the wonderful spectacle, watching the 'paper chambers flush and fill with light'. The tone changes slightly to sadness as she watches the colourful balloons rise and disappear among the stars, 'steadily forsaking us'. A more dramatic transformation occurs when the exploding balloons start 'turning dangerous'. Due to the careless human activity, fire falls from the air, causing mayhem and destruction for the vulnerable animals below. Terrified owls 'shrieked', a young rabbit is burnt to 'intangible ash' and the armadillo is reduced to 'panic'. Bishop's personal voice is filled with anger and disgust as she rages against the 'falling fire'. The italics and exclamation marks in the final stanza highlight her frustrated tone as she identifies with the unfortunate armadillo whose 'weak mailed fist/clenched ignorant against the sky' represents a useless gesture of resistance.

Examiner's Comment

A focused response that traces the development of tone in the poem. There is a real sense of well-informed engagement with the text. Short, accurate quotations are used effectively to illustrate the various changes in tone. The expression is clear, varied and controlled throughout. Grade A.

CLASS/HOMEWORK EXERCISES

1. 'In reading the poetry of Elizabeth Bishop, readers can discover moments of quiet reflection and shocking truth.' Discuss this statement in relation to 'The Armadillo', supporting the points you make with reference to the poem.

2. Copy the table below into your own notes and fill in critical comments about the last two quotations.

Key Quotes

frail, illegal fire balloons appear	Bishop's description suggests both the elegance and menace of the balloons.
rising toward a saint	Might the rising balloons be a symbol of the hopes and prayers of the local people?
they shrieked up out of sight	Sharp, onomatopoeic effects echo the high-pitched sounds made by the fleeing owls.
paper chambers flush and fill with light	
a weak mailed fist/clenched ignorant against the sky!	

7 SESTINA

September rain falls on the house.
In the failing light, the old grandmother
sits in the kitchen with the child
beside the Little Marvel Stove,
reading the jokes from the almanac,   5
laughing and talking to hide her tears.

She thinks that her equinoctial tears
and the rain that beats on the roof of the house
were both foretold by the almanac,
but only known to a grandmother.   10
The iron kettle sings on the stove.
She cuts some bread and says to the child,

It's time for tea now; but the child
is watching the teakettle's small hard tears
dance like mad on the hot black stove,   15
the way the rain must dance on the house.
Tidying up, the old grandmother
hangs up the clever almanac

on its string. Birdlike, the almanac
hovers half open above the child,   20
hovers above the old grandmother
and her teacup full of dark brown tears.
She shivers and says she thinks the house
feels chilly, and puts more wood in the stove.

It was to be, says the Marvel Stove.   25
I know what I know, says the almanac.
With crayons the child draws a rigid house
and a winding pathway. Then the child
puts in a man with buttons like tears
and shows it proudly to the grandmother.   30

But secretly, while the grandmother
busies herself about the stove,
the little moons fall down like tears

from between the pages of the almanac
into the flower bed the child   35
has carefully placed in the front of the house.

Time to plant tears, says the almanac.
The grandmother sings to the marvellous stove
and the child draws another inscrutable house.

'the child draws a rigid house'

GLOSSARY

A sestina is a traditional poetic form of six six-line stanzas followed by a final stanza of just three lines. In Bishop's 'Sestina', the same six words recur at the ends of lines in each stanza: tears, almanac, stove, grandmother, house and child. The final three-line stanza contains all six words.

4   *the Little Marvel Stove*: a heater or cooker that burns wood or coal.

5   *almanac*: calendar giving important dates, information and predictions.

7   *equinoctial*: the time when day and night are of equal length (22 September, 20 March approximately).

39   *inscrutable*: secret; impossible to understand or interpret.

EXPLORATIONS

1. Describe the atmosphere in the house. Is it happy, unhappy, relaxed, secretive? Support your response with quotation from the text.

2. Choose one image that you find particularly interesting and effective in the poem. Briefly explain your choice.

3. Write your personal response to the poem, supporting your views with reference to the text.

STUDY NOTES

'Sestina' was written between 1960 and 1965. For Elizabeth Bishop, the creative act of writing brought shape and order to experience. This poem is autobiographical, as it tells of a home without a mother or father. It is one of Bishop's first poems about her childhood and she was in her fifties, living in Brazil, when she wrote it. The complicated, restrictive structure of the poem can be seen as the poet's attempt to put order on her early childhood trauma.

The poem's **opening stanza** paints a domestic scene, which at first seems cosy and secure. The child and her grandmother sit in the evening light beside a stove. They are reading 'jokes from the almanac' and 'laughing and talking'. However, on closer observation, sadness is layered onto the scene with certain details:

'September rain', 'failing light' and the old grandmother hiding 'her tears'. Bishop adopts the point of view of adult reminiscence. She recollects; she is an observer of her own childhood and the poem's **tone is disturbing and challenging**. We are introduced to someone who looks, but never belongs. The six end-words echo chillingly throughout the poem. Here is a house full of tears with a grandmother and child together, alone.

In **stanza two** the grandmother believes that her autumn tears and the rain were 'foretold by the almanac'. There is a sense of inevitability and tired resignation in the opening lines. But normality enters: 'The iron kettle sings on the stove'. Homely domesticity is seen when the grandmother cuts some bread and says to the child: 'It's time for tea now'. **Bishop suddenly switches from being an observer to being an interpreter**, as she lets the reader see the workings of the child's mind in the **third stanza**: 'but the child/is watching the teakettle's small hard tears'. The child interprets sorrow everywhere; even droplets of steam from a kettle are transformed into the unwept tears of the grandmother. The phrase 'dance like mad' strikes a poignant note as we remember that Bishop's own mother was committed to a mental asylum when Bishop was just five years old; they never met again. A cartoon-like image of the almanac ends this stanza. We view it through the child's eyes, as 'the clever almanac'.

Stanza four focuses on the almanac. It is a **sinister presence**, personified as a bird of ill-omen: 'Birdlike' it hovers, suspended 'half open'. This mood of misgiving is heightened when we are told that the grandmother's cup is not full of tea, but of 'dark brown tears'. However, normality asserts itself again – the grandmother 'shivers' and puts wood on the fire.

Stanza five opens with the eerie personification of the Marvel Stove and the almanac. A **sense of inevitability** ('It was to be') and hidden secrets ('I know what I know') is absorbed by the child. Just as the older Bishop puts order on her traumatic childhood experiences by arranging them into the tightly knit form of the sestina, the child in the poem attempts to order her experiences by drawing houses. But the house is tense, 'rigid', inflexible. The sorrow of this childhood cannot be changed; the situation was as it was. This house can only be reached by a 'winding pathway'. Does this echo Bishop's later travels, as she searches for home? The sadness of Bishop's situation focuses on the drawing now, as the child sketches a man with 'buttons like tears'.

In **stanza six**, the tears continue to fall, now 'into the flower bed' in the child's drawing. **Fantasy and reality are mixed** in the innocent perception of the child, who feels but does not understand. The **final three lines** contain all six key words as the almanac instructs that it is 'Time to plant tears'. Is the time for regret over? Is the child planting tears that will be wept in the future? Should the grandmother and child be shedding tears now? The 'child draws another inscrutable house'. The secrecy continues. Nothing is as it seems. The future looks chilling.

ANALYSIS

Elizabeth Bishop's poetry is an emotional journey. To what extent do you agree with this? Support your views with close reference to 'Sestina'.

Sample Paragraph

I agree that the reader goes on an emotional journey with Bishop in the poem 'Sestina' as Bishop struggles to come to terms with her traumatic childhood. I think we focus with her, not on her as we observe the little child valiantly drawing 'inscrutable' houses, full of tears and secrets. Our hearts go out to the small, motherless and fatherless little girl, caught in an almost nightmare scenario, as the almanac hangs 'Birdlike' above her, almost like a bird of prey. The child feels, but does not comprehend the awful tragedy in the house and Bishop allows us to see the workings of the little mind as the child blends reality and fantasy, as stoves and books talk. Everything seems to know except the child. The chaotic experiences of Bishop's childhood are strictly contained in the formal structure of the sestina, the song of sixes, with six stanzas containing six lines ending with the same six end-words: house, grandmother, child, stove, almanac and tears. This mirrors the 'rigid' house of the little girl's drawings. Both the older and the younger Bishop are trying desperately to put order and control on this overwhelming situation. The reader experiences the poignancy through the details of the 'failing light', 'the rain that beats on the roof of the house' and the teacup 'full of dark brown tears'. Finally, the reader, like Bishop, is not left comforted, but is faced with enigma as yet another 'inscrutable' house is drawn. It is interesting to note that Bishop was unable to write about her early childhood until her fifties. Was it only then that the planted tears were harvested?

Examiner's Comment

A competent and insightful answer focusing on the emotional journey undertaken by both the poet and reader. There is a clear sense of engagement with the poem. Quotations are used effectively throughout. Grade B.

CLASS/HOMEWORK EXERCISES

1. Some critics have said that 'Sestina' is a sentimental poem. Do you agree with this? Support your views with close reference to the poem.

2. Copy the table below into your own notes and fill in critical comments about the last two quotations.

Key Quotes

laughing and talking to hide her tears	This is a poem of pretence, where nothing is as it appears. The grandmother is trying to hide her sorrow as she attempts to entertain her granddaughter.
the clever almanac	The child assumes that the almanac must know many things, since it can foretell the phases of the moon, etc. Is there a sense of desperate curiosity contained in this poem?
It was to be, says the Marvel Stove	The blurring of fantasy and reality is shown by Bishop's clever use of personification.
the little moons fall down like tears/from between the pages of the almanac	
and the child draws another inscrutable house	

[handwritten top margin: Theme - death / Tone - haunting + surreal / First experience of death for her]

8 FIRST DEATH IN NOVA SCOTIA

[handwritten left margin: Eulogy for her cousins death Arthur, written from a childs view. / language = child like. / sibilance / Focuses on objects in the room.]

In the cold, cold parlor
my mother laid out Arthur
beneath the chromographs:
Edward, Prince of Wales,
with Princess Alexandra,
and King George with Queen Mary.
Below them on the table
stood a stuffed loon
shot and stuffed by Uncle
Arthur, Arthur's father.   10

[handwritten: repetition. The repetition from the start plays a role in creating an atmosphere. It also reflects the mind of a child attempting to make sense of the world she is describing. presents a grim scene. Child is being laid out by her mum who she rarely speaks of. Body is talked about briefly. objects in room are depicted in a factual detached way. The chromographs depict Royalty. Their presence leads to a moment of importance - Rulers of Canada. Attention then moves to the stuffed loon - like Arthur it is dead. To the child everything is frozen in time - everything is motionless - the lifeless corpse, the still photo, the stuffed animal.]

[handwritten left margin: personification]
Since Uncle Arthur fired
a bullet into him,
he hadn't said a word.
[handwritten left margin: metaphor]
He kept his own counsel
on his white, frozen lake,
the marble-topped table.

[handwritten left margin: alliteration metaphor]
His breast was deep and white,
cold and caressable;
his eyes were red glass,
much to be desired.   20

[handwritten: Interest appears to lie on the bird. She personifies him by assigning him with the power of speech - although the bird has not said a word also like Arthur. She speaks of the loons silence, cold stance and contradictory everything else she speaks of is attractive. "desired". the red marble eyes are like a gem. Ideas in this stanza reoccur later - deep and white breast of the loon + later deep snow - red maple leaf, red = Arthurs hair, red royal clothes. Shows child like mind.]

'Come,' said my mother,
'Come and say good-bye
to your little cousin Arthur.'
I was lifted up and given
one lily of the valley
to put in Arthur's hand.
Arthur's coffin was
[handwritten left margin: Metaphor]
a little frosted cake,
and the red-eyed loon eyed it
[handwritten left margin: Repetition]
from his white, frozen lake.   30

[handwritten: The gaze is broken by her mothers words. The mother wishes her to look on death by placing the lily in her cousins hand. poignant, moving scene, we consider Elizabeths memory of her mother with ease. In her child like mind she imagines the coffin to be a frosted cake and now imagines the loon wanting it for himself (red eyes) may have meanings of weeping as well as perhaps greed / desires.]

Arthur was very small.
[handwritten left margin: simile]
He was all white, like a doll
that hadn't been painted yet.
[handwritten left margin: Metaphor / % coldness / coldness]
Jack Frost had started to paint him
the way he always painted   35

[handwritten: Focus on Arthur, simplistic language No sense of fear so she describes Arthurs pallor (unhealthy pale appearance) The idea of Jack Frost starting to paint him refers to the red hair J.F is also known for bringing the red to the leaves of autumn. This reminds her of the maple leaf which is red and is mentioned in the Canadian emblem. The corpse is associated with patriotism not like the forever at the end of the stanza.]

the Maple Leaf (Forever).
He had just begun on his hair,
a few red strokes, and then
Jack Frost had dropped the brush
and left him white, forever.

we have the child like images of J.F painting Arthur's hair red but stopping off to leave him white. The brush does echo the word from the anthem but here it implies

40

The gracious royal couples
were warm in red and ermine;
their feet were well wrapped up
in the ladies' ermine trains.
They invited Arthur to be
the smallest page at court.
But how could Arthur go,
clutching his tiny lily,
with his eyes shut up so tight
and the roads deep in snow?

Child imagines a fairytale ending for Arthur — to bring warmth to the poem. The couples in the two pictures have a sense of warmth + comfort + she imagines them to invite Arthur into join them in her childlike mind — she decided Ours to be Arthur's picture.

Fear comes to the child seeing this as impossible as Arthur is dead and in his coffin. How can he possibly escape? He can't open his eyes so how could he see his way to the court let alone travel on the icy roads. The question about the snow reveals further her innocence and knowledge about death.

45

50

The details "clutching", "tiny", "tight" and "deep" suggest vulnerability — the final image is of Arthur — a child all alone in the world incapable of reaching safety.

'the roads deep in snow'

GLOSSARY

1	*parlor*: room set aside for entertaining guests.	8	*loon*: great crested grebe, an aquatic diving bird.
3	*chromographs*: coloured copies of pictures.	14	*counsel*: opinion.
4	*Edward*: British Royal (1841–1910).	28	*frosted*: iced.
5	*Alexandra*: Edward's wife.	36	*the Maple Leaf*: Canadian national emblem.
6	*King George*: King George V (1865–1936).	42	*ermine*: white fur.
6	*Queen Mary*: wife of King George V (1867–1953).	46	*page*: boy attendant.

EXPLORATIONS

1. With reference to lines 1–20 of the poem, describe the mood and atmosphere in the 'parlor'.

2. The poet uses several comparisons in this poem. Select one that you found particularly interesting and comment on its effectiveness.

3. Write your personal response to this poem, referring to the text in your answer.

STUDY NOTES

'First Death in Nova Scotia' was published when Elizabeth Bishop was in her early fifties. Written entirely in the past tense, it is an extraordinarily vivid memory of a disturbing experience. In the poem, Bishop's young narrator recounts the circumstances of an even younger cousin's death.

From the outset, we visualise Cousin Arthur's wake through a child's eyes. Characteristically, Bishop sets the scene in **stanza one** using **carefully chosen** descriptive details. It is winter in Nova Scotia. The dead child has been laid out in a 'cold, cold parlor'. Above the coffin are old photographs of two deceased royal couples. Fragmented memories of unfamiliar objects add to the dreamlike atmosphere. A stuffed loon sits on the marble-topped table. The young girl – in her desperate attempt to comprehend death – describes her cousin as 'all white, like a doll/that hadn't been painted yet'.

The dead boy and the 'dead' room soon become real for the reader, as does the dilemma faced by the **living child, who seems increasingly confused**. **Stanza two** focuses on the young narrator's fixation with the stuffed bird. By thinking hard about the death of this 'cold and caressable' loon, she is trying to find a possible explanation for death. She is fascinated by the loon – perhaps an escape mechanism from the unfamiliar atmosphere in the parlour. In any case, the bird – with its desired 'red glass' eyes – might be less threatening than the dead body in the casket. Suddenly, somewhere in the child's imagination, Cousin Arthur and the personified bird become closely associated. Both share an impenetrably cold stillness, suggested by the 'marble-topped table', which is compared to a 'white, frozen lake'.

In **stanza three** the child's mother lifts her up to the coffin so that she can place a lily of the valley in the dead boy's hand. Her mother's insistent invitation ('Come and say good-bye') is chillingly remote. We sense the young girl's vulnerability ('I was lifted up') as she is forced to place the flower in Arthur's hand. In a poignantly childlike image, she compares her cousin's white coffin to 'a little frosted cake'. **The mood turns progressively surreal** when the apprehensive narrator imagines the stuffed bird as a predator ('the red-eyed loon eyed it'). As always, Bishop's imagery is direct, brisk and to the point.

Bishop continues to explore childhood innocence in **stanza four**. Using the simplest of language, the child narrator describes her dead cousin: 'He was all white, like a doll'. In a renewed burst of imagination, she creates her own 'story' to explain what has happened to Arthur. His death must be caused by the winter frost that 'paints' the autumn leaves, including the familiar maple leaf. This thought immediately brings to mind the Canadian song 'The Maple Leaf Forever'. To the child, it seems that Jack Frost started to paint Arthur, but 'dropped the brush/ and left him white, forever'. This creative **stream of consciousness highlights the child's efforts to make sense of death's mysterious reality**.

The imagery of childhood fairytales continues in **stanza five** when the narrator pictures Arthur in the company of the royal families whose pictures hang on the parlour walls. He is now 'the smallest page at court'. For the first time, the cold has disappeared and the royals are 'warm in red and ermine'. This fantasy, however, is short lived. Still shaken by the strangeness of the occasion, the young narrator questions how this could have happened – especially as Arthur could not travel anywhere 'with his eyes shut up so tight/and the roads deep in snow'. The poem's final, tender image reflects both the child's naivety and a genuine concern for her cousin. Ironically, all around are symbols of immortality – the heavenly royal images of Arthur's entrance into a new, more glorious life. But the narrator's enduring uncertainty is central to the poem. The deceased boy, like the stuffed loon, seems really dead. Perhaps the dead don't go anywhere.

ANALYSIS

'The unknowable nature of life and death is a central concern of Elizabeth Bishop's poetry.' Discuss this statement with reference to 'First Death in Nova Scotia'. Support the points you make by referring to the poem.

Sample Paragraph

In several poems I have studied, it's clear that Elizabeth Bishop addresses life's mysteries. Sometimes she does this through the eyes of a child, as in 'First Death in Nova Scotia'. The poem describes her first experience of a death and how she struggled to understand it. It is an elegy for her young cousin, Arthur, and Bishop's memories of his funeral are extraordinarily clear. Everything about it confuses her. The formal, domestic setting is uninviting – a 'cold, cold parlor' has strange chromographs of the British Royal Family on the walls and a stuffed loon bird on the marble table. The bird had been shot by the dead child's father. As a young girl, Bishop recalls being forced to place a lily in her dead cousin's cold hand. These objects add to her insecurity. Nothing is explained to her and she escapes into her own imaginary world, comparing Arthur's casket to 'a little frosted cake'. She tries to tell herself that 'Jack Frost' is responsible for leaving Arthur 'white forever'. In the last verse, she imagines her dead cousin in an afterlife – not in heaven, but in a magical royal castle, 'the smallest page at court'. However, the young Elizabeth is caught between make-believe and reason. Her final thoughts challenge her own fantasy about life after death. Common sense tells her that Arthur, 'with his eyes shut up so tight', could not go out into 'roads deep in snow'. I thought Bishop really captured the uncertainty of a young child's mind in this very moving poem. I also got the impression that she was making the point that life and death can never be fully understood, no matter what age a person is.

Examiner's Comment

A focused and sustained response, showing good engagement with the text. Starting with a succinct overview, the paragraph traces the progress of thought through the poem, using apt and accurate quotations effectively. Clear expression and a convincing personal approach also contribute to the Grade A standard.

> ## CLASS/HOMEWORK EXERCISES

1. In your opinion, does 'First Death in Nova Scotia' present a sentimental view of death? Support your argument with reference to the text of the poem.

2. Copy the table below into your own notes and use the blank spaces to fill in the missing critical comments about the last two quotations.

Key Quotes

In the cold, cold parlor/my mother laid out Arthur	The atmosphere in the 'parlor' is icy and formal, emphasised by repetition and assonance.
he hadn't said a word./He kept his own counsel	In her confusion, the child narrator personifies the stuffed bird and assumes that the loon refuses to reveal the truth about how it died.
But how could Arthur go,/ clutching his tiny lily	The child's final, poignant concern is for her dead cousin. Are her feelings sincere or sentimental?
Arthur's coffin was/a little frosted cake	
Arthur was very small./He was all white, like a doll	

Handwritten top margin: Tone - one of surprise
Theme - Discovery of the domestic side of life.

9 FILLING STATION

Handwritten left margin: Colloquial language.

Oh, but it is dirty!
- this little filling station,
oil-soaked, oil-permeated
to a disturbing, over-all
black translucency.
Be careful with that match!

Handwritten annotations: Spontaneous opening. The title has already set the scene. no intro, no explanation. The exclamation adds emphasis to the dirty. writer seems disgusted + superior to the filling station. vivid description, use of adjectives "soaked", "permeated" emphasises the extent of the oil. The place is exact & glistening. Humour in last line, certain warning.

Father wears a dirty,
oil-soaked monkey suit
that cuts him under the arms,
and several quick and saucy
and greasy sons assist him

Handwritten left margin: alliteration

(it's a family filling station),
all quite thoroughly dirty.

Handwritten annotations: Human + domestic dimension (very masculine). Every thing about them is dirty. "dirty" placed at end of stanza so we can't fail to get the point. Beyond the dirt, the words, family father + sons soften the tone, creates cosy atmosphere. sibilance = hissing sound (s) (SH)

Do they live in the station?
It has a cement porch
behind the pumps, and on it
a set of crushed and grease-
impregnated wickerwork;

Handwritten left margin: alliteration

on the wicker sofa
a dirty dog, quite comfy.

Handwritten annotations: Question shows us that the poets curiosity is aroused, begins to speculate the people here. Describes what she sees around her again bringing in the idea of "dirt". The dog completes image of family: no mention of mother. colloquial word "comfy" adds to our sense that this place is good. - a place of nurture. Male environment.

Some comic books provide
the only note of color -
of certain color. They lie
upon a big dim doily

Handwritten left margin: alliteration

draping a taboret
(part of the set), beside
a big hirsute begonia.

Handwritten annotations: More vivid description of the place + objects that grasp her attention. The comic books are the only things that have kept its original colour. The objects like their surroundings are dirty + uncared for. However the speaker can recognise the aspiration to a finer life a sense of order. The taboret is part of a set. the dim grey doily has been embroidered with a daisy stitch - somebody put time into crocheting this.

Handwritten left margin: Repetition of the word "why".

Why the extraneous plant?
Why the taboret?
Why, oh why, the doily?
(Embroidered in daisy stitch
with marguerites, I think,
and heavy with gray crochet.)

Handwritten annotations: "why" she is finally coming to the realisation that someone is caring for the filling station.

Somebody embroidered the doily. *somebody does care about this place even though their effort are futile.*

Somebody waters the plant, *she humourously suggests that the begonia*

or oils it, maybe. Somebody *gets more oil than water.*

arranges the rows of cans *That same "somebody" has taken the trouble*

so that they softly say: *to arrange the cans in some sort of order so they*

read "ESSO-SO-SO-SO" Bishop explained these

ESSO-SO-SO-SO *sounds are those used to soothe horses which*

to high-strung automobiles. *accounts for the next line. 40 it has a calming*

Somebody loves us all. *soothing effect among the work like atmosphere*

of the filling station and these busy people who

come and go.

The final line seems to encapsulate / summarise her discovery of an affectionate presence – no matter how unattractive a place is and its inhabitants maybe – there is a mother figure or somebody in the background whose affection can be seen through small detail. The family is now complete.

'it's a family filling station'   *Strongly visual poem.*

GLOSSARY

3   *oil-permeated*: soaked through with oil.
5   *translucency*: shine, glow.
8   *monkey suit*: dungarees; all-in-one working
      clothes.
10   *saucy*: cheeky, insolent.
18   *impregnated*: saturated.
24   *doily*: ornamental napkin.
25   *taboret*: drum-shaped low seat; a stool.
27   *hirsute*: hairy.
27   *begonia*: house plant with large
      multicoloured leaves.
28   *extraneous*: unnecessary, inappropriate.

31   *daisy stitch*: stitch pattern used in
      embroidery.
32   *marguerites*: daisies.
33   *crochet*: intricate knitting patterns.
39   *ESSO-SO-SO*: Esso is a brand of oil;
      reference to the careful arrangement of
      oil cans.

EXPLORATIONS

1. In your opinion, how does Bishop make the opening of this poem dynamic and interesting? Comment on her use of punctuation, direct speech and compound words, which draw us into the world of the poem. Support your response with quotation from the text.

2. Trace the development of the poet's attitude to the filling station throughout the poem. Does it change from being critical and patronising to being more positive? Illustrate your answer with close reference to the text.

3. Comment on the effectiveness of Bishop's use of repetition in lines 34–41. Refer to the text in your response.

STUDY NOTES

Elizabeth Bishop was strongly influenced by a poetic movement called imagism, which was concerned with the accurate description of a particular thing. In this poem, she gives us an iconic description of a familiar American scene, the small-town gas station. Bishop found the new culture in 1960s California bewildering and it is noteworthy that the voice in this poem is that of an outsider trying to make sense of what is observed.

The prosaic title of the poem sets the mood for this commonplace scene. The poem **opens** with a **highly strung comment, disparaging the lack of hygiene** at the little station: 'Oh, but it is dirty!' The compound words ('oil-soaked', 'oil-permeated') suggest that everything is covered in a fine film of grease. This 'black translucency' has its own particular glow. Bishop's tense, dismissive tone creates a volatile, brittle atmosphere. Another voice interrupts her reverie: 'Be careful with that match!' In a few deft lines, the poet has set the scene, established the mood and introduced her characters. She uses a series of intensely descriptive lines that gives the poem a cinematic quality as we observe the details, like close-ups on a big screen.

The busy little station is captured in the **second stanza** through the poet's critical observations as she watches the family bustle about their business. The father is wearing a 'dirty,/oil-soaked monkey suit' that is too small for him ('cuts him under the arms'). The sons are described using alliteration of the letter 's', which suggests their fluid movements as well as their oily appearance ('several quick and saucy/and greasy sons assist'). Like the poet, we also become fascinated by this unremarkable place. Bishop's critical tone becomes more strident as she comments on the sons' insolence ('saucy') and their lack of hygiene ('all quite thoroughly dirty'). **We can hear the contempt in her voice.**

The **third stanza** questions, in a disbelieving tone, whether anyone could actually reside in such an awful place: 'Do they live in the station?' The poet's eye seems to pan around her surroundings **like a film camera, picking up on small details** as she tries to piece the scene into some kind of order. She lingers on the porch and its set of 'crushed and grease-/impregnated wickerwork'. Her disdain is obvious to the reader. The dog is described as a 'dirty dog' – it is almost as if it, too, has been smeared in oil. The repetition of the dead 'd' sound emphasises the unkempt appearance of everything. Then, suddenly, the poem pivots and turns on the homely word 'comfy'. The poet is surprised to note that the dog is quite content in this place. We are reminded that because of the harrowing circumstances of her own childhood, Bishop never fully knew what home was; we are left wondering if she longed to be 'comfy' too.

In **stanzas four and five**, she begins to notice evidence of a woman's hand in this place, particularly 'a big dim doily' on the 'taboret'. She notes the colourful 'comic books' and her eye is caught by the incongruous sight of 'a big hirsute begonia'. Even the plant has masculine qualities, being big and hairy. Bishop is observing the extraordinary in the ordinary; **in the most unlikely places, there is beauty and love**. We understand her bemusement as she reflects, almost in exasperation: 'Why, oh why, the doily?' We, like the narrator, have to reassess our initial view of this cluttered gas station. On closer observation, there is care and attention to detail, including artistic embroidery. We are brought right up close to examine this marvellous 'daisy stitch'. The critical, conversational tone of the poem clearly belongs to someone who is the observer, someone who does not belong. Is this the role Bishop was forced to adopt in her own life?

The poet's disturbed tone gives way in the **final stanza** to one of comfort. The lines whisper softly with sibilant 's' sounds. 'Somebody' cares for things, arranging the cans in order 'so that they softly say:/ESSO–SO–SO–SO'. Bishop commented that 'so–so–so' was a phrase used to calm highly strung horses. It is used here to calm herself, just as the oil in the cans is used to make the engines of 'high-strung automobiles' run smoothly. The tone relaxes and a touch of humour creeps in: she notes that 'Somebody waters the plant,/or oils it, maybe'. The use of repetition is also soothing as we, like Bishop, come to realise that there is 'Somebody' who cares. **The poem concludes on a quiet note of assurance that everybody gets love from somewhere: 'Somebody loves us all'.** This is a particularly poignant ending when we consider that Elizabeth Bishop's parents were both absent from her childhood. The wonderfully comforting conclusion soothes the reader, just as a mother might quieten a cranky child.

ANALYSIS

'Elizabeth Bishop's poems are often described as deceptively casual.' Discuss this view of the poet's work, with particular reference to 'Filling Station'. Support your response with close reference to the text.

Sample Paragraph

'Filling Station' deals with a central concern of all human beings, the need to feel wanted and cared for, the need to belong. Instead of a heavy, moralising tone, Bishop adopts a deceptively casual tone in this poem from the start, with its almost colloquial, conversational opening: 'Oh, but it is dirty!' However, the carefully selected compound phrases ('oil-soaked, oil-permeated') show a carefully crafted poem. The subtle use of repetition of 'why' to suggest the increasing puzzlement of the poet as she tries to make sense of this scene also convinces me that Bishop is a master craftsperson at work, whose art conceals her effort. Similarly, the repetition of 'Somebody' at the end of the poem leaves a lasting sense of reassurance not only for the high-strung cars and their drivers, but also for us, as the poet states with deliberate calm that 'Somebody loves us all'. The tone is that of a loving parent soothing a contrary child who won't go to sleep. Here is a first-class poet skilfully communicating her message of quiet optimism. The word 'comfy' is also deceptively casual as, suddenly, the critical tone of the poem changes when the poet realises that the dog is content to be living there. Now the realisation dawns that even in the most outlandish places there is comfort and caring. I thought it was clever of the poet to use such a homely word as 'comfy' to totally change the mood of the poem. Finally, I think that Bishop shows her skill with a beautiful use of quiet, soothing music in the use of the sibilant 's' at the conclusion of the poem. Just as the oil stops the gears in a car from making noise and grating, the carefully arranged oil cans in the filling station send their message of comfort to the narrator and to us: 'Somebody loves us all'.

Examiner's Comment

This is a competent answer, which addresses the question throughout. There is some very good engagement with the poem and effective use is made of apt references. The expression is reasonably well controlled, although slightly repetitive at times. Grade B.

CLASS/HOMEWORK EXERCISES

1. 'A sense of homelessness pervades Bishop's poetry'. Comment on this statement, referring to both the content and stylistic techniques used in 'Filling Station'. Support your discussion with reference to the poem.

2. Copy the table below into your own notes and fill in critical comments about the last two quotations.

Key Quotes

Be careful with that match!	We overhear this exchange on the forecourt. Bishop draws us into the dramatic world of this small family station.
a set of crushed and grease-/ impregnated wickerwork	Precise detail helps us to visualise the grubby little station and to hear the disdainful tone of the poet's observations as she surveys the unappealing surroundings.
Why the extraneous plant?	A feeling of disbelief is captured in the question, as Bishop tries to make sense of what she sees as an incongruous detail.
so that they softly say: ESSO– SO–SO–SO	
Somebody loves us all	

10 IN THE WAITING ROOM

In Worcester, Massachusetts,
I went with Aunt Consuelo
to keep her dentist's appointment
and sat and waited for her
in the dentist's waiting room.   5
It was winter. It got dark
early. The waiting room
was full of grown-up people,
arctics and overcoats,
lamps and magazines.   10
My aunt was inside
what seemed like a long time
and while I waited I read
the *National Geographic*
(I could read) and carefully   15
studied the photographs:
the inside of a volcano,
black, and full of ashes;
then it was spilling over
in rivulets of fire.   20
Osa and Martin Johnson
dressed in riding breeches,
laced boots, and pith helmets.
A dead man slung on a pole
– 'Long Pig,' the caption said.   25
Babies with pointed heads
wound round and round with string;
black, naked women with necks
wound round and round with wire
like the necks of light bulbs.   30
Their breasts were horrifying.
I read it right straight through.
I was too shy to stop.
And then I looked at the cover:
the yellow margins, the date.   35

Suddenly, from inside,
came an *oh!* of pain

- Aunt Consuelo's voice -
not very loud or long.
I wasn't at all surprised;   40
even then I knew she was
a foolish, timid woman.
I might have been embarrassed,
but wasn't. What took me
completely by surprise   45
was that it was *me*:
my voice, in my mouth.
Without thinking at all
I was my foolish aunt,
I - we - were falling, falling,   50
our eyes glued to the cover
of the *National Geographic*,
February, 1918.

I said to myself: three days
and you'll be seven years old.   55
I was saying it to stop
the sensation of falling off
the round, turning world
into cold, blue-black space.
But I felt: you are an *I*,   60
you are an *Elizabeth*,
you are one of *them*.
Why should you be one, too?
I scarcely dared to look
to see what it was I was.   65
I gave a sidelong glance
- I couldn't look any higher -
at shadowy gray knees,
trousers and skirts and boots
and different pairs of hands   70
lying under the lamps.
I knew that nothing stranger
had ever happened, that nothing
stranger could ever happen.
Why should I be my aunt,   75
or me, or anyone?

What similarities –
boots, hands, the family voice
I felt in my throat, or even
the *National Geographic*   80
and those awful hanging breasts –
held us all together
or made us all just one?
How – I didn't know any
word for it – how 'unlikely' ...   85
How had I come to be here,
like them, and overhear
a cry of pain that could have
got loud and worse but hadn't?

The waiting room was bright   90
and too hot. It was sliding
beneath a big black wave,
another, and another.

Then I was back in it.
The War was on. Outside,   95
in Worcester, Massachusetts,
were night and slush and cold,
and it was still the fifth
of February, 1918.

'then it was spilling over'

GLOSSARY

1   *Worcester*: much of the poet's childhood
    was spent here.
9   *arctics*: waterproof overshoes.
14 *National Geographic*: international
    geography magazine.
21 *Osa and Martin Johnson*: well-known
    American explorers.

23 *pith helmets*: sun helmets made from
    dried jungle plants.
25 *'Long Pig'*: term used by Polynesian
    cannibals for human flesh.
61 *Elizabeth*: the poet is addressing herself.
95 *The War*: First World War (1914-18).

EXPLORATIONS

1. In your view, what image of women is presented in the poem? Support your
    answer with reference to the text.

2. Select two images that have a surreal or dreamlike impact in the poem.
    Comment on the effectiveness of each image.

3. Write your personal response to the poem, using textual reference.

STUDY NOTES

*'In the Waiting Room' describes a defining coming-of-age experience for the poet
when she was just six years old. While her aunt receives dental treatment, the child
narrator browses through the pages of a* National Geographic *magazine and observes
what is happening around her. In the powerful and provocative moments that follow,
she begins to acknowledge her individual sense of being female.*

   The poem opens with a specific setting recalled in vivid detail by the child
narrator. She flicks through a *National Geographic* magazine in the dentist's office
while her aunt is in the patients' surgery. Familiar images of 'grown-up people,/
arctics and overcoats' seem to convey a sense of wellbeing. It is the winter of
1918 in Worcester, Massachusetts. **The language is direct and uncomplicated,
mirroring the candid observations of a young girl** as filtered through the adult
poet's mature interpretation. Short sentences establish the fragmented flashback,

allowing the reader to identify immediately with the narrative: 'It was winter. It got dark/early'. In addition to the unguarded tone, Bishop's short lines give the poem a visual simplicity, even though the **first stanza** is composed of 35 lines.

The mood changes from **line 18** onwards, as the young girl studies the dramatic magazine photographs of an active volcano 'spilling over/in rivulets of fire'. For the first time, **she recognises the earth's destructive force**. In contrast to the earlier feeling of security in the waiting room, the atmosphere becomes uneasy. Disturbing pictures ('A dead man slung on a pole' and 'Babies with pointed heads') are as intriguing as they are shocking. The child is drawn further into an astonishingly exotic world of cannibalism and violence. Graphic images of ornamental disfigurement seem horrifying: 'naked women with necks/wound round and round with wire'. The repetition of 'round and round' emphasises the young girl's spiralling descent into an enthralling world. Caught between fascination, repulsion and embarrassment ('too shy to stop'), she concentrates on the magazine's cover in an effort to regain control of her feelings.

The child is unexpectedly startled by a voice 'from inside' (**line 36**). At first, she presumes that the sound ('an *oh!* of pain') has been made by her aunt. But then something extraordinary happens and she realises that she has made the sound herself: 'it was *me*'. This sudden awareness that the cry has come from within herself prompts a **strange, visionary experience** in which she identifies closely with her 'foolish aunt'. The scene is dramatic and dreamlike: 'I – we – were falling, falling'.

In the surreal sequence that follows, the child focuses on her approaching birthday as she tries hard to resist the sensation of fainting: 'three days/and you'll be seven years old' (**line 54**). Ironically, it is at this crucial point (on the edge of 'cold, blue-black space') that she gains an astonishing insight into her own sense of self: 'you are an *Elizabeth*,/you are one of *them*'. The idea of sharing a common female identity with her aunt and the unfamiliar women in the magazine pictures is almost overwhelming: 'nothing stranger/had ever happened' (**line 72**). To the distraught child, it seems as though **all women have lost their individuality and have merged into a single female identity**. Although she attempts to stay calm, she is plagued by recurring questions and confusion: 'Why should I be my aunt,/ or me, or anyone?' The young Elizabeth's awakening to adulthood is obviously painful. In attempting to come to terms with her destiny as both an individual and also as part of a unified female gender, she makes this hesitant statement: 'How – I didn't know any/word for it – how "unlikely" ...'.

Before she can return to everyday reality, the young girl must endure further discomfort. Her surroundings feel 'bright/and too hot' (**line 90**) and she imagines being repeatedly submerged 'beneath a big black wave', a metaphor for helplessness and disorientation. In the **final stanza**, she regains her composure in the waiting room's apparent safety, where she lists the certainties of place and time. But there is a distinct sense of life's harshness: 'The War was on' and Massachusetts is encountering 'slush and cold' (**line 97**). Such **symbols are central to our understanding of this deeply personal poem**. Just as the image of the erupting volcano seemed to signify Bishop's development, the waiting room itself is a significant location as a transition point in her self-awareness.

ANALYSIS

'An unsettling sense of not being fully in control is a central theme in the poetry of Elizabeth Bishop.' To what extent is this true of 'In the Waiting Room'? Support your answer with reference to the text of the poem.

Sample Paragraph

The theme of the trauma of growing up is central to 'In the Waiting Room'. It's unlike many nostalgic poems. They often describe childhood experiences in a sentimental way. But this one's very disturbing. It's set in a dentist's where the poet remembers waiting for 'Aunt Consuelo' who is having treatment. The atmosphere at the start is quite relaxed as the child passes the time by reading an old copy of the *National Geographic*. However, the photographs of a black volcano 'full of ashes' and of cannibals carrying a dead man ('Long Pig') are extremely upsetting. The mood becomes nervous. Photographs of African native women terrify the child as some of them wear wire necklaces. The poet compares them to 'light bulbs' – an image which immediately frightens her. The outside world is so violent and unexpected that she then goes into a trance-like state and cries out in agony. Her experience is more and more unsettled as she struggles to keep a grip on reality. Instead, she faints into 'cold, blue-black space'. The image suggests how out of control she is. However, what really unsettles her is the discovery for the very first time that she herself is a young woman and she shares this with every other female. The unusual photos of the naked African women suggest her own future and she becomes terrified. Her uneasy feelings are summed up at the end when she describes being overcome by the heat in the crowded waiting room, 'beneath a big black wave'. This leaves me feeling sympathy for this traumatised girl who is very unsure about her life and future role as a woman.

Examiner's Comment

A reasonably well-focused and sustained response, which addresses the question competently. Good use is made of quotations. The expression could be more controlled in places, particularly in the opening section. Grade B.

CLASS/HOMEWORK EXERCISES

1. 'Bishop's reflective poems combine precise observation with striking imagery.' Discuss this view with reference to 'In the Waiting Room'. Refer to the poem in your answer.

2. Copy the table below into your own notes and fill in critical comments about the last two quotations.

Key Quotes

the inside of a volcano,/black, and full of ashes	The dramatic image suggests danger and the unknown. It might also symbolise the child's coming of age.
naked women with necks/ wound round and round with wire	Graphic imagery illustrates the child's introduction to a disconcerting world. The alliteration and insistent rhythm emphasise her sense of shock.
you are an Elizabeth,/you are one of them	The alarming insight that her secure sense of uniqueness is being absorbed into a greater female identity is a moment of epiphany for the child.
It was sliding/beneath a big black wave	
Then I was back in it./The War was on	

'Elizabeth Bishop's personal poetry is filled with vivid imagery.' To what extent do you agree with this statement? Support the points you make with suitable reference to the poems by Bishop on your course.

Marking Scheme Guidelines

Candidates are free to agree and/or disagree with the given statement. Expect discussion (though not necessarily equally) on both 'personal poetry' and 'vivid imagery'. Allow for a broad range of approaches. However, responses should show clear evidence of engagement with the poems of Elizabeth Bishop on the course.

Material might be drawn from the following:

- Exaggerated/enhanced exploration of childhood, nature, death
- Detailed description of people and places, both familiar and exotic
- Atmospheres/moods created by wide-ranging images – visual, aural, tactile
- Vivid 'painterly' quality of the writing sharpens/enriches impact
- Freshness and intensity of her language, comparisons, symbols, etc.

Sample Essay

(Bishop's personal poetry is filled with vivid imagery)

1. *Elizabeth Bishop's poems are remarkably colourful and vibrant. The poet was a great traveller and was very interested in painting, so it isn't surprising that her eye for detailed observation and skill at creating varied moods are apparent in poems, such as 'Filling Station' and 'First Death in Nova Scotia'. Bishop also demonstrates her interest in people and places throughout her work. She is also a writer who treats her subjects – including nature – in a very personal and dramatic way.*

2. *In 'Filling Station', the poem's narrator – and central character, presumably Bishop herself – is looking at an everyday scene. But the speaker is an outside observer who is critical of the 'oil-soaked, oil-permeated' filling station. She reacts personally, immediately becoming involved in the small drama around her – 'Oh, but it is dirty!' I could easily picture the place as the poet described the garage family of males, the father in his 'dirty oil-soaked money suit', and his 'several quick and saucy/and greasy sons'. They almost slide off the page in their oily working clothes. Bishop's*

close focus is on the film of oil which permeates everything. She is thinking fast and highly-charged, like the car engines on the forecourt. She smokes and a terse voice shouts, 'Be careful with that match!' Not only does Bishop allow us to see this place, but also she enables us to hear its loud, rough sounds by the use of this conversational phrase.

3. *Details about this ordinary little place absorb Bishop and gets her observing – 'some comic books', 'a big hirsute begonia', 'a dirty dog, quite comfy'. This is typical of the poet whose eye for close observation really brings the garage to life and suggests that there is a relaxed atmosphere in the filling station. This humble place is a caring environment, one where people look after each other. 'Somebody embroidered the doily', 'Somebody waters the plant', the highly-strung speaker relaxes enough to even crack a joke, 'or oils it'. Just as the harsh, grating sound of the engine is lubricated to a silky purr by the oil, so the tense observer is soothed by the soft, sibilant sounds, 'ESSO-SO-SO'.*

4. *This sensation of intimate interaction with people is also evident in the poem, 'Sestina'. The whole poem is filled with shadowy secrets as the older Bishop looks back at a domestic scene: a grandmother making tea and reading to her little granddaughter. I thought it was poignant how the child tries to make sense of her experiences by drawing 'rigid' houses, and the older poet attempts to order the chaotic nature of her early childhood by using the tightly-knit form of the sestina, the 'song of sixes'. The child's house even mirrors the strict form of the poem, with its six emphatic words; 'grandmother', 'child', 'stove', 'tears', 'almanac', 'house'. These words contain the meaning of the poem, unlike the house which remains a puzzle. The older Bishop comprehends while the younger child is aware, but unknowing. The little girl feels, but does not understand the sadness in the atmosphere, so she draws 'a man with buttons likes tears'. When I read this poem, I found Bishop's personal approach to be very moving. Behind the appearance of normality in this house lurks strange secrets. The almanac, which would be in every country home for its information on calendar dates and seasons, is described as, 'Birdlike it hovers' above the child. The teacup is 'full of dark brown tears'. One thing merges into another, like a nightmare. The future looks chilling, 'Time to plant tears'. At some point this sorrow will have to be released and expressed. I found the viewpoint in this very intimate poem original and challenging.*

5. 'First Death in Nova Scotia' is an exceptionally vivid poem – almost surreal at times. Bishop recalls her early experience of seeing the dead body of her young cousin Arthur. The poet manages to create a memorable setting in the Canadian winter landscape, with 'the roads deep in snow'. The intense child's view of the 'cold parlor' where her cousin is laid out seems dreamlike, reflecting the disturbing event. There are old-fashioned pictures of royal couples and 'a stuffed loon' on the table beside the boy's body. She clearly recalls seeing her cousin's coffin, which looked like 'a little frosted cake'. Such a colourful comparison effectively illustrated Bishop's heightened experience – a mixture of confused innocence and shock. The poem ended with the child poet imagining her cousin alive and well, 'clutching his tiny lily' and with 'his eyes shut up so tight'. The room contains many images of death and the afterlife which left me wondering – just like the young narrator – about the questions associated with dying.

6. For me, Bishop is at her best when she re-creates scenes from her own life. I enjoyed her poems about nature, fishing, and travelling to strange environments. One of her great skills is in bringing characters and places to life, and leaving readers with lasting impressions of how varied and mysterious nature – and human nature – can be.

(approx. 840 words)

Examiner's Comment

A very well-focused and personal response that shows a close reading of the question. The opening paragraph provides a succinct overview of Bishop's subject matter and key stylistic features. Both elements of the question are addressed throughout, and there is effective use of a great many supportive quotes in developing discussion points. Expression is clear, varied and well controlled.

GRADE: A1

P = 14/15

C = 13/15

L = 13/15

M = 5/5

Total = 45/50

> SAMPLE LEAVING CERT QUESTIONS ON BISHOP'S POETRY

1. 'In her poems, Elizabeth Bishop reveals her own response to the natural world through the precision of her language.' Discuss this statement, referring to the poetry of Bishop on your course.

2. 'Elizabeth Bishop's poems explore issues of universal significance in a fresh and interesting style.' To what extent do you agree with this view? Support your answer with suitable reference to the poems by Bishop on your course.

3. 'Moments of discovery and a carefully controlled writing style characterise the poetry of Elizabeth Bishop.' Comment on this assessment of Bishop's poetry, supporting your answer with reference to the poems by Bishop on your course.

Sample Essay Plan (Q3)

'Moments of discovery and a carefully controlled writing style characterise the poetry of Elizabeth Bishop.' Comment on this assessment of Bishop's poetry, supporting your answer with reference to the poems by Bishop on your course.

- Intro: Bishop takes ordinary, everyday experiences and carefully reveals the insightful drama and wonder found there. Detailed, imaginative descriptions fill her poetry so that the reader journeys to self-discovery with her.

- Point 1: Based on an actual event, 'The Fish' describes a special day spent fishing. Precise similes, e.g. skin hanging 'like ancient wallpaper', allow us to examine the fish closely. The awestruck poet responds respectfully, 'rainbow, rainbow, rainbow!', reflecting her admiration and wonder.

- Point 2: 'First Death in Nova Scotia' typifies a startling first experience of death: 'Come and say good-bye/to your little cousin'. Disquieting imagery lets the reader see the event through the eyes of a child.

- Point 3: In 'The Prodigal', Bishop characteristically uses setting effectively to explore themes of degradation, alienation, resilience and redemption. Similarly, in 'The Armadillo', she discovers how defenceless animals are at risk from human carelessness.

- Point 4: The well-managed form of 'Sestina' illustrates the depth of the poet's feeling as she strains to hold chaos in order. Six key end-words in each of the six stanzas, all contained in the final rhyming triplet.

- Conclusion: Bishop's narrative and reflective poems are often journeys of discovery and realisation. The loss of innocence is a recurring theme. Her distinctive poetry is both thoughtful and thought provoking.

Sample Essay Plan (Q1)

Develop one of the above points into a paragraph.

Sample Paragraph: Point 2

Elizabeth Bishop's poetry frequently deals with the memory of specific occurrences in her life. 'First Death in Nova Scotia' is about her little cousin's death when he was five. It is the young Bishop's first experience of death, and it is clear that she does not understand the concept. The poet enables us to see the event through the eyes of the child and also allows us to see the workings of the child's mind. She carefully sets the chilling mood at Arthur's wake. The stuffed loon 'hadn't said a word' since 'Uncle Arthur fired/a bullet into him'. The image is exact, a common feature of Bishop's writing. The 'marble-topped table' becomes 'his white, frozen lake'. The 'red glass' eyes were 'much to be desired'. The poignancy of the description of the little dead boy as a 'doll/that hadn't been painted yet' is heartbreaking, as we see the child apply a childish understanding to an adult event, death. She sustains the childlike images: 'Jack Frost had started to paint him'. This is the child referencing her nursery rhymes to try to comprehend what is happening. She continues in this way. She looks at the royal picture and imagines the 'gracious royal couples' inviting the little boy 'to be/the smallest page at court'. However, as often happens in Bishop's autobiographical poems, there is a moment of revelation – in this case, it is the painful innocence of childhood experiences, particularly of death. This is shown in the final question as the young Bishop wonders 'how could Arthur go'. The child seems obsessed with her cousin's strange appearance: 'with his eyes shut up so tight/and the roads deep in snow?' I could relate to the idea of a child learning about reality the hard way – especially in the final sad image of the little girl alone and with no one explaining what is happening.

Examiner's Comment

This paragraph makes a solid attempt to address the question in a focused manner. There is a good understanding of the poem and some personal response. References and quotes are used well to discuss the child's uncertain reaction to death. Overall, expression is varied and controlled, although slightly note-like at times. Basic B grade standard.

> ## LAST WORDS

'Bishop was spectacular in being unspectacular.'

Marianne Moore

'The sun set in the sea ... and there was one of it and one of me.'

Elizabeth Bishop

'Bishop disliked the swagger and visibility of literary life.'

Eavan Boland

EMILY DICKINSON

1830–86

'Forever is composed of nows.'

Emily Dickinson was born on 10 December 1830 in Amherst, Massachusetts. Widely regarded as one of America's greatest poets, she is also known for her unusual life of self-imposed social seclusion. An enigmatic figure with a fondness for the macabre, Dickinson never married. She was a prolific letter-writer and private poet, though fewer than a dozen of her poems were published during her lifetime. It was only after her death in 1886 that her work was discovered. It is estimated that she wrote about 1,770 poems, many of which explored the nature of immortality and death, with an almost mantric quality at times. Ultimately, however, she is remembered for her distinctive style, which was unique for the era in which she wrote. Her poems contain short lines, typically lack titles and often ignore the rules of grammar, syntax and punctuation, yet she expressed far-reaching ideas within compact phrases. Amidst paradox and uncertainty, her poetry has an undeniable capacity to move and provoke.

Prescribed Poems

[handwritten annotations at top:]
Theme : enduring power
power + hope is seen through the bird
optimistic and cheerful.
Through the poem she is giving hope the celebration it deserves.

'HOPE' IS THE THING WITH FEATHERS

[handwritten:] = simile, comparing hope to a thing with feathers.
authoritive, a vivid, direct statement.

[left margin handwritten:] Abstract concept "hope" is portrayed through the concrete image of the bird.

'Hope' is the thing with feathers— *a bird can fly and is something*
That perches in the soul— *feathers = warmth, comfort. Hope is now our spiritual. that can lift our spirits like hope.*
And sings the tune without the words— *No words can element*
And never stops—at all— *describe hope, it goes beyond*
dash represents its continuity. all logic + its always there.

[left margin:] In our most turmoil time hope is at its sweetest.

[handwritten: terror, difficult time you go through]
And sweetest—in the Gale—is heard— *Gale + storm are the hard*
And sore must be the storm— *moments in life and where hope is strong. Gale + storm ; mental*
That could abash the little Bird *it shows the strength states of*
That kept so many warm— *of the bird (hope), it looks people.*

[left margin:] Universal poem.
Even though there might be a tiny bit of hope, it still protects us from the storms.

I've heard it in the chillest land— *own personal experience.*
And on the strangest Sea— *metaphor for her own mental state.*

[left margin:] emphasises "never".
Yet, never, in Extremity, *In the times of extreme crisis, hope*
It asked a crumb—of Me. *never asked for anything back.*

[handwritten:] Poem is telling us to always have hope, its absolute and everlasting.

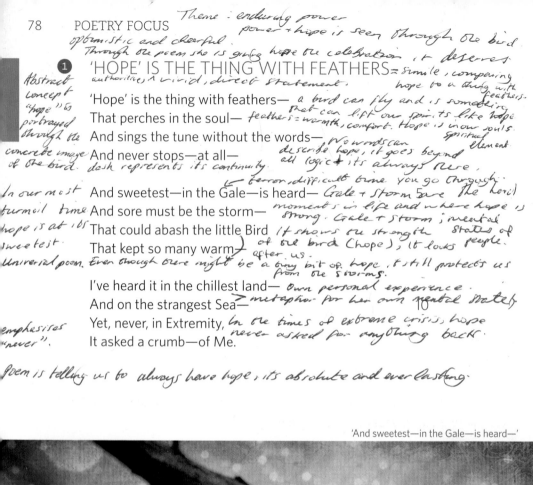

'And sweetest—in the Gale—is heard—'

GLOSSARY

5 *And sweetest—in the Gale—is heard:* hope is most comforting in times of trouble.

7 *abash:* embarrass; defeat.
11 *in Extremity:* in terrible times.

EXPLORATIONS

1. What are the main characteristics of the bird admired by Dickinson? Does the image help or hinder your understanding of the meaning of hope? Refer to the poem in support of your opinions.

2. Would you consider Dickinson to be an optimist or a pessimist? How does the poem contribute to your view?

3. In your view, what is the purpose of the poem – to instruct, to explain, to express a feeling? Support your response by reference to the text.

A bird can fly therefore it compares to hope as our spirits are being lifted

STUDY NOTES

Few of Emily Dickinson's poems were published during her lifetime and it was not until 1955, 69 years after her death, that an accurate edition of her poems was published, with the original punctuation and words. This didactic poem explores the abstraction, hope. It is one of her 'definition' poems, wherein she likens hope to a little bird, offering comfort to all.

The dictionary definition of hope is an expectation of something desired. The Bible refers to hope, saying, 'Hope deferred maketh the heart sick', while the poet Alexander Pope (1688–1744) declares that 'Hope springs eternal in the human breast'. In **stanza one**, Dickinson explores hope by using the **metaphor of a little bird** whose qualities are similar to those of hope: non-threatening, calm and powerful. Just like the bird, hope can rise above the earth with all its troubles and desperate times. Raised in the Puritan tradition, Dickinson, although rejecting formal religion, would have been aware of the religious symbolism of the dove and its connection with divine inspiration and the Spirit or Holy Ghost, as well as the reference to doves in the story of Noah's Ark and the Flood. Hope appears against all odds and 'perches in the soul'. But this hope is not easily defined, so she refers to it as 'the thing', an inanimate object.

This silent presence is able to **communicate** beyond reason and logic and far **beyond the limitations of language**: 'sings the tune without the words'. Hope's permanence is highlighted by the unusual use of dashes in the punctuation: 'never stops—at all—'. This effective use of punctuation suggests the ongoing process of hope.

Stanza two focuses on the tangible qualities of hope (sweetness and warmth) and shows the spiritual, emotional and psychological **comfort found in hope**. The 'Gale' could refer to the inner state of confusion felt in the agony of despair. The little bird that comforts and shelters its young offers protection to 'so many'. The vigour of the word 'abash' suggests the buffeting wind of the storm against which the little bird survives. The last two lines, which run on, convey the welcoming, protective circle of the little bird's wing.

A **personal experience of hope in times of anguish** ('I've heard') is referred to in **stanza three**. Extreme circumstances are deftly sketched in the phrases 'chillest land' and 'strangest Sea'. This reclusive poet, who spent most of her life indoors in her father's house, deftly catches an alien, foreign element. She then explains that hope is not demanding in bad times; it is generous, giving rather than taking: 'Yet, never, in Extremity,/It asked a crumb—of Me.' The central paradox of hope is expressed in the metaphor of the bird, delicate and fragile, yet strong and indomitable. The tiny bird is an effective image for the first stirring of hope in a time of despair. In the solemn ending, the poet gives hope the dignified celebration it deserves.

Dickinson is a unique and original talent. She used the metre of hymns. She also uses their form of the four-line verse. Yet this is not conventional poetry, due to Dickinson's use of the dash to slow the line and make the reader pause and consider. Ordinary words like 'at all' and 'is heard' assume a tremendous importance and their position is to be considered and savoured. **Her unusual punctuation has the same effect, as it highlights the dangers ('Gale', 'Sea').** The alliteration of 's' in 'strangest Sea' and the run-on line to suggest the circling comfort of the little bird all add to the curious music of Dickinson's poems. The buoyant, self-confident tone of the poem is in direct contrast to the strict Puritanical tradition of a severe, righteous God, with which she would have been familiar in her youth and which she rejected, preferring to keep her Sabbath 'staying at home'.

'Emily Dickinson's poetry contains an intense awareness of the private, inner self.' Discuss how Dickinson gives expression to this interior world in her poetry. Support your exploration with quotations from her prescribed poems.

Sample Paragraph

Everyone has experienced the 'dark night of the soul' when it seems nothing is ever going to go right again. Dickinson, with her simple image of the bird singing in the soul, derived from psalms, provides the perfect optimistic antidote to this dark interior state of mind, '"Hope" is the thing with feathers'. She then develops this metaphor throughout the poem, comforting us with the thought that the bird/hope can communicate with us without the need for the restrictions of language, 'sings the tune without words'. There is no end to hope 'And never stops—at all'. She understands the darkness of despair, 'in the Gale', 'the strangest Sea'. The use of capitalisation by the poet seems to me to point out the terror of the individual struggling to survive. But the bird of hope provides comfort and warmth, 'And sweetest'. I like the poet's use of enjambment in the lines 'That could abash the little Bird/That kept so many warm'. It is as if the protection of hope encircles the individual, just as the wing of the little bird protects her young in the nest. This is an optimistic, buoyant poem in which Dickinson appears to be instructing the reader that one should never despair. The phrase 'perches in the soul' suggests to me that the poet regards hope as coming of its own volition, it just appears, there is a sense of otherworldliness about it. Hope, she tells us, is generous, never demanding, always giving, 'Yet, never, in Extremity,/It asked a crumb—of Me'. I think the use of the capital for 'Me' shows the heightened concern of someone for him/herself when the feeling of despair envelops.

Examiner's Comment

This response shows an awareness of the poet's style and content. It is a solid B-grade response. However, it lacks the in-depth analysis required for an A-grade answer.

CLASS/HOMEWORK EXERCISES

1. 'Dickinson is a wholly new and original poetic genius.' Do you agree or disagree with this statement? Support your response with reference to the poems on your course.

2. Copy the table below into your own notes and fill in critical comments about the last two quotations.

Key Quotes

'Hope' is the thing with feathers	The image of the bird is used to represent hope.
And sweetest—in the Gale	Hope is needed most in times of trouble.
I've heard it in the chillest land	
Yet, never, in Extremity,/It asked a crumb—of Me	

poem of despair, picturing depression as a nature landscape.
poem of an abstract feeling and concrete idea.
It explores the negative relationship toward man and Emily Dickinson   83
God.

② THERE'S A CERTAIN SLANT OF LIGHT

= light doesn't signify positivity in this context.

Melancholic mood within the poem.

There's a certain Slant of light,
Winter Afternoons—

Simile = linking the winter light + church music.

That oppresses, like the Heft
Of Cathedral Tunes—

The winter light is oppressive intensify the negative outlook negative relationship.

paradox

Heavenly Hurt, it gives us—
We can find no scar,
But internal difference,
Where the Meanings, are—

awareness of mortality we don't live forever.

The effects of the sunlight, mentally. Heavenly Hurt = fear of judgement day. There are no physical scars but there are scars in our souls, that mean deep down we know we will eventually die. Universal touch.

None may teach it—Any—
'Tis the Seal Despair—
An imperial affliction
Sent us of the Air—

sense of hopelessness

The meaning of life cannot be explained. Inevitably we will die   10

Evokes the harshness of God's will.

It's sent from a higher place which we can't explain. Her presenting God as royalty/powerful.

When it comes, the Landscape listens
Shadows—hold their breath—
When it goes, 'tis like the Distance
On the look of Death—

personification. When death comes, it not only effects us but the world around us.

we don't know the minute, the hour, whenever it will be. How long is left until we die.

Final dash: lifeline from start to finish. We don't know when our time is up. Mental anguish she was going through made her worry about death. When her spirits lift that worry fades.

'Heavenly Hurt, it gives us'

GLOSSARY

1   *Slant*: incline; fall; interpretation.
3   *oppresses*: feels heavy; overwhelms.
3   *Heft*: strength; weight.
9   *Any*: anything.

10 *Seal Despair*: sign or symbol of hopelessness.
11 *imperial affliction*: God's will for mortal human beings.

EXPLORATIONS

1. Describe the mood and atmosphere created by the poet in the opening stanza.

2. Comment on Dickinson's use of personification within the poem.

3. Write your own personal response to the poem, supporting your views with reference or quotation.

STUDY NOTES

Dickinson was a keen observer of her environment, often dramatising her observations in poems. In this case, a particular beam of winter light puts the poet into a mood of depression as the slanting sunlight communicates a sense of despair. The poem typifies her creeping fascination with mortality. But although the poet's subject matter is intricate and disturbing, her own views are more difficult to determine. Ironically, this exploration of light and its effects seems to suggest a great deal about Dickinson's own dark consciousness.

From the outset, Dickinson creates an uneasy atmosphere. The setting ('Winter Afternoons') is dreary and desultory. Throughout **stanza one**, there is an underlying sense of time weighing heavily, especially when the light is compared to solemn cathedral music ('Cathedral Tunes'). We usually expect church music to be inspirational and uplifting, but in this case, its 'Heft' has a burdensome effect which simply 'oppresses' and adds to the **downcast mood.**

In **stanza two**, the poet considers the significance of the sunlight. For her, its effects are negative, causing pain to the world: 'Heavenly Hurt, it gives us'. The paradoxical language appears to reflect Dickinson's ironic attitude that **human beings live in**

great fear of God's power. Is there a sense that deep down in their souls ('Where the Meanings, are'), people struggle under the weight of God's will, fearing death and judgement?

This feeling of humanity's helplessness is highlighted in **stanza three**: 'None may teach it' sums up the predicament of our limitations. Life and death can never be fully understood. Perhaps this is our tragic fate – our 'Seal Despair'. Dickinson presents **God as an all-powerful royal figure** associated with suffering and punishment ('An imperial affliction'). Is the poet's tone critical and accusatory? Or is she simply expressing the reality of human experience?

Stanza four is highly dramatic. **Dickinson personifies a terrified world** where 'the Landscape listens'. The earlier sombre light is now replaced by 'Shadows' that 'hold their breath' in the silence. The poet imagines the shocking moment of death and the mystery of time ('the Distance'). While the poem's ending is open to speculation, it seems clear that Dickinson is exploring the transition from life into eternity, a subject that is central to her writing. The only certain conclusion is an obvious one – that death is an inescapable reality beyond human understanding, as mysterious as it is natural. The poet's final tone is resigned, almost relieved. The 'Slant of light' offers no definitive answers to life's questions and the human condition is as inexplicable as death itself.

Throughout the poem, Dickinson's fragmented style is characterised by her **erratic punctuation and repeated use of capital letters**. She uses the dash at every opportunity to create suspense and drama. For the poet, the winter light is seen as an important sign from God, disturbing the inner 'Landscape' of her soul. In the end, the light (a likely metaphor for truth) causes Dickinson to experience an inner sadness and a deep sense of spiritual longing.

ANALYSIS

In your view, what is the central theme in this poem? Support the points you make with suitable reference to the text.

Sample Paragraph

I think that death is the main theme in all of Emily Dickinson's poems, including this one. The poem is very atmospheric, but the light coming through the church window can be interpreted as a symbol of God, hope for the world. However, Dickinson's language is quite negative and it could be argued that our human lives are under pressure and that fear of eternal damnation is also part of life. The phrases 'Heavenly Hurt' and 'imperial affliction' suggest that we are God's subjects, trying to avoid sin in this life in order to find salvation after death. One of the central points in the poem is the fear of dying that people have. It is outside of our control. All humans can do is 'hold their breath'. I believe that the central message of Dickinson's poem is that death comes to us all and we must accept it. The mood throughout the poem is oppressive, just like the sunlight coming in through the church window and the depressing 'Cathedral Tunes' the poet hears. The poet's distinctive punctuation, using dashes and abrupt stops and starts, is part of the tense mood of the poem. Dickinson's theme is quite distressing and the broken rhythms and disturbing images such as 'scar', 'Seal Despair' and 'Shadows' add to the uneasiness of the theme that death is unavoidable.

Examiner's Comment

A well-sustained response which attempted to stay focused throughout. In the main, references and quotations were used effectively and there were some worthwhile attempts to show how features of the poet's style enhanced the presentation of her central theme. Grade A.

CLASS/HOMEWORK EXERCISES

1. How would you describe the dominant mood of the poem? Is it positive in any way? Explain your response, supporting the points you make with suitable reference to the text.

2. Copy the table below into your own notes and fill in critical comments about the last two quotations.

Key Quotes

Winter Afternoons	The oppressive mood is reinforced through the setting itself and suggested by the use of this assonant phrase.
But internal difference	Dickinson believes that the pain of being mortal is an inner one, both psychological and spiritual.
Heavenly Hurt	
Shadows—hold their breath	

death and mental anguish.

③ I FELT A FUNERAL, IN MY BRAIN   *Her own funeral in her brain that she imagines or she suffocated feeling of a mental breakdown*

personal poem, no universality

Alliteration
Run on lines
highlighting T
the word.

I felt a Funeral, in my Brain,   *Unusual dramatic statement. Some intense*
And Mourners to and fro   *psychological suffering to make her imagine this.*
Kept treading—treading—till it seemed   *Mourners coming may lead to some kind of understanding or that the ability*
That Sense was breaking through—   *to think rationally was breaking and she was losing it.*

smile
Repetition

And when they all were seated,   *The mourners became peaceful.*
A Service, like a Drum—   *Her experience of this thought was constant like*
Kept beating—beating—till I thought   *the beating of a drum.*
My Mind was going numb—   *It's sooner power she felt her mind was going numb. Sense of oppression associated with the gradual disintegration of sanity.*

And then I heard them lift a Box   *Describing the carrying of the coffin to the grave.*
And creak across my Soul   10
With those same Boots of Lead, again,   *Suggest the movement is uncomfortable.*
Then Space—began to toll,   *It intensifies the sense of oppression toll suggests a mournful sad mood, the clash can represent emptiness which leads to a mental breakdown.*

Metaphor

As all the Heavens were a Bell,   *The entire universe is reduced to one sound of one funeral bell.*
And Being, but an Ear,   *As she is just reduced to hearing she still feels isolated.*
And I, and Silence, some strange Race   *She's transitioning from one life to the next.*
Wrecked, solitary, here—   *She's trapped in a limbo almost*
sibilance

Alliteration
Repetition

And then a Plank in Reason, broke,
And I dropped down, and down—
And hit a World, at every plunge,
And Finished knowing—then—   20

'And then a Plank in Reason, broke'

GLOSSARY

3 *treading*: crush by walking on.
4 *Sense*: faculty of perception; the senses (seeing, hearing, touching, tasting, smelling); sound, practical judgement.

12 *toll*: ring slowly and steadily, especially to announce a death.
13 *As all*: as if all.
14 *And Being, but an Ear*: all senses, except hearing, are now useless.

EXPLORATIONS

1. Do you find the images in this poem frightening, macabre or coldly realistic? Give reasons for your answer, supported by textual reference.

2. What is the dominant tone in the poem? Where is the climax of the poem, in your opinion? Refer to the text in your answer.

3. Consider the rhyme scheme of the poem. In your view, why does the poet rhyme words like 'Drum'/'numb' and 'Soul'/'toll'? In your opinion, why does the rhyme scheme break down in the last stanza?

STUDY NOTES

This poem is thought to have been written in 1861, at a time of turbulence in Dickinson's life. She was having religious and artistic doubts and had experienced an unhappy time in a personal relationship. This interior landscape paints a dark picture of something falling apart. It is for the reader to decide whether it is a fainting spell, a mental breakdown or a funeral. That is the enigma of Dickinson.

The startling perspective of this poem in **stanza one** can be seen as the view experienced by a person in a coffin, if the poem is read as an **account of the poet imagining her death**. Alternatively, it could refer to the suffocating feeling of the breakdown of consciousness, either through fainting or a mental breakdown. Perhaps it is the dearth of artistic activity. Whichever reading is chosen, and maybe all co-exist, the **interior landscape of awareness is being explored**. The use of the personal pronoun 'I' shows that this is a unique experience, although it has relevance for all. The relentless pounding of the mourners walking is reminiscent of a blinding migraine headache. The repetition of the hard-sounding 't' in the verb 'treading—treading' evocatively describes this terrible experience. The 'I' is undergoing an intense trauma beyond understanding: 'Sense was breaking through'. This repetition and disorientation are synonymous with psychological breakdown.

Stanza two gives a **first-person account of a funeral**. The mourners are seated and the service has begun. Hearing ('an Ear') is the only sense able to perceive. All the verbs refer to sound: 'tread', 'beat', 'heard', 'creak', 'toll'. The passive 'I' receives the experience, hearing, not listening, which is an active process. The experience is so overwhelming that 'I' thought the 'Mind was going numb', unable to endure any more. The use of the past tense reminds the reader that the experience is over, so is the first-person narrative told from beyond the grave? Is this the voice of someone who has died? Or is it the voice of someone in the throes of a desperate personal experience? The reader must decide.

The reference to 'Soul' in **stanza three** suggests a **spiritual dimension** to the experience. The 'I' has started to become disoriented as the line dividing an external experience and an internal one is breaking. The mourners 'creak across my Soul'. The oppressive, almost suffocating experience is captured in the onomatopoeic phrase 'Boots of Lead' and space becomes filled with the tolling bell. Existence in **stanza four** is reduced totally to hearing. The fearful transitory experience of crossing from awareness to unconsciousness, from life to death, is being imagined. The 'I' in stanza four is now stranded, 'Wrecked', cut off from life. The person is in a comatose state, able to comprehend but unable to communicate: 'solitary, here'. The word 'here' makes the reader feel present at this awful drama.

Finally, in **stanza five**, a new sensation takes over, **the sense of falling uncontrollably**. The 'I' has finished knowing and is now no longer aware of surroundings. Is this the descent into the hell of the angels in *Paradise Lost*? Is it the descent of the coffin into the grave? Or is it the descent into madness or oblivion? The 'I' has learned something, but it is not revealed. The repetition of 'And' advances the movement of the poem in an almost uncontrollable way, mimicking the final descent. The 'I' is powerless under the repetitive verbs and the incessant rhythm punctuated by the ever-present dash. This poem is extraordinary, because before the study of psychology had defined it, it is a step-by-step description of mental collapse. Here is 'the drama of process'.

ANALYSIS

'This poem is a detailed exploration of the experience of death.' Discuss this statement, using references from the text to support your views.

Sample Paragraph

When I first read Emily Dickinson's poem 'I felt a Funeral, in my Brain', I was reminded of the macabre pictures of Salvador Dali, where everything is real, but not quite right. It also reminded me of the films of Tim Burton, such as *The Nightmare Before Christmas*. All the elements are there, but nothing is totally right, it is surreal. This imagined funeral in the poem suggests to me the losing of the grip on life by the individual 'I'. The incessant noise, 'treading', 'beating', induces an almost trance-like state as the brain cannot function any more, and so becomes numb. In death, the senses are supposed to shut down, sight is one of the first to go, so I think it is very clever of the poet to suggest that being is just reduced to the one sense hearing – 'an Ear'. I also find the perspective of the poem chilling, the idea that this is the view of someone lying in the coffin observing their funeral is macabre in the extreme. But the most compelling line in the poem is 'And then a Plank in Reason, broke'. This graphically conveys the snap of reason as the 'I' finally loses a grip on consciousness and slips away, hurtling uncontrollably into another dimension. Even the punctuation, with the use of the two commas, conveys this divided reality. But the most unnerving word is yet to come, 'then'. Does the poet know now? What does the poet know, is it about the existence or non-existence of an afterlife? Where is the poet standing now – here or there, alive or dead?

Examiner's Comment

An unusual, individual reading of the poem, and generally well supported by reference to the text. There are some weaknesses in expression and the paragraph is not fully focused on the question. Overall, a B-grade response.

CLASS/HOMEWORK EXERCISES

1. 'She seems as close to touching bottom here as she ever got.' Discuss this view of Emily Dickinson with reference to the poem 'I felt a Funeral, in my Brain'.

2. Copy the table below into your own notes and fill in critical comments about the last two quotations.

Key Quotes

That Sense was breaking through	This enigmatic line could refer to the breakdown of the five senses, or that reason was collapsing or coming.
My Mind was going numb	The narrator in the poem is presented as a passive recipient who can no longer endure this traumatic experience. This is enhanced by assonance.
And creak across my Soul	
And then a Plank in Reason, broke	

4 A BIRD CAME DOWN THE WALK

A Bird came down the Walk—
He did not know I saw—
He bit an Angleworm in halves
And ate the fellow, raw,

And then he drank a Dew   5
From a convenient Grass—
And then hopped sidewise to the Wall
To let a Beetle pass—

He glanced with rapid eyes
That hurried all around—   10
They looked like frightened Beads, I thought—
He stirred his Velvet Head

Like one in danger, Cautious,
I offered him a Crumb
And he unrolled his feathers   15
And rowed him softer home—

Than Oars divide the Ocean,
Too silver for a seam—
Or Butterflies, off Banks of Noon
Leap, plashless as they swim.   20

'He glanced with rapid eyes'

GLOSSARY

3 *Angleworm*: small worm used as fish bait by anglers.

17 *the Ocean*: Dickinson compares the blue sky to the sea.

18 *silver*: the sea's surface looks like solid silver.

18 *a seam*: opening; division.

20 *plashless*: splashless; undisturbed.

EXPLORATIONS

1. In your view, what does the poem suggest about the relationship between human beings and nature?

2. What effect does Dickinson's use of humour in the poem have? Does it let you see nature in a different way? Support the points you make with reference to the text.

3. From your reading of the poem, what impression of Emily Dickinson herself is conveyed? Refer to the text in your answer.

STUDY NOTES

In this short descriptive poem, Dickinson celebrates the beauty and wonder of animals. While the bird is seen as a wild creature at times, other details present its behaviour and appearance in human terms. The poem also illustrates Dickinson's quirky sense of humour as well as offering interesting insights into nature and the exclusion of human beings from that world.

The poem begins with an everyday scene. Because the bird is unaware of the poet's presence, it behaves naturally. **Stanza one** demonstrates the **competition and danger of nature**: 'He bit an Angleworm in halves'. Although Dickinson imagines the bird within a human context, casually coming 'down the Walk' and suddenly eating 'the fellow, raw', she is amused by the uncivilised reality of the animal kingdom. The word 'raw' echoes her self-deprecating sense of shock. Despite its initial elegance, the predatory bird could hardly have been expected to cook the worm.

The poet's comic portrayal continues in **stanza two**. She gives the bird certain social qualities, drinking from a 'Grass' and politely allowing a hurrying beetle to pass. The tone is relaxed and playful. The slender vowel sounds ('convenient') and soft sibilance ('sidewise', 'pass') add to the seemingly refined atmosphere. However, the mood changes in **stanza three**, reflecting the bird's cautious fear. Dickinson observes the rapid eye movement, 'like frightened Beads'. Such **precise detail increases the drama of the moment**. The details of the bird's prim movement and beautiful texture are wonderfully accurate: 'He stirred his Velvet Head'. The simile is highly effective, suggesting the animal's natural grace.

The danger becomes more explicit in **stanza four**. Both the spectator and the observed bird are 'Cautious'. The crumb offered to the bird by the poet is rejected, highlighting the **gulf between their two separate worlds**. The description of the bird taking flight evokes the delicacy and fluidity of its movement: 'And he unrolled his feathers/And rowed him softer home'. The confident rhythm and emphatic alliteration enrich our understanding of the harmony between the creature and its natural environment. The sensual imagery captures the magnificence of the bird, compared to a rower moving with ease across placid water.

Stanza five develops the metaphorical description further, conveying the bird's poise and mystery: 'Too silver for a seam'. Not only was its flying seamless, it was smoother than that of butterflies leaping 'off Banks of Noon' and splashlessly swimming through the sky. The **breathtaking image and onomatopoeic language** remind us of Dickinson's admiration for nature in all its impressive beauty and is one of the most memorable descriptions in all of Dickinson's writing.

ANALYSIS

In your view, does Dickinson have a sense of empathy with the bird? Support your response with reference to the poem.

Sample Paragraph

It is clear from the start of the poem that Emily Dickinson is both fascinated and amused by the appearance of a small bird in her garden. She seems surprised and almost honoured that out of nowhere 'A Bird came down the Walk'. When it suddenly swallows a worm 'raw', she becomes even more interested. The fact that she admits 'He did not know I saw' tells me that she really has empathy for the bird. Her tone suggests that she feels privileged to watch and she certainly doesn't want to disturb it in its own world. The poet also finds the bird's antics funny. Although it devours the snail, it still behaves very mannerly towards the beetle. Towards the end, Dickinson shows her feelings for the bird when it becomes frightened and she notices its 'rapid eyes'. She sees that it is 'in danger'. The fact that she offered it a crumb also shows her empathy. At the very end, she shows her admiration for the beauty and agility of the bird as it flies off to freedom – to its 'softer home'. The descriptions of it like a rower or a butterfly also suggest that she admires its grace.

Examiner's Comment

Apt references and short quotations are used very well to illustrate the poet's regard for the bird. The answer ranges well over much of the poem. Some further discussion on the poet's tone would have been welcome. A good grade B.

CLASS/HOMEWORK EXERCISES

1. Comment on Dickinson's use of imagery in 'A Bird came down the Walk'. Support the points you make with the aid of suitable reference.

2. Copy the table below into your own notes and fill in critical comments about the last two quotations.

Key Quotes

He did not know I saw	Dickinson is excited at the opportunity to view the bird in its natural element.
And then he drank a Dew	The poet's comic observation recognises signs of social etiquette in the bird's behaviour.
And rowed him softer home	
plashless as they swim	

my name...deals with...fascination with death.
Imagining her dying again.

Poem Depicts a death bed scenario
Deeply personal poem.

5   I HEARD A FLY BUZZ—WHEN I DIED

may be symbolic of negativity towards death.

The buzzing of a fly seems insignificant around the time of death

I heard a Fly buzz—when I died— *Strange connection, the buzzing highlights*
The Stillness in the Room *the stillness and silence.*
Was like the Stillness in the Air— *Heave - suggest the strength of the storm, the upset of the deceased.*
Between the Heaves of Storm— *Comparison to the midst of a storm.*

The fly trivialises a very unique moment.

The Eyes around—had wrung them dry— *You can feel the intensity of*
And Breaths were gathering firm *the grieving, they're holding their breaths with anticipation preparing for death.*
For that last Onset—when the King *Anticipation of the presence of God*
Be witnessed—in the Room— *in the room. Solemnly waiting for it to happen. suggests their strong religious beliefs.*

The fly gets between the moment just before death

I willed my Keepsakes—Signed away *The aspect of the will of the deceased.*
What portion of me be *She signed away what she could except for her soul (belongs to God)*
Assignable—and then it was *Just as they were waiting for death,*
There interposed a Fly— *a fly arrived in. It may be a symbol for the decay about to happen to the dead body.*

Blue may suggest the "Blue Bottle"

With Blue—uncertain stumbling Buzz— *The fly has accidentally stumbled in and disturbed an important occasion.*
Between the light—and me— *It comes between the source of light and the dying person.*
And then the Windows failed—and then *Metaphor - eyes closing*
I could not see to see— *No more light & plunged into the darkness of death.*

what light has the fly come between? The Natural light? OR the Divine light? Sense of confusion.

'The Stillness in the Room/Was like the Stillness in the Air—'

GLOSSARY

4   *Heaves*: lift with effort.
7   *Onset*: beginning.
7   *the King*: God.

9   *Keepsakes*: gifts treasured for the sake of the giver.
12   *interposed*: inserted between or among things.

EXPLORATIONS

1. How would you describe the atmosphere in the poem? Pick out two phrases which, in your opinion, are especially descriptive and explain why you chose them.

2. Do you think Dickinson uses contrast effectively in this poem? Discuss one contrast you found particularly striking.

3. Look at the last line of the poem. What, in your view, is the poet suggesting to us about a person's fate after death?

STUDY NOTES

Dickinson was fascinated by death. This poem examines the moment between life and death. At that time, it was common for family and friends to be present at deathbed vigils. It was thought that the way a person behaved or looked at the moment of death gave an indication of the soul's fate.

The last moment of a person's life is a solemn and often sad occasion. The perspective of the poem is that of the person dying and this significant moment is dominated by the buzzing of a fly in the room in the **first stanza**. This is **absurdly comic and strangely distorts** this moment into something grotesque. Surely the person dying should be concerned with more important matters than an insignificant fly: 'I heard a Fly buzz—when I died'. The room is still and expectant as the last breaths are drawn, a stillness like the moments before a storm. All are braced for what is to come. The word 'Heaves' suggests the force of the storm that is about to break.

The **second stanza** shows us that the mourners had now stopped crying and were holding their breath as they awaited the coming of the 'King' (God) into the room at the moment of death. The phrase 'Be witnessed' refers to the dying person and the mourners who are witnessing their faith, and it conjures up all the solemnity of a court. The word 'firm' also suggests these people's steadfast religious beliefs. The **third stanza** is concerned with putting matters right. The dying person has made a will – 'What portion of me be/Assignable' – and what is not assignable belongs to God. The person is awaiting the coming of his/her Maker, 'and then it was/There interposed a Fly' – the symbol of decay and corruption appeared. Human affairs cannot be managed; real life intervenes. The **fly comes between ('interposed') the dying person and the moment of death, which trivialises** the event.

The fractured syntax of the last stanza shows the **breakdown of the senses** at the moment of death: 'Between the light—and me'. Sight and sound are blurring. The presence of the fly is completely inappropriate, like a drunken person at a solemn ceremony, disturbing and embarrassing and interrupting proceedings. The fly is now between the dying person and the source of light. Does this suggest that the person has lost concentration on higher things, distracted by the buzzing fly? The sense of sight then fails: 'And then the Windows failed'. The moment of death had come and gone, dominated by the noisy fly. Has the fly prevented the person from reaching another dimension? Is death emptiness, just human decay, as signified by the presence of the fly, or is there something more? Do we need comic relief at overwhelming occasions? Is the poet signalling her own lack of belief in an afterlife with God? Dickinson, as usual, intrigues, **leaving the reader with more questions than answers**, so that the reader, like the dying person, is struggling to 'see to see'.

ANALYSIS

'Dickinson's poems on mortality often lead to uncertainty or despair.' Would you agree or disagree with this statement after reading the poem 'I heard a Fly buzz—when I died'? Discuss this statement, using references from the text to support your views.

Sample Paragraph

This first-person, reminiscent narrative takes us through a series of images, inside and outside the head, showing us confused feelings and insurmountable problems, leading to an inconclusive ending. The view of this deathbed scene is from the dying person's perspective. The problem is that when all should be focused on the last drawing of breath, all are distracted by the inappropriate arrival of a noisy fly! Life won't be managed, nor death – both are lived and experienced. Life and death are not a play, a work of art; they are messy and disorganised, which goes against the human desire for order and control: 'Signed away/What portion of me be/Assignable'. I feel that the poet may be suggesting that the dying person, distracted by the silly fly, does not reach the understanding and knowledge appropriate at this great moment, and is therefore cheated in some way. The momentous moment has passed, dominated by a buzzing fly. This was no dress rehearsal; you can only die once. Life and death happen. Are we being told that we often lose concentration at important moments, for absurd reasons, and so lose valuable insight? Dickinson is not a reassuring poet in this poem. Instead, she coldly and dispassionately draws a deathbed scene and lets us 'see to see'. Can we? Or are we, like the dying person, distracted and unable to still ourselves at the appropriate time to achieve greater wisdom? The divided voice, that of the person dying and that of the person after death, leaves us with mysteries, and so this poem of Dickinson's on mortality leaves me with bleak uncertainties about the human condition and its ability to control and order.

Examiner's Comment

This response is considered and shows a very good discursive treatment of the question. Expression is varied and fluent, and apt quotations are used effectively throughout the answer. Grade A.

CLASS/HOMEWORK EXERCISES

1. Comment on how Dickinson's style contributes to the theme or message in this poem. Quote from your prescribed poems to support your opinions.

2. Copy the table below into your own notes and fill in critical comments about the last two quotations.

Key Quotes

I heard a Fly buzz	The dying person is distracted from this significant moment by the noise made by a fly.
And Breaths were gathering firm/For that last Onset	The narrator is aware that those present are bracing themselves for the important moment of death, which for believers is associated with the coming of God.
And then the Windows failed	
and then/I could not see to see	

6 THE SOUL HAS BANDAGED MOMENTS

The Soul has Bandaged moments—
When too appalled to stir—
She feels some ghastly Fright come up
And stop to look at her—

Salute her—with long fingers— 5
Caress her freezing hair—
Sip, Goblin, from the very lips
The Lover—hovered—o'er—
Unworthy, that a thought so mean
Accost a Theme—so—fair— 10

The soul has moments of Escape—
When bursting all the doors—
She dances like a Bomb, abroad,
And swings upon the Hours,

As do the Bee—delirious borne— 15
Long Dungeoned from his Rose—
Touch Liberty—then know no more,
But Noon, and Paradise—

The Soul's retaken moments—
When, Felon led along, 20
With shackles on the plumed feet,
And staples, in the Song,

The Horror welcomes her, again,
These, are not brayed of Tongue—

'As do the Bee—delirious borne'

GLOSSARY

1 *Bandaged moments*: painful experiences.
2 *appalled*: shocked, horrified.
2 *stir*: act; retaliate.
10 *Accost*: address.
11 *Escape*: freedom.
13 *like a Bomb*: dramatically.
13 *abroad*: in unusual directions.

16 *Dungeoned*: imprisoned in the hive.
20 *Felon*: criminal.
21 *shackles*: chains, ropes.
21 *plumed*: decorated.
22 *staples*: fastenings.
24 *brayed*: inarticulate.

EXPLORATIONS

1. What details in the poem evoke the feelings of 'ghastly Fright' experienced by the soul? Support your answer with quotation or reference.

2. Choose one comparison from the poem that you find particularly effective. Explain your choice.

3. Comment on Dickinson's use of dashes in this poem, briefly explaining their effectiveness.

STUDY NOTES

Throughout much of her poetry, Dickinson focuses on the nature of consciousness and the experience of being alive. She was constantly searching for meaning, particularly of transient moments or changing moods. This search is central to 'The Soul has Bandaged moments', where the poet takes us through a series of dramatic images contrasting the extremes of the spirit and the conscious self.

Stanza one introduces the soul as being fearful and vulnerable, personified as a terrified female who 'feels some ghastly Fright', with the poem's stark opening line suggesting restriction and pain. Dickinson's language is extreme: 'Bandaged', 'appalled'. The **tone is one of helpless desperation and introspection**. Yet while the dominant mood reflects suffering and fear, the phrase 'Bandaged moments' indicates the resilient soul's ability to recover despite being wounded repeatedly.

Stanza two is unnervingly dramatic. The poet creates a mock-romantic scene between the victimised soul and the 'ghastly Fright' figure, now portrayed as a hideous goblin and her would-be lover, their encounter depicted in terms of gothic horror. The soul experiences terrifying fantasies as **the surreal sequence becomes increasingly menacing** and the goblin's long fingers 'Caress her freezing hair'. The appearance of an unidentified shadowy 'Lover' is unexpected. There is a sense of the indecisive soul being caught between two states, represented by the malevolent goblin and the deserving lover. It is unclear whether Dickinson is writing about the choices involved in romantic love or the relationship between herself and God.

The stanza ends inconclusively, juxtaposing two opposites: the 'Unworthy' or undeserving 'thought' and the 'fair' (worthy) 'Theme'. The latter might well refer to the ideal of romantic love. If so, it is confronted by erotic desire (the 'thought'). Dickinson's disjointed style, especially her frequent use of dashes within stanzas, isolates key words and intensifies the overwhelmingly **nightmarish atmosphere**.

The feeling of confused terror is replaced with ecstatic 'moments of Escape' in **stanzas three** and **four**. The soul recovers in triumph, 'bursting all the doors'. This **explosion of energy** ('She dances like a Bomb') evokes a rising mood of riotous freedom. Explosive verbs ('bursting', 'dances', 'swings') and robust rhythms add to the sense of uncontrollable excitement. Dickinson compares the soul to a 'Bee— delirious borne'. After being 'Long Dungeoned' in its hive, this bee can now enjoy the sensuous delights of 'his Rose'.

The mood is short-lived, however, and in **stanzas five** and **six**, 'The Horror' returns. The soul becomes depressed again, feeling bound and shackled, like a 'Felon led along'. **Dickinson develops this criminal metaphor** – 'With shackles on the plumed feet' – leaving us with an ultimate sense of loss as 'The Horror welcomes her, again'. Is this the soul's inevitable fate? The final line is unsettling. Whatever horrible experiences confront the soul, they are simply unspeakable: 'not brayed of Tongue'.

As always, Dickinson's poem is open to many interpretations. Critics have suggested that the poet is dramatising the turmoil of dealing with the loss of creativity. Some view the poem's central conflict as the tension between romantic love and sexual desire. Others believe that the poet was exploring the theme of depression and mental instability. In the end, readers must find their own meaning and decide for themselves.

ANALYSIS

Comment on the dramatic elements that are present in the poem, supporting the points you make with reference to the text.

Sample Paragraph

'The Soul has Bandaged moments' is built around a central conflict between two opposing forces, the 'Soul', or spirit, and its great enemy, 'Fright'. Emily Dickinson sets the dramatic scene with the Soul still recovering – presumably from the last battle. It is 'Bandaged' after the fight with its arch enemy. The descriptions of the soul's opponent are startling. Fright is 'ghastly', a 'Horror' and a sleazy 'Goblin' who is trying to seduce the innocent soul. Some of Dickinson's images add to the dramatic tension. In the seduction scene, the goblin is described as having 'long fingers'. His intended victim is seen as helpless, petrified with fear. The goblin uses its bony claws to 'Caress her freezing hair'. Both characters seem to have come out of an old black-and-white horror movie. I find the whole situation disturbing. The drama continues right to the end of the poem. The soul is compared to a 'Felon' who has just been recaptured and is being led away in 'shackles'. Such images have a distressing impact in explaining the pressures on the soul to be free. Finally, Dickinson's stop-and-start style is also unsettling. Broken rhythms and her condensed use of language increase the edgy atmosphere throughout this highly dramatic poem.

Examiner's Comment

An assured and focused A-grade response, showing a clear understanding of the poem's dramatic elements. The answer addresses both subject matter and style, using back-up illustration very effectively. Expression throughout is also impressive.

CLASS/HOMEWORK EXERCISES

1. How would you describe the dominant tone of 'The Soul has Bandaged moments'? Use reference to the text to show how the tone is effectively conveyed.

2. Copy the table below into your own notes and fill in critical comments about the last two quotations.

Key Quotes

Bandaged moments	While the adjective indicates hurt and weakness, there is also a sense of healing and recovery.
The Lover—hovered—o'er	The verb suggests menace, typical of a poem where almost every image is tinged with fear and uncertainty.
Caress her freezing hair	
The Horror welcomes her, again	

7   I COULD BRING YOU JEWELS—HAD I A MIND TO

I could bring You Jewels—had I a mind to—
But You have enough—of those—
I could bring You Odors from St. Domingo—
Colors—from Vera Cruz—

Berries of the Bahamas—have I—   5
But this little Blaze
Flickering to itself—in the Meadow—
Suits Me—more than those—

Never a Fellow matched this Topaz—
And his Emerald Swing—   10
Dower itself—for Bobadilo—
Better—Could I bring?

'Never a Fellow matched this Topaz—'

GLOSSARY

3 *Odors*: fragrances, perfumes.
3 *St. Domingo*: Santo Domingo in the Caribbean.
4 *Vera Cruz*: city on the east coast of Mexico.
5 *Bahamas*: group of islands south-east of Florida.

6 *Blaze*: strong fire or flame; very bright light.
11 *Dower*: part of her husband's estate allotted to a widow by law.
11 *Bobadilo*: braggart; someone who speaks arrogantly or boastfully.

EXPLORATIONS

1. Does the poet value exotic or homely gifts? In your opinion, which phrases suggest this contrast most effectively?

2. Slant rhyme is when words almost rhyme, as in 'those' and 'Cruz'. Identify another example of slant rhyme in the poem and suggest why, in your opinion, the poet chooses to rhyme the words in this way. (Consider emphasis, order and music.)

3. What is the tone in this poem: arrogant, humble, gentle, strident, confident? Quote in support of your opinion.

STUDY NOTES

Although described as a recluse, Dickinson had a wide circle of friends. She wrote letter-poems to them, often representing them as flowers, 'things of nature which had come with no practice at all'. This poem is one without shadows, celebratory and happy, focusing out rather than in as she concentrates on a relationship.

In the **first stanza**, the poem opens with the speaker **considering the gift she will give** her beloved, 'You'. The 'You' is very much admired, and is wealthy ('You have enough'), so the gift of jewels is dismissed. The phrase 'had I a mind to' playfully suggests that maybe the 'I' doesn't necessarily wish to present anything. There is a certain coquettish air evident here. A world of privilege and plenty is shown as, one after another, expensively exotic gifts are considered and dismissed. These include perfumes and vibrant colours from faraway locations, conjuring up images of romance and adventure: 'Odors from St. Domingo'.

The **second stanza** continues the list, with 'Berries of the Bahamas' being considered as an option for this special gift, but they are not quite right either. The tense changes to 'have I' and the laconic listing and dismissing stops. A small wildflower 'in the Meadow', 'this little Blaze', is chosen instead. This 'Suits Me'. Notice that it is not that this suits the other person. **This gift is a reflection of her own unshowy personality.** The long lines of considering exotic gifts have now given way to shorter, more decisive lines.

In the **third stanza**, the speaker has a definite note of conviction, as she confidently states that 'Never a Fellow matched' this shining gift of hers. No alluring, foreign gemstone, be it a brilliant topaz or emerald, shines as this 'little Blaze' in the meadow. The gift glows with colour; it is natural, inexpensive and accessible. The reference to a dower might suggest a gift given by a woman to a prospective husband. This **gift is suitable** for a Spanish adventurer, a 'Bobadilo'. The assured tone is clear in the word 'Never' and the jaunty rhyme 'Swing' and 'bring'. The final rhetorical question suggests that this is the best gift she could give. The poem shows that **the true value of a present cannot be measured in a material way**.

ANALYSIS

'Dickinson is fascinated by moments of change.' Discuss this statement using the poem 'I could bring You Jewels—had I a mind to' as a reference.

Sample Paragraph

Unlike many of Dickinson's poems on our course, this poem turns outwards, as the speaker considers what present would be suitable to give to her 'Bobadilo'. The happy, celebratory tone continues right through the poem. This is a confident, assured woman listing and dismissing exotic gifts in a world of privilege and wealth. The 'Odors' from St. Domingo, the 'Colors' from Vera Cruz, the 'Berries' from the Bahamas are looked at and discarded by this knowing woman, 'had I a mind to'. The moment of change here is when the speaker chooses a gift that is natural and unassuming and, more importantly, which is to her liking: 'Suits Me'. It will convey something of her personality to the recipient, the swaggering 'Bobadilo'. This 'little Blaze/Flickering to itself' reflects the hidden qualities of the woman. Although it is not directly stated what this little shining gift is exactly, I think it is likely a meadow flower. It is free and easily picked, but how it shines! This is brighter than any precious stone of 'Topaz' or 'Emerald'. As the decision is reached, the long lines in which the speaker is considering her choice of gift change with her decision. Now short, crisp lines ring out with the self-belief of a woman who knows best. Even the rhyme changes from the slant rhyme where she is considering her options ('those'/'Cruz') in the first stanza to the more definite jaunty full rhyme of 'Swing' and 'bring' in the final stanza. I read that Dickinson's favourite chapter in the Book of Revelations was the description of Jerusalem as a jewel. In this poem, jewels are rejected for something more precious than material worth: beauty. I really enjoyed how Dickinson explored the very feminine trait of considering everything, and then finally deciding after humorous vacillating. This is the moment of change in the poem.

Examiner's Comment

A lucid, fluent response to the question, backed up with a convincing use of quotation, ensures a grade A. The point about the change in line length was interesting. Varied vocabulary is impressive throughout.

CLASS/HOMEWORK EXERCISES

1. 'Dickinson disrupts and transforms our accepted view of things.' What is your opinion of this statement? Refer to 'I could bring You Jewels—had I a mind to' in support of your response.

2. Copy the table below into your own notes and fill in critical comments about the last two quotations.

Key Quotes

I could bring You Jewels—had I a mind to	The speaker is confidently considering her options.
But this little Blaze/Flickering to itself	The gift chosen is simple and natural, but it is warm, vivid and beautiful, as conveyed by the lively onomatopoeia.
Dower itself	
Better—Could I bring?	

8   A NARROW FELLOW IN THE GRASS

A narrow Fellow in the Grass
Occasionally rides—
You may have met Him—did you not
His notice sudden is—

The Grass divides as with a Comb—   5
A spotted shaft is seen—
And then it closes at your feet
And opens further on—

He likes a Boggy Acre
A Floor too cool for Corn—   10
Yet when a Boy, and Barefoot—
I more than once at Noon
Have passed, I thought, a Whip lash
Unbraiding in the Sun
When stooping to secure it   15
It wrinkled, and was gone—

Several of Nature's People
I know, and they know me—
I feel for them a transport
Of cordiality—   20

But never met this Fellow
Attended, or alone
Without a tighter breathing
And Zero at the Bone—

'His notice sudden is—'

GLOSSARY

6 *a spotted shaft*: patterned skin of the darting snake.
13 *Whip lash*: sudden, violent movement.
14 *Unbraiding*: straightening out, uncoiling.

19 *transport*: heightened emotion.
20 *cordiality*: civility, welcome.
24 *Zero at the Bone*: cold terror.

EXPLORATIONS

1. Select two images from the poem that suggest evil or menace. Comment briefly on the effectiveness of each.

2. How successful is the poet in conveying the snake's erratic sense of movement? Refer to the text in your answer.

3. Outline your own feelings in response to the poem.

STUDY NOTES

In this poem, one of the few published during her lifetime, Dickinson adopts a male persona remembering an incident from his boyhood. Snakes have traditionally been seen as symbols of evil. We still use the expression 'snake in the grass' to describe someone who cannot be trusted. Central to this poem is Dickinson's own portrayal of nature – beautiful, brutal and lyrical. She seems fascinated by the endless mystery, danger and unpredictability of the natural world.

The opening lines of **stanza one** casually introduce a 'Fellow in the Grass'. (Dickinson never refers explicitly to the snake.) **The conversational tone immediately involves readers** who may already 'have met Him'. However, there is more than a hint of warning in the postscript: 'His notice sudden is'. This underlying wariness now appears foreshadowed by the menacing adjective 'narrow' and by the disjointed rhythm and slightly awkward word order.

Dickinson focuses on the volatile snake's dramatic movements in **stanza two**. The verbs 'divide', 'closes' and 'opens' emphasise its dynamic energy. The snake suddenly emerges like a 'spotted shaft'. The poet's **comparisons are particularly effective**, suggesting a lightning bolt or a camouflaged weapon. Run-on lines, a forceful rhythm and the repetition of 'And' contribute to the vivid image of the snake as a powerful presence to be treated with caution.

Stanza three reveals even more about the snake's natural habitat: 'He likes a Boggy Acre'. It also divulges the speaker's identity – an adult male remembering his failed boyhood efforts to capture snakes. The memory conveys something of the intensity of childhood experiences, especially of dangerous encounters with nature. The boy's innocence and vulnerability ('Barefoot') contrasts with the 'Whip lash' violence of the wild snake. **Dickinson's attitude to nature is open to interpretation.** Does the threat come from the animal or the boy? Did the adult speaker regard the snake differently when he was young? The poet herself clearly appreciates the complexities found within the natural world and her precisely observed descriptions ('Unbraiding', 'It wrinkled') provide ample evidence of her interest.

From the speaker's viewpoint in **stanza four**, nature is generally benign. This positive image is conveyed by the affectionate tribute to 'Nature's People'. The familiar personification and personal tone underline the mutual 'cordiality' that exists between nature and human nature. Despite this, **divisions between the two worlds cannot be ignored.** Indeed, the focus in **stanza five** is on the sheer horror people experience when confronted by 'this Fellow'. The poet's sparse and chilling descriptions – 'tighter breathing', 'Zero at the Bone' – are startling expressions of stunned terror.

As in other poems, Dickinson attributes human characteristics to nature – the snake 'Occasionally rides', 'The Grass divides' and the bogland has a 'Floor'. One effect of this is to highlight the **variety and mystery of the natural environment**, which can only ever be glimpsed within limited human terms. The snake remains unknowable to the end, dependent on a chance encounter, a fleeting glance or a trick of light.

ANALYSIS

Comment on the effectiveness of Dickinson's use of the male persona voice in 'A narrow Fellow in the Grass'. Support the points you make with reference to the poem.

Sample Paragraph

In some of her poems, Emily Dickinson chose to substitute her own voice with that of a persona, a fictional narrator. This is the case in 'A narrow Fellow in the Grass', where she uses a country boy to tell the story of his experiences trying to catch snakes when he was young. It is obvious that he has a great love for nature, but neither is he blind to the cold fear he felt when he came face to face with the 'spotted shaft'. Dickinson's use of language emphasises his youthful terror. She lets him remember his encounter exactly as it happened. The images she uses are powerful and disturbing: 'a tighter breathing'. The boy remembers shuddering with uncontrollable fright, 'Zero at the Bone'. The description is dramatic and I found I could relate to the boy's sense of horror. The poem is all the more effective for being centred around one terrified character, the young boy. I can visualise the child in his bare feet trying to catch a frightened snake in the grass. It is only later that he realises the great danger he was in and this has taught him a lifelong lesson about nature. By using another speaker's persona, Dickinson explores the excitement and danger of nature in a wider way that allows readers to imagine it more clearly.

Examiner's Comment

Although the answer drifts at times from the central question, there is good personal engagement and a great deal of insightful discussion. Quotations are well used throughout the answer to provide a very interesting response. Grade A.

CLASS/HOMEWORK EXERCISES

1. In your opinion, how does Dickinson portray nature in 'A narrow Fellow in the Grass'? Support your points with reference to the poem.

2. Copy the table below into your own notes and fill in critical comments about the last two quotations.

Key Quotes

His notice sudden is	The awkward syntax used to describe the snake's jerky movements adds to our sense of unease.
And then it closes at your feet	Dickinson highlights the lethal unpredictability of the snake.
Nature's People	
And Zero at the Bone	

theme: celebration of life.

Dashes used throughout represent her delight.

A lot of nature imagery. The inspiration it gives her.

9 I TASTE A LIQUOR NEVER BREWED

Being drunk on the appreciation of life.

paradox statement ↑

Central metaphor: Intoxication on the delight of life.

I taste a liquor never brewed— *Intensity portrayed moment for her*
From Tankards scooped in Pearl— *Pearl is a beautiful image and it makes it more special.*
Not all the Vats upon the Rhine *Hyperbole, the joy she feels from this*
Yield such an Alcohol! *alcohol couldn't be supplied by all the vats on the Rhine.* [alcohol : Happiness]

Inebriate of Air—am I— *Using images of intoxication.*
And Debauchee of Dew— *She recklessly intoxicated.* 5
Reeling—thro endless summer days— *It's the beauty of her*
From inns of Molten Blue— *surroundings that brings on her intoxication.*

Metaphor: going from one pub to another.

Melting blue skies of the summer.

When 'Landlords' turn the drunken Bee *Very playful + cheerful.*
Out of the Foxglove's door— *Heightens the appeal of the poem.* 10
Compares Foxglove flower to be a pub.
When Butterflies—renounce their 'drams'— *Metaphor for people*
I shall but drink the more! *When the butterflies have enough getting kicked out of pubs, she will keep intoxicating herself on joy.*

Heavenly experience.

Till Seraphs swing their snowy Hats— *She is in a state of drunken*
And Saints—to windows run— *bliss, she is extatically happy.*
To see the little Tippler *Alcohol Reference. Saints + Angels run to see the Tippler and the sense of*
Leaning against the—Sun— *freedom that she's found.*

The mention of angels + saints reinforce the idea of Heaven. Sun is something optimistic, we associate it with life.

Sibilance: Adds a musical quality.

'Not all the Vats upon the Rhine/Yield such an Alcohol!'

GLOSSARY

2 *Tankards*: one-handled mugs, usually made of pewter, used for drinking beer.
3 *Vats*: large vessels used for making alcohol.
6 *Debauchee*: someone who has overindulged and neglected duty.

13 *Seraphs*: angels who are of the highest spiritual level.
15 *Tippler*: a person who drinks often, but does not get drunk.

EXPLORATIONS

1. What is the mood in this poem? Does it intensify or change? Use references from the text in your response.

2. Which stanza appeals to you? Discuss both the poet's style and content in your answer, using quotations from the poem as evidence for your views.

3. Look at the final dash in the poem. Why do you think the poet ended the poem with this punctuation? What is it suggesting about the little tippler? Does it add a sense of fun?

STUDY NOTES

This 'rapturous poem about summer' uses the metaphor of intoxication to capture the essence of this wonderful season. Dickinson's family were strict Calvinists, a religion that emphasised damnation as the consequence of sin. Her father supported the Temperance League, an organisation that warned against the dangers of drink.

This poem is written as a **joyful appreciation of this wonderful life**. The tone is playful and exaggerated from the beginning, as the poet declares this drink was never 'brewed'. The reference to 'scooped in Pearl' could refer to the great, white frothing heads of beer in the 'Tankards'. The poet certainly conveys the merriment of intoxication, as the poem reels along its happy way. The explanation for all this drunkenness is that the poet is drunk on life ('Inebriate', 'Debauchee'). The pubs are the inns of 'Molten Blue', i.e. the sky (**stanza two**). It is like a cartoon, with little drunken bees being shown the door by the pub owners as they lurch about in delirious ecstasy. The drinkers of the natural world are the bees and butterflies, but she can drink more than these: 'I shall but drink the more!' This roots the poem in reality, as drunken people always feel they can manage more.

But this has caused uproar in the heavens, as the angels and saints run to look out at this little drunk, 'the little Tippler'. She stands drunkenly leaning against the 'Sun', a celestial lamppost. The final dash suggests the crooked stance of the little drunken one. **There is no heavy moral at the end of this poem. In fact, there seems to be a slight note of envy for the freedom and happiness being experienced by the intoxicated poet.** Are the angels swinging their hats to cheer her on in her drunken rebellion? Is this poem celebrating the reckless indulgence of excess? Or is the final metaphor of the sun referring to Christ or to the poet's own arrival in heaven after she indulgently enjoys the beauty of the natural world?

Nature is seen as the spur for high jinks and good humour. The riddle of the first line starts it off: how was the alcohol 'never brewed'? The exaggerated imagery, such as the metaphor of the flower as a pub and the bee as the drunk, all add to the **fantasy land atmosphere**. The words 'Inebriate', 'Debauchee' and 'renounce' are reminiscent of the language which those disapproving of the consumption of alcohol might use for those who do indulge. Is the poet having a sly laugh at the serious Temperance League to which her father belonged? The ridiculous costumes, 'snowy Hats', and the uproar in heaven ('swing' and 'run') all add to the impression of this land of merriment. The juxtaposition of the sacred ('Seraphs') and the profane ('Tippler') in **stanza four** also adds to the comic effect. However, it is the verbs that carry the sense of mad fun most effectively: 'scooped', 'Reeling', 'drink', 'swing', 'run' and 'Leaning'. The poem lurches and flows in an almost uncontrollable way as the ecstasy of overindulging in the delirious pleasure of nature is vividly conveyed.

There are two different types of humour present in this irrepressible poem – the broad humour of farce and the more **subversive humour of irony**. She even uses the steady metre of a hymn, with eight syllables in lines one and three and six syllables in lines two and four. Dickinson seems to be standing at a distance, smiling wryly, as she gently deflates.

ANALYSIS

'Dickinson was always wary of excess, even of joy.' Discuss this statement in relation to the above poem, using references from the text to support your answer.

Sample Paragraph

I don't agree. I think this is a funny poem and the poet is enjoying herself getting very drunk. But she is not drunk on beer. She is drunk on nature. I think it is very funny when the angels are waving their white caps, egging her on. I think this is a good poem, the best poem I ever red, as it makes me want to red more of Dickinson's poems. There is a good metaphor for drinking all through. Some of it is definately full of joy EG the bee. The part on the tippler leaning against the paling post is also joyful. I think everyone should enjoy Emily's absolutely brilliant poem as it has many good joyful images such as the drinking bee and little tippler.

Examiner's Comment

This short answer shows very little knowledge of or engagement with the poem. There is no substantial referencing. The language used is repetitive, expression is flawed and there are mechanical mistakes. The over enthusiastic ending is not convincing. A basic D-grade standard.

CLASS/HOMEWORK EXERCISES

1. 'Hypersensitivity to natural beauty produced Dickinson's poetry.' Do you agree or disagree with this statement? Refer to the poem 'I taste a liquor never brewed' in your response.

2. Copy the table below into your own notes and fill in critical comments about the last two quotations.

Key Quotes

From tankards scooped in Pearl	This line, with its use of the descriptive verb, suggests the outlining of the tankard in white, foaming beer.
Inebriate of Air—am I	The narrator in the poem is confessing to drunkenness due to an excessive indulgence in the beauty of nature.
Till Seraphs swing their snowy hats	
Leaning against the—Sun	

10   AFTER GREAT PAIN, A FORMAL FEELING COMES

After great pain, a formal feeling comes—
The Nerves sit ceremonious, like Tombs—
The stiff Heart questions was it He, that bore,
And Yesterday, or Centuries before?

The Feet, mechanical, go round—   5
Of Ground, or Air, or Ought—
A Wooden way
Regardless grown,
A Quartz contentment, like a stone—

This is the Hour of Lead—   10
Remembered, if outlived,
As Freezing persons, recollect the Snow—
First—Chill—then Stupor—then the letting go—

'First—Chill—then Stupor'

GLOSSARY

1 *formal*: serious; exact.
2 *ceremonious*: on show.
3 *He*: the stiff Heart, or possibly Christ.
3 *bore*: endure; intrude.
6 *Ought*: anything.

9 *Quartz*: basic rock mineral.
10 *Hour of Lead*: traumatic experience.
13 *Stupor*: numbness; disorientation.

EXPLORATIONS

1. Comment on the poet's use of personification in the opening stanza.

2. How does the language used in the second stanza convey the condition of the victim in pain?

3. Write your own short personal response to the poem.

STUDY NOTES

Dickinson wrote 'After great pain' in 1862, at a time when she was thought to have been experiencing severe psychological difficulties. The poet addresses the effects of isolation and anguish on the individual. Ironically, the absence of the personal pronoun 'I' gives the poem a universal significance. The 'great pain' itself is never fully explained and the final lines are ambiguous. Like so much of Dickinson's work, this dramatic poem raises many questions for consideration.

From the outset, Dickinson is concerned with the emotional numbness ('a formal feeling') that follows the experience of 'great pain'. The poet's authoritative tone in **stanza one** reflects a first-hand knowledge of trauma, with the adjective 'formal' suggesting self-conscious recovery from some earlier distress. Dickinson personifies the physical response as order returns to body and mind: 'The Nerves sit ceremonious, like Tombs'. The severe pain has also shocked the 'stiff Heart', which has become confused by the experience. Is the poet also drawing a parallel with the life and death of Jesus Christ (the Sacred Heart), crucified 'Centuries before'? The images certainly suggest timeless suffering and endurance. This **sombre sense of loss** is further enhanced by the broad vowel assonance of the opening lines.

The feeling of stunned inertia continues into **stanza two**. In reacting to intense pain, 'The Feet, mechanical, go round'. It is as if the response is unfocused and indifferent, lacking any real purpose. Dickinson uses two **analogies to emphasise the sense of pointless alienation**. The reference to the 'Wooden way' might be interpreted as a fragile bridge between reason and insanity, or this metaphor could be associated with Christ's suffering as he carried his cross to Calvary. The level of consciousness at such times is described as 'Regardless grown', or beyond caring. Dickinson's second comparison is equally innovative: 'A Quartz contentment' underpins the feeling of complete apathy that makes the victims of pain behave 'like a stone'. Is she being ironic by suggesting that the post-traumatic state is an escape, a 'contentment' of sorts?

There is a disturbing sense of resignation at the start of **stanza three**: 'This is the Hour of Lead'. The dull weight of depression is reinforced by the insistent monosyllables and solemn rhythm, but the devastating experience is not 'outlived' by everyone. Dickinson outlines the aftermath of suffering by using one final comparison: 'As Freezing persons'. This shocking simile evokes the unimaginable hopelessness of the victim stranded in a vast wasteland of snow. The poem's last line traces the tragic stages leading to oblivion: 'First—Chill—then Stupor—then the letting go—'. The inclusion of the dash at the end might indicate a possibility of relief, though whether it is through rescue or death is not revealed. In either case, **readers are left with an acute awareness of an extremely distraught voice**.

ANALYSIS

One of Dickinson's great achievements is her ability to explore the experience of deep depression. To what extent is this true of her poem 'After great pain, a formal feeling comes'? Refer closely to the text in your answer.

Sample Paragraph

'After great pain' is a very good example of Emily Dickinson's skill in addressing controversial and distressing subjects, such as mental breakdown. Although she never really explains what she means by the 'pain' referred to in the first line, she deals with the after-effects of suffering throughout the poem. The loss of a loved one can cause very great anguish. What Dickinson does very well is to explain how depression can lead to people becoming numb, beyond all emotion. I believe this is what she means by 'a formal feeling'. She uses an interesting image of a sufferer's nerves sitting quietly in a church at a funeral service. They 'sit ceremonious'. This same idea is used to describe the mourners following the hearse – 'Feet mechanical'. I get the impression that grief and mourning can destroy people's confidence and make them numb. They go beyond grief. Dickinson's images are compelling and suggest the coldness experienced by patients who have suffered depression. They are 'like a stone'. The best description is at the end, when she compares sufferers to being lost in the snow. They will slowly fade into a 'stupor' or death wish. I think Dickinson is very good at using images and moods to explore depression. She is very good at suggesting shock in this poem.

Examiner's Comment

Although the expression is awkward in places, there are a number of worthwhile points in the paragraph. There is also some good personal engagement with the poem and references are used well in support. A basic B-grade standard.

CLASS/HOMEWORK EXERCISES

1. In your opinion, what is the dominant mood in 'After great pain, a formal feeling comes'? Is it one of depression, sadness or acceptance? Refer closely to the text in your answer.

2. Copy the table below into your own notes and fill in critical comments about the last two quotations.

Key Quotes

a formal feeling comes	Dickinson states that the reaction to the experience of intense suffering is stiff and self-conscious.
A Quartz contentment, like a stone	After experiencing trauma, sufferers retreat within themselves, feeling lifeless and inhuman.
A Wooden way/Regardless grown	
First—Chill—then Stupor— then the letting go	

LEAVING CERT SAMPLE ESSAY

'Emily Dickinson's distinctive style of poetry reflects a wide range of powerful emotions.' Discuss this view, supporting the points you make with suitable reference to the poems by Dickinson on your course.

Marking Scheme Guidelines

Candidates are free to agree and/or disagree with the given statement. However, they should show clear evidence of personal engagement with Dickinson's poetry. The key terms ('distinctive style' and 'wide range of powerful emotions') should be addressed either implicitly or explicitly. Allow for a wide range of approaches in the answering.

Material might be drawn from the following:

- Startling treatment of recurring themes: consciousness, death, nature
- Dramatic moments of crucial experiences
- Widely varying moods/atmospheres of anguish/celebration
- Unconventional punctuation and syntax highlight emotions
- Realistic/pessimistic attitudes, etc.

Sample Essay

(Dickinson's distinctive style of poetry reflects a wide range of powerful emotions)

1. *Emily Dickinson is probably best known for her unique use of language. She is usually associated with short phrases, broken rhythms, capital letters and the constant use of dashes in place of ordinary punctuation. Many of her condensed poems are like puzzles where the reader is forced to seek through odd sentences in order to find the poet's true meaning. I found Dickinson's poetry intriguing because of this. However, her poems about nature were quirky and even humorous at times. On other occasions, she seemed edgy, obsessed with death and depression.*

2. *The oddness of Dickinson's poetry would, I feel, appeal to many young people of my age group. She is an original writer – and her eccentric style seems strangely modern. In the dramatic poem 'Slant of Light', Dickinson takes an unlikely approach. When one thinks of light, one normally imagines brightness and joy. But the winter*

light in this poem is coldly oppressive, suggesting Dickinson's deep despair. A sense of finality is present throughout – particularly in the chill setting. It is the end of the year –'Winter afternoons' so the light is fading. Dickinson immediately expresses religious doubts. The 'Cathedral Tunes' offer no comfort – instead, the church music is harsh. The poet's fearful fascination with death is clearly evident in her portrayal of a merciless, vengeful God subjecting humans to 'Heavenly Hurt, it gives us'.

3. This sense of terror is a recurring emotion in Dickinson's poetry. 'I felt a Funeral, in my Brain' is especially harrowing. Using nightmarish imagery, she imagines the experience of her own burial, with 'Mourners to and fro'. Her helplessness and isolation is powerfully conveyed through the repeated references to sounds 'threading—threading'. The funeral drum haunts her – 'beating—beating'. This awful alienation is forcefully expressed by a pounding rhythm which echoes the funeral march and reminds us of the poet's panic. The stark image of a coffin being lowered into a grave is suggested in the final stanza – 'And I dropped down, and down'. Dickinson's fragmented syntax reinforces the powerlessness of the 'solitary' speaker who is being lowered into her final resting place. There is something surreal about the graveyard scene which Dickinson creates, but she manages communicate some of the trauma surrounding the disturbing subject of death.

4. However, in other poems, such as 'Hope is the thing with Feathers', Dickinson reveals a more cheerful side to her character. This poem explores the abstract topic of hope by comparing it to a small, mysterious bird. The celebration of human resilience in the face of constant difficulty is in contrast to the poet's reputation as someone who only writes about anguish and despair. For Dickinson, the feeling of hope 'perches in the soul'. The verb suggests vitality. Dickinson maintains the comparison by referring to the bird (of hope) weathering 'the Gale' and surviving hard times even though 'sore must be the storm'. The final stanza is personal to the poet herself who admits her reliance on hope – 'I've heard it in the chilliest land'. The metaphorical language emphasises the importance of feeling hopeful. Dickinson expresses her gratitude for this simple human quality which has always helped her to cope: 'Yet never, in Extremity,/It asked a Crumb — of Me'.

5. Emily Dickinson's individual style of writing is seen in another nature poem, 'A Narrow Fellow in the Grass'. In this seemingly ordinary domestic drama, Dickinson

takes a young boy's perspective to express the excitement and shock of seeing a snake that frightened him – 'His notice sudden is'. The snake is personified and unpredictable – a 'spotted shaft'. I thought the poet was really expressing feelings of surprise when confronted with the unexpected. Everyone experiences shock at some time in their lives. Short, sharp sentences add to the drama and are typical of the poet's condensed writing style. Dickinson ranges over a variety of emotional responses throughout this narrative poem, firstly accepting the snake as another fascinating part of the natural world, but later reacting with complete terror – feeling 'Zero at the Bone'. She is clearly horrified by it but is still intrigued by the possibility of what the deadly snake might do.

6. Dickinson's poem's covered a great many emotions. She even sees the natural world in a comic way – particularly in 'A Bird came down the Walk.' The oddness of her poems really enticed me, the more I read them. She is a highly imaginative poet who can see animals in human terms. The bird 'drank a dew/From a convenient grass'. But the same bird soon reminds the poet that nature can be dangerous and should be treated with caution – 'He bit an Angleworm in halves/And ate the fellow, raw'. I liked the way Dickinson switches moods and expresses contrasting feelings. For me, she is a really fresh and original poetic voice who is always realistic about life.

(approx. 800 words)

Examiner's Comment

This is a good personal response that tries hard to remain focused on the question. While some of the points are slightly forced, there is close engagement with both the content and style of poems used for discussion. Intelligent use of quotations throughout. Overall, the expression is varied, fluent and well managed.

GRADE: B1

P = 12/15

C = 11/15

L = 12/15

M = 5/5

Total = 40/50

SAMPLE LEAVING CERT QUESTIONS ON DICKINSON'S POETRY

(45/50 MINUTES)

1. 'Emily Dickinson's unique poetic style is perfectly suited to the extraordinary experiences which she explores in her poems.' Do you agree with this assessment of Dickinson's poetry? Support your answer with suitable reference to the poems by Dickinson on your course.

2. 'A dark, eccentric vision is at the heart of Emily Dickinson's most dramatic poems.' Discuss this view, supporting the points you make with reference to the poems by Dickinson on your course.

3. 'Underlying all of Emily Dickinson's original poetry is a deep exploration of life's mysteries.' Write a response to this statement, supporting your answer with reference to the poems by Dickinson on your course.

Sample Essay Plan (Q1)

'Emily Dickinson's unique poetic style is perfectly suited to the extraordinary experiences which she explores in her poems.' Do you agree with this assessment of Dickinson's poetry? Support your answer with suitable reference to the poems by Dickinson on your course.

- Intro: Dickinson is an original voice who addresses abstract subject matter, such as states of consciousness, hope, death and the relationship between nature and human nature. Her energetic style is in keeping with the intensity of her experiences.

- Point 1: '"Hope" is the thing with feathers' – metaphorical language reflects the small bird's presence to illustrate and highlight various aspects of hope and human resilience.

- Point 2: Dramatic atmospheres in 'I felt a funeral, in my Brain' and 'I Heard a Fly Buzz—when I Died'. Surreal imagery, haunting aural effects and fragmented rhythms effectively convey disorientation and powerlessness.

- Point 3: The poet's strangely realistic view of nature evident in 'A Bird came down the Walk'. Use of odd, precise details, onomatopoeic language and comic moments enhance the reader's understanding of Dickinson's attitude.

- Point 4: Extended metaphor of drunkenness to reflect the poet's celebration of nature in 'I taste a liquor never brewed' reveals an idiosyncratic sense of humour. Strikingly imaginative images, forceful rhythms and enthusiastic tones all echo the poet's response to natural beauty.

- Conclusion: Condensed poetic forms, compressed syntax and daring language use is entirely appropriate to Dickinson's insightful reflections and dramatisations. Readers can engage more immediately with the intensity of the poet's heightened experiences.

Sample Essay Plan (Q1)

Develop one of the above points into a paragraph.

Sample Paragraph: Point 2

In both 'I felt a funeral, in my Brain' and 'I Heard a Fly Buzz—when I Died', Emily Dickinson creates a disturbing account of the sensation of dying. The two poems are dramatic, with a central speaker experiencing death through terrifying images. I thought the poet's style is perfectly in keeping with this alarming subject in 'I felt a funeral', especially her presentation of the 'Mourners' who keep 'treading' as the coffin is lowered into the grave – ' I dropped down, and down'. Repetition – the unreal drum 'beating—beating' – and short, broken phrasing emphasised the feeling of sheer dread and helplessness. Dickinson's vivid imagery and sounds add to the feeling of being overpowered. There is a more absurd atmosphere in 'I heard a Fly buzz—when I died'. The whole exaggerated scene seems distorted, particularly when the insignificant insect became the centre of attention, an 'uncertain stumbling Buzz'. Is Dickinson suggesting that human life is no more important than that of the unseen fly? The typically broken sentences also conveyed the confusion of the scene. From the dying person's perspective, there are 'Eyes around', 'Stillness in the Air' and thoughts about the afterlife, 'that last Onset'. The ending is sharp and stops abruptly, 'I could not see to see', a line suggesting the dreadful frustration and struggle, a desperation for clarity. I find that Dickinson's dramatic language conveys the reality of such troubling experiences very effectively.

Examiner's Comment

As part of a full examination essay, this is a clear personal response that addresses the question directly. The sustained focus on Dickinson's language use is aptly supported with very effective use of quotation. Both poems were treated succinctly and included some thoughtful discussion. Well-controlled expression added to the quality of the response. Grade A.

LAST WORDS

'The Dickinson dashes are an integral part of her method and style ... and cannot be translated ... without deadening the wonderful naked voltage of the poems.'

Ted Hughes

'The Brain—is wider than the Sky—
The Brain is deeper than the sea—'

Emily Dickinson

(On her determination to hide secrets) 'The price she paid was that of appearing to posterity as perpetually unfinished and wilfully eccentric.'

Philip Larkin

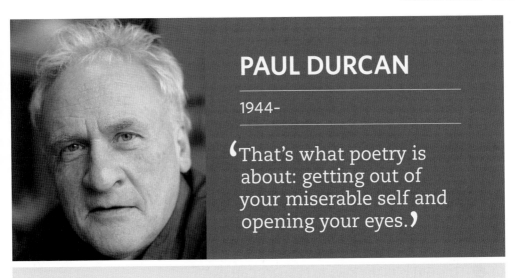

1944-

‘That's what poetry is about: getting out of your miserable self and opening your eyes.’

P aul Durcan is one of modern Ireland's foremost and most prolific poets. He is known for his controversial, comic and deeply moving poems. An outspoken critic of his native country, he has traced its emergence from the repressions of the 1950s to the contradictions of the present day.

Born in Dublin in 1944, Durcan spent much of his childhood with relatives in County Mayo. He was educated at University College Cork, where he studied archaeology and medieval history. In 1967, he met Nessa O'Neill. The couple later married and had two daughters. The marriage ended in 1984.

Among Durcan's many poetic influences are Eliot, Hopkins and Kavanagh. Significantly, his first solo collection of poetry, *O Westport in the Light of Asia Minor*, won the Patrick Kavanagh Award in 1975.

A variety of voices can be heard throughout Durcan's distinctive work, by turns hilarious, humane and heartbreaking. He uses many different forms, including dramatic monologues, ballads, mock news reports, songs and even prayers. His poetry can be surreal, mystical, passionate and ironic.

The subject matter of Paul Durcan's poems ranges widely, from explorations of cultural change in contemporary Ireland to intimate studies of family relationships. He is constantly observing the world around him, challenging authority and expressing human vulnerability. Many of the narrative poems he writes are autobiographical, often filled with black humour and satirical jibes. They seem to be carefully designed for oral appreciation.

Prescribed Poems

6 ' "Windfall", 8 Parnell Hill, Cork'

This long poem recounts both the happiness of family love and domesticity and the bitter consequences of a marriage. The intensity of the pain of separation is searing as Durcan discloses the disintegration of important relationships: 'The most subversive unit in society is the human family'. **162**

7 'Six Nuns Die In Convent Inferno'

In this lengthy narrative poem about a fire that destroyed a Dublin convent in 1986, Durcan characteristically transforms the details of the tragedy into an extended exercise in spiritual reflection. The elderly nun who narrates the moving story of this disaster reveals the personal choices she had made and her memories of happier times: 'fluttering up and down the beach'. **174**

8 'Sport'

Another painfully autobiographical poem in which Durcan recalls a football match from his youth and explores the troubled relationship he had with his father. With disarming honesty, the poet accepts the unhappy estrangement between father and son: 'More than anybody/ it was you/I wanted to mesmerise'. **185**

9 'Father's Day, 21 June 1992'

On a crucial train journey from Dublin to Cork, the poet confronts the erosive effects of time on his role as a husband and father. The poem alternates between tragicomedy, surreal scenes and moments of devastating self-awareness. By the end of this poignant journey, however, Durcan accepts that he no longer has any reason to celebrate Father's Day. **192**

10 'The Arnolfini Marriage'

This dramatic monologue was inspired by the famous Jan Van Eyck oil painting, which is believed to represent a rich Italian merchant and his wife. Durcan assumes the personas of the married couple, 'We are the Arnolfinis', as they reflect on marriage and their good fortune. Characteristically, boundaries are blurred throughout the poem and we are left to guess at the poet's real feelings. **199**

❶ NESSA

I met her on the first of August
In the Shangri-La Hotel,
She took me by the index finger
And dropped me in her well.
And that was a whirlpool, that was a whirlpool,   5
And I very nearly drowned.

Take off your pants, she said to me,
And I very nearly didn't;
Would you care to swim? she said to me,
And I hopped into the Irish Sea.   10
And that was a whirlpool, that was a whirlpool,
And I very nearly drowned.

On the way back I fell in the field
And she fell down beside me,
I'd have lain in the grass with her all my life   15
With Nessa:
She was a whirlpool, she was a whirlpool,
And I very nearly drowned.

O Nessa my dear, Nessa my dear,
Will you stay with me on the rocks?   20
Will you come for me into the Irish Sea
And for me let your red hair down?
And then we will ride into Dublin City
In a taxi-cab wrapped up in dust.
Oh you are a whirlpool, you are a whirlpool,   25
And I am very nearly drowned.

'And that was a whirlpool'

GLOSSARY

2   *Shangri-La*: legendary location often used in a similar context to the Garden of Eden to represent a hidden paradise. The Shangri-La Hotel was located in Dalkey, Co. Dublin.

3   *index finger*: forefinger, pointer finger, trigger finger; often used to make a warning gesture.

5   *whirlpool*: swirling body of water produced by the meeting of opposing currents.

20   *on the rocks*: a phrase describing a drink served with ice cubes; also refers to a disaster at sea.

EXPLORATIONS

1. What impression of Nessa do you get from reading the poem? Refer to the text in your answer.

2. Comment on the effectiveness of the poet's use of the whirlpool image.

3. Write your own personal response to the poem, highlighting the impact it made on you.

STUDY NOTES

This well-known love poem comes from Paul Durcan's second collection, O Westport in the Light of Asia Minor *(1975). The poet has said that he first met Nessa O'Neill in the bar of the Shangri-La Hotel in Dalkey when he was at a wedding reception there in August 1967. Soon afterwards, the couple moved to London and married. 'Nessa' includes elements of the* aisling *(dream vision) poetry tradition, which dates from late 17th-century Gaelic literature, when Ireland was often represented by an enchanting female figure. Durcan's poem is centred around swimming, an extended metaphor conveying both the delights and dangers of falling in love.*

The poem's title and dramatic **opening lines** emphasise the significance of meeting Nessa 'on the first of August'. This date also marks the traditional Celtic harvest festival, a time for celebrations and arranging marriages. The Irish term *Lughnasa* even echoes Nessa's own name. From the outset, Durcan's first-person presentation associates the woman who was to be his soul mate with mythology. Their introduction 'In the Shangri-La Hotel' seems a suitably exotic setting, suggesting the close spiritual union the couple would share. However, **line 3** foreshadows the uncertainty of romance as the poet recalls being led 'by the index finger'. Durcan uses the poem's central **metaphor of swimming to express exhilaration and risk-taking**. The lovers' intimacy is evoked in the erotic image of the wishing well, 'a whirlpool' in which he 'very nearly drowned'. The repetition and insistent rhythm of **line 5** reflects the continuing fascination of this unforgettable turning point in the poet's life.

The tone is a mixture of colloquial intimacy and self-mocking incantation. From the outset, Durcan highlights Nessa's power to enchant. His **wry humour** is apparent in the self-deprecating comments about his initial nervousness: 'Take off your pants, she said to me,/And I very nearly didn't'. The breathless enthusiasm of their first encounter is evident in lively phrasing: 'I hopped into the Irish Sea' (**line 10**). The poet's signature use of refrain forces the reader to appreciate the personal upheaval caused by his relationship with Nessa.

Line 13 marks a noticeable change of mood. Durcan focuses on the aftermath ('the way back') of that first swim when Nessa 'fell down beside me'. The **enduring remorse of knowing and losing love** is clear in the regretful line 'I'd have lain in the grass with her all my life'. The contrasting brevity and precise lyrical simplicity of **line 16** ('With Nessa') is almost immediately undermined by the stark realisation of the whirlpool symbol as the poet faces the reality of love's impermanence. The poem's **richly textured final section** is particularly tender: 'O Nessa my dear, Nessa my dear' (**line 19**). Durcan delicately repeats his wife's name. Ironically, his plaintive desire for her to 'stay with me on the rocks' reveals a yearning for a marriage that was inevitably doomed. The poet's powerful vision of Nessa encompasses elements of both dreams and nightmares. Imagining her as an idealised heroic creature ('for me let your red hair down'), he wonders if she can still be with him in the sea. The heart-rending fantasy is abruptly replaced by a darker image of the couple journeying through Dublin 'In a taxi-cab wrapped up in dust' (**line 24**). An unmistakable sense of death – coupled with the acceptance of lost love – is tinged with the notion that their kindred spirits are united forever.

The hypnotic rhythm of the last two lines brings the poet's reflection of that special day when he met his beloved Nessa up to date. Using the present tense verb, Durcan emphasises the ongoing and relentless hurt of the relationship breakdown: 'I am very nearly drowned'. Such **an honest expression of emotion and personal vulnerability** is characteristic of the poet. It has been said that the tragedy at the heart of Paul Durcan's writing is that he cannot accept tragedy. This is undoubtedly the case in 'Nessa', leaving readers with the lasting impression of a man who is still profoundly shocked by the enduring power of romantic love.

ANALYSIS

'What often defines Paul Durcan's poetry is an underlying sense of failure in personal relationships.' Do you agree with this view? Give reasons for your response, referring to Durcan's poem 'Nessa'.

Sample Paragraph

While Paul Durcan's poem, 'Nessa', is primarily a loving tribute to his ex-wife, it is also a warning that love doesn't always last. The suggestion of a relationship failing is suggested in the first stanza when Durcan describes their 'whirlpool' romance. This dramatic image indicates the wildness of their feelings and that they were taking a chance in marrying. A whirlpool is exciting, but also precarious. Durcan uses the refrain at the end of each stanza to reinforce the idea of being unsuccessful in love. Looking back on their marriage, he seems to be really reprimanding himself for his own carelessness. As though he took love for granted when he 'hopped into the Irish Sea'. I think he blames the failure of the relationship on himself, as suggested by the phrase 'I fell'. Durcan's tone of longing – 'Will you stay with me on the rocks?' – is very well expressed in this tragic poetic metaphor. Nessa is pictured as a beautiful and mysterious woman whose 'red hair' mesmerised the poet. The end of the poem really brings out the tragic disappointment of the couple's separation as Durcan makes it clear that the distress still exists – 'you are a whirlpool'. His tone at the end is of anguish and disillusionment. The loss of true love will remain with him forever.

Examiner's Comment

This is a focused personal response that addresses the question directly by tracing the progress of thought through the poem. The critical discussion touches on several interesting aspects relating to the predominant sense of failure. Supportive quotes are integrated effectively into the answer. Although the vocabulary is impressive, some of the expression is slightly awkward. Grade B.

CLASS/HOMEWORK EXERCISES

1. 'Durcan's inventive poetry is filled with dramatic tension.' Discuss this statement in relation to 'Nessa'.

2. Copy the table below into your own notes and fill in critical comments about the last two quotations.

Key Quotes

the Shangri-La Hotel	Durcan still associates the seaside hotel where he met Nessa with the mysterious utopian world of legend where the lovers would be destined to find perfect happiness. Ironically, he was to be disappointed.
And I hopped into the Irish Sea./And that was a whirl-pool	The exuberant rhythm and choice of the playful verb 'hopped' suggest a childlike enthusiasm. In retrospect, is the poet sensing that love was a dangerous game?
Will you stay with me on the rocks?	
we will ride into Dublin City/ In a taxi-cab wrapped up in dust	

2 THE GIRL WITH THE KEYS TO PEARSE'S COTTAGE

to John and Judith Meagher

When I was sixteen I met a dark girl;
Her dark hair was darker because her smile was so bright;
She was the girl with the keys to Pearse's Cottage;
And her name was Cáit Killann.

The cottage was built into the side of a hill;   5
I recall two windows and cosmic peace
Of bare brown rooms and on whitewashed walls
Photographs of the passionate and pale Pearse.

I recall wet thatch and peeling jambs
And how all was best seen from below in the field;   10
I used sit in the rushes with ledger-book and pencil
Compiling poems of passion for Cáit Killann.

Often she used linger on the sill of a window;
Hands by her side and brown legs akimbo;
In sun-red skirt and moon-black blazer;   15
Looking toward our strange world wide-eyed.

Our world was strange because it had no future;
She was America-bound at summer's end.
She had no choice but to leave her home –
The girl with the keys to Pearse's Cottage.   20

O Cáit Killann, O Cáit Killann,
You have gone with your keys from your own native place.
Yet here in this dark – El Greco eyes blaze back
From your Connemara postman's daughter's proudly mortal face.

'El Greco eyes blaze back'

GLOSSARY

3 **Pearse's Cottage**: Pádraic Pearse, Irish
teacher and political activist who was one
of the leaders of the 1916 Easter Rising,
owned a small cottage in Rosmuc,
Connemara. Pearse believed that the key
to national identity and independence was
knowledge of the language.

6 **cosmic**: endless, universal.
9 **jambs**: wooden doorframes.
11 **rushes**: marsh plants.
11 **ledger-book**: book used to keep records.
14 **akimbo**: standing confidently.
23 **El Greco**: Spanish Renaissance painter
famous for his fantastical portraits.

EXPLORATIONS

1. Why, in your opinion, is it important that the poem's setting is a cottage that belonged to Pádraic Pearse? Use reference from the text to support your views.

2. Describe the atmosphere of country life that the poet creates in lines 5–10.

3. Select one image from the poem that you find particularly interesting. Briefly explain your choice.

STUDY NOTES

'The Girl with the Keys to Pearse's Cottage' was published in Paul Durcan's first poetry collection, O Westport in the Light of Asia Minor, *in 1975. Themes of identity, belonging and the instability of place are frequently addressed in Durcan's work. The concept of home is a recurring concern. In this case, the poet narrates a poem of love and loss which includes some elements of the traditional Irish ballad. The poetic voice incorporates both the poet's 16-year-old self and his mature adult attitude to the painful legacy of emigration.*

The poem's **opening lines** immediately bring the reader back to a bittersweet moment in Durcan's life: 'When I was sixteen I met a dark girl'. **The strong visual awareness and effective use of repetition** ('dark', 'dark hair', 'darker') suggest the native Irish colouring of the young girl. Her dazzling smile is captured in the long line that culminates with the monosyllabic adjective 'bright', perhaps mirroring sudden sunshine bursting from the clouds over Western Ireland. We learn that the young woman held the 'keys to Pearse's Cottage'. Had she the means to unlock the secret of his house as well as enabling visitors to enter there? Reverently, the narrator reveals the identity of his lost love: 'And her name was Cáit Killann'.

The **second stanza** describes Pearse's cottage in remarkable detail: 'built into the side of a hill'. Durcan draws the reader into a romanticised place of 'cosmic peace'. He makes effective use of alliteration to emphasise the **simplicity and lack of ostentation** of the two-bedroomed house, with its 'bare brown rooms' and 'whitewashed walls'. In stark contrast to this are the photographs of the fiery nationalist politician himself, 'the passionate and pale Pearse'.

Stanza three delves further into the poet's memory ('I recall wet thatch and peeling jambs') as the ordinary opens up its secrets under the poet's observant gaze. This is a place that is past its best days, tired and weary. Is this how the people of the countryside regarded their environment? The **personal autobiographical detail** is conveyed in the picture of the young poet who sits 'in the rushes with ledger-book and pencil'. Instead of creating accounts, he compiles 'poems of passion' for the girl he loves. Again, alliteration suggests the copious number of poems the infatuated young poet wrote. The naive awkwardness of expressing his feelings in a book dedicated to dry statistics reflects the engaging sincerity of youth.

In **stanza four**, Durcan lyrically recalls Cáit Killann's languid grace: 'she used linger on the sill of a window'. The slender vowel 'i' delineates her confident movements. Suddenly, the pen portrait erupts into colour – 'brown legs', 'sun-red skirt', 'moon-black blazer'. These compound words indicate both her extraordinary effect on the poet and also **her effortless harmony with the native environment.** The beautiful Cáit belongs here. She gazes 'wide-eyed' and innocent 'toward our strange world'. Readers are left to wonder what she is about to discover.

The adult poet's answer in the **penultimate stanza** is that 'Our world was strange because it had no future'. His tone is suddenly bitter in response to the bleak realisation that emigration engulfs this crumbling place. 'She was America-bound at summer's end', almost as if she was a migratory bird. The stark political reality becomes a personal experience: 'She had no choice but to leave her home'. **Durcan has always addressed public issues** and he leaves us in no doubt of his own deep awareness that Irish life is lived in transit. Our young migrants become the diaspora scattered around the globe.

The **final stanza** is defined by a grief-stricken poetic voice lamenting the departure of someone who is loved. The poet repeats Cáit's name tenderly. **Plaintive assonant sounds** echo the traditional mourning or keening that was once found in the West of Ireland: 'O Cáit Killann, O Cáit Killann'. Now that she has left her 'own native place', it is as though a young plant was roughly torn from the Irish soil and transplanted elsewhere to bloom. The poet clearly regards Ireland as a 'dark' country, yet the memory of Cáit's vivid 'El Greco eyes' remains. In celebrating the alluring looks of the 'postman's daughter', Durcan has coloured the ordinariness of Connemara with the exotic fascination of international artistic beauty. El Greco, the Spanish painter, dared to view the world his way, sometimes representing it through exquisite portraits of intriguing women with shining eyes.

For Durcan, Cáit Killann also carried her own extraordinary light. The intensity of her gaze is conveyed in the explosive alliterative phrase 'blaze back' from her 'proudly mortal face'. Just like the poet, we mourn her loss. Through his use of metaphor, Durcan has transformed this native Irish girl into a striking icon. In addition, he has brought the reader to a different vantage point from which to view **the tragedy of emigration,** which is such an intrinsically Irish experience. Is this realistic viewpoint similar to the perspective from which Pearse's cottage might be perceived: 'all was best seen from below in the field'? Does something have to be viewed from a distance in order to understand it correctly? Have we been brought to a moment of epiphany as we contemplate the sombre reality of exile? At any rate, Cáit Killann remains a powerfully sad and realistic symbol of Irish emigration, an ironic reminder of what has become of Pearse's idealistic dreams.

ANALYSIS

'In the poetry of Paul Durcan, reality is frequently shaped by the imagination.' Discuss this statement in relation to the poem 'The Girl with the Keys to Pearse's Cottage'. Support your views with close reference to the text.

Sample Paragraph

Durcan's keen observation of mundane detail, 'wet thatch', 'peeling jambs', 'bare brown rooms', 'whitewashed walls', etc., all root the poem firmly in the reality of rain-soaked Connemara. All is calm, 'cosmic peace', on the surface. Yet bubbling beneath this seeming ordinariness, strong feelings flow, portrayed vividly in the photographs of the 'passionate and pale Pearse' who once inhabited this place. The longing of a sixteen-year-old boy for the beautiful 'postman's daughter' can be sensed as he sat 'in the rushes' while 'Compiling poems of passion' for her. The girl of the 'sun-red skirt' and 'moon-black blazer' is brought into another world through Durcan's inspired reference to her 'El Greco eyes'. The ordinary is opened up by his inventive metaphor. The Spanish painter, El Greco, saw things in a unique way – exactly like Cáit, 'Looking toward our strange world wide-eyed'. She seems surprised or perplexed at what she sees, perhaps because she is being forced to leave her native land, 'America-bound at summer's end'. Despite the sacrifice of the 1916 Rising, of which Pearse was a leader, this country is still unable to support its own people. But is the girl truly gone? Does her spirit still remain 'in this dark' as her eyes 'blaze back'? From my reading of the poem, I believe that she exists only in the poet's memory. Suddenly the reality of this little place in the West of Ireland has been formed by the imagination of the poet to represent the tragedy of emigration.

Examiner's Comment

A good personal response, engaging well with the poem. Carefully considered terms, such as 'inventive' and 'inspired', indicate a sustained focus on addressing the question directly. Overall, the expression is very well managed and accurate quotations are effectively integrated into the critical discussion. Grade A.

CLASS/HOMEWORK EXERCISES

1. 'Paul Durcan's poetry is often concerned with the world of the Irish countryside that has now disappeared.' Discuss this statement in relation to 'The Girl with the Keys to Pearse's Cottage'. Support the points you make with reference to the text.

2. Copy the table below into your own notes and fill in critical comments about the last two quotations.

Key Quotes

When I was sixteen I met a dark girl	The tone of the opening line is reminiscent of an old traditional Irish ballad. The adjective 'dark', suggesting beauty, might also be foreboding.
In sun-red skirt and moon-black blazer	Compound descriptions literally show what the girl is wearing, but also suggest how closely attuned she is to her surroundings since her appearance reflects nature.
Our world was strange because it had no future	
El Greco eyes blaze back/From your Connemara postman's daughter's proudly mortal face	

3 THE DIFFICULTY THAT IS MARRIAGE

We disagree to disagree, we divide, we differ;
Yet each night as I lie in bed beside you
And you are faraway curled up in sleep
I array the moonlit ceiling with a mosaic of question marks;
How was it I was so lucky to have ever met you?   5
I am no brave pagan proud of my mortality
Yet gladly on this changeling earth I should live for ever
If it were with you, my sleeping friend.
I have my troubles and I shall always have them
But I should rather live with you for ever   10
Than exchange my troubles for a changeless kingdom.
But I do not put you on a pedestal or throne;
You must have your faults but I do not see them.
If it were with you, I should live for ever.

'I array the moonlit ceiling with a mosaic
of question marks'

GLOSSARY

Difficulty: challenge, complication, problem.

Marriage: formal union of a man and woman; a close blend or mixture of two things.

4   *array*: adorn, arrange in an impressive way.

4   *mosaic*: pattern, montage.

6   *pagan*: unbeliever, atheist.

6   *mortality*: humanity, transience, death.

7   *changeling*: secretly exchanged.

9   *troubles*: afflictions, difficulties.

11   *exchange*: swap, substitute.

12   *pedestal*: raised platform, exalted position.

13   *faults*: failings, weaknesses.

EXPLORATIONS

1. Why, in your opinion, would Paul Durcan regard marriage as a difficulty? Refer to the poem to support your response.

2. Choose one image from the poem that you thought was particularly effective and explain your choice.

3. Would you consider the poet to be realistic or romantic in his view of marriage? Refer to the text in your answer.

STUDY NOTES

Paul Durcan published 'The Difficulty that is Marriage' in his collection Teresa's Bar *(1976). In considering his relationship with his wife, the poet's lyrical voice clearly reflects his intense personal romanticism. He observes and explores a small everyday event, a married couple sharing a bed together, but who are estranged from each other. Reflecting on his upbringing, Durcan once said, 'We were educated to believe that women were, on the one hand, untouchable and pure and on the other hand, that they were the source of all evil … women represent and embody freedom … living in much closer harmony with their true selves.' The title of this very personal poem suggests that while true love is not immune from problems, it will endure despite such obstacles.*

The **opening line** of this dramatic monologue is broken into abrupt staccato sections by its frequent punctuation marks and the deadening alliterative letter 'd': 'We disagree to disagree, we divide, we differ'. Durcan cleverly pinpoints the destructive conflict in a marriage as two separate individuals try to live as part of a couple. In this case, they cannot even agree that they can disagree. Instead, they are distinct, they deviate, they argue. After this turmoil of daily married life, three run-on lines smoothly convey, in unforced conversational tones, the stillness of the marriage bed: 'each night as I lie in bed beside you'. But while the couple are physically present in the one space, mentally and emotionally they are worlds apart. She is 'faraway curled up in sleep', content and at peace with herself. In contrast, the poet is lying awake, thinking, wondering, questioning. **Durcan's strong visual sensibility is evident** in the descriptive 'I array the moonlit ceiling with a mosaic of question marks'. The image has the immediacy of a snapshot coupled with surrealism as the reader views the ceiling bathed in the romantic moonlight patterned with the question marks of uncertainties: 'How was it I was so lucky to have ever met you?' Is the relationship broken into countless pieces by constant soul-searching and argument? Is the poet trying to reassemble the fragments into an ideal shape? The world with which he is so familiar seems to be undermined by such secret moments of human doubt and disbelief.

Durcan has always portrayed himself as an admirer of women, and on numerous occasions has cast his wife, Nessa, in a heroic role as someone to be admired, the one person who provides stability in his insecure life. In **line 6**, he expresses the male pain of never doing well enough, criticising his own character: 'I am no brave pagan proud of my mortality'. He is not an audacious savage delighted with his transient humanity. The self-deprecating tone changes to one of deep romanticism in his declaration that he would live forever 'on this changeling earth' if he could be 'with you, my sleeping friend'. There is a strong underlying sense that the poet feels uncomfortable in this world. In Irish folklore, a changeling refers to a child who has been secretly exchanged by the fairies for the parents' real child.

Line 9 reveals the dark side of Durcan's personality, 'I have my troubles', which is a common Irish euphemism for serious problems. Durcan has spoken of being committed by his family, against his will, to a range of psychiatric treatments, including electric convulsive therapy. He subsequently suffered from depression and has admitted, 'I think I came out of it with a kind of melancholia.' **Is the poet casting himself here in the role of sacrificial victim?** His father, with whom he had a difficult relationship, predicted that he would never be free of misfortune:

'Nemesis will follow you all the days of your life.' Is this why Durcan sees this earth as a 'changeling' place? Three words resonate: 'changeling', 'exchange' and 'changeless'. Is he willing to swap his longing for peace if he can always be with his beloved? 'But I should rather live with you for ever/Than exchange my troubles for a changeless kingdom'.

Paradoxically, while the poet denies that he exaggerates his feelings for his wife by exalting her 'on a pedestal or throne' (**line 12**) as if she were a saint or queen, at the same time he appears to worship her. He declares that 'You must have your faults', yet disarmingly admits, 'but I do not see them'. This short, introspective poem concludes with a statement of heightened romanticism: 'If it were with you, I should live for ever'. The **reverential tone** suggests a strong sense of the spiritual fulfilment he receives from their relationship. Yet although this poem shows such high regard for his wife, Durcan remains the leading man throughout, demanding to be noticed despite all his charming self-criticism. Alternatively, it is possible to read the poem more generously in the light of another of the poet's statements: 'Heaven is other people: a house where there are no women and children is a very empty house.'

ANALYSIS

'Paul Durcan has the gift of being able to make something out of nothing.' Discuss this statement with reference to his poem 'The Difficulty that is Marriage'. Support the points you make with reference to the text.

Sample Paragraph

'The Difficulty that is Marriage' explores the deep gulf between couples and the challenges they face. This is a universal theme that very many people can relate to. The obstacles to a successful relationship are vividly conveyed in the alliterative, broken opening line, 'We disagree to disagree, we divide, we differ'. The couple engage in aggressive, complicated wordplay as they attempt to score points off each other. The woman's ability to be content with herself is evident in the simple phrase, 'faraway curled up in sleep'. In contrast, the man's anxiety is revealed in the imaginative line, 'I array the moonlit ceiling with a mosaic of question marks'. Ironically, this married couple appear close, but really inhabit different universes. Durcan addresses a crucial issue, the reality of complicated human relationships. Using the direct language of genuine emotion, the husband longs to be 'with you for ever'. We are left wondering if, instead of outlining differences, did the poet convey these feelings to his partner? Or can he only address her like this because she is his 'sleeping friend'? I wonder did he ever tell her 'How was it I was so lucky to have ever met you'? Or did he just paint patterns on the ceiling? Perhaps this is the real difficulty of marriage, no one really knows for certain what the other is thinking or feeling. Durcan skilfully presents an ordinary occurrence, a married couple at night, one awake, one asleep, and creates a very important something out of a very mundane nothing.

Examiner's Comment

This is a competent response to a challenging question. There is a good personal approach throughout that shows engagement with the poem. Among several interesting points is the focus on the complexity of relationships. Effective use is made of accurate quotation. Expression is also clear and well controlled. Grade A.

CLASS/HOMEWORK EXERCISES

1. 'Poetry has to be fundamentally cinematic, painterly and musical.' Discuss this view in relation to Durcan's poem 'The Difficulty that is Marriage'. Refer closely to the text in your answer.

2. Copy the table below into your own notes and fill in critical comments about the last two quotations.

Key Quotes

I array the moonlit ceiling with a mosaic of question marks	This visual representation of the poet's troubled mind is portrayed as if an artist were making a work of art, decorating a ceiling from broken coloured pieces.
But I should rather live with you for ever/Than exchange my troubles for a changeless kingdom	The contrasting wordplay of 'exchange' and 'changeless' in these two run-on lines emphasises the poet's emotive assertion that nothing would make him happier than being with his beloved for all time.
I do not put you on a pedestal or throne	
You must have your faults but I do not see them	

❹ WIFE WHO SMASHED TELEVISION GETS JAIL

'She came home, my Lord, and smashed in the television;
Me and the kids were peaceably watching *Kojak*
When she marched into the living room and declared
That if I didn't turn off the television immediately
She'd put her boot through the screen;   5
I didn't turn it off, so instead she turned it off –
I remember the moment exactly because Kojak
After shooting a dame with the same name as my wife
Snarled at the corpse – Goodnight, Queen Maeve –
And then she took off her boots and smashed in the television;   10
I had to bring the kids round to my mother's place;
We got there just before the finish of *Kojak*;
(My mother has a fondness for *Kojak*, my Lord);
When I returned home my wife had deposited
What was left of the television into the dustbin,   15
Saying – I didn't get married to a television
And I don't see why my kids or anybody else's kids
Should have a television for a father or mother,
We'd be much better off all down in the pub talking
Or playing bar-billiards –   20
Whereupon she disappeared off back down again to the pub.'
Justice O'Brádaigh said wives who preferred bar-billiards to family television
Were a threat to the family which was the basic unit of society
As indeed the television itself could be said to be a basic unit of the family
And when as in this case wives expressed their preference in forms of
    violence   25
Jail was the only place for them. Leave to appeal was refused.

'peaceably watching *Kojak*'

GLOSSARY

1   *my Lord*: official form of address to a judge in court.

2   *Kojak*: American TV crime drama starring Telly Savalas. The series was popular in Ireland during the mid-1970s.

9   *Queen Maeve*: legendary Irish queen with a colourful reputation.

20 *bar-billiards*: group table game in which short cues are used.

26 *appeal*: review to challenge a court sentence.

EXPLORATIONS

1. In your opinion, what is the main point or message of this poem? Refer to the text in your response.

2. Comment on Durcan's use of irony throughout the poem, supporting the points you make with reference to the text.

3. Write a paragraph outlining your own feelings in response to this poem. Refer to the text in your answer.

STUDY NOTES

In his hard-hitting critiques of Irish society, one of Paul Durcan's signatures is the poem written as pseudo-reportage, where an unlikely event is depicted in a seemingly journalistic style. Humour has always been an essential component of the distinctive Durcan style. This poem is divided into two sections: the first 21 lines in the voice of the husband and the final five-line report of the judge's opinion and verdict. The poet's father was a circuit court judge.

The news headline title and matter-of-fact simplicity of the **opening lines** add all the more to their dramatic impact. There is an instantaneous quality to the initial evidence presented by the aggrieved husband who acts as a witness in the matter of his wife's prosecution, protesting that at the moment the act of violence occurred, 'Me and the kids were peaceably watching *Kojak*'. Unable to see the irony of viewing a violent TV drama, the man is immediately **ridiculed and mocked** by Durcan. His assertive wife is identified as 'Queen Maeve' solely because the husband describes Kojak as 'shooting a dame with the same name' (**line 8**). This instantly associates her with one of the great legendary symbols of female power – a queen of Connaught in the Ulster Cycle of Irish myths. However, in the real patriarchal world of Durcan's Ireland, the modern Maeve is merely seen as a deranged troublemaker.

The husband proceeds to condemn himself further by boasting that instead of taking his wife seriously, he has still not come to terms with the interruption to one of his favourite TV programmes. It is unsurprising to learn that he rushes off to seek comfort from his mother, who shares his 'fondness for *Kojak*' (**line 13**). However, aggressive as his wife's actions may be, it soon becomes clear that it is **her words and attitudes that serve to justify her condemnation.** As the story unfolds, Durcan slips effortlessly from the real to the surreal, often to inspired comic effect. When the distressed husband returns home, he discovers that his wife has dumped 'What was left of the television into the dustbin' (**line 15**).

In direct opposition to her uncommunicative husband and children, she boldly states: 'I don't see why my kids or anybody else's kids/Should have a television for a father or mother' (**lines 17–18**). **Durcan's bizarre humour is laced with unsmiling undertones.** For him, TV violence and escapism compete with the less glamorous facts of real life. As a result, any interference with the illusions that television creates can now be treated as serious crimes. The reader's sympathy for the eponymous wife is further generated by exposing the dramatic delusions of the male judge.

In the poem's **final lines**, the satire becomes much more intense. Durcan undermines the astounding moral certainty in the arrogant speech delivered by 'Justice O'Brádaigh', who declares that 'the television itself could be said to be a basic unit of the family' (**line 24**). The unashamed verdict promotes the idea that **virtual violence has a rightful place at the heart of family life**, a reason for the judge to state that 'Jail was the only place' for transgressors such as Maeve, who will not be allowed to challenge her sentence since 'Leave to appeal was refused'. The snarling tone of such a dismissive ruling is in keeping with Justice O'Brádaigh's prevailing mindset of disdainful self-delusion.

What sustains the tragicomic structure of this poem is Durcan's skilful depiction of the contrasting characters who are party to the scene: the precious husband, his frustrated wife and the condescending judge. Significantly, the wife herself is never directly heard. **Durcan is uncompromising in exposing negative attitudes towards voiceless women** – especially women who dare to resist the bounds of rigid expectations. His disapproval of the conventional pieties of Ireland's conspiratorial, male-dominated society is characteristic of his poetry. However, a close reading of 'Wife Who Smashed Television Gets Jail' reveals that it is not the medium of television, but its abuse that Durcan calls into question. As usual, in addressing such cultural issues, the poet entertains and gives pause for thought.

ANALYSIS

'Paul Durcan's deep sense of outrage is often evident in his poetry.' Discuss this view in relation to 'Wife Who Smashed Television Gets Jail', using references from the poem to support your answer.

Sample Paragraph

Paul Durcan has a reputation for producing what appear to be light-hearted poems, but his anger is never far from the surface. This is true of 'Wife Who Smashed Television Gets Jail' where he confronts society's ignorance and hypocrisy. The idea of a wife being taken to court by a man who gives more attention to his TV seems ridiculous, but the real point is that women have very little power. I could easily imagine Durcan's anger at the man's superior tone – 'Me and the kids were peaceably watching *Kojak*'. Even his comment about the detective 'shooting a dame' is a reminder that it's a man's world, both on TV and in real life. Underneath the absurd courthouse scene, Durcan barely conceals his rage that men – the husband, the TV hero and the influential judge – all represent a macho world. I thought the last line – 'Leave to appeal was refused' – summed up the poet's appreciation of how women in Irish society are marginalised. Durcan also makes effective use of the mock newspaper style. The serious courtroom atmosphere almost convinced me to take what was happening seriously. The poet seems to be saying that it is nearly impossible not to be part of the patriarchal culture that prevents many women from expressing the view that emotions and communication are more important than escapist TV violence. The outrage was present throughout the poem especially during the comic scenes.

Examiner's Comment

This is a clearly focused personal response showing good engagement with the poem. The focus on the dominance of male characters provided worthwhile support. Valuable use was also made of suitable references, particularly the *Kojak* quotation, which was very effective. Expression was well controlled throughout. Grade A.

CLASS/HOMEWORK EXERCISES

1. 'Humour and surrealism are Durcan's most powerful satirical weapons.' Discuss this statement with reference to the poem 'Wife Who Smashed Television Gets Jail'.

2. Copy the table below into your own notes and fill in critical comments about the last two quotations.

Key Quotes

she marched into the living room	The husband's self-pitying tone is reflected in this military image, which suggests a belligerent character similar to Queen Maeve.
I remember the moment exactly	There is obvious irony in the fact that family time is now marked by television shows and that the husband is oblivious to the lack of personal interaction.
We'd be much better off all down in the pub talking	
television itself could be said to be a basic unit of the family	

5 ## PARENTS

A child's face is a drowned face:
Her parents stare down at her asleep
Estranged from her by a sea:
She is under the sea
And they are above the sea: 5
If she looked up she would see them
As if locked out of their own home,
Their mouths open,
Their foreheads furrowed –
Pursed-up orifices of fearful fish –   10
Their big ears are fins behind glass
And in her sleep she is calling out to them
    Father, Father
    Mother, Mother
But they cannot hear her: 15
She is inside the sea
And they are outside the sea.
Through the night, stranded, they stare
At the drowned, drowned face of their child.

'And in her sleep she is calling out to them'

GLOSSARY

3	*Estranged*: separated.
9	*furrowed*: wrinkled.
10	*Pursed-up orifices*: open-shaped mouths.
18	*stranded*: abandoned.

EXPLORATIONS

1. Write a paragraph giving your own immediate reaction to reading 'Parents'. Refer to the poem in your answer.

2. Select one image from the poem that you find particularly unsettling and briefly explain your choice.

3. Using reference to the text, comment on the poem's dramatic features.

STUDY NOTES

'Parents' was published in Paul Durcan's 1978 collection, Sam's Cross. The poem raises interesting questions about parent–child communication, a recurring theme in Durcan's work. Characteristically, some of the poet's perceptions have a disturbing quality, which convey shock as well as intensity.

The poem's opening metaphor – 'A child's face is a drowned face' – has a startling effect. The devastating image represents every parent's greatest fear and introduces an **overwhelmingly anxious mood** that will dominate the entire poem. Durcan develops the sea metaphor in **lines 2–3**, creating a desperate scene of helplessness, as the parents can only stare down at their precious child, 'Estranged from her by a sea'. The lack of intimate communication – symbolised by the impenetrable ocean – is a central theme. There is something unsettling about the parents' realisation that they are already detached from their newborn child and that they can never know her as much as they would wish.

Lines 4–5 reflect their sense of shock at the unfathomable gulf that exists between them and the child: 'She is under the sea/And they are above the sea'. The separate lines emphasise the obstacle. Repetition and a deliberate rhythm further underline Durcan's sombre tone. For the first time in the poem, the child's perspective is presented when she imagines her parents being 'locked out of their own home' (**line 7**). Just as she is no longer within the security of the womb, they are also leading independent lives. Her growing understanding of the world is described in a series of increasingly distorted images. The 'furrowed' looks on her parents' foreheads are unnerving. The **surreal underwater sequence** becomes even more grotesque when Durcan compares the concerned adult expressions to 'Pursed-up orifices of fearful fish'. To the confused and frightened infant, the parents' ears are 'fins behind glass'.

Through **lines 12–14**, the developing drama of the parent–child exchange becomes all the more poignant. Durcan's dark vision of the child's distressed cry for attention ('Father, Father/Mother, Mother') transcends the moment and highlights the trauma of unfulfilled relationships between parents and children, lasting perhaps throughout entire lifetimes. For the poet, however, there is no denying the harsh fact revealed in **line 15**: 'But they cannot hear her'. An overpowering mood of desolation dominates the poem. The subdued tone and ironic alliteration echo **Durcan's sad acceptance that there will always be barriers between parents and children.** Throughout his writing career, the poet has explored his own troubled relationships, particularly with his father, who was a stern and distant figure.

There is a restrained **sense of resignation** in **lines 16–19**. Durcan repeats the stark truth about separation between individuals, contrasting the child 'inside the sea' with her parents, who are 'outside'. The final elegiac mood is achieved by the exaggerated illustration of the ever-watchful parents, who are left 'stranded', faced with the challenge of coming to terms with 'the drowned, face of their child'. The repetition of 'drowned' in the long final line leaves readers thinking of the many questions raised in this short poem. As always, Durcan has addressed important issues, not just about how individual human beings interact, but about the mystery of life itself.

ANALYSIS

'Paul Durcan writes well about detachment and isolation.' Discuss this view, with particular reference to 'Parents'. Refer closely to the text in your response.

Sample Paragraph

Durcan addresses interesting aspects of human experience in his poetry, and this is certainly the case in 'Parents'. The poem focuses on one set of unnamed parents and their young child, but takes a very negative view of the relationship. From the start, the parents are disconnected from their baby daughter, imagining that her sleeping face is 'a drowned face'. Their imagined fear of her death immediately suggests that her life is outside of their control. Durcan uses shocking sea images all through the poem to show the lack of close contact with the child who appears to be 'under the sea'. This gap exists between them and they can never know her completely. Their panic is conveyed very effectively in nightmarish terms. The child sees them as alien, almost intimidating, like 'fearful fish'. She calls to them but 'they cannot hear her'. I felt this was a really heartbreaking moment, especially as the poet repeated her frantic words, 'Father, Father/Mother, Mother'. The separation they feel in never fully communicating is seen at the end of the poem where the parents are 'stranded' – another seas image – 'Through the night'. This tragic insight into the distances between people is reinforced in the last line by the repetition of 'drowned' – a final reminder of detachment and alienation.

Examiner's Comment

A successful response that tackles the question directly. Suitable references and quotations sustain the focused discussion of Durcan's treatment of isolation. There is some good personal engagement and the answer traces the development of thought in the poem very effectively. Expression is varied and assured throughout. Grade A.

CLASS/HOMEWORK EXERCISES

1. 'Durcan's most compelling poems often raise significant questions about the complexity of human relationships.' To what extent is this true of 'Parents'? Support your answer with reference to the poem.

2. Copy the table below into your own notes and fill in critical comments about the last two quotations.

Key Quotes

A child's face is a drowned face	This emphatic opening metaphor is both dramatic and startling. The assured tone and use of repetition add to the poem's ominous tone.
Pursed-up orifices of fearful fish	The child's view of her parents is suggested by this exaggerated image of the strangely distorted fish. Edgy sound effects contribute to the sense of agitation.
in her sleep she is calling out to them	
Through the night, stranded	

6 'WINDFALL', 8 PARNELL HILL, CORK

But, then, at the end of day I could always say –
Well, now, I am going home.
I felt elected, steeped, sovereign to be able to say –
I am going home.
When I was at home I liked to stay at home;   5
At home I stayed at home for weeks;
At home I used sit in a winged chair by the window
Overlooking the river and the factory chimneys,
The electricity power station and the car assembly works,
The fleets of trawlers and the pilot tugs,   10
Dreaming that life is a dream which is real,
The river a reflection of itself in its own waters,
Goya sketching Goya among the smoky mirrors.
The industrial vista was my Mont Sainte-Victoire.
While my children sat on my knees watching TV   15
Their mother, my wife, reclined on the couch
Knitting a bright-coloured scarf, drinking a cup of black coffee,
Smoking a cigarette – one of her own roll-ups.
I closed my eyes and breathed in and breathed out.

It is ecstasy to breathe if you are at home in the world.   20
What a windfall! A home of our own!
Our neighbours' houses had names like 'Con Amore',
'Sans Souci', 'Pacelli', 'Montini', 'Homesville'.
But we called our home 'Windfall'.
'Windfall', 8 Parnell Hill, Cork.   25
In the gut of my head coursed the leaf of tranquillity
Which I dreamed was known only to Buddhist Monks
In lotus monasteries high up in the Hindu Kush.
Down here in the dark depths of Ireland,
Below sea level in the city of Cork,   30
In a city as intimate and homicidal as a Little Marseilles,
In a country where all the children of the nation
Are not cherished equally
And where the best go homeless, while the worst
Erect block-house palaces – self-regardingly ugly –   35
Having a home of your own can give to a family
A chance in a lifetime to transcend death.

At the high window, shipping from all over the world
Being borne up and down the busy, yet contemplative, river;
Skylines drifting in and out of skylines in the cloudy valley; 40
Firelight at dusk, and city lights;
Beyond them the control tower of the airport on the hill –
A lighthouse in the sky flashing green to white to green;
Our black-and-white cat snoozing in the corner of a chair;
Pastels and etchings on the four walls, and over the mantelpiece 45
'Van Gogh's Grave' and 'Lovers in Water';
A room wallpapered in books and family photograph albums
Chronicling the adventures and metamorphoses of family life:
In swaddling clothes in Mammy's arms on baptism day;
Being a baby of nine months and not remembering it; 50
Face-down in a pram, incarcerated in a high chair;
Everybody, including strangers, wearing shop-window smiles;
With Granny in Felixstowe, with Granny in Ballymaloe;
In a group photo in First Infants, on a bike at thirteen;
In the back garden in London, in the back garden in Cork; 55
Performing a headstand after First Holy Communion;
Getting a kiss from the Bishop on Confirmation Day;
Straw hats in the Bois de Boulougne, wearing wings at the seaside;

Mammy and Daddy holding hands on the Normandy Beaches;
Mammy and Daddy at the wedding of Jeremiah and Margot; 60
Mammy and Daddy queuing up for *Last Tango in Paris*;
Boating on the Shannon, climbing mountains in Kerry;
Building sandcastles in Killala, camping in Barley Cove;
Picnicking in Moone, hide-and-go-seek in Clonmacnoise;
Riding horses, cantering, jumping fences; 65
Pushing out toy yachts in the pond in the Tuileries;
The Irish College revisited in the Rue des Irlandais;
Sipping an *orange pressé* through a straw on the roof of the Beaubourg;
Dancing in Père Lachaise, weeping at Auvers.
Year in, year out, I pored over these albums accumulating, 70
My children looking over my shoulder, exhilarated as I was,
Their mother presiding at our ritual from a distance –
The far side of the hearthrug, diffidently, proudly.
Schoolbooks on the floor and pyjamas on the couch –
Whose turn is it tonight to put the children to bed? 75

Our children swam about our home
As if it was their private sea,
Their own unique, symbiotic fluid
Of which their parents also partook.
Such is home – a sea of your own –   80
In which you hang upside down from the ceiling
With equanimity, while postcards from Thailand on the mantelpiece
Are raising their eyebrow markings benignly:
Your hands dangling their prayers to the floorboards of your home,
Sifting the sands underneath the surfaces of conversations,   85
The marine insect life of the family psyche.
A home of your own – or a sea of your own –
In which climbing the walls is as natural
As making love on the stairs;
In which when the telephone rings   90
Husband and wife are metamorphosed into smiling accomplices,
Both declining to answer it;
Initiating, instead, a yet more subversive kiss –
A kiss they have perhaps never attempted before –
And might never have dreamed of attempting   95
Were it not for the telephone belling.
Through the bannisters or along the bannister rails
The pyjama-clad children solemnly watching
Their parents at play, jumping up and down in support,
Race back to bed, gesticulating wordlessly: 100
The most subversive unit in society is the human family.

We're almost home, pet, almost home...
Our home is at...
I'll be home...
I have to go home now...   105
I want to go home now...
Are you feeling homesick?
Are you anxious to get home?...
I can't wait to get home...
Let's stay at home tonight and...   110
What time will you be coming home at?...
If I'm not home by six at the latest, I'll phone...
We're nearly home, don't worry, we're nearly home...

But then with good reason
I was put out of my home: 115
By a keen wind felled.
I find myself now without a home
Having to live homeless in the alien, foreign city of Dublin.
It is an eerie enough feeling to be homesick
Yet knowing you will be going home next week;   120
It is an eerie feeling beyond all ornithological analysis
To be homesick knowing that there is no home to go home to:
Day by day, creeping, crawling,
Moonlighting, escaping,
Bed-and-breakfast to bed-and-breakfast;   125
Hostels, centres, one-night hotels.

Homeless in Dublin,
Blown about the suburban streets at evening,
Peering in the windows of other people's homes,
Wondering what it must feel like   130
To be sitting around a fire –
Apache or Cherokee or Bourgeoisie –
Beholding the firelit faces of your family,
Beholding their starry or their TV gaze:
Windfall to Windfall – can you hear me?   135
Windfall to Windfall…
We're almost home, pet, don't worry anymore, we're almost home.

'Lovers in Water'

GLOSSARY

Windfall: something good received unexpectedly; something the wind has blown down.

3 *elected, steeped, sovereign*: slang terms for being very lucky.

7 *winged*: high-backed chair; capable of flight.

11 *life is a dream*: play by the Spanish playwright Calderon, which deals with the problems of distinguishing between illusion and reality.

13 *Goya*: Spanish romantic painter whose works contain a subversive imaginative element.

13 *smoky mirrors*: a reference to a painting by Goya of a Spanish king with his family containing an image of Goya himself in a dark mirror looking out at the viewer. The message is one of underlying corruption and decay.

14 *Mont Sainte-Victoire*: beautiful French mountain often painted by Paul Cézanne.

27 *Buddhist Monks*: monks who live a simple meditative life. They believe that married couples should respect each other's beliefs and privacy.

28 *lotus*: sacred. The lotus refers to an exotic water lily and to a fruit that causes dreamy forgetfulness.

28 *Hindu Kush*: mountain range stretching from Afghanistan to Pakistan, meaning 'Kills the Hindu', a reference to the many Indian slaves who perished there from harsh weather conditions.

31 *Marseilles*: oldest city in France, a Mediterranean port that suffered many sieges and where 'La Marseillaise', the French national anthem, came from. It had a colony of famous artists and is now a gateway for immigrants from the African continent.

35 *block-house palaces*: a disparaging reference to new high-rise buildings that sprang up in modern Ireland.

46 *'Van Gogh's Grave'*: Vincent van Gogh (1853–90) is a famous Dutch post-Impressionist painter who suffered, like Durcan, from depression. He was a tortured soul who lived for his art.

46 *'Lovers in Water'*: a reference to a painting by modern artist Francine Scialom Greenblatt that refers to a private place made public.

49 *swaddling*: strips of cloth wrapped around a newborn child to calm it; also a reference to how the infant Jesus is described in the gospel account.

61 *Last Tango in Paris*: romantic movie (1972) about a love affair that ends in tragedy.

68 *Beaubourg*: small, stylish hotel in Paris.

69 *Père Lachaise*: largest cemetery in Paris, containing the graves of many famous people.

69 *Auvers*: village where Van Gogh lived.

78 *symbiotic*: safe, secure; similar to the natural pre-birth environment.

82 *equanimity*: composure, calmness.

83 *benignly*: compassionately, favourably.

86 *psyche*: consciousness; soul.

91 *metamorphosed*: changed.

91 *accomplices*: partners – usually in crime.

93 *subversive*: unsettling, rebellious.

100 *gesticulating*: gesturing dramatically.

116 *keen*: sharp, biting.

118 *alien*: unfamiliar, strange.

119 *eerie*: scary, unnatural.

121 *ornithological*: scientific study of birds.

132 *Apache*: Native American tribe from Arizona.

132 *Cherokee*: Native American tribe from the southern United States.

132 *Bourgeoisie*: conservative middle class, chiefly concerned with wealth.

EXPLORATIONS

1. In your opinion, what is Durcan's central theme or point in this poem? Briefly explain your response.

2. The poet uses conversational language throughout the poem. What effect do you think this has on the reader?

3. Comment on the tone of the concluding line, 'We're almost home, pet, don't worry anymore, we're almost home'. Does the poet really believe this or is there a darker meaning?

STUDY NOTES

'"Windfall", 8 Parnell Hill, Cork' was published in Paul Durcan's collection The Berlin Wall Café *(1985). It chronicles not only the happy domesticity Durcan enjoyed in his marriage with his wife, Nessa, and his two girls, but also the bitter consequences of the break-up of that marriage for the poet. The intensity of the pain of separation is searing as the ex-husband unflinchingly discloses the disintegration of his relationship. Paul Durcan has commented, 'Hardly a day goes by that I don't think about our marriage ... I put the breakdown of our marriage down to my stupidity.'*

The **opening line** is written in the past tense and expresses a possibility for the future. The poet used to be able to say, 'Well, now, I am going home', as if all the ills of the world could be left outside when he retreated to his one safe place of contentment. Durcan explains how good he felt that he could make that statement: 'I felt elected, steeped, sovereign'. He felt chosen, 'steeped' in luck, free and dominant. But there is a note of regret here, clearly suggesting that he can no longer return home. The importance of home is emphasised by continual repetition: 'When I was at home I liked to stay at home;/At home I stayed at home for weeks'. From his privileged position in his 'winged chair', the poet could survey the familiar sights of the city port, 'the river and the factory chimneys'. He meditates, 'Dreaming that life is a dream which is real'. For Durcan, however, reality becomes uncertain, unfocused, 'The river a reflection of itself in its own waters'. His mind turns to a painting by Goya where the painter has depicted himself in a 'smoky' mirror behind a group of people peering out at the viewer. The industrial vista of Cork seems every bit as important for the poet as Mont Sainte-Victoire was for another artist, Paul Cézanne. A happy picture of domesticity soon replaces the fluid, unsettling river images. We see Durcan and his family forming a secure, close-knit group: 'my children sat on my knees watching TV'. It is a picture of indolence. Their mother is described separately, as if not quite belonging to this unit. In contrast to the poet, she is much more engaged, 'Knitting', 'drinking', 'Smoking'. But Durcan is oblivious and blissfully happy in his comfortable habitat: 'I closed my eyes and breathed in and breathed out'.

Section 2 (line 20) conveys the heights of emotion, 'ecstasy', that is felt when an individual is at ease in the right place, 'at home in the world'. The poet describes this as a 'windfall', something good that has been received unexpectedly. The tone is complacent – almost cynical – when he recalls the names of his neighbours' homes: 'Con Amore' (with love), 'Sans Souci' (without worries), 'Homesville'. Some other houses are called after popes, suggesting the controlling religious influence on the local community. Durcan points out that he and his wife were above all that – 'But we called our home "Windfall"', as though nature itself had provided this haven for his family. Already there is an underlying suggestion that he took too much for granted. He still feels a sense of deep serenity in the depths of his being, 'the leaf of tranquillity', known only to the ascetic monks who lived in Asia's remote mountain ranges. The exotic image of 'lotus monasteries' evokes the **idealised state of wistful forgetfulness** enjoyed both by the monks and the poet himself. But this restful dreamscape is rudely torn apart by the shocking reality of bourgeois Ireland's 'dark depths'. Cork city is 'intimate', private and personal, but also 'homicidal', murderous, just like the subversive city of Marseilles, where the French Revolution started. Characteristically, Durcan makes a bitter reference to the Irish Constitution, which had not fulfilled its promises and instead produced 'a country where all the children of the nation/Are not cherished equally'. He ridicules the greed of the rising moneyed classes and their 'block-house palaces'. This section concludes **(lines 36–37)** that 'Having a home of your own' allows a family to 'transcend death'. Some of the poet's ancestors had once been evicted from their holding in County Mayo. Durcan has said that in his own family, 'There was only one value and that was money.'

The dreamy sight of changing skies opens the poem's **third section (line 38)**. Tall ships are 'drifting in and out of skylines in the cloudy valley'. **Family harmony**

appears to reign: 'Our black-and-white cat snoozing in the corner of a chair'. The living room is filled with pictures and old photo albums that record in detail the changes in family life over two generations. But another disturbing note is struck as the poet describes early pictures of himself 'Face-down in a pram, incarcerated in a high chair'. Durcan was once regarded by his own relations as the black sheep of the family and at one time he was even confined to a mental institution. As he studies the albums, he feels betrayed by the false expressions: 'shop-window smiles'. The seemingly random collection of memories ranges widely over significant times and various places at home, at school and on holiday. The young Durcan is seen behaving wildly, 'Performing a headstand after First Holy Communion'. But he seems more forlorn than bitter. Is the concluding image, 'wearing wings at the seaside', a reference to his innocence or his wish to escape?

The **fourth section (line 59)** continues with a hypnotic refrain, 'Mammy and Daddy'. Is the poet now openly sneering at the irony of these misleadingly happy photos? He has placed himself centre stage of two family units, as though watching himself growing from childhood to parenthood. For years, he has 'pored over these albums' with his children, who seem equally 'exhilarated' by these glimpses into the past. It is yet another irony that the 'hearthrug' – which used to signify domestic warmth – is now a symbol of the void at the heart of the house. Strangely, **his wife is excluded**, almost sidelined as the adult in the scene coolly looking on, 'presiding'. The poet's wife is described as self-effacing, but she looks on 'proudly'. Does the poet consider that he made the mistake of taking her for granted? She was the family breadwinner while Durcan remained at home caring for their two children and writing. He has since said, 'I sometimes think Nessa missed out. She was out working while I was with the girls'. At times, the tone wavers between condemnation and remorse, with the conflicting preoccupations of the couple's time together remaining unresolved. In the midst of the rough and tumble of family life, 'Schoolbooks on the floor and pyjamas on the couch', her cool voice echoes, 'Whose turn is it tonight to put the children to bed?'

An allegorical **dream scene** reveals the spiritual and emotional aspects of ordinary domestic life in **section five (line 76)**: 'Our children swam about our home/As if it was their private sea'. The idyllic, unrestrained happiness of the family is caught in the image of the 'symbiotic fluid' of which everyone 'partook'. Durcan believed that home was a place where one could be at liberty without consequences, even hanging 'upside down from the ceiling/With equanimity'. However, the sibilant line 'Sifting the sands underneath the surfaces of conversations' sounds a warning note. Is someone scrutinising, negatively reviewing? The couple are happy when they are partners in crime, 'smiling accomplices', preferring to continue kissing rather than answer the phone. There are signs that the poet could only relate to his wife when she was not behaving as a responsible adult. Meanwhile, the children watch their 'parents at play' sharing another 'subversive kiss' before running 'wordlessly' to bed. But from his intense study of the 'family psyche', Durcan has learned that **the challenges of an intimate relationship can be destructive**. His ringing assertion that 'The most subversive unit in society is the human family' abruptly contradicts any nostalgic homesickness he may have been experiencing.

In the **sixth section (line 102)**, a reassuring parental voice is heard: 'We're almost home, pet, almost home'. The poet follows up with a litany of everyday phrases, some hanging unfinished, and all containing the word 'home'. It is as if this ubiquitous term – the crucial concept of 'home' and belonging – highlights the **overwhelming sense of security and safety he associates with family life**: 'If I'm not home by six at the latest, I'll phone...' The comforting tone concludes this short section as if Durcan himself and his family have almost made it 'home'. As always, the immediacy of his poetic voice resonates with readers, reinforcing the universal importance of close family relationships.

Inevitably, however, all the celebration of domesticity – whether real or imagined – is shattered in the **penultimate section (line 114)**: 'But then with good reason/I was put out of my home'. The poet no longer refers to 'our home', as in the previous section, but to 'my home'. Does he think he has an absolute right to be there? Durcan frankly admits that he was expelled 'with good reason'. But what was this reason – depression, alcoholism, a refusal to mature? Is he assuming the manipulative posture of the bad boy, disarmingly admitting his faults so that he will be immediately forgiven? There is more than a hint of self-pity in the claim that he was finally brought down 'By a keen wind'. Is this sharp, biting force really his wife? Typically self-absorbed, the poet goes on to describe his experience of being without a home. He now has to live in the 'alien, foreign city of Dublin', a frightening, disorienting experience. He has discovered how strange it is to be 'homesick' and regards it as totally unnatural, 'beyond all ornithological analysis' if 'there is no home to go home to'. **Short lines effectively convey the aimless wanderings of a homeless man.** 'Day by day' he spends his time 'creeping, crawling,/Moonlighting, escaping'. What a contrast to his previous idyllic existence, when he was in control of his home in his 'winged chair', surveying his own 'Mont Sainte-Victoire' with his happy children on his knees. Now he moves restlessly from 'Bed-and-breakfast to bed-and breakfast;/Hostels, centres, one-night hotels'.

The poem's **final section (line 127)** refers again to a 'Windfall', but now the word is said with bitter irony. It no longer refers to his comfortable home, but to himself as a rootless object 'Blown about the suburban streets at evening'. Longingly, he peers 'in the windows of other people's homes,/Wondering what it must feel like/To be sitting around a fire'. This basic experience is enjoyed by all races and societies, 'Apache or Cherokee' or the middle-class 'Bourgeoisie'. They all have the privilege of looking at their families' faces illuminated by firelight, whether they gaze at the stars or the TV screen. The poet now resembles a distressed vessel that had been cast adrift. He is calling frantically for assistance: 'can you hear me?' At this point, the calming tones of a parent return, tenderly reassuring a distracted child: 'We're almost home, pet, don't worry anymore, we're almost home'. Is this longing so deeply ingrained in Durcan that he takes refuge in convincing himself that it is still a possibility? Or is the reality the awful truth that he can never again go back to '"Windfall", 8 Parnell Hill, Cork'?

ANALYSIS

'Paul Durcan charms readers with his self-critical revelations while concealing his own self-centredness.' Discuss this statement in relation to the poem '"Windfall", 8 Parnell Hill, Cork'. Refer closely to the text in your response.

Sample Paragraph

In this poem, Paul Durcan charms us by presenting memorable images of cosy domesticity, 'my children sat on my knees watching TV', 'Our children swam about our home'. I did feel sympathy for him when I heard his graphic account of homelessness, 'creeping and crawling' as though he was unwanted, going from one anonymous place to another, 'Hostels, centres, one-night hotels'. He appears rootless, a windfall, belonging nowhere, 'Blown about the suburban streets at evening'. But his admission of being 'put out' of his home 'with good reason' seems as if he is condemning himself just to get pity. His wife is seen busily 'Knitting'. She is 'presiding' while the poet and his children look at old pictures of him 'Dancing' in a Paris graveyard. She is the breadwinner and the adult in the relationship, 'Whose turn is it tonight to put the children to bed?' Is he placing his wife in the role of a person who didn't understand him? I believe that his wife was becoming frustrated, 'Sifting the sands underneath the surfaces of conversations'. She snapped and finally refused to accept her husband's selfish behaviour. In my opinion, this poem is not really about Durcan's home, but about himself. He does attempt to hide his self-centred character. At the same time, I still feel sorry for him. He ends up as a very lonely man who has lost all, reduced to the pitiful state of peering into other people's homes and who can never say 'Well, now, I am going home'.

Examiner's Comment

The paragraph touches on interesting aspects of how the poet appears to readers and there is a good attempt at addressing the crucial relationship between Durcan and his wife. Points are well illustrated with accurate quotations and there is clear evidence of personal engagement. Expression is generally controlled, but is a little note-like. Grade B.

CLASS/HOMEWORK EXERCISES

1. 'In many of his poems, Paul Durcan relishes conflict and exhibitionism.' Discuss this statement in relation to '"Windfall", 8 Parnell Hill, Cork'. Support the points you make with suitable reference.

2. Copy the table below into your own notes and fill in critical comments about the last two quotations.

Key Quotes

I used sit in a winged chair by the window	This image vividly conveys the comfortable position of the husband in his home while also referring to his belief that he is a gifted artist who can soar to great heights. But is Durcan really mocking his own earlier self-importance?
The most subversive unit in society is the human family	This controversial assertion challenges the popular belief that it is the family that holds society together. The poet is stating that family tensions are the cause of all our discontent.
But then with good reason/I was put out of my home	
We're almost home, pet, don't worry anymore, we're almost home	

❼ SIX NUNS DIE IN CONVENT INFERNO

To the
happy memory of six Loreto nuns
who died
between midnight and morning of
2 June 1986

I

We resided in a Loreto convent in the centre of Dublin city
On the east side of a public gardens, St Stephen's Green.
Grafton Street – the *paseo*
Where everybody *paseo*'d, including even ourselves –
Debouched on the north side, and at the top of Grafton Street,   5
Or round the base of the great patriotic pebble of O'Donovan Rossa,
Knelt tableaus of punk girls and punk boys.
When I used pass them – scurrying as I went –
Often as not to catch a mass in Clarendon Street,
The Carmelite Church in Clarendon Street   10
(Myself, I never used the Clarendon Street entrance,
I always slipped in by way of Johnson's Court,
Opposite the side entrance to Bewley's Oriental Café),
I could not help but smile, as I sucked on a Fox's mint,
That for all the half-shaven heads and the martial garb   15
And the dyed hair-dos and the nappy pins
They looked so conventional, really, and vulnerable,
Clinging to warpaint and to uniforms and to one another.
I knew it was myself who was the ultimate drop-out,
The delinquent, the recidivist, the vagabond,   20
The wild woman, the subversive, the original punk.
Yet, although I confess I was smiling, I was also afraid,
Appalled by my own nerve, my own fervour,
My apocalyptic enthusiasm, my other-worldly hubris:
To opt out of the world and to   25
Choose such exotic loneliness,
Such terrestrial abandonment,
A lifetime of bicycle lamps and bicycle pumps,
A lifetime of galoshes stowed under the stairs,
A lifetime of umbrellas drying out in the kitchens.   30

I was an old nun – an agèd beadswoman –
But I was no daw.

I knew what a weird bird I was, I knew that when we
Went to bed we were as eerie an aviary as you'd find
In all the blown-off rooftops of the city: 35
Scuttling about our dorm, wheezing, shrieking, croaking,
In our yellowy corsets, wonky suspenders, strung-out garters,
A bony crew in the gods of the sleeping city.
Many's the night I lay awake in bed
Dreaming what would befall us if there were a fire: 40
No fire-escapes outside, no fire-extinguishers inside;
To coin a Dublin saying,
We'd not stand a snowball's chance in hell. Fancy that!
It seemed too good to be true:
Happy death vouchsafed only to the few.   45
Sleeping up there was like sleeping at the top of the mast
Of a nineteenth-century schooner, and in the daytime
We old nuns were the ones who crawled out on the yardarms
To stitch and sew the rigging and the canvas.
To be sure we were weird birds, oddballs, Christniks,   50
For we had done the weirdest thing a woman can do –
Surrendered the marvellous passions of girlhood,
The innocent dreams of childhood,
Not for a night or a weekend or even a Lent or a season,
But for a lifetime.   55
Never to know the love of a man or a woman;
Never to have children of our own;
Never to have a home of our own;
All for why and for what?
To follow a young man – would you believe it –   60
Who lived two thousand years ago in Palestine
And who died a common criminal strung up on a tree.

As we stood there in the disintegrating dormitory
Burning to death in the arms of Christ –
O Christ, Christ, come quickly, quickly –   65
Fluttering about in our tight, gold bodices,
Beating our wings in vain,
It reminded me of the snaps one of the sisters took
When we took a seaside holiday in 1956
(The year Cardinal Mindszenty went into hiding   70
In the US legation in Budapest.

He was a great hero of ours, Cardinal Mindszenty,
Any of us would have given our right arm
To have been his nun - darning his socks, cooking his meals,
Making his bed, doing his washing and ironing.)   75
Somebody - an affluent buddy of the bishop's repenting his affluence -
Loaned Mother Superior a secluded beach in Co. Waterford -
Ardmore, along the coast from Tramore -
A cove with palm trees, no less, well off the main road.
There we were, fluttering up and down the beach,   80
Scampering hither and thither in our starched bathing-costumes.
Tonight, expiring in the fire, was quite much like that,
Only instead of scampering into the waves of the sea,
Now we were scampering into the flames of the fire.

That was one of the gayest days of my life,   85
The day the sisters went swimming.
Often in the silent darkness of the chapel after Benediction,
During the Exposition of the Blessed Sacrament,
I glimpsed the sea again as it was that day.
Praying - daydreaming really -   90
I became aware that Christ is the ocean
Forever rising and falling on the world's shore.
Now tonight in the convent Christ is the fire in whose waves
We are doomed but delighted to drown.
And, darting in and out of the flames of the dormitory,   95
Gabriel, with that extraordinary message of his on his boyish lips,
Frenetically pedalling his skybike.
He whispers into my ear what I must do
And I do it - and die.
Each of us in our own tiny, frail, furtive way   100
Was a Mother of God, mothering forth illegitimate Christs
In the street life of Dublin city.
God have mercy on our whirring souls -
Wild women were we all -
And on the misfortunate, poor fire-brigade men   105
Whose task it will be to shovel up our ashes and shovel
What is left of us into black plastic refuse sacks.
Fire-brigade men are the salt of the earth.

Isn't it a marvellous thing how your hour comes
When you least expect it? When you lose a thing,   110
Not to know about it until it actually happens?
How, in so many ways, losing things is such a refreshing experience,
Giving you a sense of freedom you've not often experienced?
How lucky I was to lose – I say, lose – lose my life.
It was a Sunday night, and after vespers   115
I skipped bathroom so that I could hop straight into bed
And get in a bit of a read before lights out:
Conor Cruise O'Brien's new book *The Siege*,
All about Israel and superlatively insightful
For a man who they say is reputedly an agnostic –   120
I got a loan of it from the brother-in-law's married niece –
But I was tired out and I fell asleep with the book open
Face down across my breast and I woke
To the racket of bellowing flame and snarling glass.
The first thing I thought was that the brother-in-law's married niece   125
Would never again get her Conor Cruise O'Brien back
And I had seen on the price-tag that it cost £23.00:
Small wonder that the custom of snipping off the price
As an exercise in social deportment has simply died out;
Indeed a book today is almost worth buying for its price,   130
Its price frequently being more remarkable than its contents.

The strange Eucharist of my death –
To be eaten alive by fire and smoke.
I clasped the dragon to my breast
And stroked his red-hot ears.   135
Strange! There we were, all sleeping molecules,
Suddenly all giving birth to our deaths,
All frantically in labour.
Doctors and midwives weaved in and out
In gowns of smoke and gloves of fire.   140
Christ, like an Orthodox patriarch in his dressing gown,
Flew up and down the dormitory, splashing water on our souls:
Sister Eucharia; Sister Seraphia; Sister Rosario;
Sister Gonzaga; Sister Margaret; Sister Edith.
If you will remember us – six nuns burnt to death –   145
Remember us for the frisky girls that we were,
Now more than ever kittens in the sun.

II

When Jesus heard these words at the top of Grafton Street
Uttered by a small, agèd, emaciated, female punk
Clad all in mourning black, and grieving like an alley cat,   150
He was annulled with astonishment, and turning round
He declared to the gangs of teenagers and dicemen following him:
'I tell you, not even in New York City
Have I found faith like this.'

That night in St Stephen's Green,   155
After the keepers had locked the gates,
And the courting couples had found cinemas themselves to die in,
The six nuns who had died in the convent inferno,
From the bandstand they'd been hiding under, crept out
And knelt together by the Fountain of the Three Fates,   160
Reciting the Agnus Dei: reciting it as if it were the torch song
Of all aid – Live Aid, Self Aid, Aids, and All Aid –
Lord, I am not worthy
That thou should'st enter under my roof;
Say but the word and my soul shall be healed.   165

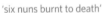
'six nuns burnt to death'

GLOSSARY

Inferno: uncontrollable fire, conflagration.

3   *paseo*: pedestrian area where people can take a leisurely stroll.

5   *Debouched*: emerged into the open.

6   *O'Donovan Rossa*: Jeremiah O'Donovan Rossa (1831–1915) was a prominent Irish Republican. Durcan refers to his stone memorial as a 'pebble'.

7   *tableaus*: groups posing as though in a stage freeze.

15   *martial garb*: military-style clothes.

18   *warpaint*: heavy make-up.

20   *recidivist*: undesirable character.

24   *apocalyptic*: ruinous.

24   *hubris*: excessive pride or arrogance.

32   *daw*: jackdaw, noisy crow.

34   *aviary*: enclosure or large cage for birds.

47   *schooner*: fast sailing ship.

48   *yardarms*: parts of a mast from which sails are hung.

49   *rigging*: ropes and other supports for sails.

50   *Christniks*: fans of Jesus; a pun on the word 'Beatniks'.

54   *Lent*: six-week period of penance leading up to Easter in Christian liturgy.

60   *young man*: a reference to Jesus.

68   *snaps*: photographs.

70   *Cardinal Mindszenty*: József Mindszenty (1892–1975), leader of the Catholic Church in Hungary. He was jailed for opposing communism.

76   *affluence*: wealth, privileged circumstances.

87   *Benediction*: Catholic religious service of blessing.

88   *Exposition of the Blessed Sacrament*: prayerful part of Catholic devotion to the Blessed Sacrament (the consecrated bread and wine believed to be the real presence of Jesus Christ).

96   *Gabriel*: angel who served as God's messenger.

97   *Frenetically*: frantically, wildly.

118   *Conor Cruise O'Brien*: prominent Irish politician, writer and academic (1917–2008).

120   *agnostic*: religious sceptic.

132   *Eucharist*: Thanksgiving; refers to the Mass and Holy Communion (the consecrated bread and wine).

134   *dragon*: mythical creature representing fire.

136   *molecules*: body particles.

141   *Orthodox patriarch*: leader of the Eastern Orthodox Church, the second largest Christian Church in the world.

149   *emaciated*: skinny, skeletal.

152   *dicemen*: street performers, mime artists.

160   *Fountain of the Three Fates*: St Stephen's Green statue of the Three Fates or Graces controlling human destiny.

161   *Agnus Dei*: Lamb of God (Latin), referring to Christ, a contemplative prayer.

162   *Live Aid, Self Aid*: popular charities.

162   *Aids*: acquired immune deficiency syndrome, a syndrome caused by human immunodeficiency virus (HIV).

EXPLORATIONS

1. Based on your reading of the poem, what is your impression of convent life in Ireland? Refer to the text in your answer.

2. Briefly describe Durcan's attitude to the nuns and their way of life. Is he always sympathetic to them? Explain your response.

3. Choose one short section of the poem that you consider particularly dramatic and rich in imagery. Discuss the poet's language use, commenting on its effectiveness.

STUDY NOTES

Paul Durcan has a reputation for being an incisive social commentator. His journalistic approach ranges widely over contemporary events, defining him as a poet of the present moment. But the poet is never content with mere reportage. This long narrative poem about a fire that destroyed a Dublin convent in 1986 characteristically transforms the details of the tragedy into an extended exercise in spiritual reflection. He focuses on one elderly nun who narrates the story of this disaster and reveals the personal choices she had made and her memories of happier times.

Durcan's poems are predominantly narrative in form, but they often combine incidents, impressions and flights of fancy. In this case, the title juxtaposes the dramatic newspaper heading, 'Six Nuns Die in Convent Inferno', with the poignant memorial celebrating the women who dedicated their lives to Christ. What is most evident in the **opening lines** of Part I is the spirited voice of the nun who provides a short history of the Loreto convent where she 'resided'. The **gentle, self-deprecating humour** of the sisters joining the Grafton Street crowds and 'scurrying' past punks who 'Knelt' indicates a lively sense of irony.

The narrator is particularly amused by the displays of youthful rebelliousness she notices: 'the half-shaven heads' and 'dyed hair-dos' (**lines 15-16**). She is also convinced that **her 'subversive' choice of vocation** makes her 'the ultimate drop-out'. In retrospect, she is still shocked by her decision to 'opt out of the world' and follow the religious life in all its 'exotic loneliness'. But despite the long 'lifetime' of 'bicycle pumps' and 'umbrellas drying out', she always understood the significance of her alternative calling as a nun: 'I knew what a weird bird I was' (**line 33**). From her 'agèd beadswoman' perspective, stooped and dressed in black, she is able to imagine how she must appear to outsiders, who might compare her eccentric appearance in full religious habit to 'a daw' – not that any criticism dampens her enthusiasm. Durcan develops the bird metaphor – 'we were as eerie an aviary as you'd find', suggesting the enclosed convent environment.

The speaker's **reflections become increasingly surreal** when she recalls occasional fears ('what would befall us if there were a fire') and the accompanying prospect of a 'Happy death'. Durcan uses a dramatic sailing image to bring to mind the thought of being accidentally killed while 'sleeping at the top of the mast/ Of a nineteenth-century schooner'. His attitude to the nuns, encompassing both admiration and astonishment, shows how closely he himself identifies with these unusual women who have 'Surrendered the marvellous passions of girlhood'. He also acknowledges the contribution made by the Loreto nuns in Ireland to providing spiritual guidance and education. Their essential work is compared to the sailors who 'stitch and sew the rigging and the canvas'. The poet's trademark repetition emphasises their sacrifice and isolation: 'Never to have children ... Never to have a home of our own' (**lines 57–58**).

Many of Durcan's more loosely structured poems are composed by 'cutting' and 'reassembling' various narrative scenes. In **line 63**, the speaker remembers the 'disintegrating dormitory' and the terrifying ecstasy of 'Burning to death in the arms of Christ'. Amid the chaos – accentuated by exclamatory language – there is **the unsettling sense of souls desperate to emerge as angels**: 'Beating our wings in vain'. In another sudden change of space and time, the narrator associates this crucial moment with an earlier experience when the nuns 'took a seaside holiday in 1956'. The nostalgia for a simpler, old-fashioned era is apparent in the innocent hero worship of Cardinal Mindszenty and the youthful pleasures of carefree times, 'scampering into the waves'. However, the fond memory is short lived and the secluded beach abruptly becomes the raging fire that consumed the sisters: 'Now we were scampering into the flames'.

Nevertheless, the elation experienced by the speaker during moments of devout prayer is expressed in terms of the 'day the sisters went swimming'. Durcan uses the nun's elegiac recollection to emphasise the central importance of unconditional Christian faith. Her **visionary account** equates Christ with all of the natural world, including 'the fire in whose waves/We are doomed but delighted to drown' (**lines 93–94**). A touch of black humour is added to her portrait when she imagines the 'boyish' angel Gabriel, 'Frenetically pedalling his skybike'. Her childlike sincerity is also obvious when she worries about the 'poor fire-brigade men' and the loss of a book she borrowed from her niece – 'it cost £23.00'.

Throughout the poem, Durcan promotes the radical Christian values of charity, piety and the achievement of sanctity through suffering, all virtues epitomised in Christ's own life on earth. The nun who narrates this tragic story readily accepts her fate as God's will: 'The strange Eucharist of my death' (**line 132**). In trying to make sense of the horrific event, the poet interweaves an ingenious series of random insights ('all sleeping molecules') and nightmarish images ('I clasped the dragon to my breast'). The inferno itself is personified, dramatising this central moment of Christian renewal – the paradoxical transition into the spiritual afterlife from earthly existence, 'giving birth to our deaths'. But we are never allowed to forget that at the heart of this sacrifice is the reality of human loss: 'six nuns burnt to death'. As the individual names are recorded precisely, readers can share **Durcan's tender and sad compassion**. The narrator's modest request – to be remembered as 'the frisky girls that we were' (**line 146**) – is particularly moving. Characteristically playful to the end, she chooses a universal image of childhood innocence to describe her vision of eternal happiness: 'Now more than ever kittens in the sun'.

The 18 lines that make up Part II of the poem are told as third person narrative. The didactic tone echoes countless gospel stories. Durcan imagines the aftermath of the tragedy, with Jesus relocated to Grafton Street, where he is humbled by the story of the grieving nun, now in the persona of 'a small, agèd, emaciated, female punk' (**line 149**). His shocked reaction ('annulled with astonishment') reflects the poet's well-documented objections to current Catholic teaching on aspects of marriage breakdown. Within this framework, linking the six nuns' deaths to the vulnerability of some women today, **Durcan achieves a bizarre satirical effect**. But while he mocks Ireland's conservative Catholic lawmakers, he shows the highest regard for the unshakable faith of individuals, such as the victims of the convent fire.

The poem ends where it began, back in St Stephen's Green, where a final dramatic scenario is played out under cover of darkness. Trancelike, the dead nuns kneel 'by the Fountain of the Three Fates' happily chanting the Agnus Dei (**line 161**) 'as if it were the torch song' at an outdoor music festival. **The words of this Communion prayer are spoken in preparation for the Divine encounter** – sentiments that are entirely in keeping with the faith of the six Loreto sisters. Durcan's tone of conviction and use of italics reflect the significance of recognising human unworthiness and the acceptance of divine healing love.

From the outset, the poet has venerated the nuns who lost their lives, articulating their religious impulses in particular. The poem's surreal and theatrical elements broaden our understanding of Durcan's subject matter, increasing the clarity of **his imaginative vision**. In blending psychological and physical impressions, he has managed to translate the sensational newspaper story of the inferno into an incisive exploration of individual religious experience.

ANALYSIS

'Durcan's unique poetic voice is particularly evident in his elegies for victims.' Discuss this view based on your reading of 'Six Nuns Die in Convent Inferno', supporting the points you make with reference to the poem.

Sample Paragraph

Paul Durcan's poetry is always accessible and his distinctive voice is evident in the tragic poem, 'Six Nuns Die in Convent Inferno'. Religious topics are often found in Durcan's writing. This elegy shows his great sympathy for the unfortunate victims of the 1986 fire, but also shows their deaths in the true religious sense. The nuns are now with God. The rambling anecdotal style is typical of Durcan. His narrator is one of the nuns who died, a jolly person, still childish and mischievous. She sees herself as a comic character and refers to the O'Donovan Rossa memorial as 'the patriotic pebble'. I liked the way her personality was gradually revealed, showing that she was never disappointed with life. She saw death – even the terrible inferno – as a 'very strange Eucharist', a release. The poem wandered in and out of times in her life, mixing the fire scene with her everyday walks around Stephen's Green and vivid memories of a holiday in Tramore. Durcan always uses names to create a sense of place. His respect for the nuns was obvious in his use of prayers. The whole poem paid tribute to the nuns' deep faith, suggesting that they are more or less obsessed with religion. Durcan's conclusion was dreamlike and emotional, showing the spirits of the six nuns celebrating their entry to Heaven through a vivid image of dancing in the dark. I thought the tribute was sincere without being sentimental, another good feature of Paul Durcan's poems.

Examiner's Comment

This fresh response shows clear personal engagement with the poem and touches on several interesting points, focusing particularly well on characteristics of Durcan's style. The expression is satisfactory, but more use could be made of supportive quotations (the two included are slightly inaccurate). Grade B.

CLASS/HOMEWORK EXERCISES

1. 'Durcan makes effective use of surrealistic effects in addressing religious themes.' Discuss this statement based on your reading of 'Six Nuns Die in Convent Inferno'. Support the points you make with reference to the poem.

2. Copy the table below into your own notes and fill in critical comments about the last two quotations.

Key Quotes

although I confess I was smiling, I was also afraid,/Appalled by my own nerve	The elderly nun has conflicting feelings about her rebellious decision to choose a religious vocation. She recognises the irony of still not coming to terms with it.
We are doomed but delighted to drown	Durcan identifies the paradoxical nature of Christian faith. The believer must surrender this life for eternal spiritual happiness after death.
Suddenly all giving birth to our deaths,/All frantically in labour	
Remember us for the frisky girls that we were	

⑧ SPORT

There were not many fields
In which you had hopes for me
But sport was one of them.
On my twenty-first birthday
I was selected to play   5
For Grangegorman Mental Hospital
In an away game
Against Mullingar Mental Hospital.
I was a patient
In B Wing.   10
You drove all the way down,
Fifty miles,
To Mullingar to stand
On the sidelines and observe me.

I was fearful I would let down   15
Not only my team but you.
It was Gaelic football.
I was selected as goalkeeper.
There were big country men
On the Mullingar Mental Hospital team,   20
Men with gapped teeth, red faces,
Oily, frizzy hair, bushy eyebrows.
Their full forward line
Were over six foot tall
Fifteen stone in weight.   25
All three of them, I was informed,
Cases of schizophrenia.

There was a rumour
That their centre-half forward
Was an alcoholic solicitor   30
Who, in a lounge bar misunderstanding,
Had castrated his best friend
But that he had no memory of it.
He had meant well – it was said.
His best friend had had to emigrate   35
To Nigeria.

To my surprise,
I did not flinch in the goals.
I made three or four spectacular saves,
Diving full stretch to turn   40
A certain goal around the corner,
Leaping high to tip another certain goal
Over the bar for a point.
It was my knowing
That you were standing on the sideline   45
That gave me the necessary motivation –
That will to die
That is as essential to sportsmen as to artists.
More than anybody it was you
I wanted to mesmerise, and after the game –   50
Grangegorman Mental Hospital
Having defeated Mullingar Mental Hospital
By 14 goals and 38 points to 3 goals and 10 points –
Sniffing your approval, you shook hands with me.
'Well played, son.'   55

I may not have been mesmeric
But I had not been mediocre.
In your eyes I had achieved something at last.
On my twenty-first birthday I had played on a winning team
The Grangegorman Mental Hospital team.   60
Seldom if ever again in your eyes
Was I to rise to these heights.

'I had achieved something'

GLOSSARY

Sport: an activity involving effort and skill in which an individual or team compete; also refers to a person who behaves in a good way in response to teasing or defeat.

1   *fields*: pitches, areas, disciplines.

7   *away game*: played at an opponent's place, seen as an advantage to the opposing team.

14   *observe*: examine, consider, scrutinise.

27   *schizophrenia*: long-term mental disorder with symptoms including emotional instability, detachment from reality and withdrawal into self.

32   *castrated*: removed testicles; deprived of power, made docile.

38   *flinch*: cower, dodge, shy away.

46   *motivation*: reasons to act and be enthusiastic.

50   *mesmerise*: fascinate, captivate.

54   *Sniffing*: snorting, showing contempt for.

56   *mesmeric*: brilliant, hypnotic.

57   *mediocre*: only average, amateurish, ordinary.

EXPLORATIONS

1. Based on an initial reading of the poem, what is your impression of Paul Durcan's father? Refer closely to the text in your response.

2. Trace the changing tones of voice as the poem progresses. Support your answer with appropriate reference.

3. Are you sympathetic or not to the character of Durcan himself that emerges from the poem? Refer to the text to support the points you make.

STUDY NOTES

'Sport' is from Paul Durcan's collection Daddy, Daddy, *for which he was awarded the Whitbread Prize (1990). This poem is painfully autobiographical, as he not only recalls a difficult time in his youth, but also explores the troubled relationship he had with his father. Durcan has remarked: 'My father would say, "Paul is a sissy. Come on, be a man." I was aware of his deep disappointment.'*

The poet's father was a judge in the circuit court. He was an introverted man, apparently ill-suited to the legal profession. Nevertheless, Durcan shared 'many rich moments' with him in early childhood. But in the mid-1950s, 'the picture darkened'

when the young Durcan was about 10. Paul began to receive beatings and there was
pressure about exam performance. He contracted a serious bone disease at 13, which
ended his athletic career. Because of difficulties with his behaviour in his late teens,
members of his wider family had him committed to a mental hospital.

The poem **opens** candidly, with Durcan addressing his father directly. He immediately registers an acute awareness of his father's disappointment with him in many areas: 'There were not many fields/In which you had hopes for me/ But sport was one of them'. Sometimes, when men find it hard to communicate, they can relate through sport. They can express their emotions as they discuss the winning or losing of a match without being considered odd. The Gaelic football game Durcan recalls was played on his twenty-first birthday, the day he becomes a man. In **line 6, the chilling context of this occasion** is revealed. It was an 'away game' between the inmates of 'Grangegorman Mental Hospital' and 'Mullingar Mental Hospital'. Durcan is 'a patient/In B Wing', a vulnerable individual. He acknowledges his father's efforts to attend the match, driving 'Fifty miles,/To Mullingar to stand/On the sidelines'. The inference is that the father was never really involved in the poet's life. Durcan also suggests his father's judgemental character when he is described as coming to 'observe me'. It is almost as if his son was a laboratory specimen. The curt tone clearly indicates that **his father's attendance was far from supportive**.

Nevertheless, there is no denying the son's extreme anxiety to impress: 'I was fearful I would let down/Not only my team but you' (**lines 15–16**). The young man was obviously keen to please his father in this unlikely Gaelic match, where he had been 'selected as goalkeeper'. Durcan's fondness for dark humour is evident in his exaggerated description of the opposition players. The Mullingar team had 'gapped teeth, red faces,/Oily, frizzy hair, bushy eyebrows'. They scarcely seemed human. **Odd details reflect the poet's visual alertness.** The opposing team consisted of 'big country men' whose 'full forward line/Were over six foot tall/ Fifteen stone in weight'. These three suffered from schizophrenia, a withdrawal from reality into fantasy. As if the situation was not surreal enough already, Durcan recounts the 'rumour' (**line 28**) about another member of the Mullingar team, 'an alcoholic solicitor' who had mindlessly 'castrated his best friend'. Readers are left with an uneasy sense of absurd comedy based on uncontrollable male violence.

As for the game itself, the poet is amazed by his own performance: 'To my surprise,/I did not flinch in the goals'. The dramatic jargon of sports writing is used, perhaps self-mockingly, to describe his exploits on the field of play, making 'spectacular saves' that were at 'full stretch'. Action-packed verbs convey his tremendous agility – 'Diving', 'Leaping' – and all for the sake of his father, 'knowing/That you were standing on the sideline'. Durcan makes a revealing comment in **line 47** that **both artists, such as himself, and sportsmen must have absolute motivation –** 'That will to die'. They will give their all and risk everything in their desire to succeed. The young man's need to make an impact on his father accelerates: 'it was you/I wanted to mesmerise'. Characteristically, the overwhelmingly decisive triumph of Durcan's team is recorded with mock-heroic pride: '14 goals and 38 points to 3 goals and 10 points'. Despite this great triumph, however, the father's minimal response, his monosyllabic ruling, is less than enthusiastic: 'Well played, son'. There is no embrace. Instead, a formal handshake takes place. The disappointment of the young man contrasts with the emotionally stilted father 'Sniffing ... approval'. Is he suggesting that his son is merely satisfactory, damning him with faint praise? Of course, we see everything from the son's perspective. During the early 1960s, a father's function in Irish society was to fund and guide his family. Overt displays of affection were not common between parents and children, especially sons. Is Durcan's forensic examination of the father–son relationship almost as unhealthy as his father's scrutiny of him? Are both tragically locked into damaging behavioural attitudes?

In the poem's concluding section, Durcan ruefully admits, 'I may not have been mesmeric' (**line 56**). Yet he also asserts 'But I had not been mediocre' and had indeed 'achieved something at last'. The phrase 'at last' forcefully expresses how intensely aware the poet is of his father's lack of confidence in him. After all, he had accomplished something, playing on a 'winning team'. It was, however, a mental hospital patients' team. Does this matter greatly to the father – and to the son? **The poem ends on a poignant note**: 'Seldom if ever again in your eyes/Was I to rise to these heights'. Dark shadows of family relationships were cast by the father's continuing disappointment with his son. The son is still devastated about what it means to be a man and always to feel not quite good enough. As the poet himself has stated elsewhere, even though the father 'loved books', it was always clear that 'the more it looked like I was going to be a writer, the more he was against it'.

ANALYSIS

'Durcan's poetry is not just revealing, it also has a shockingly frank quality.' Discuss this statement in relation to the poem 'Sport'. Refer closely to the text in your answer.

Sample Paragraph

The highly personal poem 'Sport' comes from Durcan's collection *Daddy, Daddy*, whose title is a reference to the American poet Sylvia Plath's cry to her father, 'Daddy, daddy, you bastard, I'm through'. I think the lines in 'Sport' are almost as shocking. They convey, in a frank manner, the longing of the young son for his father's approval. Durcan reveals his lack of confidence in lines such as, 'I was fearful I would let down/Not only my team but you'. He was willing, as Christ was, to make the ultimate sacrifice for his father, 'That will to die'. Like most young men, he desperately wanted to 'mesmerise' his uncommunicative father. The urgent tone seems to me to suggest the spellbinding effect he wishes to make on him. I thought the father's lukewarm response was hurtful, especially when he shook hands and uttered the cold words 'Well played, son'. The poet does not shy away from disclosing that just as his father stood on 'the sidelines' to 'observe' him, he now appears obsessed with studying his father and is still trying to understand him after so many years. I believe he feels just as let down by his father's behaviour as his father is by his: 'But I had not been mediocre'. His continuing disappointment with this man mirrors his father's feelings towards him as he sadly notes in the run-on concluding lines of the poem, 'Seldom if ever again in your eyes/Was I to rise to these heights'. Durcan is actually quite brave to detail the awkward relationship he had with his father with such devastating honesty.

Examiner's Comment

A well-written paragraph that uses suitable reference and quotations to outline the poet's central thought. The use of pertinent descriptive terms, such as 'uncommunicative', 'lukewarm' and 'devastating', helps to define the strained relationship between Durcan and his father. There is clear evidence throughout of close engagement with the poem. Grade A.

CLASS/HOMEWORK EXERCISES

1. 'Paul Durcan blends fact, fiction and fantasy to create a realistic view of the world.' Discuss this viewpoint in relation to the poem 'Sport'. Support your opinions with close reference to the text.

2. Copy the table below into your own notes and fill in critical comments about the last two quotations.

Key Quotes

On my twenty-first birthday/I was selected to play/For Grangegorman Mental Hospital/In an away game/Against Mullingar Mental Hospital	The matter-of-fact tone and run-on lines calmly emphasise the extraordinary circumstances in which the young man found himself. This is a bizarre reality.
I was selected as goalkeeper	By focusing on the verb 'selected', Durcan conveys the young man's pride in being carefully chosen. It also communicates that he was under some other person's control and that he had not been chosen for much else in life.
Diving full stretch to turn/A certain goal around the corner	
On my twenty-first birthday I had played on a winning team	

⑨ FATHER'S DAY, 21 JUNE 1992

Just as I was dashing to catch the Dublin–Cork train,
Dashing up and down the stairs, searching my pockets,
She told me that her sister in Cork wanted a loan of the axe;
It was late June and
The buddleia tree in the backyard   5
Had grown out of control.
The taxi was ticking over outside in the street,
All the neighbours noticing it.
'You mean that you want me to bring her down the axe?'
'Yes, if you wouldn't mind, that is –'   10
'A simple saw would do the job, surely to God
She could borrow a simple saw.'
'She said that she'd like the axe.'
'OK. There is a Blue Cabs taxi ticking over outside
And the whole world inspecting it,   15
I'll bring her down the axe.'
The axe – all-four-and-a-half feet of it –
Was leaning up against the wall behind the settee –
The fold-up settee that doubles as a bed.
She handed the axe to me just as it was,   20
As neat as a newborn babe,
All in the bare buff.
You'd think she'd have swaddled it up
In something – if not a blanket, an old newspaper,
But no, not even a token hanky   25
Tied in a bow round its head.
I decided not to argue the toss. I kissed her goodbye.

The whole long way down to Cork
I felt uneasy. Guilt feelings.
It's a killer, this guilt.   30
I always feel bad leaving her
But this time it was the worst.
I could see that she was glad
To see me go away for a while,
Glad at the prospect of being   35
Two weeks on her own,
Two weeks of having the bed to herself,

Two weeks of not having to be pestered
By my coarse advances,
Two weeks of not having to look up from her plate   40
And behold me eating spaghetti with a knife and fork.
Our daughters are all grown up and gone away.
Once when she was sitting pregnant on the settee
It snapped shut with herself inside it,
But not a bother on her. I nearly died.   45

As the train slowed down approaching Portarlington
I overheard myself say to the passenger sitting opposite me:
'I am feeling guilty because she does not love me
As much as she used to, can you explain that?'
The passenger's eyes were on the axe on the seat beside me.   50
'Her sister wants a loan of the axe ...'
As the train threaded itself into Portarlington
I nodded to the passenger 'Cúl an tSúdaire!'
The passenger stood up, lifted down a case from the rack,
Walked out of the coach, but did not get off the train.   55
For the remainder of the journey, we sat alone,
The axe and I,
All the green fields running away from us,
All our daughters grown up and gone away.

'the train threaded itself into Portarlington'

GLOSSARY

Father's Day: an important family occasion in honour of male parenting, traditionally celebrated on the third Sunday of June.

5   *buddleia tree*: colourful flowering shrub; butterfly bush.

23   *swaddled*: wrapped.

25   *token*: symbolic, nominal.

27   *argue the toss*: dispute the issue.

35   *prospect*: expectation.

38   *pestered*: bothered.

39   *coarse advances*: unrefined sexual demands.

53   *Cúl an tSúdaire*: Irish name for Portarlington (literally 'back of the tanner', referring to the tannery once located there). Durcan might well be making a snide comment about the town's humble origins.

EXPLORATIONS

1. In your opinion, what does the poem's first stanza reveal about the relationship between the poet and his wife? Refer closely to the text in your answer.

2. Select one image (or line) that has a surreal or bizarre impact in the poem. Briefly explain your choice.

3. Comment on the significance of the poem's final line: 'All our daughters grown up and gone away'.

STUDY NOTES

Because so much of his poetry has been autobiographical, Durcan's insecure relationships are already widely known. 'Father's Day, 21 June 1992' is taken from A Snail in my Prime (1993) and recounts a crucial train journey when the poet confronts the adverse effects of time on his role as a husband and father. Typically, the poem alternates between tragicomedy, surreal scenes and devastating self-awareness. The abrupt changes of tone and mood are likely to be disconcerting for readers, who can never be completely sure about the poet's true feelings.

In the anecdotal **opening lines**, Durcan assumes the persona of a slightly befuddled figure 'dashing' about the house. From the outset, there are suggestions of marriage difficulties, particularly in his petulant account of his wife's attitude towards him: 'She told me that her sister in Cork wanted a loan of the axe'. Everyone involved in this uneasy family drama seems slightly eccentric. **Durcan often finds grim humour in the most unexpected circumstances.** Is he suggesting that his sister-in-law is dangerously deranged? The poet's mention of the garden shrub that is now 'out of control' adds to the unstable atmosphere. Could this be a reference to his officious wife and her sister? Or is the marriage itself veering close to crisis? Meanwhile, the waiting taxi is 'ticking over', another possible symbol of the explosive domestic situation.

The strained exchange between the couple (**lines 9–16**) illustrates their barely concealed frustration with each other. Although the poet is reluctant to bring an axe on public transport, his wife is politely insistent: 'if you wouldn't mind'. She seems to be a strangely disembodied presence, reflecting the considerable lack of communication in the marriage. In choosing to do as he is asked on this occasion – 'I decided not to argue the toss' – Durcan indicates a history of marital disagreements. Almost as a defence mechanism to block out the truth about a relationship under threat, **Durcan's description of the scene becomes increasingly trancelike**. He exaggerates the importance of the axe – 'all-four-and-a-half feet of it' – comparing it to 'a newborn babe' (**line 21**). The simile has a poignant association with happier times, when his infant children represented what was truly meaningful about Father's Day. In a blurred state of distorted memories and nostalgic self-pity, the poet personifies the axe and wonders why it could not have been 'swaddled' or at least gift-wrapped with 'a bow round its head'.

Durcan's small family narrative develops in the poem's **second stanza**. On the train journey from Dublin to Cork, his tone is much more reflective as he laments his guilty mood: 'I always feel bad leaving her'. Acknowledging that his wife is 'glad' to be alone, he indulges in mock-serious self-recrimination. Not only will she will welcome a fortnight's break from his 'coarse advances', but she will no longer have to endure his irritating table manners, 'eating spaghetti with a knife and fork' (**line 41**). Whether such overstated self-accusation is totally sincere is, of course, open to question. At any rate, whatever humour that exists is soon replaced with **the stark reality of loss** that is at the heart of the poet's unhappiness: 'Our daughters are all grown up and gone away'. This heartbreaking admission, enhanced by broad assonant effects, provides a momentary explanation for the couple's failing marriage. However, in a sudden change in tone, the poet recalls another comic occasion when his young wife was pregnant and almost got trapped in the fold-up settee. Ironically, the memory does not lessen the deep sense of disappointment that he is experiencing.

The poem's **third stanza** is set at Portarlington Station, where Durcan seems overwhelmed by profound feelings of sorrow. However, the normality of his situation quickly turns into an anarchic event. In a dreamlike sequence, the poet imagines confiding in another passenger about his guilt 'because she does not love me/As much as she used to'. **The surreal sense of disorientation grows** when the encounter is viewed from the perspective of the stranger, whose 'eyes were on the axe on the seat beside me'. Needless to say, when Durcan calls out the station name in Irish, 'Cúl an tSúdaire', the frightened passenger leaves the coach as quickly as possible. Again, the farcical episode is underpinned with underlying heartbreak. In the **final lines**, we see a broken human being abandoned in a bizarre world of utter isolation: 'we sat alone,/The axe and I'. The ending is particularly lyrical, evoking the sadness of innocent times gone forever: 'All the green fields running away from us'. Durcan often uses the metaphor of travel to express significant changes in his life. The train journey to Cork is a remarkably sombre one, depicting a forlorn man who is still struggling to come to terms with the effects of time and the devastating fact that 'All our daughters' are 'grown up and gone away'. The concluding mood is one of estrangement and desolation. Durcan is only too aware that he no longer has a reason to celebrate Father's Day.

ANALYSIS

'Father's Day, 21 June 1992' is one of Paul Durcan's most personal and revealing poems. What aspects of the poem affected you most?

Sample Paragraph

After studying 'Father's Day, 21 June 1992', I had mixed feelings. In some ways, the poem is a desperately sad memory of the time when Durcan realised his marriage was ending. The cold conversation about bringing an axe to Cork was only amusing on the surface. The couple seemed like strangers and Durcan isn't in the mood for another argument – 'I decided not to argue the toss'. The mood in the family home is awkward. The discussion about bringing an axe on the train seems ludicrous, but it's difficult not to have sympathy for both the poet and his wife. There is a distance between them, evident in the ironic comment, 'I kissed her goodbye'. For me, the most moving part of the poem is Durcan's acknowledgement 'Our daughters are all grown up and gone away'. The serious tone, slow rhythm of this long thoughtful line, filled with mournful assonance, emphasises the poet's essential depression. He now accepts that there is nothing to keep his marriage alive and the poem's concluding lines left me genuinely sympathetic. Father's Day has lost all meaning for Durcan. The image of 'All our green fields running away from us' is very appropriate. As he looks out of the train window, the beauty of the Irish countryside is out of reach for the ageing poet. I thought this was a very moving symbol of his empty life – and I felt it was in keeping with the elegiac mood throughout this memorable poem.

Examiner's Comment

A very good personal response, showing true engagement with the poem. The focus throughout is on the emotional interaction with the poet's experience of failure and loss. Effective use was made of supportive quotes that showed illustrative aspects of various stylistic features, including tone and imagery. Expression is also clear and varied. Grade A.

CLASS/HOMEWORK EXERCISES

1. 'The use of humour in Paul Durcan's poems provides revealing insights into his complex personal relationships.' Discuss this view, with particular reference to 'Father's Day, 21 June 1992'.

2. Copy the table below into your own notes and fill in critical comments about the last two quotations.

Key Quotes

The buddleia tree in the backyard/Had grown out of control	Durcan's reference to the wild garden shrub reflects the manic atmosphere inside the family home. The image also typifies his dry humour in describing a world that is increasingly absurd.
I kissed her goodbye	The subdued tone of this routine act suggests much about the coolness between husband and wife. Any romance and tenderness seem to have disappeared from the marriage.
'I am feeling guilty because she does not love me/As much as she used to, can you explain that?'	
All the green fields running away from us	

THE ARNOLFINI MARRIAGE

after Jan Van Eyck

We are the Arnolfinis.
Do not think you may invade
Our privacy because you may not.

We are standing to our portrait,
The most erotic portrait ever made,   5
Because we have faith in the artist

To do justice to the plurality,
Fertility, domesticity, barefootedness
Of a man and a woman saying 'we':

To do justice to our bed   10
As being our most necessary furniture;
To do justice to our life as a reflection.

Our brains spill out upon the floor
And the terrier at our feet sniffs
The minutiae of our magnitude.   15

The most relaxing word in our vocabulary is 'we'.
Imagine being able to say 'we'.
Most people are in no position to say 'we'.

Are you? Who eat alone? Sleep alone?
And at dawn cycle to work   20
With an Alsatian shepherd dog tied to your handlebars?

We will pause now for the Angelus.
Here you have it:
The two halves of the coconut.

'We are the Arnolfinis'

GLOSSARY

The Arnolfini Marriage: Painted by the Dutch artist Jan Van Eyck in 1434 and regarded as a masterpiece, it has become a well-known symbol of marriage yet it retains its mystery.

1   *Arnolfinis*: Generally believed to represent the Italian merchant Giovanni and his wife Constanza, possibly in their home in the Flemish city of Bruges, perhaps undertaking a civil marriage ceremony. It was commissioned a year after Constanza died.

2   *invade*: infringe, violate, intrude on.

3   *privacy*: undisturbed time, secrecy.

5   *erotic*: sensual, suggestive.

6   *faith*: complete trust.

7   *To do justice*: to be fair and reasonable.

7   *plurality*: range, various meanings, truth.

8   *barefootedness*: In 15th-century Flanders, it was traditional to remove shoes for a wedding ceremony. This emphasised the marriage rite's blessedness and inviolability.

12   *reflection*: light thrown back from a surface; image formed by a reflection; a serious thought.

15   *minutiae*: small, precise details.

15   *magnitude*: greatness, importance.

22   *Angelus*: Christian devotional prayers commemorating the announcement to Mary that she was going to give birth to Jesus, the son of God.

24   *coconut*: fruit of the coconut palm, consisting of a hard fibrous husk and white inner core.

EXPLORATIONS

1. Based on your reading of the poem, do you think that the speakers are trying to shock or discomfort the reader? Briefly explain your views.

2. What, in your opinion, is Durcan's attitude towards the Arnolfinis? Refer to the poem in your answer.

3. Select one image from the poem that you found particularly interesting. Comment on its effectiveness.

STUDY NOTES

Paul Durcan's poetry collection Give Me Your Hand *(1994) was inspired by paintings in London's National Gallery. He has taken some of the most famous paintings in the world and interpreted them with his own distinctive poetic voice. We see the artwork 'through the prism of his imagination' as he projects himself into the famous characters of the paintings, slipping in and out of the pictures and 'sending us on flights of our own'. 'The Arnolfini Marriage' was inspired by the Jan Van Eyck oil painting, which is believed to represent a rich Italian merchant and his wife. It was painted in Bruges in 1434, 'in its own way new and revolutionary ... For the first time in history, the artist became the perfect eye-witness'.*

The **opening line** of this dramatic monologue simply states, 'We are the Arnolfinis', a confident declaration by an assured, well-to-do couple. Durcan assumes their persona. The regular form of the poem – eight three-line stanzas – mirrors the orderly composition of the portrait. The speakers issue a stern warning to the reader: 'Do not think you may invade/Our privacy because you may not'. The formal tone contains more than a suggestion that Durcan is casting a satirical eye on the prim couple. Although this painting has become a famous symbol of marriage, representing the Arnolfinis in the intimate environment of their home, it conceals as much as it reveals. It is, however, an utterly convincing picture of a room as well as the people who inhabit it. Argument rages over the original painting, but the most recent view suggests that the couple are Giovanni and Constanza Arnolfini. Some critics maintain that the woman is simply holding up her full-skirted dress in the contemporary fashion. Although the wife looks pregnant, there are no recorded children for this couple. In the painting, the man's hand is raised as if taking an oath. Is it a record of a marriage contract in the form of a painting? **Durcan is clearly fascinated – both by the questions raised and by the answers we will never know**, since we cannot 'invade' the couple's 'privacy'.

The announcement at the start of the **second stanza** is also intriguing: 'We are standing to our portrait'. It is as if they are taking up position in readiness for military action. Is the poet suggesting that marriage can also have its share of conflict? Nonetheless, the speakers describe the painting as the 'most erotic portrait ever made'. It is certainly a sensual, stimulating picture celebrating the couple's sexual relationship as well as the sanctity of marriage. Throughout **stanza three**, Durcan emphasises the faith the Arnolfinis have in the artist's ability 'To do justice to the plurality' of their married lives. **There are many aspects to a man and woman saying 'we'.** A chance of having children, 'Fertility', is now possible. The challenge of living together as man and wife, 'domesticity', must now be faced. The removal of shoes, 'barefootedness', could suggest the vulnerability of laying bare one's soul to another in an intimate relationship. Going barefoot also means landing on the forefoot, the centre of gravity. This guarantees optimum balance and increased stability – but is this true for every marriage?

In **stanza four**, the Arnolfinis assert that they want the artist to 'do justice' and be objective in his depiction of their 'bed/As being our most necessary furniture'. It is central to their marriage. They hope the artist will execute a work of integrity, 'to our life as a reflection'. They want a true likeness. **Durcan's fondness for the surreal** becomes evident in the **fifth stanza** with the introduction of a more disturbing image: 'Our brains spill out upon the floor'. Does this suggest the suppressed aggression within the relationship? Meanwhile, the little dog, usually a symbol of loyalty, is sniffing 'The minutiae of our magnitude', the small details that reveal the couple's sense of their importance. In the **sixth stanza**, the repetition of 'we' shows the complacency of the couple now that they are man and wife: 'The most relaxing word in our vocabulary is "we"'. They luxuriate in their ability to say it: 'Imagine being able to say "we"'. Then they realise that most people are not so fortunate – 'are in no position to say "we"'. Durcan has used the process of repetition to develop this thought. But is he also thinking about his own marriage and that he never expected it to fail?

The tone of the **seventh stanza** sharply challenges us with the uncomfortable question: 'Are you?' The solitary state of the reader is highlighted by the emphatic 'Who eat alone? Sleep alone?' Durcan sketches some of the mundane routines of modern life for people who 'at dawn cycle to work'. **What a contrast to the opulence of the Arnolfinis.** He uses another surreal image ('an Alsatian shepherd dog tied to your handlebars') to exaggerate the insecurity of our contemporary world.

In the **last stanza**, the couple 'pause now for the Angelus'. This Christian act of devotion commemorates the occasion when the angel Gabriel declared to Mary that she was to conceive the son of God: 'blessed is the fruit of thy womb, Jesus'. Here is the good news, the possibility of redemption. A final dreamlike image is presented when the two figures in the portrait are seen as 'The two halves of the coconut'. Is Durcan laughing at the Arnolfinis? Or does this naive metaphor refer to the Hindu custom of breaking a coconut at a wedding to ensure the blessing of the gods? In some other societies, the coconut is regarded as the tree that provides all the necessities of life. As always, the poem (like the Van Eyck painting) shows and conceals equally. Once again, **boundaries are blurred** as the reader is challenged to view the accepted norms relating to married life in a different way.

ANALYSIS

'Durcan's poetry celebrates plurality of perspective.' Discuss this statement in relation to the poem 'The Arnolfini Marriage'. Refer closely to the text in your response.

Sample Paragraph

In 'The Arnolfini Marriage', Paul Durcan, in my opinion, clearly demonstrates the important role the artist adopts in showing how necessary it is to hold more than one view on things, 'we have faith in the artist/To do justice to the plurality'. I think Durcan wants us to consider this portrait of the Arnolfinis as a symbol of marriage and all it entails. Is it a battlefield, 'We are standing to our portrait'? Is it a contented, cosy state, 'The most relaxing word in our vocabulary is "we"'? This poem reminds me of the cult of celebrity in our times. We see someone's image and we feel we know this person intimately. Durcan warns us of this blinkered, one-sided view, 'Do not think you may invade/our privacy'. Because you may not, warn the Arnolfini couple through the poet. Although we see these people in the most intimate of settings, beside a bed with the curtains drawn open, we do not know the real purpose of the painting. A surreal image concludes the poem, 'two halves of the coconut'. Is this a dismissive reference to the self-important couple? Is it a reference to a blessing of a wedding? As usual, the nonconformist Durcan has succeeded in showing us that there are many ways to view someone or something. He has challenged our fixed notions of the way things are. After all, who goes to work with 'an Alsatian shepherd dog tied' to a bicycle? The puzzles in the poem show the complexity of humanity. He has raised many interesting questions with this 'reflection'.

Examiner's Comment

Overall, a well-focused response that addresses a demanding question. There is effective use of quotation throughout and some good personal engagement with the poem. Apart from an over-reliance on questions, the paragraph offers several interesting discussion points about Durcan's perspective. Grade B.

CLASS/HOMEWORK EXERCISES

1. 'Durcan does verbally what painting does visually.' Discuss this view, using suitable reference to the poem 'The Arnolfini Marriage'.

2. Copy the table below into your own notes and fill in critical comments about the last two quotations.

Key Quotes

Because we have faith in the artist/To do justice	The poet repeats this phrase to emphasise the important role the artist has to represent the many aspects in a situation. The religious overtones of the language stress the strong conviction of the couple.
Our brains spill out upon the floor	Durcan uses several surreal images that blur the lines between reality and fantasy, allowing the reader to take a fresh approach.
Most people are in no position to say 'we'	
Here you have it:/The two halves of the coconut	

11   ROSIE JOYCE

I

That was that Sunday afternoon in May
When a hot sun pushed through the clouds
And you were born!

I was driving the two hundred miles from west to east,
The sky blue-and-white china in the fields   5
In impromptu picnics of tartan rugs;

When neither words nor I
Could have known that you had been named already
And that your name was Rosie –

Rosie Joyce! May you some day in May   10
Fifty-six years from today be as lucky
As I was when you were born that Sunday:

To drive such side-roads, such main roads, such ramps, such roundabouts,
To cross such bridges, to by-pass such villages, such towns
As I did on your Incarnation Day.   15

By-passing Swinford – Croagh Patrick in my rear-view mirror –
My mobile phone rang and, stopping on the hard edge of P. Flynn's highway,
I heard Mark your father say:

'A baby girl was born at 3.33 p.m.
Weighing 7 and a 1/2 lbs in Holles Street.   20
Tough work, all well.'

II

That Sunday in May before daybreak
Night had pushed up through the slopes of Achill
Yellow forefingers of Arum Lily – the first of the year;

Down at the Sound the first rhododendrons   25
Purpling the golden camps of whins;
The first hawthorns powdering white the mainland;

The first yellow irises flagging roadside streams;
Quills of bog-cotton skimming the bogs;
Burrishoole cemetery shin-deep in forget-me-nots;   30

The first sea pinks speckling the seashore;
Cliffs of London Pride, groves of bluebell,
First fuchsia, Queen Anne's Lace, primrose.

I drove the Old Turlough Road, past Walter Durcan's Farm,
Umbrella'd in the joined handwriting of its ash trees;   35
I drove Tulsk, Kilmainham, the Grand Canal.

Never before had I felt so fortunate
To be driving back into Dublin city;
Each canal bridge an old pewter brooch.

I rode the waters and the roads of Ireland,   40
Rosie, to be with you, seashell at my ear!
How I laughed when I cradled you in my hand.

Only at Tarmonbarry did I slow down,
As in my father's Ford Anglia half a century ago
He slowed down also, as across the River Shannon   45

We crashed, rattled, bounced on a Bailey bridge;
Daddy relishing his role as Moses,
Enunciating the name of the Great Divide

Between the East and the West!
We are the people of the West,   50
Our fate to go East.

No such thing, Rosie, as a Uniform Ireland
And please God there never will be;
There is only the River Shannon and all her sister rivers

And all her brother mountains and their family prospects.   55
There are higher powers than politics
And these we call wildflowers or, geologically, people.

Rosie Joyce – that Sunday in May
Not alone did you make my day, my week, my year
To the prescription of Jonathan Philbin Bowman –   60

Daymaker!
Daymaker!
Daymaker!

Popping out of my daughter, your mother –
Changing the expressions on the faces all around you –   65
All of them looking like blue hills in a heat haze –

But you saved my life. For three years
I had been subsisting in the slums of despair,
Unable to distinguish one day from the next.

                              III
On the return journey from Dublin to Mayo   70
In Charlestown on Main Street
I meet John Normanly, organic farmer from Curry.

He is driving home to his wife Caroline
From a Mountbellew meeting of the Western Development Commission
Of Dillon House in Ballaghadereen.   75

He crouches in his car, I waver in the street,
As we exchange lullabies of expectancy;
We wet our foreheads in John Moriarty's autobiography.

The following Sunday is the Feast of the Ascension
Of Our Lord into Heaven: 80
Thank You, O Lord, for the Descent of Rosie onto Earth.

'There is only the River Shannon'

GLOSSARY

6   *impromptu*: spontaneous, spur-of-the-moment.

15   *Incarnation Day*: Rosie's day of birth, seen by Durcan as blessed.

16   *Croagh Patrick*: Co. Mayo mountain and place of religious pilgrimage.

17   *P. Flynn's highway*: satirical reference to an impressive new road in the constituency of a former government minister, Padraig Flynn.

20   *Holles Street*: Dublin maternity hospital.

24   *Arum Lily*: colourful flower.

25   *the Sound*: the small village of Achill Sound on Achill Island.

25   *rhododendrons*: vivid shrubs that flower in springtime.

26   *whins*: gorse; wild bushes with yellow flowers.

27   *hawthorns*: thorny hedgerow bushes that usually have white flowers.

29   *Quills of bog-cotton*: stems of sedge plants with flower heads resembling tufts of cotton.

31:   *sea pinks*: grass-like stalks with pink flowers.

32   *London Pride*: long-stemmed evergreen plant that flowers in pale pink clusters.

33   *fuchsia*: widely cultivated bush with brilliant deep purplish-reddish colours.

33   *Queen Anne's Lace*: tall plant with fern leaves and bright white flowers.

39   *pewter*: dark grey-coloured metal.

44   *Ford Anglia*: brand of family car.

46   *Bailey bridge*: small temporary bridge.

47   *relishing*: delighting in, appreciating.

47   *Moses*: Biblical figure and religious prophet chosen by God to lead the Jewish people out of slavery.

57   *geologically*: geographically, in natural history.

60   *Jonathan Philbin Bowman*: journalist and broadcaster.

61   *Daymaker*: Durcan repeats a comment used by Philbin Bowman about people who made him feel more cheerful.

68   *subsisting*: struggling to live.

78   *wet our foreheads*: colloquial expression for having a celebratory drink (based on baptising a newborn child).

78   *John Moriarty*: Irish philosopher and mystic.

79   *Feast of the Ascension*: important Christian day commemorating the bodily ascension of Jesus into heaven.

EXPLORATIONS

1. Based on your reading of Section I of the poem, describe Paul Durcan's mood as he drives to Dublin. Support your answer with reference to the text.

2. What does Durcan reveal about his attitude to Ireland in Section II? In your response, use suitable reference to the poem.

3. Vivid imagery is a recurring feature of this poem. Select one image that you consider particularly striking and comment briefly on your choice.

'Rosie Joyce' (taken from Paul Durcan's 2004 collection, The Art of Life*) celebrates the birth of the poet's granddaughter. Her arrival into the world represents a wonderful new beginning in the poet's life. He has frequently used the motif of travel to signify self-renewal, opportunities to reflect on change and emotional development. In this case, Durcan recalls a car journey he took in May 2001 from County Mayo to Dublin. Along the way, images of landscape and movement reveal his newfound sense of optimism.*

The casual, narrative opening of Section I is typical of so many of Durcan's autobiographical poems. There is a nostalgic quality to the description of that golden Sunday afternoon: 'a hot sun pushed through the clouds' (**line 2**). Rosie's birth is immediately symbolised through images drawn from the world of nature. **The idyllic setting reflects Durcan's euphoric tone** perfectly. Breathless exclamatory lines ('And you were born!') and the repetition of the child's name convey the poet's immense joy. Run-on lines underpin the insistent rhythm. It is Rosie's 'Incarnation Day' (**line 15**), a special occasion on which the poet feels truly blessed.

Driving 'two hundred miles from west to east', Durcan is intensely aware of the newness of nature that is reflected all around him. Seeing the world through a child's eyes, he takes great delight in listing everything he notices: 'such side-roads, such main roads, such ramps, such roundabouts'. His deeply satisfying sense of freedom to travel through the country at large is palpable. By persistently naming local places ('By-passing Swinford – Croagh Patrick in my rear-view mirror'), **Durcan acknowledges their equally distinctive importance**. He recounts the crucial details of the telephone message alerting him of Rosie's birth. The simple facts recording the baby's weight and time of birth – 'A baby girl was born at 3.33 p.m.' (**line 19**) – contrast sharply with Durcan's highly emotional response.

Section II focuses on the Irish landscape in summertime. Durcan highlights the colourful diversity and energy of an island in bloom: 'Yellow forefingers of Arum Lily – the first of the year' (**line 24**). **The sense of regeneration is everywhere**: 'the first rhododendrons', 'first hawthorns', ' first yellow irises'. Repetition suggests the widespread growth and the careful choice of forceful verbs ('powdering', 'skimming', 'speckling') adds to our understanding of the vivid power of nature at its height. Everywhere he looks, Durcan sees the shrubs and flowers celebrating

Rosie's birth – even the graveyard at Burrishoole is 'shin-deep in forget-me-nots' (**line 30**). The poet mentions more of the place-names on his cross-country route: 'the Old Turlough Road, past Walter Durcan's Farm'. The intimacies of setting and the poet's enthusiastic voice carry into reflections of his excitement: 'Never before had I felt so fortunate' (**line 37**). Indeed, his great desire to be with Rosie seems almost biblical: 'I rode the waters and the roads of Ireland'.

The poet's careful observation of rural villages reminds him of a journey he once took 'half a century ago'. During that earlier drive, he remembers his father 'relishing his role as Moses' as he named the River Shannon as 'the Great Divide/Between the East and the West' (**lines 48–49**). Durcan takes the opportunity of his granddaughter's birth to present his own view: 'No such thing, Rosie, as a Uniform Ireland'. The poet develops his plea for tolerance and acceptance by emphasising the diversity of the country's geography: 'There is only the River Shannon and all her sister rivers/And all her brother mountains'. With simple clarity ('There are higher powers than politics'), **the poet dismisses the boundaries of class, religion and gender that have often divided Irish people.** After emphatically expressing devotion to his '*Daymaker*' granddaughter, Durcan names Rosie as his personal saviour in a tone that is manifestly reverential: 'you saved my life. For three years/I had been subsisting in the slums of despair' (**lines 67–68**).

In Section III, the mood is much more subdued as the poet recounts details of his 'return journey from Dublin to Mayo'. The daily social routines that mark small communities are illustrated by the chance meeting in Charlestown between Durcan and an old friend, an 'organic farmer from Curry'. Somewhat typically of Irish people's behaviour, their encounter is not without its awkward nuances: 'He crouches in his car, I waver in the street' (**line 76**). Before long, however, the two men share a drink in honour of the new baby. They discuss the life of Co. Kerry poet and philosopher, John Moriarty. This seemingly mundane moment represents what is best about Ireland's cultural and communal identity. **Rosie Joyce has now been accepted into her new natural and spiritual environment.** The cycle of life and death continues. In the poem's **final lines**, Durcan returns to his earlier religious mood with a formal offering of thanksgiving for his granddaughter's life. The motif becomes deliberately whimsical and prayer-like, building to a high point: 'Thank you, O Lord, for the Descent of Rosie onto Earth'.

ANALYSIS

'Paul Durcan frequently uses journeys as a metaphor for reflection or soul-searching.' Discuss this statement with particular reference to 'Rosie Joyce'. Support your answer with reference to the poem.

Sample Paragraph

Paul Durcan's love of travel is clearly evident in 'Rosie Joyce'. Journeys are often metaphors for new insights into life. In the early lines, Durcan reflects on how lucky he is to be able to love a new family member. Everything on the route fills him with joy – and his upbeat tone is emphatic as he drives past 'such villages, such towns'. He is particularly excited by the colourful spring vegetation – 'the first rhododendrons/Purpling the golden camps of whins'. The variety and energy of nature thrills him. But the journey also reminds him of his youth when his father would tell him how the River Shannon was the 'Great Divide/Between the East and the West'. However, Durcan no longer agrees and his message to his granddaughter is a resounding one: 'No such thing, Rosie, as a Uniform Ireland'. The trip across country has given the poet a chance to clarify his own views on the Ireland that Rosie will know. I thought Durcan's description of the island as a place of great scenic variety was the central idea in the poem – 'There is only the River Shannon and all her sister rivers/And all her brother mountains'. He is welcoming the child into a pluralist Ireland – where he accepts all its cultural diversity. He sees people as being equal, above politics and other such labels. This lesson that he offers Rosie is the best gift he can give her. On a personal note, he sees Rosie as bringing joy to his spirit – 'you saved my life'. The sincerity of Durcan's reverential tone is quite moving. His journey has been physical and spiritual – one of great happiness and discovery – a glimpse of how the first Christians felt when they celebrated the birth of Jesus.

Examiner's Comment

This clearly written response focuses effectively on the significance of the poet's journey, both on a personal and cultural level. Useful quotations support key discussion points and the expression is generally well handled (although dashes are over-used). There is also some good engagement with the poem, especially when discussing Durcan's powerful varied tones. Grade A.

CLASS/HOMEWORK EXERCISES

1. 'Durcan's poems can be challenging at times, but they provide a singularly refreshing view of Ireland.' Discuss this view with particular reference to 'Rosie Joyce'. Support the points you make with reference to the poem.

2. Copy the table below into your own notes and fill in critical comments about the last two quotations.

Key Quotes

a hot sun pushed through the clouds	From the start, Durcan emphasises the idea of his newborn granddaughter's eagerness for life and her closeness to nature. The image of physical birth is a recurrent feature of the poem.
Umbrella'd in the joined handwriting of its ash trees	This imaginative description of the farm is couched in metaphorical details that graphically suggest the sheltered farmland and its surrounding rows of ash trees.
No such thing, Rosie, as a Uniform Ireland	
Thank You, O Lord, for the Descent of Rosie onto Earth	

12 THE MACBRIDE DYNASTY

What young mother is not a vengeful goddess
Spitting dynastic as well as motherly pride?
In 1949 in the black Ford Anglia,
Now that I had become a walking, talking little boy,
Mummy drove me out to visit my grand-aunt Maud Gonne   5
In Roebuck House in the countryside near Dublin,
To show off to the servant of the Queen
The latest addition to the extended family.
Although the eighty-year-old Cathleen Ni Houlihan had taken to her bed
She was keen as ever to receive admirers,   10
Especially the children of the family.
Only the previous week the actor MacLiammóir
Had been kneeling at her bedside reciting Yeats to her,
His hand on his heart, clutching a red rose.
Cousin Séan and his wife Kid led the way up the stairs,   15
Séan opening the door and announcing my mother.
Mummy lifted me up in her arms as she approached the bed
And Maud leaned forward, sticking out her claws
To embrace me, her lizards of eyes darting about
In the rubble of the ruins of her beautiful face.   20
Terrified, I recoiled from her embrace
And, fleeing her bedroom, ran down the stairs
Out onto the wrought-iron balcony
Until Séan caught up with me and quieted me
And took me for a walk in the walled orchard.   25
Mummy was a little but not totally mortified:
She had never liked Maud Gonne because of Maud's
Betrayal of her husband, Mummy's Uncle John,
Major John, most ordinary of men, most
Humorous, courageous of soldiers,   30
The pride of our family,
Whose memory always brought laughter
To my grandmother Eileen's lips. 'John,'
She used cry, 'John was such a gay man.'
Mummy set great store by loyalty; loyalty   35
In Mummy's eyes was the cardinal virtue.
Maud Gonne was a disloyal wife
And, therefore, not worthy of Mummy's love.
For dynastic reasons we would tolerate Maud,
But we would always see through her.   40

'In the rubble of the ruins of her beautiful face'

GLOSSARY

1   *vengeful*: vindictive.

1   *goddess*: deity, powerful creature.

2   *Spitting*: hissing.

2   *dynastic*: old established family superiority.

5   *Maud Gonne*: English-born Irish revolutionary who had a stormy relationship with W.B. Yeats. She married Major John MacBride, with whom she had one son.

9   *Cathleen Ni Houlihan*: Cathleen is an old woman of Ireland who mourns the loss of her four provinces, which have been taken by the English. Maud Gonne played her in Yeats's famous play.

12   *MacLiammóir*: Micheál MacLiammóir, a flamboyant English-born Irish actor.

13   *Yeats*: famous Irish poet who celebrated Maud Gonne in his poetry throughout his life.

15   *Cousin Séan*: Séan MacBride was Maud and Major John's only son. He went on to win a Nobel Peace Prize.

19   *lizards*: reptiles with rough, prickly skin.

21   *recoiled*: jumped back, flinched.

23   *wrought-iron*: tough form of iron fashioned into swirling shapes.

26   *mortified*: embarrassed, uncomfortable.

28   *Uncle John*: Major John MacBride was the uncle of Paul Durcan's mother. He was executed by the British for his part in the 1916 Rising.

36   *cardinal*: greatest, essential.

37   *disloyal*: treacherous, unfaithful.

39   *tolerate*: endure, accept.

40   *see through*: see the reality, realise the truth about.

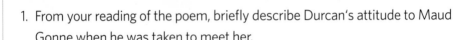

EXPLORATIONS

1. From your reading of the poem, briefly describe Durcan's attitude to Maud Gonne when he was taken to meet her.

2. Surreal imagery is a feature of Paul Durcan's poetry. Choose one surreal image from the poem that made an impact on you and discuss its effectiveness.

3. Comment on Durcan's use of repetition in this poem. Support your answer with reference to the text.

STUDY NOTES

'The MacBride Dynasty' was published in Paul Durcan's 2007 collection, The Laughter of Mothers. *These poignant poems commemorate his mother, Sheila MacBride Durcan. They contrast sharply with the many withering poems about his father, Judge John Durcan. The poet's mother was the niece of one of the renowned martyrs of 1916, Major John MacBride, the husband of Maud Gonne. This poem relates the time Durcan's mother made a personal journey back to her hometown to introduce her young son, ('the latest addition' to the family dynasty), to her uncle's famous wife.*

The **opening lines** dramatically pose an intriguing question with mock solemnity: 'What young mother is not a vengeful goddess/Spitting dynastic as well as motherly pride?' The epic reference suggests the angry response to a slur on the family name. **The MacBrides regarded themselves as a family of significance** in the Mayo region, as can be seen from the poem's title. They were a dynasty, a prominent and powerful family who retained their power and influence through several generations. If an injustice is perceived to have been done to one of the family, the other members close ranks against the outsider. The onomatopoeic verb 'Spitting' graphically depicts the mythical outrage of the young mother. Precise details root the visit to 'grand-aunt Maud' firmly in reality: 'In 1949 in the back Ford Anglia'. At that time, most people in Ireland could not afford to own a car. Broad-vowelled assonance ('walking, talking') mimics the babbling of the five-year-old Durcan as the proud mother drives to Roebuck House to show off her young son to Maud. A sly reference is made to Gonne's autobiography,

A Servant of the Queen, which refers to a vision she had of the Irish queen of old, Cathleen Ni Houlihan. The reference is also ironic since Gonne was an Irish nationalist who rejected the British queen.

The lengthy run-on **line 9** describes how the 80-year-old Maud had 'taken to her bed'. Is there a suggestion that she is a self-indulgent woman? She is referred to as the mythical character she played in Yeats's drama. In this personal narrative, **Durcan seems to be slowly dismantling the popular image of Maud Gonne** as a beautiful young woman, the feminist Irish activist loved by Yeats. Her vanity is obvious: 'She was keen as ever to receive admirers'. The rarefied, overly dramatic world she existed in is cleverly demonstrated by the intimate anecdote showing the famous Irish actor MacLiammóir on his knees at her bedside, 'clutching a red rose' while reciting the poetry of Yeats to her. Is the tone slightly disapproving? The formal, almost regal atmosphere of the house is captured in the description of how 'Cousin Séan and his wife Kid led the way up the stairs' as the door was opened and the arrival of Durcan's mother was announced. But the young Durcan is no MacLiammóir. He does not pay court, but runs away, terrified at this monster 'sticking out her claws' and whose 'lizards of eyes' flitted quickly about. With this bizarre image, the leading lady of nationalistic politics is reduced to a crumbling wreck as the devastation of her beauty by the cruel hand of time is laid bare 'In the rubble of the ruins of her beautiful face' (**line 20**). The alliteration stresses the poignancy of this devastating portrait.

Maud Gonne's relationship with the MacBrides was intricate. She had turned down Yeats's offers of marriage and had married Major John in Paris in 1903. When the marriage ended, she made allegations of domestic violence. She raised her son in Paris until MacBride's execution and then returned to Ireland. The run-on lines (**lines 21–25**) convey the alarm of a little boy terrified out of his wits until his uncle calms him down with a 'walk in the walled orchard'. The long vowel 'a' and the gentle 'w' alliteration produce a soothing effect. **Line 26** carefully records his mother's subtle reaction to his behaviour: 'a little but not totally mortified'. **Was she secretly glad that her little son had not behaved well to a woman she did not respect?** The poet candidly reveals the source of his mother's distaste for Gonne: her 'Betrayal of her husband'. In contrast, a much more favourable picture is painted of Major John, not only through the poet's voice, but also his mother's. He is the 'pride of our family'. His light-heartedness is also noted: 'he 'always brought laughter/To my grandmother Eileen's lips'.

Durcan's ability to capture Irish speech is shown in **line 35**: 'Mummy set great store by loyalty'. The admirable characteristic is repeated: 'loyalty/In Mummy's eyes was the cardinal virtue'. But Maud had committed the cardinal sin of being 'a disloyal wife', for which there is no forgiveness. The repetition of the word 'Mummy' – delivered in a highly sarcastic tone – shows how the poet is influenced by his mother's judgement that Maud was 'not worthy of Mummy's love'. **Is Durcan also critical of his intolerant mother**, who adopts a superior attitude to the infamous Maud? Once again, the underlying MacBride tensions are exposed. The family ('we') would accept her grudgingly, but only 'For dynastic reasons'. The chilling qualification is in the **final line**: 'But we would always see through her'. History might well be fooled by Maud's mythical status, but the family knew what she truly was. Has Durcan succeeded in debunking another official state myth? No person or thing is immune to criticism or satirical comment. As a challenging poetic voice, he has always 'seen through' falseness. He believes language in Ireland has been abused 'by poets as much as by gunmen and churchmen'. Is he also criticising Yeats?

ANALYSIS

Paul Durcan is regarded as the 'Public Poet'. How is this shown in the poem 'The MacBride Dynasty'? Refer closely to the poem in your response.

Sample Paragraph

From the title of the poem to the slyly humorous last line, Durcan captures what others miss. He does not shy away from questioning popular, widely accepted beliefs. In this poem, he exposes not only the power struggles within a self-important family, the 'MacBride Dynasty', but also he reveals the real Maud Gonne as she is in the ill-health and arrogance of her later years, 'She was keen as ever to receive admirers'. The poet publicly deals with private matters and personally comments on some famous Irish public figures. The one-sided stance adopted by the MacBride family is clear for all to see in the flattering portrait of 'Uncle John'. His mother's critical attitude to the 'disloyal' Maud is revealed. She would 'tolerate' this woman, but only for 'dynastic reasons'. The poet reveals the elderly Maud Gonne to the public gaze, 'In the rubble of the ruins of her beautiful face'. Her power to influence has disappeared. In a way, she is a pathetic figure. She is now seen as a reptile with 'claws' and 'lizards of eyes darting about'. The absurdity between reality and image is being exposed through this fantasy. She is no longer the woman Yeats worshipped. A great myth has been exposed to the public. Now, not only Durcan and his mother, but we too can 'see through' and are not fooled by the artifice of 'a red rose'. In 'The MacBride Dynasty', Durcan has dared to express the unthinkable.

Examiner's Comment

This is a very good attempt at addressing a challenging question. There is good engagement with the poem and a clear thematic response. Overall, points are effectively supported by useful reference and quotation. Ideas are expressed fluently throughout. Grade A.

CLASS/HOMEWORK EXERCISES

1. 'Poetry is a form of entertainment, but it is not cheap.' Discuss this statement made by Durcan in relation to the poem 'The MacBride Dynasty'. Support your views with suitable reference to the text.

2. Copy the table below into your own notes and fill in critical comments about the last two quotations.

Key Quotes

To show off to the servant of the Queen	Durcan's mother's pride as well as her disapproval of Gonne are cleverly captured in this reference to Maud Gonne's complex Anglo-Irish background.
ran down the stairs/Out onto the wrought-iron balcony	The comic description of the boy's headlong flight from the ageing Maud Gonne is vividly captured. Durcan's poems often move in such rapid rhythms.
loyalty/In Mummy's eyes was the cardinal virtue	
But we would always see through her	

13 THREE SHORT POEMS

Paul Durcan's enigmatic two-line poems are sharp and epigrammatic. They are also characteristic of his richly textured work in accommodating his contradictory responses to Ireland and to personal relationships. Durcan's intense poetry often focuses on memories of loneliness. Even when he is being ironic, the essential bleakness of his poetic vision is still evident.

EN FAMILLE, 1979

Bring me back to the dark school – to the dark school of childhood:
To where tiny is tiny, and massive is massive.

'En Famille, 1979' almost appears to be a cry for help, as though the poet has never come to terms with the traumatic effects of his earliest experiences. The 'dark school' presents **a disturbing metaphor of his boyhood** and the force of his most intimate hopes and fears. Repetition and the exaggerated extremes of 'tiny' and 'massive' suggest childhood innocence. Durcan's use of the French title phrase (meaning 'with one's family' or 'at home') is heartbreakingly poignant. Yet he remains obsessed with the past. His unsettled childhood, particularly his painful relationship with his father, has marked much of his poetry.

MADMAN

Every child has a madman on their street:
The only trouble about *our* madman is that he's our father.

'Madman' offers further evidence that Paul Durcan's **poetry can encompass nightmares as well as dreams**. Despite this poem's humorous whimsy and surface levity, there is something harrowing about the admission. Terms such as 'madman' are often used casually. Within the immediate family context, however, the word takes on a much greater personal significance. Durcan's short poem raises interesting questions about our own perception of 'madness' and its effects on individuals.

IRELAND 2002

Do you ever take a holiday abroad?
No, we always go to America.

'Ireland 2002' is typical of those small 'nutshell poems' that aim to encapsulate a given period of recent history or define Irish contemporary life. The piece is usually read as a **trenchantly satirical criticism of the country's moneyed classes**, for whom America isn't considered 'abroad'. It could also refer to Ireland's history of emigration to the United States and that our diaspora no longer seems foreign. The poem is a reminder of how Ireland has become so culturally influenced by US fashions and attitudes over recent times. Durcan's glib tone echoes the self-absorbed nature of complacent Celtic Tiger Ireland at its height.

PAUL DURCAN: THE PUBLIC POET

Paul Durcan has always assumed the role of the public poet. Whether questioning Irish politics or simply documenting his day-to-day encounters with shopkeepers and bank clerks, his poems essentially attempt to capture what most people seem to miss.

Throughout his long career, Durcan has given mesmerising poetry recitals of his work to audiences in Ireland and internationally. He seems to enjoy the role of poet-as-storyteller and his readings have been extraordinarily popular. He has also recorded and released readings of his poems.

He has said, 'People have called me a performance poet – a phrase I deeply dislike. But to me, it's another part of the work – or rather, the fulfilment of it. The poem has to work on the page, but it has to be spoken as well.'

The poet's objections to being categorised are understandable. Such labels take away from the serious themes he explores and his inventive use of language. He is widely recognised for his authentic sense of Irish speech.

Surrealism is one of his most powerful satirical devices. Seemingly random flights of fantasy are recurring features of his narrative poems, highlighting incongruities between reality and an imaginary – often a bizarre – world. While such surreal scenes can be highly comic and entertaining, the poet's underlying sense of outrage can sometimes break through his verbal control.

Durcan himself has an expressive voice that rises and falls with emotion, always displaying perfect timing. He whispers some lines, sings others. He has even been known to shout. It all adds up to the powerful impact of his public readings.

'Durcan's mastery of tone, his manic confidentiality, his blithe expositions of the seemingly unthinkable, his hypnotic repetitions of what other poets would hardly dare utter once ... give an air of audacious authority unique in contemporary poetry.'

Brendan Kennelly

'Paul Durcan's poetry dares to explore the hidden areas of life in a confidential yet authoritative manner.' Discuss this view, supporting your response with suitable reference to the poems by Durcan on your course.

Marking Scheme Guidelines

Candidates are free to agree and/or disagree with the statement. The key terms ('dares to explore the hidden areas of life' and 'confidential yet authoritative manner') should be addressed either explicitly or implicitly. Evidence of genuine engagement with the poems should be rewarded. Allow for a wide range of approaches in the answering.

Material might be drawn from the following:
- Provocative treatment of key themes, such as history, love, family
- Convincing treatment of compelling personal disclosures
- Addresses revealing aspects of relationships and identity
- Confident plurality of perspectives challenge views of readers
- Repetition as a process for epiphany and self-discovery
- Sense of place and community adds authenticity
- Effective use of surreal imagery, symbolism, colloquial language, etc.

Sample Essay
(Durcan's poetry dares to explore the hidden areas of life)

1. *Paul Durcan probes dark, bitter themes of contemporary Irish life, emigration and strained relationships. His meditations and monologues challenge the accepted views on Irish life as he keenly observes and elusively slides into surreal images to examine this odd world of ours. Like one of his favourite poets, Kavanagh, he sees the extraordinary in the ordinary and he enables readers to view life, as his character Cáit does, 'Looking toward our strange world wide-eyed'.*

2. *The poet addresses the sombre reality of emigration in 'The Girl with the Keys to Pearse's Cottage'. The young Irish girl's future was 'America-bound at summer's end'. This was no fun-filled adventure, no world-exploring gap year. 'She had no choice but to leave her home'. She was so much part of her landscape with her 'sun-red skirt and moon-black blazer', yet she is torn from her native environment.*

Her intriguing character is caught in the surprising alliterative image, 'El Greco eyes blaze back'. The piercing eyes, so similar to the exotic Spanish painter's portraits, illuminate the darkness felt by the poet at his personal loss. I was urged by the poet to view Ireland's history of exile as the shocking reality that after all the sacrifices of 1916, this country cannot support its own. Durcan bitterly laments his loss with the repetitive phrase, 'O Cáit Killann, O Cáit Killann'. I was convinced by his obvious frustration in his account of the hidden tragedy of emigration which pulls people from their homes and shatters families.

3. *Durcan is not afraid to expose intimate family relationships in all their complexities. 'Sport' explores the troubled relationship he had with his father. The devastation he experienced as a young man desperately attempting to impress his father is evident in the bleak phrases 'I was fearful I would let you down', 'Seldom if ever again in your eyes/Was I to rise to these heights'. Durcan had just played a game of football on the side of Grangegorman Mental Hospital to which he had been committed. The poet's efforts in this game is described in the typically heightened language of sports writing, 'I did not flinch', 'spectacular saves', 'Diving at full stretch'. However, he was met by his father 'Sniffing' his 'approval' as he coldly 'shook hands' with his son. I felt the aching longing of the poet to be regarded and praised, 'I may not have been mesmeric/But I had not been mediocre'. Durcan made me realise the hurt that is caused by the lack of close communication between family members. He is obviously hurt in his feelings of never being quite good enough to satisfy.*

4. *Marriage is successfully scrutinised in several Durcan poems, including 'The Arnolfini Marriage', after the famous Dutch painting of a self-assured young couple. He uses the language of military combat, 'We are standing to our portrait' to suggest that marriage can be a battle of wills. The vulnerability of this intimate relationship is conveyed by the detail of the couple's bare feet, 'barefootedness'. Durcan shows the complacent contentment of the married couple basking in the embrace of their togetherness, 'The most relaxing word in our vocabulary is "we"'. A series of sharp staccato questions blast out as the poet questions 'Who eat alone? Sleep alone?' – contrasting the individual life of the reader with the cosy intimacy of the two Arnolfinis. In presenting different views on married life, the poet challenged me to look again at the accepted norms of marriage.*

5. *Characteristically, Durcan spares neither himself nor the reader when he exposes the shocking consequences of a marriage break-up. 'Nessa' examines his personal*

relationship with his wife through the extended metaphor of a whirlpool, which is at once exciting and dangerous. Nessa is described as if she were an enchantress in an old Irish *aisling* leading the hopelessly devoted lover away, 'She took me by the index finger'. Her intoxicating attraction is echoed in the poet's hypnotic phrase, 'She was a whirlpool, she was a whirlpool'. The poem's central metaphor is a powerful literary device for reflecting on the contradictions of married life. Once again, Durcan is showing us contrasting views of romantic love. There is the thrill and exhilaration of Nessa seducing him, 'for me let your red hair down'. But there is also the destruction of the individual self, 'And I very nearly drowned'. The poem ends with a series of poignant questions reflecting Durcan's deep sense of loss – 'Will you stay with me on the rocks', 'Will you come for me into the Irish Sea'. This honest expression of emotion and admission of personal vulnerability act as a reminder that serious relationships can be overwhelming. The poet made me question whether love, no matter how romantic, should require the total sacrifice of self.

6. *Paul Durcan, with audacious authority, has stirred up accepted views by peering under the stones of society's accepted norms on such universal themes as emigration and relationships. He has allowed me to see the familiar world in a new light which enabled me to question and challenge. His 'bittersweet clowning' has produced intimate poems which truly reveal the essential oddness at the heart of the everyday secret areas of life.* (approx. 865 words)

Examiner's Comment

A solid personal answer showing some clear personal interaction with Durcan's poetry. Generally focused on addressing the question. Most main points are dealt with effectively and there is good use of apt quotation. Some of the poems discussed, such as 'Sport', would have benefitted from a more thorough treatment of the striking techniques (e.g. varying tones and irony) that are used to expose the poet's preoccupations.

GRADE: A2
P = 13/15
C = 12/15
L = 13/15
M = 5/5
Total = 43/50

SAMPLE LEAVING CERT QUESTIONS ON DURCAN'S POETRY

(45/50 MINUTES)

1. 'Paul Durcan's poetry reflects a broad range of powerful feelings communicated through thought-provoking imagery.' Do you agree with this assessment of his poetry? Your answer should focus on the poet's themes and the way he expresses them. Support the points you make with suitable reference to the poems by Durcan on your course.

2. 'Durcan's vision of life is conveyed in poems that are both interesting and atmospheric.' Discuss this statement, supporting your answer with suitable reference to the poetry of Durcan on your course.

3. 'The poetry of Paul Durcan explores the tensions of modern life in an inventive and insightful fashion.' Write a response to this statement, supporting your points with reference to the poems by Durcan on your course.

Sample Essay Plan (Q1)

'Paul Durcan's poetry reflects a broad range of powerful feelings communicated through thought-provoking imagery.' Do you agree with this assessment of his poetry? Your answer should focus on the poet's themes and the way he expresses them. Support the points you make with suitable reference to the poems by Durcan on your course.

- Intro: Identify the elements of the question to be addressed ('broad range of powerful feelings', 'thought-provoking imagery'). Introduce Durcan as a searingly honest poet who lays himself bare in the exploration of strong emotions arising from personal experiences. Communicates different aspects of the situations through precise and surreal imagery delivered in a variety of tones.

- Point 1: Despair and frustration at the common Irish experience of emigration, 'The Girl with the Keys to Pearse's Cottage'. Arresting image 'El Greco eyes blaze back' captures the essence of the girl and highlights the poet's deep yearning.

- Point 2: Fear of change is emphasised in '"Windfall", 8 Parnell Hill, Cork'. Different aspects of home are examined in similes such as 'a city as intimate and homicidal as a Little Marseilles'.

- Point 3: The challenge of being oneself when in a troubled relationship is shown in his deep disappointment at the cold response of his father in 'Sport'. An image of precise detail conveys the moment 'Sniffing your approval'.

- Point 4: Durcan is joyful as he is deeply moved by the lasting power of love in 'Nessa'. The image of a whirlpool expresses the excitement and danger of a close romantic relationship.

- Point 5: Bizarre imagery and a variety of tones allow Durcan to explode icons and myths in 'The MacBride Dynasty'.

- Point 6: Durcan's fascination with married life is explored in 'The Arnolfini Marriage'. The dramatic monologue conveys the intricacies of marriage. Using surreal imagery ('The two halves of the coconut'), the poet explores the contrasting aspects of this state.

- Conclusion: The sensitive poet, Durcan, illuminates our complex world, challenging us to view and reconsider its multifaceted aspects.

Sample Essay Plan (Q1)

Develop one of the above points into a paragraph.

Sample Paragraph: Point 5

The disapproving feeling of Paul Durcan's mother towards her relative, Maud Gonne, and her pride in her own family is provocatively conveyed in the poem 'The MacBride Dynasty'. Maud Gonne was a revered figure in early 20th-century Irish history, beloved of the poet W.B. Yeats and wife of Major John MacBride, a patriot of the 1916 Rising. She was greatly admired and the 'actor MacLiammóir/Had been kneeling at her bedside reciting Yeats to her'. Through two intimate perspectives, Durcan's mother's and his five-year-old self, a different picture of this symbolic woman emerges. The young Durcan's terror of this iconic woman is revealed through surreal imagery. He cruelly paints a devastating portrait of the once-beautiful Maud, 'sticking out her claws/ To embrace me, her lizards of eyes darting about'. Through this monstrous imagery, Durcan challenges the accepted view of this famous woman. A similarly negative portrait of Maud is shown through the dismissive comment delivered at the conclusion of the poem, 'But we would always see through her'. She had been viewed and judged by the family as unworthy because of her behaviour towards her husband, the relative of Durcan's mother who 'set great store by loyalty' and Maud had not matched up. The cutting tone of this line slashes through the veneer of Maud's greatness.

Examiner's Comment

As part of a full essay, this is a solid B-grade response that is well rooted in the text. Quotes are integrated effectively and expression is both varied and assured throughout. Some points could have been more focused on how language, particularly Durcan's ironic and satirical tones, is used to convey the 'powerful feelings' expressed in the poem.

LAST WORDS ”

'His songs celebrate our small mercies and tender decencies in a world that favours the corrupt.'

Paula Meehan

'He makes particularly engaging poems out of passing conversations - "You're looking great – are you going to a wedding?"/"Oh God no – I'm coming back from a wake."'

Deirdre Collins

'Like all first-class comedians, he is deadly serious.'

Terry Eagleton

T.S. ELIOT

1888-1965

'Humankind cannot stand very much reality.'

Thomas Stearns Eliot, the American-British poet, playwright and literary critic, was born in St Louis, Missouri, in 1888. He was educated at Harvard and did graduate work at various European universities before settling in England, where he worked as a teacher and publisher. In 1927, Eliot took British citizenship at about the same time he became an Anglican.

T.S. Eliot is one of the most daring innovators of modern literature. Indeed, his experiments in diction, style and versification revitalised English poetry. Throughout his life, he believed that poetry should aim at a representation of the complexities of modern civilisation and that such representation necessarily leads to difficult poetry. Despite this, his influence on modern poetic diction has been immense. His poetry collections, from *Prufrock* (1917) to the *Four Quartets* (1943), largely reflect the development of a Christian poet and dramatist.

Eliot's early and experimental writing depicts a bleak and barren soullessness, often in spare yet finely crafted modern verse. Much of his work deals with unsettling and haunting themes of individual consciousness and spiritual desolation against the decline of civilisation. His poems, which often lack any obvious narrative structure, include numerous cultural and historical allusions.

Although some critics found his poetry esoteric and disconnected, he has been increasingly praised for his originality and craftsmanship and is now widely recognised as one of the most significant poetic voices of the 20th century.

An intensely private man, Eliot separated from his first wife in 1933 following an unhappy marriage. He remarried in 1956. T.S. Eliot received the Nobel Prize for Literature in 1948 and died in London in 1965.

Prescribed Poems

❶ 'The Love Song of J. Alfred Prufrock'

Eliot's most famous poem touches on fascinating aspects of human experience. For many people in the 1920s, Prufrock seemed to summarise the frustration and uncertainty of the modern individual. He is a man who feels isolated and incapable of decisive action. His poignant monologue is filled with irony since this is not a conventional love song. Prufrock would like to speak of love to a woman, but he does not dare. The poet traces this wretched man's journey through an unnamed city to the woman's apartment. Hopelessly insecure about rejection and fearful of old age, Prufrock is never able to assert himself by asking the mysterious 'overwhelming question'.   **232**

❷ 'Preludes'

Throughout the four sections of this atmospheric poem, Eliot presents a dark vision of the failure of modern secular society, exploring human despair and feelings of failure. Using a stream of consciousness style, the poet reveals a variety of solitary lives that are played out against the backdrop of a dispiriting urban setting. Typically, the mood is overpoweringly downbeat and the poet's language is as negative as his attitude to 20th-century urban life.   **245**

❸ 'Aunt Helen'

In this satirical glimpse into a disappearing world of genteel rituals, Eliot's unusually accessible poem portrays a prim 'maiden aunt'. Even after her death, there was 'silence in heaven'. The poet's gentle ridicule is particularly directed at the cultural lifelessness and self-satisfaction of Miss Helen Slingsby's sterile lifestyle.   **252**

❹ *from* 'The Waste Land': II. 'A Game of Chess'

Using numerous literary allusions, Eliot focuses on the failure of relationships in contrasting social settings. In this chilling vision, human interaction is reduced to a mere set of movements on a checkerboard. Characteristically, the poet depicts a false and meaningless world, in keeping with his disillusioned view of modern life as a wasteland without love or moral values.   257

5 **'Journey of the Magi'**
Eliot's version of the three kings who visited the newborn Messiah in Bethlehem is narrated by one of the elderly magi. Christ's birth marked the end of their old pagan religion. The uncertain and painful transition mirrors the poet's own doubts about his spiritual conversion to Christianity. This dramatic monologue is notable for its ambiguity. Throughout the poem, Eliot interweaves the real and symbolic journeys of life and death.   267

6 *from* **'Landscapes': III. 'Usk'**
This evocative landscape sketch records Eliot's response to the Welsh landscape after a short holiday there. The countryside is closely associated with the legend of King Arthur. However, the most likely reading of this 11-line poem sees it as a search for faith, which typified much of Eliot's later writing.   274

7 *from* **'Landscapes': IV. 'Rannoch, by Glencoe'**
Written after a visit to the Scottish Highlands, Eliot's short poem evokes the enduring atmosphere of the remote moor, which provides a compelling backdrop to the poet's message that historical events and old conflicts become entrenched in the places where they once occurred.   279

8 *from* **'Four Quartets': 'East Coker IV'**
This didactic poem is another illustration of Eliot's critical view of Christianity. The poet focuses on life, death and the continuity between the two. He uses the field hospital as a compelling metaphor for the world's suffering patients who are in the hands of Jesus, the 'wounded surgeon'. Striking imagery and thought-provoking paradoxes emphasise the poet's severe view of the Christian experience.   284

① THE LOVE SONG OF J. ALFRED PRUFROCK

S'io credesse che mia risposta fosse
a persona che mai tornasse al mondo,
questa fiamma staria sanza più scosse;
ma però che già mai di questo fondo
non tornò vivo alcun, s'i'odo il vero,
sanza tema d'infamia ti rispondo.

Let us go then, you and I,
When the evening is spread out against the sky
Like a patient etherised upon a table;
Let us go, through certain half-deserted streets,
The muttering retreats   5
Of restless nights in one-night cheap hotels
And sawdust restaurants with oyster-shells:
Streets that follow like a tedious argument
Of insidious intent
To lead you to an overwhelming question…   10
Oh, do not ask, 'What is it?'
Let us go and make our visit.

In the room the women come and go
Talking of Michelangelo.

The yellow fog that rubs its back upon the window-panes,   15
The yellow smoke that rubs its muzzle on the window-panes,
Licked its tongue into the corners of the evening,
Lingered upon the pools that stand in drains,
Let fall upon its back the soot that falls from chimneys,
Slipped by the terrace, made a sudden leap,   20
And seeing that it was a soft October night,
Curled once about the house, and fell asleep.

And indeed there will be time
For the yellow smoke that slides along the street
Rubbing its back upon the window-panes;   25
There will be time, there will be time
To prepare a face to meet the faces that you meet;
There will be time to murder and create,

And time for all the works and days of hands
That lift and drop a question on your plate;   30
Time for you and time for me,
And time yet for a hundred indecisions,
And for a hundred visions and revisions,
Before the taking of a toast and tea.

   In the room the women come and go   35
Talking of Michelangelo.

   And indeed there will be time
To wonder, 'Do I dare?' and, 'Do I dare?'
Time to turn back and descend the stair,
With a bald spot in the middle of my hair –   40
(They will say: 'How his hair is growing thin!')
My morning coat, my collar mounting firmly to the chin.
My necktie rich and modest, but asserted by a simple pin –
(They will say: 'But how his arms and legs are thin!')
Do I dare   45
Disturb the universe?
In a minute there is time
For decisions and revisions which a minute will reverse.

   For I have known them all already, known them all –
Have known the evenings, mornings, afternoons,   50
I have measured out my life with coffee spoons;
I know the voices dying with a dying fall
Beneath the music from a farther room.
   So how should I presume?

   And I have known the eyes already, known them all –   55
The eyes that fix you in a formulated phrase,
And when I am formulated, sprawling on a pin,
When I am pinned and wriggling on the wall,
Then how should I begin
To spit out all the butt-ends of my days and ways?   60
   And how should I presume?

   And I have known the arms already, known them all –
Arms that are braceleted and white and bare

(But in the lamplight, downed with light brown hair!)
Is it perfume from a dress   65
That makes me so digress?
Arms that lie along a table, or wrap about a shawl.
    And should I then presume?
    And how should I begin?

          .   .   .   .   .

    Shall I say, I have gone at dusk through narrow streets   70
And watched the smoke that rises from the pipes
Of lonely men in shirt-sleeves, leaning out of windows?...

    I should have been a pair of ragged claws
Scuttling across the floors of silent seas.

        .   .   .   .   .

    And the afternoon, the evening, sleeps so peacefully!   75
Smoothed by long fingers,
Asleep ... tired ... or it malingers,
Stretched on the floor, here beside you and me.
Should I, after tea and cakes and ices,
Have the strength to force the moment to its crisis?   80
But though I have wept and fasted, wept and prayed,
Though I have seen my head (grown slightly bald) brought in upon a platter,
I am no prophet – and here's no great matter;
I have seen the moment of my greatness flicker,
And I have seen the eternal Footman hold my coat, and snicker,   85
And in short, I was afraid.

    And would it have been worth it, after all,
After the cups, the marmalade, the tea,
Among the porcelain, among some talk of you and me,
Would it have been worth while,   90
To have bitten off the matter with a smile,
To have squeezed the universe into a ball
To roll it towards some overwhelming question,
To say: 'I am Lazarus, come from the dead,
Come back to tell you all, I shall tell you all' –   95
If one, settling a pillow by her head,

Should say: 'That is not what I meant at all.
That is not it, at all.'

   And would it have been worth it, after all,
Would it have been worth while,   100
After the sunsets and the dooryards and the sprinkled streets,
After the novels, after the teacups, after the skirts that trail along the floor –
And this, and so much more? –
It is impossible to say just what I mean!
But as if a magic lantern threw the nerves in patterns on a screen: 105
Would it have been worth while
If one, settling a pillow or throwing off a shawl,
And turning toward the window, should say:
    'That is not it at all,
     That is not what I meant, at all.'   110

.   .   .   .   .

   No! I am not Prince Hamlet, nor was meant to be;
Am an attendant lord, one that will do
To swell a progress, start a scene or two,
Advise the prince; no doubt, an easy tool,
Deferential, glad to be of use,   115
Politic, cautious, and meticulous;
Full of high sentence, but a bit obtuse;
At times, indeed, almost ridiculous –
Almost, at times, the Fool.

   I grow old ... I grow old ...   120
I shall wear the bottoms of my trousers rolled.

   Shall I part my hair behind? Do I dare to eat a peach?
I shall wear white flannel trousers, and walk upon the beach.
I have heard the mermaids singing, each to each.

I do not think that they will sing to me.   125

I have seen them riding seaward on the waves
Combing the white hair of the waves blown back
When the wind blows the water white and black.

We have lingered in the chambers of the sea
By sea-girls wreathed with seaweed red and brown   130
Till human voices wake us, and we drown.

'Should I, after tea and cakes and ices,
Have the strength to force the moment to its crisis?'

GLOSSARY

Epigraph: 'If I thought that my response would be to someone who would ever return to earth, this flame would remain without further movement; but as no one has ever returned alive from this depth, if what I hear is true, I can answer you with no fear of disgrace.' This Italian epigraph is taken from Dante's *Inferno*. The speaker was imprisoned in hell and is filled with hopelessness.

1   **you and I**: the public self and the inner man represent Prufrock's divided personality.

3   **etherised upon a table**: anaesthetised and unconscious on an operating table.

5   **retreats**: places of security.

7   **sawdust restaurants with oyster-shells**: cheap hotels with sawdust on the floor and oyster shells as ashtrays.

9   **insidious intent**: deceptive purpose.

14   **Michelangelo**: famous Italian Renaissance artist who portrayed heroic figures.

15   **yellow**: cowardly; London was also known for its dense fogs.

16   **muzzle**: animal's nose and mouth.

23   **And indeed there will be time**: biblical reference to each event having a correct time; 'A time to be born, and a time to die' (Book of Ecclesiastes).

42   **morning coat**: a formal tailed coat.

52   **dying fall**: Shakespearean reference to fading music; 'That strain again, it had a dying fall' (*Twelfth Night*).

56   **formulated phrase**: prepared, dismissive expression.

60   **butt-ends**: discarded cigarette remains.

66   **digress**: stray from the point.

73   **a pair of ragged claws**: dismembered image of a crab.

77   **malingers**: pretends to be ill.

82 *my head ... upon a platter*: biblical reference to John the Baptist, whose head was the price Salome demanded for performing her dance (Matthew).

85 *the eternal Footman*: Death.

89 *porcelain*: fine chinaware.

92 *squeezed the universe into a ball*: literary reference; 'Let us roll all our strength ... into one ball' ('To His Coy Mistress' by Andrew Marvell).

94 *Lazarus*: Biblical reference to a man Jesus brought back to life.

101 *dooryards*: American gardens.

105 *magic lantern*: instrument used to project enlarged moving images.

111 *Prince Hamlet*: the indecisive hero of Shakespeare's tragic play.

113 *swell a progress*: make up part of the crowd.

115 *Deferential*: courteous, submissive.

116 *Politic*: diplomatic, expedient.

116 *meticulous*: scrupulously careful, fussy.

117 *Full of high sentence*: speaking in a pompous way (a literary reference to a character in Chaucer's *Canterbury Tales*).

117 *obtuse*: dull, insensitive.

119 *Fool*: in Shakespearean drama, the court jester or clown often spoke wisely.

124 *I have heard the mermaids singing*: literary reference to a poem by John Donne where the mermaids symbolise romance and danger.

EXPLORATIONS

1. Eliot once considered 'Prufrock among the Women' as the title for this poem. Would you prefer that title or the present one, 'The Love Song of J. Alfred Prufrock'? Give reasons for your choice.

2. Choose a short section of the poem that you consider particularly rich in sensuous lyrical language. Discuss the sound patterns (rhyme, assonance, alliteration) used by Eliot and comment on their effectiveness.

3. Comment briefly on the three settings used in this poem: the seedy cityscape, the elegant drawing room and the romantic seashore.

STUDY NOTES

'The Love Song of J. Alfred Prufrock' (commonly known as 'Prufrock') was first published in 1915. This period saw Europe lose an entire generation of young men during World War I. The British Empire was breaking up and the certainty of Victorian ideals was still being shaken by the evolutionary theories of Darwin. Society

seemed to be in crisis, with signs that cultural and spiritual values were crumbling in the new urban age. Eliot's dramatic monologue traces Prufrock's uneasy stream of consciousness. Through a series of compulsive cadences, the poem explores the tortured soul of modern man: educated, eloquent, alienated and emotionally paralysed by indecisiveness.

The **title** immediately raises the question about who is being addressed: possibly the unnamed woman in the poem, or Prufrock himself, or even the reader. What is not in doubt is that the name 'J. Alfred Prufrock' suggests a conceited, pretentious character, one who wishes to be seen as more important than he actually is. The epigraph (from Dante's *Inferno*) makes us think that the love song is not being sung in the real world at all, but in an interior 'Hell' of Prufrock's own making. From the outset, there are signs that the protagonist's torment comes from the division of his own self into a timid public person and a passionate private individual.

This is certainly suggested in the opening section (**lines 1–12**), where Prufrock proposes setting out on a journey: 'Let us go then, you and I'. The two pronouns might well refer to his divided personality: the reserved, careful outer man and the colourful, emotional inner soul. The initial mood is lethargic. Eliot uses a startling simile to describe the evening sky ('Like a patient etherised upon a table'), emphasising its distant, lifeless quality. Prufrock's own emotional state informs what he sees. There is **an uncomfortable sense of restlessness and dissatisfaction about Prufrock's life**, as though he is struggling with dark secrets. The impersonal streetscape suggests meaningless encounters 'in one-night cheap hotels'. Sea imagery ('oyster-shells') also seems slightly distasteful within the context of the furtive setting. Eliot's unsettling image of the 'half-deserted streets' compared to 'a tedious argument/Of insidious intent' conveys the agitation of modern living. Run-on lines lead Prufrock to momentarily think about an undisclosed 'overwhelming question' that is just too unbearable to consider at length.

Lines 13–14 stand alone. The **location has changed to a more sophisticated world** – probably a fashionable social event – where the smart conversation centres on an important sculptor of heroic figures: 'In the room the women come and go/Talking of Michelangelo'. The almost childlike jingling rhythm and rhyme raise the possibility that these cultured socialites are affected and frivolous.

But why should Prufrock be intimidated by a group of sophisticated women discussing Renaissance art? Perhaps he fears that if these people are interested in the celebrated artist Michelangelo, they could never relate to somebody as undistinguished as himself. This disquieting feeling of exclusion becomes an increasingly defining characteristic of Prufrock.

In **lines 15–22**, the scene changes again, moving away from the trivial conversation of the social gathering. Using **a developed metaphor**, Eliot describes the foggy urban district through which Prufrock walks in terms of the sinuous movement of a cat through sensuous verbs: 'rubs', 'licked', 'lingered', 'slipped', 'curled' and 'fell asleep'. Images suggesting the sleek movements of the cat combine with soft 'l' and 's' sounds to create a soporific mood. Does the 'yellow fog' convey the blurred vision of humanity in the 20th century?

Prufrock hypnotically repeats the phrase 'there will be time' to adopt a public mask that he can use to 'meet the faces that you meet'. **Lines 23–34** convey a feeling of irritation with his surroundings and the people he encounters in public. He seems unnerved by the 'smoke that slides along the street' and his thoughts turn to the stark choices that any individual might face in extreme circumstances, 'to murder and create'. **The pressing rhythm marks Prufrock's growing nervousness** as he looks forward to but also fears meeting with the woman, when he will 'lift and drop a question on your plate'. Anxiously, he delays, hesitating and considering a 'hundred visions and revisions' before concluding with the mock-heroic action of 'the taking of a toast and tea'.

Lines 35–36 repeat the rhymed couplet, 'In the room the women come and go', further emphasising **the tedium of the women's conversation** as they endlessly discuss the same topic. The refrain might also indicate Prufrock's own inability to join in the social discourse of the elegant drawing room.

He becomes progressively more self-conscious in **lines 37–48**, mainly about his own insecurity ('Do I dare?'). Seemingly obsessed by his ageing appearance, Prufrock speculates about the way other people view him. He particularly **fears hearing the truth**, even about the most trivial matters: 'How his hair is growing thin!' For a moment, he tries to bolster his confidence by relating how carefully he pays attention to the details of his dress: 'My necktie rich and modest, but asserted by a simple pin'. However, the women's gaze seems relentless to Prufrock, who cannot stop imagining their derogatory comments: 'how his arms and legs are thin'. He exaggerates dramatically in the broken line, 'Do I dare/Disturb the universe?' Characteristically, the irony of his pretentious question reflects his self-deprecating humour. But as always, he is tormented by an uncontrollable inadequacy and paralysed by over-thinking. Despite all his self-delusion about future plans, Prufrock does nothing at all but sit and watch as time goes by.

Lines 49–54 present the first of three arguments against asking the 'overwhelming question'. Prufrock is only too aware that his complete lack of confidence stems from the **meaningless life** he leads. Its pointless routine is demonstrated by the repetition of the listless, broad-vowelled phrasing, 'For I have known them all already, known them all'. His earlier apprehension has gradually been replaced by the disillusionment of his wasted years: 'I have measured out my life with coffee spoons'. There is something acutely dismal about the admission of an entirely ineffective existence. Prufrock's social phobias now prevent any type of spontaneity. Feeling so distanced from human contact, he has reached the stage where he is no longer sure about anything, even the right to ask 'So how should I presume?'

This **sensation of personal failure** increases in **lines 55–61**. Prufrock is constantly afraid of appearing foolish, which in itself always makes him feel that way. He is terrified of the contemptuous eyes of the women around him, who 'fix you in a formulated phrase'. He feels reduced to an insignificant insect pinned and coldly dissected as if in a laboratory experiment. His pointless lifestyle is further diminished, comparable to an ashtray filled with discarded cigarettes: 'the butt-ends of my days and ways'. Even the forlorn repetition of the question 'And how should I presume?' peters out. For Prufrock, the second argument against addressing the significant question is that he cannot face any further ridicule. It is typical of Eliot's portrayal that while we have sympathy for this pathetic man, we are also irritated by him.

Lines 62–69 reveal the third reason why Prufrock avoids life's most serious questions: he is both **attracted and repulsed** by the physical reality of the women around him. While he admires the perfect ideal of 'Arms that are braceleted and white and bare', he is also put off by the fact that they are 'in the lamplight, downed with light brown hair'. The poet's description of the apparently disembodied woman is impersonal. The sensuous movement of their arms 'that lie along a table, or wrap about a shawl' recalls the feline grace of the yellow fog. Caught between such thoughts of romance and revulsion, Prufrock's dilemma is unresolved. Yet again, he finds himself unable to do anything: 'And how should I begin?'

This intense sense of helplessness persists throughout **lines 70-74**. Prufrock rehearses what he might say if forced to make conversation. He wonders whether he might describe the 'narrow streets' he has just passed through and the 'lonely men in shirt-sleeves, leaning out of windows'. But his line of thought diminishes into silence, concluding with an ellipsis. It is as though **he is crushed by all the isolation he sees around him** – a feeling that accurately mirrors his own alienation. As always, in moments of desperate self-loathing, he reverts to using sea imagery: 'I should have been a pair of ragged claws'. Comparing himself to a crab scavenging on the floor of the ocean reduces him even further to an inanimate object, the very opposite of his present excruciating position. The renewed onomatopoeic effect of 'Scuttling' and the hauntingly alliterative 'silent seas' clearly depict this fantastical image of self-disgust. Prufrock's random reflections continue in **lines 75-86**, which introduce a soft, trance-like, reflective atmosphere. The afternoon 'sleeps', 'malingers', is 'Stretched on the floor' like the earlier cat-like fog. Not for the first time, he debates whether he can ever have sufficient courage to display his true feelings and desires. For an instant, Prufrock imagines himself as a biblical figure, but soon dismisses this idea, accepting that his personal humiliation is simply ridiculous, especially when compared to such a celebrated martyr as John the Baptist. Arguably, this is the turning point of the poem, marking **the protagonist's stark realisation that his life is essentially insignificant**. His brief 'flicker' of youth and hope has gone. Death is all that lies ahead, personified as a sneering 'eternal Footman' who mocks Prufrock's unproductive past and his fear of the unknown.

Lines 87-98, however, mark yet another of the protagonist's attempts to excuse his failure to take control of his life. Prufrock tries to convince himself that the stylish setting – 'Among the porcelain', a delicate and easily damaged china – inhibits him. In such refined surroundings, an immense effort would be required to express his secret desires openly and 'squeeze the universe into a ball', a self-mocking reference to a poem by Andrew Marvell, who believed in seizing the moment and enjoying life's pleasures. But the **fear of rejection keeps restraining Prufrock**. He has become so self-deluded that he exaggerates his predicament, comparing his task of tackling his questions about the meaning of life to Lazarus coming back from the dead. Tortured by incessant thoughts of failure, he imagines an embarrassing misunderstanding between himself and an unnamed woman who tells him, 'That is not what I meant at all'. Once again, the pained awkwardness of the invented scene stops Prufrock in his tracks.

An edgy mood of growing frustration dominates **lines 99–119**. The sensuous language and fragmented style become even more evident as Prufrock cries out in exasperation at his inability to communicate: 'It is impossible to say just what I mean!' Almost completely demoralised, he creates an image of his true personality projected onto a screen by a 'magic lantern' for the derision of the woman he wishes to impress. He also admits that **he is no hero** like Prince Hamlet, even though they both share the common characteristic of indecisiveness. If anything, Prufrock feels that he is more like the uncharismatic 'attendant lord' Polonius, a relatively minor Shakespearean character who talks too much and is 'almost ridiculous'. In the end, he accepts that he is much more like 'the Fool' (or court jester), another dramatic stereotype whose quick wit often contained serious criticisms of life's absurdity.

The poem's closing lines (**lines 120–131**) **show a man anxiously trying to come to terms with ageing and death**: 'I grow old … I grow old'. Having completely failed to confront the 'overwhelming question', the only decision Prufrock will make is about his appearance: 'I shall wear the bottoms of my trousers rolled'. Nonetheless, in this agonising postscript, he indulges in one last flight of fancy set on an idyllic beach.

To the end, however, Eliot seems intent on trivialising the anxieties of a man who knows he is facing death but still cannot 'dare to eat a peach'. Yet, whatever time he has left may not be taken up entirely with mundane considerations. Prufrock can also dream of hearing the seductive 'mermaids singing'. Eliot's mysterious image – possibly symbolising both desire and danger – signals that Prufrock has come close to experiencing something wonderful, yet ultimately unattainable. A single line (the only isolated one in the entire poem) highlights the sad truth for this unfortunate individual: 'I do not think that they will sing to me'.

It could be argued that having the courage to dream is Prufrock's only triumph. Dramatic run-on lines depict a magnificent picture of the elusive mermaids through haunting sound effects: 'riding seaward on the waves/Combing the white hair of the waves blown back'. Their ability to enjoy the moment in harmony with their environment is the very antithesis of the neurotic Prufrock. Like so much of this mesmerising poem, **the conclusion is open to various interpretations**. It seems that Prufrock's divided self becomes united in the plural personal pronoun 'we'. He is suddenly awakened from his vision of 'sea-girls wreathed with seaweed red and brown'. The heart-rending **final line** ends Prufrock's tragic fantasy and he is brought back to reality by 'human voices'. With his last words, 'we drown', he invites us into his own private hell. Is Eliot suggesting that all of us are lost in daydreams and desires that we can never realise?

Most critics agree that 'The Love Song of J. Alfred Prufrock' offers **a pessimistic vision of the modern spiritual condition**. The anti-hero of Eliot's ironic love song glimpses redemptive beauty, but settles for a life of indecision and triviality rather than boldly searching for personal fulfilment. This is likely to reflect the poet's own disenchanted outlook on modern secular civilisation, increasingly empty of any religious faith or meaningful love, and paralysed by anxiety. Yet nothing is resolved in this poem. Perhaps it is easier not to ask the 'overwhelming question' about life's meaning after all – particularly if there is no satisfactory answer.

ANALYSIS

'The sense of isolation and detachment in personal relationships is agonisingly evoked in the poetry of T.S. Eliot.' Do you agree with this view? Give reasons for your response, referring to Eliot's poem, 'The Love Song of J. Alfred Prufrock'.

Sample Paragraph

Eliot's poignant poem, 'The Love Song of J. Alfred Prufrock', is closely associated with a new kind of modern 20th-century poetry. It depicts the character of modern man weakened by over-analysis into a paralytic state of inaction: 'Do I dare/Disturb the universe?' Literary and biblical references emphasised the central character's alienation. Prufrock is an insecure loner, warped by uncertainty, but constantly searching for answers. His scattered thoughts wander from the important philosophical questions about life's meaning to the trivial reality of his mundane existence: 'Is it perfume from a dress/That makes me so digress?' The desperate tone of his random question reveals an inner trauma. In addition, free association, everyday speech and sharp irony show a lonely figure who is caught between conflicting forces of desire, weakness and a devastating sense of personal failure. Prufrock's intense self-examination as he fails to ask the 'overwhelming question' reminds me of modern-day films where the main characters sink beneath the weight of psychological analysis:

'we drown'. The tone of loathing and self-disgust is conveyed in excruciating detail: 'When I am pinned and wriggling on the wall'. Fear of rejection keeps isolating Prufrock, 'That is not what I meant at all', and prevents him from even making the attempt to communicate. 'Let us go then, you and I' invites the reader to accompany Prufrock on this journey into his interior consciousness – but the excursion becomes a series of painful disappointments, leaving both the protagonist and reader feeling severed and isolated.

Examiner's Comment

A well-supported response that addresses the question directly. There is a clear attempt to place the central character within the early 20th-century context. Revealing quotes illustrate Prufrock's distressing loneliness effectively and the comments on tone show a good understanding of the poem. Expression is impressive, varied and well controlled throughout. Grade A.

CLASS/HOMEWORK EXERCISES

1. 'T.S. Eliot's distinctive poetic voice presents troubled characters in an unsettled world.' Write a response to this statement with reference to both the subject matter and style of 'The Love Song of J. Alfred Prufrock'.

2. Copy the table below into your own notes and fill in critical comments about the last two quotations.

Key Quotes

There will be time to murder and create	Eliot's carefully chosen verbs not only convey the harshness of the modern world, with its emphasis on massacre (as witnessed in World War I), but they also refer to the state of flux as new inventions and ideas spring up in the 20th-century.
one that will do/To swell a progress, start a scene or two	Prufrock realises with chilling clarity that he is not an important character even in the story of his own life, but is merely there to make up the crowd.
I do not think that they will sing to me	
Till human voices wake us, and we drown	

PRELUDES

I

The winter evening settles down
With smell of steaks in passageways.
Six o'clock.
The burnt-out ends of smoky days.
And now a gusty shower wraps   5
The grimy scraps
Of withered leaves about your feet
And newspapers from vacant lots;
The showers beat
On broken blinds and chimney-pots,   10
And at the corner of the street
A lonely cab-horse steams and stamps.

And then the lighting of the lamps.

II

The morning comes to consciousness
Of faint stale smells of beer   15
From the sawdust-trampled street
With all its muddy feet that press
To early coffee-stands.

With the other masquerades
That time resumes,   20
One thinks of all the hands
That are raising dingy shades
In a thousand furnished rooms.

III

You tossed a blanket from the bed,
You lay upon your back, and waited;   25
You dozed, and watched the night revealing
The thousand sordid images
Of which your soul was constituted;
They flickered against the ceiling.
And when all the world came back   30
And the light crept up between the shutters

And you heard the sparrows in the gutters,
You had such a vision of the street
As the street hardly understands;
Sitting along the bed's edge, where   35
You curled the papers from your hair,
Or clasped the yellowed soles of feet
In the palms of both soiled hands.

IV

His soul stretched tight across the skies
That fade behind a city block,   40
Or trampled by insistent feet
At four and five and six o'clock;
And short square fingers stuffing pipes,
And evening newspapers, and eyes
Assured of certain certainties,   45
The conscience of a blackened street
Impatient to assume the world.

I am moved by fancies that are curled
Around these images, and cling:
The notion of some infinitely gentle   50
Infinitely suffering thing.

Wipe your hand across your mouth, and laugh;
The worlds revolve like ancient women
Gathering fuel in vacant lots.

'The conscience of a blackened street'

GLOSSARY

Prelude: an introductory event that precedes something longer and more important; a short introductory piece of music.	22 *dingy shades*: soiled window blinds.
	23 *furnished rooms*: small apartments, often rented for a short time.
5 *gusty shower*: strong windy rush of rain.	27 *sordid*: filthy, sleazy.
8 *vacant lots*: empty or abandoned building sites.	28 *constituted*: brought together, composed.
	36 *papers*: small papers used as hair curlers.
14 *consciousness*: awareness.	45 *Assured*: secure, confident.
19 *masquerades*: pretences.	47 *assume*: take responsibility; pretend.
	48 *fancies*: dreams, fantasies, illusions.

EXPLORATIONS

1. Based on your reading of Part I of 'Preludes', describe the atmosphere and mood Eliot creates in this opening section. Refer closely to the text in your answer.

2. Choose one interesting image from the poem that you found particularly effective. Briefly justify your choice.

3. Write your own personal response to this poem, referring closely to the text in support of the points you make.

STUDY NOTES

'Preludes' was composed between 1910 and 1911 and published in Prufrock and Other Observations *(1917). Eliot considered these early poems 'the most satisfactory to myself'. Four sections of uneven, irregular verse provide a stream of consciousness literal and impressionistic view of various solitary lives as they play out against the backdrop of a seedy urban setting. There is an underlying awareness of the failure of modern secular civilisation throughout the sequence. Each prelude refers to the city as it moves from dusk to morning to night and back to dusk again.*

The **first prelude** begins with vivid personification, 'The winter evening settles down', reminiscent of 'The Love Song of J. Alfred Prufrock'. Eliot blends various sensuous images, imagining the customary end of another unremarkable day. The 'smell of steaks in passageways' exemplifies the monotonous nature of city life and establishes the **dejected tone** for the rest of the poem. Repeated sibilant 's' sounds conjure up the habitual evening rituals of countless urban inhabitants. This is a place of conformity, where both the people and the day itself are exhausted, aptly evoked through the cigarette metaphor: 'burnt-out ends of smoky days'. An unrelenting sense of wasteful neglect and futile living is found everywhere within the dismal urban landscape, with its 'withered leaves' and 'vacant lots'.

Run-on lines mimic the relentless wintry weather while the abrupt rhyming of 'wraps' and 'scraps' suggests the recurring hardships of modern living. The explosive alliteration in **lines 9–10**, 'showers beat/On broken blinds', forcefully captures the insistent downpour of rain. Eliot presents readers with a range of symbols of alienation and helpless frustration, introducing the 'lonely cab-horse' waiting impatiently at a deserted street corner. Into this **uncomfortable scene of ugly sterility**, a flicker of hope appears in the standalone line, 'And then the lighting of the lamps'. Is something about to happen? Will something change? Or is the night closing in?

Eliot opens the **second prelude** by personifying a new day: 'The morning comes to consciousness'. Ironically, instead of a fresh start, **images of decay and desolation** amplify the weariness of modern city living. Precisely descriptive language denotes emptiness, depression and quiet despair, a recurring theme throughout much of Eliot's poetry. This is skilfully evoked through the detail of 'faint stale smells of beer' left over from the previous night's drinking. Under pressure to conform to society's expectations, the anonymous occupants of the 'thousand furnished rooms' continue their daily routines, perhaps to mask their own unhappiness. The headlong rush of everyday life is suggested by the forward movement of run-through lines and the crushing verbs 'trampled' and 'press'.

Within all this urban chaos, individuality is submerged. People slavishly perform the same action at the same time: 'all the hands ... raising dingy shades'. The poet clearly regards their routine lifestyles as 'masquerades', a daily pretence. It is as if they are raising a theatrical curtain on their artificial, unreal lives in this **soulless setting** of 'a thousand furnished rooms'. The rhyme of 'masquerades' and 'shades' reinforces this theme of pretence. By describing the people as mere body parts – 'feet', 'hands' – the individuals are depersonalised.

The **third prelude** addresses an unnamed woman who is plainly ill at ease: 'You tossed a blanket from the bed'. Eliot's description of her robotic movements develops the growing mood of despair. Indolent verbs describe a restless night: 'lay', 'waited' and 'dozed'. There is a disturbing sense of the woman's personal degeneration, disclosed by flickering patterns – 'The thousand sordid images' of which her soul is composed. Repetition of the conjunction 'And' in **lines 30–32** emphasises the monotony of an unfulfilled existence. The morning's intrusion into this bedroom is unwelcome: 'the light crept up between the shutters'. Not unexpectedly, the early morning birdsong ('sparrows in the gutters') only adds to the atmosphere of gloom in this disreputable place. Meanwhile, a somewhat vulnerable and pathetic figure, the woman sits 'along the bed's edge' with her artificially curled hair, 'yellow soles' and 'soiled hands'. Once again, Eliot focuses on the **absence of personal identity**, reducing her to a mere collection of body parts. As morally degraded as her drab environment, she is only capable of a 'vision of the street/As the street hardly understands'.

The poet introduces a surreal image of spiritual torture in the **fourth prelude**: 'His soul stretched tight across the skies'. The monosyllabic 'tight' is precisely placed in the centre of **line 39**, suggesting that the tension is so great that it might snap at any moment. It is dusk and the unrelenting march of time is highlighted – 'At four and five and six o'clock' – as people return home from work. The ritual of pipe-filling is conveyed by the close-up image of 'short square fingers stuffing pipes' as the city's male inhabitants seek to relax after a day's toil and begin to read their newspapers. Eliot points out **the irony of their monotonous lives, where they are fed 'certain certainties'**. Does this suggest that these people always accept what they are told? Are they so powerless that they never question anything? Is their environment so 'blackened' that they 'assume the world' and accept it without any real understanding?

Lines 48–51 mark another change of mood to a **dreamlike atmosphere**. For the first time in the poem, a more personal voice emerges: 'I am moved by fancies'. Is this Eliot himself wondering if human life might have some worthwhile significance after all? Does he feel sympathy for all those people who have lost touch with their spiritual selves? Some critics have linked the 'infinitely gentle' reference to the presence of a Christ-like saviour destined to redeem a sinful world. But whatever it is that causes the poet to be 'moved' is wounded: 'Infinitely suffering thing'.

The momentary sense of hopefulness is quickly dismissed in the **last three lines**. Eliot reverts to cynicism, heralded by the derisive gesture 'Wipe your hand across your mouth', as if a gross appetite has just been satisfied. The vacant lot from the opening section is here again, and now old women are rummaging through the litter of urban desolation. We are left with **a bleak vision of an indifferent universe**, completely devoid of spiritual growth or optimism. The women look downwards.

ANALYSIS

'T.S. Eliot presents a penetrating and downbeat portrayal of the human condition.' Discuss this statement in relation to the poem 'Preludes', supporting your views with suitable reference and quotation.

Sample Paragraph

In his poem 'Preludes', Eliot offers a pessimistic view about the lack of individuality, and the impossibility for spiritual growth in modern society. The poem's mood is particularly depressing, set in the all-pervading sleaze of a godless urban environment, which reminded me of Prufrock's dismal surroundings. With sharp, vividly realised imagery, this poet painted for me a disturbing picture of the stagnant paralysis of city life. Nauseating odours ('smell of steaks in passageways', 'faint stale smells of beer'), dirty rooms ('dingy shades') and repugnant characters ('clasped the yellow soles of feet/ In the palms of both soiled hands') convey a sordid picture of this unglamorous lifestyle. The human condition is described as one of conformity, where everyone is expected to put on an act all the time, whether they are rushing with 'muddy feet that press/To early coffee-stands' or 'raising dingy shades/ In a thousand furnished rooms'. No one seems capable of looking upwards to something better. The woman character in Prelude 3 only sees 'The thousand sordid images' which make up her soul. Similarly, in the final prelude, the man's soul is 'stretched tight across the skies' as if about to break at any moment. The conclusion of the poem reminds me of a scene from *Waiting from Godot* as people scavenge among discarded rubbish in an effort to survive. This memorable image of old women hunting for fuel to keep them warm is truly startling. In Eliot's dispiriting vision, they are drawn downward, not gazing upward for the growth of the soul.

Examiner's Comment

A very well-focused personal response that tackles this straightforward question confidently. The range of accurate quotations are used effectively to support discussion points. Cross-references to other settings in Eliot's work broaden the scope of the answer. The writing is clear, fluent and assured throughout. Grade A.

CLASS/HOMEWORK EXERCISES

1. 'T.S. Eliot believed that human love offered rescue from a lifetime of misery and isolation.' Discuss this view with reference to 'Preludes'.

2. Copy the table below into your own notes and fill in critical comments about the last two quotations.

Key Quotes

A lonely cab-horse steams and stamps	This vivid visual detail captures the sense of urban alienation as the horse impatiently waits for its next fare. Alliteration reinforces the muggy, oppressive atmosphere.
With the other masquerades/ That time resumes	Eliot is interested in the disparity between appearance and reality. He regards the city's inhabitants' lives as unreal and spiritually devoid of growth. Time dictates the rhythm of their lives in a dictatorial manner.
You had such a vision of the street/As the street hardly understands	
Wipe your hand across your mouth, and laugh	

❸ AUNT HELEN

Miss Helen Slingsby was my maiden aunt,
And lived in a small house near a fashionable square
Cared for by servants to the number of four.
Now when she died there was silence in heaven
And silence at her end of the street.   5
The shutters were drawn and the undertaker wiped his feet –
He was aware that this sort of thing had occurred before.
The dogs were handsomely provided for,
But shortly afterwards the parrot died too.
The Dresden clock continued ticking on the mantelpiece,   10
And the footman sat upon the dining-table
Holding the second housemaid on his knees –
Who had always been so careful while her mistress lived.

'my maiden aunt'

GLOSSARY

Aunt Helen: a wealthy, unmarried lady who lived in a stylish Boston neighbourhood.

8   *handsomely provided for*: supplying sufficient money to ensure a comfortable life.

10   *Dresden clock*: superior china clock from the German town of Dresden.

12   *second housemaid*: servant whose duties included cleaning and polishing.

EXPLORATIONS

1. In your opinion, what is the speaker's attitude to Miss Helen Slingsby? Refer to the text in support of your views.

2. Consider the image of the footman and housemaid. How does it contrast with the life Aunt Helen lived? Support your response with reference to the poem.

3. Based on your reading of the poem, do you think that T.S. Eliot is mocking respectable middle-class society? Explain your response.

STUDY NOTES

'Aunt Helen' is included in T. S. Eliot's poetry collection Prufrock and Other Observations, *published in 1917. The poet paints a satirical portrait of the rigid, conventional society of upper-class Boston in this short piece. What's left unsaid is almost as important as what is said. Boston offended Eliot's sensibilities. He regarded this world as 'quite uncivilised, but refined beyond the point of civilisation'. His critical view of polite society is from an insider's perspective and highlights its tragicomic outcome.*

The poem's title, 'Aunt Helen', suggests a close family relationship between the poet and this lady, yet this is immediately dispelled by the formal address in the opening line, 'Miss Helen Slingsby'. Her unmarried status is carefully noted: 'maiden aunt'. This woman lived her life alone without close intimate relationships. Was she too proud to marry? Was she not asked? Her life is described in a three-line sentence that details where she lived. Aunt Helen did not reside in a large house, as Boston society would deem this vulgar and ostentatious. Her home was not on the 'fashionable square', but 'near' it. Such discretion was called for. **She carefully observed all the nuances of the secret codes of her social class.** However, there is no mention of friends. Nobody looks after Helen Slingsby except those she paid: 'servants to the number of four'. Eliot's quaint expression mirrors the old-world aunt and her affected language. Rolling 'r' and 'o' sounds allow the reader to hear the genteel tones of this superior person.

A series of short sentences deal with **the impact of the old lady's death**. The momentous adverb 'Now' in **line 4** announces her passing. The poet adopts the persona of a detached observer rather than a regretful nephew, dryly observing that his aunt's death caused 'silence in heaven'. Is the silence indifference on the part of heaven to the death of this self-absorbed lady? Or does the silence suggest hushed awe at the passing of an important individual? We are left to wonder about who, apart from herself, might have regarded Miss Slingsby as a person of note. Eliot humorously concludes that there was 'silence at her end of the street'. Was her death really of sufficient importance to bring the whole street to stillness?

The poet details the correct observance of the expected conventions: 'The shutters were drawn'. However, we are told that the undertaker 'wiped his feet'. Is this a dismissive act? Or is the visitor carefully cleaning his shoes before he enters the house, as the aunt might have demanded? The undertaker's dryly sarcastic attitude ('He was aware that this sort of thing had occurred before') clearly diminishes the aunt's social status. Everyone is equal in death. The tone of the poem so far has been listless and stiff, rather like the passive, submissive woman who bowed to all the strict conventions of her time. The combination of unoriginal rhymes ('before', 'for'), awkward rhythm and uneven lines captures the spirit of Miss Slingsby's stale, inward-looking society. Eliot finds it easy to satirise this cultural lifelessness and smug righteousness of his aunt's sterile world.

Line 8 cleverly suggests where the nephew's real interest lay: 'The dogs were handsomely provided for'. What was left to him is omitted. Is it likely that he was left out of her will? We also learn that his aunt's parrot died. A pet parrot spends its life imitating its owner. Was this action in sympathy with the elderly lady's passing? Or does it suggest that the aunt's and the parrot's deaths were equally insignificant? Again, the emphasis is on a woman's empty, barren life, which was spent concerned with protocol and etiquette rather than with people.

Eliot reminds us that **everyday life continues** in the extended **line 10**: 'The Dresden clock continued ticking on the mantelpiece'. Aunt Helen's fine possessions survived her passing implacably. The poem's somewhat humorous and risqué ending conveys a picture of sound, movement and life ('And the footman sat upon the dining-table/Holding the second housemaid on his knees'), clearly showing that the aunt's distorted sense of values does not survive. The servants ('Who had always been so careful while her mistress lived') are finally free of the confines of the aunt's lifeless, artificial world. A new order has been established in the remnants of this proper world. The repeated sibilant 's' mirrors the hushing secrecy upheld while the aunt lived.

In this unusual poem, **Eliot, the dramatist, creates a caricature caught up in her own world from a few detailed images**. He even captures the pompous tones of the aunt in phrases such as 'fashionable square' and 'this sort of thing'. Through the use of a distorted sonnet structure, one line short of the conventional 14-line form, Eliot reflects the failed notions of Aunt Helen's sense of her own importance and grandeur. The random, prosaic rhymes ('four', 'before', 'for') accentuate the dreary tone, leaving readers with an uneasy sense of the old lady's empty existence. Nevertheless, there is an underlying mischief and optimism in the poem's final lines. Now that Miss Slingsby has gone, at least the servants can begin to enjoy life.

ANALYSIS

'Eliot's poetry unveils a sharply observant picture of humankind.' Discuss this statement with reference to 'Aunt Helen'.

Sample Paragraph

I agree that Eliot draws a very revealing caricature of a lady who is trapped inside the confines of a rigid, conservative society. The poet launches a quietly blistering attack on the joyless life and times of the self-absorbed Miss Slingsby, who required 'servants to the number of four' to look after her in her 'small house near a fashionable square'. Using just a few concise details, the poet captures her upper-class voice in the repeated 'r' and 'o' sounds. She is not described, but her possessions are – her 'Dresden clock', her parrot and her dogs. Her real lack of importance is evident in the fact that there was silence in heaven at her passing and the undertaker 'was aware that this sort of thing had occurred before'. The odd length of the poem, one line short of the usual 14 lines, conveys acutely the skewed values of this self-serving woman. In two contrasting sets of run-on lines, the poet describes her dull existence, 'And lived in a small house ... number of four', and the contrasting exuberance and vitality of her servants, 'And the footman ... on his knees'. T.S. Eliot wryly captures a sobering portrait of humanity when it prefers convention and conformity over the careless dynamic of life.

Examiner's Comment

This well-focused paragraph shows a very close reading of the poem. Suitable quotations are effectively used to highlight the poet's portrayal of the central character's lonely life. The reference to the poem's unusual structure is effective. The fluent, controlled expression is sustained throughout. Grade-A standard.

CLASS/HOMEWORK EXERCISES

1. 'Eliot's poetry is filled with quiet despair.' Discuss this statement in relation to 'Aunt Helen'.

2. Copy the table below into your own notes and fill in critical comments about the last two quotations.

Key Quotes

And lived in a small house near a fashionable square	Eliot's extended line suggests the inflated notions of superiority the aunt had of herself and her position in polite society.
The dogs were handsomely provided for	The cynical tone clearly shows how the poet regards the aunt's concern for animals over people.
The Dresden clock continued ticking on the mantelpiece	
Who had always been so careful while her mistress lived	

FROM *THE WASTE LAND*: II. A GAME OF CHESS

The Chair she sat in, like a burnished throne,
Glowed on the marble, where the glass
Held up by standards wrought with fruited vines
From which a golden Cupidon peeped out
(Another hid his eyes behind his wing)   5
Doubled the flames of sevenbranched candelabra
Reflecting light upon the table as
The glitter of her jewels rose to meet it,
From satin cases poured in rich profusion.
In vials of ivory and coloured glass   10
Unstoppered, lurked her strange synthetic perfumes,
Unguent, powdered, or liquid – troubled, confused
And drowned the sense in odours; stirred by the air
That freshened from the window, these ascended
In fattening the prolonged candle-flames,   15
Flung their smoke into the laquearia,
Stirring the pattern on the coffered ceiling.
Huge sea-wood fed with copper
Burned green and orange, framed by the coloured stone,
In which sad light a carvèd dolphin swam.   20
Above the antique mantel was displayed
As though a window gave upon the sylvan scene
The change of Philomel, by the barbarous king
So rudely forced; yet there the nightingale
Filled all the desert with inviolable voice   25
And still she cried, and still the world pursues,
'Jug Jug' to dirty ears.
And other withered stumps of time
Were told upon the walls; staring forms
Leaned out, leaning, hushing the room enclosed.   30
Footsteps shuffled on the stair.
Under the firelight, under the brush, her hair
Spread out in fiery points

Glowed into words, then would be savagely still.

'My nerves are bad tonight. Yes, bad. Stay with me.   35
Speak to me. Why do you never speak? Speak.
    What are you thinking of? What thinking? What?
I never know what you are thinking. Think.'

I think we are in rats' alley
Where the dead men lost their bones.   40

'What is that noise?'
                The wind under the door.
'What is that noise now? What is the wind doing?'
                Nothing again nothing.

                                        'Do   45
You know nothing? Do you see nothing? Do you remember
Nothing?'

    I remember
Those are pearls that were his eyes.
'Are you alive, or not? Is there nothing in your head?'   50
                                        But
O O O O that Shakespeherian Rag –
It's so elegant
So intelligent
'What shall I do now? What shall I do?   55
I shall rush out as I am, and walk the street
With my hair down, so. What shall we do tomorrow?
What shall we ever do?'
                The hot water at ten.
And if it rains, a closed car at four.   60
And we shall play a game of chess,
Pressing lidless eyes and waiting for a knock upon the door.

When Lil's husband got demobbed, I said –
I didn't mince my words, I said to her myself,
HURRY UP PLEASE ITS TIME   65
Now Albert's coming back, make yourself a bit smart.
He'll want to know what you done with that money he gave you
To get yourself some teeth. He did, I was there.
You have them all out, Lil, and get a nice set,
He said, I swear, I can't bear to look at you.   70
And no more can't I, I said, and think of poor Albert,
He's been in the army four years, he wants a good time,
And if you don't give it him, there's others will, I said.
Oh is there, she said. Something o' that, I said.
Then I'll know who to thank, she said, and give me a straight look.   75
HURRY UP PLEASE ITS TIME
If you don't like it you can get on with it, I said.
Others can pick and choose if you can't.
But if Albert makes off, it won't be for lack of telling.
You ought to be ashamed, I said, to look so antique.   80
(And her only thirty-one.)
I can't help it, she said, pulling a long face,
It's them pills I took, to bring it off, she said.
(She's had five already, and nearly died of young George.)
The chemist said it would be all right, but I've never been the same.   85
You *are* a proper fool, I said.
Well, if Albert won't leave you alone, there it is, I said,
What you get married for if you don't want children?
HURRY UP PLEASE ITS TIME
Well, that Sunday Albert was home, they had a hot gammon,   90
And they asked me in to dinner, to get the beauty of it hot –
HURRY UP PLEASE ITS TIME
HURRY UP PLEASE ITS TIME
Goonight Bill. Goonight Lou. Goonight May. Goonight.
Ta ta. Goonight. Goonight.   95
Good night, ladies, good night, sweet ladies, good night, good night.

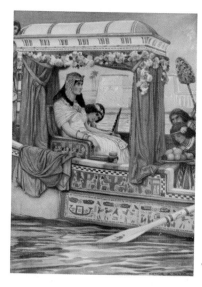

'The Chair she sat in'

GLOSSARY

A Game of Chess: Eliot's poem is based on two plays by the Jacobean playwright Thomas Middleton: *A Game of Chess* and *Women Beware Women*. In the second play, a young woman is seduced while her mother-in law unknowingly plays a game of chess with another woman who has facilitated the seduction. Every move in the game of chess represents a stage in the seduction. The audience sees both scenes at once as the action takes place in a gallery above the chess game.

1 **The Chair she sat in**: a paraphrase of the description of Cleopatra's barge from Shakespeare's play of love and betrayal, *Antony and Cleopatra*: 'The barge she sat in, like a burnished throne/Burned on the water'. Antony decides to marry another woman for political reasons and Cleopatra commits suicide.

3 **standards**: banners, upright supports.

3 **wrought**: twisted, formed.

4 **Cupidon**: Cupid, the young god of love in classical mythology.

6 **candelabra**: large branched candlestick.

10 **vials**: small containers.

11 **Unstoppered**: opened.

11 **synthetic**: artificial, fake.

12 **Unguent**: balm, ointment.

16 **laquearia**: panelled ceiling referencing the story of the Queen of Carthage, Dido, and her betrayal by Aeneas in Virgil's famous Latin poem, 'The Aeneid'. The ceiling of the hall in which Dido gave a banquet for Aeneas is described: 'flaming torches hang from the gold-panelled ceiling, and the night is pierced by the flaming lights'.

17 **coffered**: decorated with sunken panels.

22 **sylvan scene**: a wooded area. In John Milton's great poem, 'Paradise Lost', Satan sees a similar scene upon entering the Garden of Eden. Corruption and treachery ensue.

23 **Philomel**: an allusion to Ovid's epic poem 'Metamorphoses', which tells the tragic story of Philomel's rape and mutilation by her brother-in-law, Tereus, the King of Thrace. He cut off her tongue to prevent

her telling, but she communicated the horrific event to his wife, her sister Procne, by weaving a tapestry. She killed their son and fed him to Tereus in a terrible act of revenge. The gods then turned Philomel into a nightingale and she fills the desert with her song.

25 *inviolable*: secure, beyond corruption.

27 *Jug Jug*: way of representing birdsong in Elizabethan poetry; also a crude expression for lovemaking.

34 *Glowed into words*: reference to Dante's 'Inferno', where the damned souls can only speak through the tip of the flame that engulfs them.

39 *rats' alley*: slang term for World War I trenches.

40 *the dead men lost their bones*: soldiers felt great anguish when their fallen comrades were left unburied.

41 *What is that noise?*: from the revenge tragedy, *The Duchess of Malfi*; the

duchess's brother sends madmen to torment her.

49 *Those are pearls that were his eyes*: reference to Shakespeare's *The Tempest*, referring to the transformation of the dead into something beautiful and magical.

52 *that Shakespeherian Rag*: a popular American tune from Ziegfeld Follies (1912).

63 *demobbed*: demobilised, retired from the army.

65 *HURRY UP PLEASE ITS TIME*: the call of bartenders at closing time in British pubs.

90 *gammon*: cured ham.

96 *Good night, ladies*: Ophelia's poignant farewell before she commits suicide in Shakespeare's *Hamlet*. She has been driven mad by the deception and corruption of people around her.

EXPLORATIONS

1. Eliot's poem includes many allusions of misplaced love and its tragic consequences. Pick one example that made a strong impression on you and give reasons for your choice.

2. The poet introduces us to various characters whose voices we hear. In your opinion, are they happy or unhappy? Explain your answers with reference to the poem.

3. Write your own personal response to the poem, highlighting its impact on you.

'A Game of Chess' is the second section in T.S. Eliot's masterpiece, The Waste Land. It was written in 1921, when the poet was recovering from a nervous breakdown in Lausanne, Switzerland. Section II, 'A Game of Chess', explores themes of misdirected love and its destructive consequences. It also examines the insistent march of time and how the past haunts the present. The poem's fragmentary form, irregular punctuation and content respond to the mayhem and devastation caused by World War I. Eliot's many cultural and literary references universalise his themes. This modernist approach in literature also occurred in art with Pablo Picasso and in music with Arnold Schonberg. Such artists struggled to find a voice for this frenetic world of the post-war period. As Eliot's friend, the American poet Ezra Pound, commented, they were attempting to 'make it new'.

The poem presents us with two main scenes, both of which are concerned with deception and betrayal. On an initial reading, there appear to be striking differences between the characters of the first and the second drama in terms of social class, wealth and education. On closer examination, however, interesting similarities emerge. The **first half** of the poem shows an unnamed, sophisticated woman surrounded by beautiful furnishings – resembling props in a stage play. Eliot's **opening line** rephrases the account of Cleopatra's arrival on her magnificent barge in Shakespeare's play, *Antony and Cleopatra*. The **elaborate language** ('burnished', 'marble', 'wrought') suggests the lavish opulence of the setting. In **line 4**, the poet describes the mirror decorated with a 'golden Cupidon', like Cleopatra's 'smiling Cupids'. The atmosphere is formal and oppressive. But why is one of the Cupid figurines depicted as hiding 'his eyes behind his wing'? Is there a suggestion of something inappropriate or illicit?

The reference to the 'sevenbranched candelabra' shows Eliot mixing images of the sacred with the profane. God had ordered the Temple of Jerusalem to be furnished with a golden chair and seven ornate candles. The elegant diction is filled with such a 'rich profusion' of lush images that the reader is almost disoriented. However, an **unsettling note** is struck when the woman's 'synthetic perfumes' are described as 'Unstopped' on her dressing table. Something seems wrong and out of control in this seemingly luxurious setting. It is likely that the reader becomes 'troubled, confused'. Eliot depicts a stale, stifling atmosphere through the stressed extended sentences of the **first nine lines** and the evocative assonance of 'Unguent, powdered, or liquid'.

The sumptuously decorated ceiling (the 'laquearia') alludes to the tragic story of the mythical Queen of Carthage. Dido gave a splendid banquet for her lover, Aeneas, who subsequently deserted her. She then threw herself onto a funeral pyre as his ship sailed out of the harbour. Eliot is illustrating how **tragedy and destruction follow misplaced love**. This is an unavoidable reality for the stylish modern woman who is central to the poem's opening section. At every stage, she is viewed in terms of threat and betrayal. With the reference to Philomel (**line 23**), readers are introduced to another legendary scene of corruption as the seduced heroine, whose tongue was cut off, is eventually changed into a nightingale, allowing her to sing 'with inviolable voice'. Is Eliot himself like the songbird revealing the truth about deception and how it inevitably destroys relationships?

The emphasis on the present tense in **line 26** ('still the world pursues') suggests that nothing changes. Beauty and love will always be tainted. The bird's pure song is caught in the Elizabethan 'Jug Jug', yet to 'dirty ears', it has a vulgar sexual meaning.

The disappointments of real life are emphasised. Suddenly, the gaudy decorations are dismissed for what they really are – 'withered stumps of time'. **This is the infertility of the wasteland.** Is Eliot also expressing his cynicism towards those people who possess wonderful works of art but who don't really appreciate them? Is he hinting that the modern world is unaware of its rich cultural inheritance? There is no denying the poet's sharper tone as the earlier longer lines of lavish description now give way to curt expressions in **lines 27–30**.

Line 32 focuses on the modern woman, showing her under severe emotional strain while she sits alone. A surreal image, 'her hair/Spread out in fiery points', seems to speak: 'Glowed into words'. This frightening Medusa-like figure appears to be trapped in her own personal hell as she retreats into neurotic silence: 'savagely still'. Anonymous and faceless, she seems to lose control over the safe space of her beautiful dressing room when she hears 'Footsteps shuffle on the stair' – her husband, presumably. She begins to voice her paranoid concerns: 'My nerves are bad tonight'. Her nervous tension is played out in a **staccato rhythm** with the jumpy, erratic repetition of 'Speak', 'What' and 'Think'. Aimless questions and panicky commands show the lack of purpose in her speech. Is Eliot suggesting that she is just like Cleopatra and Dido, an emotional wreck who is depending on the attentions of a man?

The man's response is indirect and dismissive, indicating that he thinks but does not voice a reply to the petulant woman. Caught in his own desperate psychological state, **he is haunted by images of death**: 'I think we are in rats' alley', a reference to World War I trenches. The woman's whining voice intrudes as she wonders, 'What is that noise?' He thinks 'Nothing again nothing' and retreats from the tense questions, blotting out her voice with snippets of Shakespeare and an American hit tune. The syncopated rhythm of ragtime is indicated by the repetition of 'O O O O' and the extra syllable 'he' in 'Shakespeherian' (**line 52**). Such erratic movement and trite rhyme ('elegant'/'intelligent') reflect the couple's obvious inability to interconnect.

The woman becomes even more hysterical and threatens to 'rush out' and 'walk the street/With my hair down'. Her anxious questioning, 'What shall we ever do?', is characteristic of Eliot's recurring commentary on **the loss of religion and spirituality in modern life**. The sense of meaninglessness is emphasised when the man contemplates the banality of his daily routine. He will rise late, as if to shorten the day, 'hot water at ten' (**line 59**) before going for a pointless car ride in the rain and playing another dull game of chess. Is he simply waiting, with 'lidless' eyes, for something to happen? Who will make the 'knock upon the door'? Death, perhaps? The boredom and lack of communication of this living hell are enacted by the frightening, loveless woman and the self-centred, nihilistic man.

The **second scene** opens in a typical working-class British pub (**line 63**): 'When Lil's husband got demobbed'. A prayer-like mantra of 'I said' breaks up the bar room monologue in which the speaker recalls an earlier dialogue between herself and her friend, Lil. The snapshot of post-war British society places ordinary individuals in difficult situations, just like pieces in a game of chess. Marriage between Lil and her husband Albert is reduced to a sexual level. She is advised to 'make yourself a bit smart', otherwise she risks losing her man, who is returning from the war. Albert had given her money to buy false teeth, but she had used it for an abortion: 'She's had five already, and nearly died of young George'. Her relationship is as unsatisfactory as those mentioned in the first section of the poem. **Loneliness and human misery are shared by all social classes.** It is clear from the gossip that the speaker is sympathising with 'poor Albert'. Is this another case of 'Women Beware Women'? Is the speaker taking a perverse delight in Lil's predicament, almost blaming her in advance for what might happen: 'You *are* a proper fool' (**line 86**)?

The barman's insistent call, 'HURRY UP PLEASE ITS TIME', stresses the sinister absence of hope. Ironically, this urgency is not picked up by any of the other pub characters as they bid each other 'Goonight' (**line 95**). The bleak ending echoes one of Shakespeare's most unfortunate victims, the naive Ophelia, who dies by suicide, surrounded by heartless manipulation and betrayal. Like so much in the poem, these final lines depict a false and meaningless world, in keeping with Eliot's dark vision of modern life as a wasteland devoid of lasting love or moral values.

ANALYSIS

'T.S. Eliot's challenging poetic voice makes him inaccessible to the modern reader.' Discuss this view with reference to 'A Game of Chess'.

Sample Paragraph

From my study of 'A Game of Chess', I can understand the criticism of Eliot as a difficult poet whose use of allusions and fragmented writing style can make his work seem obscure. However, this is what is so interesting about his fresh 'modernist' early 20th-century voice, through which he comments on the frightening post-war era. I enjoyed his references to Cleopatra, 'The Chair she sat in, like a burnished throne', and to the unfortunate Dido and Philomel. By referring to these mythical women and then comparing them to Lil, the unhappy modern wife, I think Eliot succeeded in exploring the theme of sexuality very effectively. All of these women try to defy this cruel world with a determined search for love and real communication: 'Speak to me'. But man seems to be determined not to allow communication. Tereus cut off Philomel's tongue to prevent her speaking. The self-absorbed modern man blots out the woman's attempts to connect by responding to her questions with unspoken thoughts: 'we shall play a game of chess'. In my opinion, Eliot is playing a game of chess with his reader as he moves his women, the pawns in this game of love or sex, through their stories. He involves readers by asking them to examine the allusions, whether it is the jagged rhythm of ragtime, 'O O O O that Shakespeherian Rag', or the barman's insistent call for time, 'HURRY UP PLEASE ITS TIME'. Eliot is making us aware of the cruel reality of this frantic, mortal world. We have to realise that, like Ophelia, when the 'knock' comes at the door, we will have to say 'Good night'. Indirectly this poet converses, unlike the males in his poem, through his modernist, allusive masterpiece.

Examiner's Comment

This is a good personal response that takes a clear thematic view in support of Eliot's use of cultural and literary allusions. The focus is sustained throughout and aided effectively with accurate quotations. Expression is also varied, fluent and well controlled. Grade A.

CLASS/HOMEWORK EXERCISES

1. 'Eliot's poem, "A Game of Chess", moves characters like chess pieces towards destinations they cannot see as they perform in a drama they do not control or understand.' Discuss this statement with reference to the text.

2. Copy the table below into your own notes and fill in critical comments about the last two quotations.

Key Quotes

Doubled the flames of seven-branched candelabra	This vivid description of grandeur suggests the deception and duplicity of the stories that follow as Eliot mixes holy and secular imagery, with references to Cleopatra and the Jewish faith.
withered stumps of time	The evocative adjective 'withered' evokes a barren landscape, symbolising the worst of modern life, while the noun 'stumps' alludes to classical stories where barbarous acts of mutilation occurred.
HURRY UP PLEASE ITS TIME	
good night, sweet ladies, good night, good night	

⑤ JOURNEY OF THE MAGI

'A cold coming we had of it,
Just the worst time of the year
For a journey, and such a long journey:
The ways deep and the weather sharp,
The very dead of winter.'   5
And the camels galled, sore-footed, refractory,
Lying down in the melting snow.
There were times we regretted
The summer palaces on slopes, the terraces,
And the silken girls bringing sherbet.   10
Then the camel men cursing and grumbling
And running away, and wanting their liquor and women,
And the night-fires going out, and the lack of shelters,
And the cities hostile and the towns unfriendly
And the villages dirty and charging high prices: 15
A hard time we had of it.
At the end we preferred to travel all night,
Sleeping in snatches,
With the voices singing in our ears, saying
That this was all folly.   20

Then at dawn we came down to a temperate valley,
Wet, below the snow line, smelling of vegetation,
With a running stream and a water-mill beating the darkness,
And three trees on the low sky.
And an old white horse galloped away in the meadow.   25
Then we came to a tavern with vine-leaves over the lintel,
Six hands at an open door dicing for pieces of silver,
And feet kicking the empty wine-skins.
But there was no information, so we continued
And arrived at evening, not a moment too soon   30
Finding the place; it was (you may say) satisfactory.

All this was a long time ago, I remember,
And I would do it again, but set down
This set down
This: were we led all that way for   35
Birth or Death? There was a Birth, certainly,

We had evidence and no doubt. I had seen birth and death,
But had thought they were different; this Birth was
Hard and bitter agony for us, like Death, our death.
We returned to our places, these Kingdoms,   40
But no longer at ease here, in the old dispensation,
With an alien people clutching their gods.
I should be glad of another death.

'and such a long journey'

GLOSSARY

Magi: wise men, believed to be kings who travelled from the east to honour the birth of Jesus in Bethlehem. (Magi is the plural of magus, a wise man.)

6 *galled*: irritated by the chafing of a saddle.

6 *refractory*: difficult to control, unmanageable.

10 *sherbet*: sweet fruit juice drink.

20 *folly*: foolishness.

24 *three trees on the low sky*: the three crosses on Calvary, where Christ was crucified.

25 *old white horse*: Christ the conqueror rides on a white horse (according to the Book of Revelations).

26 *lintel*: horizontal supporting stone over a doorway.

27 *dicing for pieces of silver*: betrayal of Christ by Judas for 30 pieces of silver; soldiers dicing for Christ's clothes at his crucifixion.

28 *wine-skins*: container for holding wine made from animal skins.

41 *dispensation*: prevailing religion.

42 *clutching*: retaining, clinging to.

EXPLORATIONS

1. In your opinion, what is the mood of the magi as revealed in lines 19–20?

2. The poem is filled with striking imagery. Choose the image that most appeals to you and briefly explain why you found it interesting.

3. Based on your reading of the poem, what does the speaker mean when he declares: 'I should be glad of another death'? In your response, consider whether he is referring to physical or spiritual death – or both.

STUDY NOTES

'Journey of the Magi' was published in 1927 as part of a selection of poems that were to be included later in a series of Christmas cards. T.S. Eliot had converted to Anglicanism in August of that year and had been baptised into his new faith. The poem reflects Eliot's state of mind in transition between his old and new faiths. It fuses past and present as one of the magi, now an old man, recalls his experience of the journey undertaken to witness the birth of Jesus. This dramatic monologue is riddled with ambiguity. Throughout the narrative, Eliot interweaves the real and symbolic journeys of life and death.

The poem recreates the story of the three magi who travelled to Bethlehem from the east to honour the infant Jesus. Eliot's version is based on the gospel of St Matthew and takes the form of a dramatic monologue describing **a painful and life-changing experience**. The opening section (**lines 1–20**) recounts the arduous journey through the persona of one of the unnamed kings. He is caught between the past and present, no longer at ease in his old world, yet unsure about his new Christian life choice. The narrative tone is tired and unenthusiastic, as though the ageing magus has already told the story too many times.

Eliot's first five lines are based on a celebrated sermon given by an English clergyman, the Bishop of Winchester, on Christmas Day 1622: 'A cold coming we had of it,/Just the worst time of the year/For a journey'. Such strong **colloquial phrases ground the account of this extraordinary journey in reality**, although the gruelling trek itself was undertaken to find a mystery that was impenetrable to human wisdom. The details of the suffering camels, 'galled, sore-footed, refractory', add to the authenticity of the account.

Lines 11–16 contrast the **world of ease and luxury** that the magi had left behind with the challenging expedition and uncertainty ahead. They had rejected all their earlier comfort and sensuous pleasure: 'The summer palaces on slopes, the terraces,/And the silken girls bringing sherbet'. Frequent pauses in these lines convey the unhurried pace of their former lives. The recurring soft letter 's' floats as effortlessly as the youthful girls, enabling the language to glide by – a stark contrast to the hazardous mountain journey. This is vividly captured by the strikingly familiar imagery and run-on lines mimicking the fleeing camel men. Their coarse speech is graphically caught by the emphatic hard 'c' sound and broad assonance in the phrase 'cursing and grumbling'.

Memories tumble from the elderly magus, who reminisces on the various hardships endured: 'And the cities hostile and the towns unfriendly/And the villages dirty and charging high prices'. The impetus of the narrative is driven forward by an insistent rhythm emphasised by the evident repetition of 'And'. A short monosyllabic line curtly sums up his frustration: 'A hard time we had of it'. For the magi, however, there were more serious concerns than the physical discomforts. Along the way, all three kings faced agonising moments of self-doubt: 'voices singing in our ears, saying/That this was all folly'. In many ways, **their difficult experience symbolises every individual's search for spiritual meaning**, particularly Eliot's own painful journey into the Anglican faith.

The poem's second stanza (**lines 21–31**) describes the arrival of the three wise men. Eliot's version of events is unusual for all the well-known details it omits. There is no talk of a stable or any mention of gold, frankincense and myrrh. Instead, **present and future time blends** as Christ's adult life is predicted. The early morning descent into the 'temperate valley' evokes three significant Christian events: the nativity, Easter and the Second Coming of Christ. A bewildering range of images follows. Some are positive, such as the 'running stream', 'meadow' and 'vine-leaves', all of which suggest hope, freedom and fruitfulness. However, these are juxtaposed with negative imagery: the winter's 'low sky', the horse 'galloped away', 'feet kicking'.

Ambiguity fills this vivid dream-like state. **Eliot liked to use symbolism to represent philosophical ideas** through simple images. His description of 'three trees on the low sky', for example, implies the spiritual truth of the future (the skies lowered and heaven opened). The trees, of course, are likely representations of the three crosses on Calvary, where Jesus was to be crucified alongside two common criminals. Does the 'old white horse' signify Christ the conqueror? And if so, why is it galloping away? Might the poet be suggesting that true faith is always elusive? Are the 'Six hands ... dicing for pieces of silver' foreshadowing the betrayal of Christ by Judas?

The magi eventually found 'the place' where the new Messiah was born. There is a clear impression of anticlimax: 'it was (you may say) satisfactory'. All of the prophecies had been fulfilled, but there is an edge, an uncertain reticence in tone. The event was no more than adequate or acceptable. The material discomfort of the poem's opening section is replaced by **a growing awareness of a more mysterious discomfort**. Why is the magus so unsure about the importance of what he has witnessed? Undoubtedly, something crucial has happened, but there is a lingering sense of loss. The reader is also left wondering. Why was there no sense of the joyous excitement, which is recounted in the Bible, at the birth of the infant Jesus?

The final section, **lines 32–43**, of this typically multi-layered poem conveys the enduring effect that the journey had on the three magi. Emphatic repetition is used to stress that Christ's Nativity must be recorded carefully: 'but set down/ This set down/This'. The unusual line placing echoes the breakdown of the old order resulting from this recent event. Eliot highlights **the poem's central paradox**: 'were we led all that way for/Birth or Death?' For the poet, both experiences are inseparable. The birth of Christ marked the death of all previous religious beliefs. Through the experience of the three kings, Eliot also reveals the trauma of his personal spiritual journey. To an extent, this reflective monologue is that of any individual who has made his choice and achieved belief in the Incarnation, but who is still linked to the life that Christianity has come to replace.

The poem's conclusion is one of acceptance of a destiny that is the only possible answer, but still seems unbearably painful. The elderly magus admits that he 'should be glad of another death'. After they returned home, the three kings felt 'no longer at ease'. The new order that they witnessed makes them regard 'our places' as full of 'alien people clutching their gods'. The ageing narrator grows to understand that the birth of the Christ child changed everything. He has reached the end of his old pagan life, but despite his acknowledgment of the epiphany, he is still faced with the overwhelming mystery of his new Christian faith. The poem ends on a note of **mystified resignation**, serving as a metaphor for Eliot's own search to find meaning in the modern world.

ANALYSIS

'Eliot's fondness for using references can make his poetry seem difficult and dense.' Discuss this statement in relation to 'Journey of the Magi'.

Sample Paragraph

I would agree that 'The Journey of the Magi' can be demanding and intricate, particularly its fluid timeline, but I did not find it baffling. Its references are condensed, but they are not impenetrable. T.S. Eliot explores two journeys simultaneously, that undertaken by the magi as they travel to witness the birth of Jesus who was to bring in a new 'dispensation', a new religion. The second journey is Eliot's own spiritual conversion to Anglicanism. He was realising, just as the magi had, that when moving from one faith to another, there is regret for the old familiar ways – 'The summer palaces on slopes' – and he highlights this deep loss of belonging: 'no longer at ease here'. Both Eliot and the magi found 'an alien people clutching their gods'. The old ways no longer satisfied them. I found the poem's content complex, but it is understandable. Similarly, its many images, while ambiguous (such as 'an old white horse galloped away in the meadow') are by no means totally obscure. This biblical reference suggests that Christianity leads a person in an unexpected direction. True faith is an ongoing process, striving towards perfection. The 'three trees on the low sky' represent the lush vegetation of the 'temperate valley', the promise of heaven. But they also contain a foreshadowing of the crucifixion on Calvary. Eliot makes good use of a 'flashing phrase which never deserts the memory'. For me, his poetry is lucid and fluent in its treatment of difficult themes and ingenious in his use of imagery.

Examiner's Comment

This succinct paragraph addresses a challenging question effectively. Evaluative points are clear and coherently expressed. There is a good sense of confident engagement with the poem's central theme. Impressive use is made of relevant quotations and the expression is well controlled throughout. Grade-A standard.

CLASS/HOMEWORK EXERCISES

1. 'Eliot's poetry is modern in outlook yet old in allusions.' Do you agree or disagree with this assessment of his poetry? Support your opinions with close reference to the poem.

2. Copy the table below into your own notes and fill in critical comments about the last two quotations.

Key Quotes

And the villages dirty and charging high prices	Eliot brings the wearisome journey of the magi directly to the world of the reader with these realistic details.
it was (you may say) satisfactory	The poet conveys the experience of the Nativity through the jaded tone of the old magus. It satisfied all the conditions of the prophecy that had led them on the journey. But why use the bracketed phrase? Is the reader in receipt of a better view of the event than the old priest?
I had seen birth and death,/ But had thought they were different	
I should be glad of another death	

6 *FROM* LANDSCAPES: III. USK

Do not suddenly break the branch, or
Hope to find
The white hart behind the white well.
Glance aside, not for lance, do not spell
Old enchantments. Let them sleep.   5
'Gently dip, but not too deep',
Lift your eyes
Where the roads dip and where the roads rise
Seek only there
Where the grey light meets the green air   10
The hermit's chapel, the pilgrim's prayer.

'The white hart behind the white well'

GLOSSARY

Usk: small town in South Wales located on the river Usk, an ancient crossing point. Caerleon-Upon-Usk is reputed to be the site of the legendary court of King Arthur.

3 *hart*: male adult deer, associated with Arthurian legends.

3 *white well*: St Cybi's Well was a place of pilgrimage, where the water was reputed to cure various ailments.

4 *Glance aside*: have a quick look secretly.

4 *lance*: a long spear used by horsemen when jousting in medieval tournaments.

5 *Old enchantments*: legends and superstitions.

6 *'Gently dip, but not too deep'*: do not pry. The quotation comes from an Elizabethan play, *The Old Wives' Tale*, about old superstitions.

7 *Lift your eyes*: 'I will lift up mine eyes onto the hills from whence cometh my help.' (Psalm 21, Old Testament)

11 *hermit's chapel*: prayer-room of someone who lives alone for religious reasons.

11 *pilgrim*: traveller who goes on a spiritual journey to a holy place.

EXPLORATIONS

1. In the poem 'Usk', Eliot uses some effective images to create the atmosphere of the Welsh countryside. Choose one image that you particularly liked and explain its impact.

2. Sound effects such as alliteration, assonance and rhyme are used in this brief lyric. In your opinion, what contribution do they make?

3. Did you find the conclusion of the poem satisfactory or not? Give reasons for your view, supporting it with reference to the poem.

STUDY NOTES

'Usk' is the third of five short lyrics by Eliot entitled 'Landscapes', published in 1935. Each poem describes a specific place steeped in history. This evocative landscape sketch records Eliot's response to the Welsh landscape after a 10-day holiday spent there. It is the climax of the sequence, representing summer to autumn, symbolising the speaker's search for true tranquillity and spiritual happiness through prayer. The theme of spiritual fulfilment occupies much of Eliot's later poetry.

This is one of Eliot's least well-known and most puzzling poems. Typically, it can be seen as a conversation, both with the reader and the poet himself. To an extent, it is simply a very short landscape or pastoral description of the Welsh countryside around Usk. There was also a pub here called The White Hart Inn and behind it a once-whitewashed well that was so shallow that water was procured by dipping a container in. However, **Eliot's poem is primarily spiritually instructive**. The **first line** opens with an abrupt command, 'Do not', rather in the manner of an instruction given to a wayward child. Readers are warned not to seek romantic fantasy in such a landscape. The harsh alliteration ('break the branch') introduces the poet's attitude to 'Old enchantments'. We are strongly advised not to pursue the traditions and superstitions of the past: 'white hart', 'white well', 'lance'. All these symbols figure prominently in the Arthurian legend of the Quest for the Holy Grail. Eliot clearly mocks the medievalism of some of his contemporaries with a self-assured tone suggesting that his advice comes from one who is confident about his own religious faith.

Line 4 issues another ringing instruction, 'Glance aside', its internal rhyme echoing the medieval word 'lance' and emphasising that the old superstitious beliefs must be avoided: 'Let them sleep'. But **line 6** introduces a second thought with the quotation, 'Gently dip, but not too deep'. This forms the pivotal point of the poem. This quotation from an old Elizabethan play that satirised popular romantic dramas of the time has a mysterious head appear from a well warning not to intrude too closely. As far as the poet is concerned, **legend and tradition are appealing, but should be treated with caution**. In a recording of the poem, Eliot spoke this line in a sing-song voice reminiscent of a remembered childhood song. The jaunty rhythm forces readers forward. Is the poet suggesting that our relationship with the landscape should not be escapist or full of romantic fantasy, but should lead us towards the spiritual?

Unlike the restless opening, with its recurring musical effects, the **second half** of the poem begins with a prayer-like exhortation from the Old Testament: 'Lift your eyes'. The reader is being invited to go on a pilgrimage, a spiritual journey, 'Where the roads dip and where the roads rise', a reference to the smooth rolling countryside of Brecon. The repetition of 'Where' emphasises the need to seek 'The hermit's chapel, the pilgrim's prayer'. But these will only be found 'Where the grey light meets the green air'. This evocative phrase conjures up the misty countryside and green forest, a place of light and space, insubstantial. The confident triple rhyme ('there', 'air', 'prayer') reinforces the sense that the destination is within sight. Is this the symbolical meeting of the two traditions, Arthurian legend and Christianity? While the early section of the poem included repeated punctuation breaks, giving it a disruptive force, the second part flows much more smoothly through several run-on lines. **The poem concludes with a note of hope, firmly rooted in Christian imagery.** Characteristically, Eliot demonstrates his skill at evoking the reverential atmosphere of the 'hermit's chapel'.

The poem's principal tone is one of incantation – 'Hope to find', 'Lift your eyes', 'Seek only there' – which is emphasised by insistent rhyme. Eliot makes good use of both end-rhyme (such as 'well' and 'spell') and internal rhyme ('find', 'behind'). The colours used suggest peace and rejuvenation. White is usually associated with brightness and purity. The 'grey light' hints at the misty past, while 'green' is a natural, soothing shade. **Eliot creates a mysterious, mystical atmosphere** by blending simple images with sibilant sounds.

Some critics have argued that 'Usk' reflects the poet's continuing search for an answer to the 'overwhelming question' first asked in 'The Love Song of J. Alfred Prufrock'. If we accept that **the search for spiritual meaning is central to the poem**, then the chapel of the hermit would seem to represent the pilgrim's destination and the poet's confidence in the 'spell' of Christian faith.

ANALYSIS

'T.S. Eliot's search for meaning and his regard for making a spiritual journey are important elements in his poetry.' Discuss this statement in relation to his poem 'Usk'.

Sample Paragraph

This melodic poem, which vividly conjures up the Welsh landscape, warns that the 'Old enchantments' should be left in peace – 'Let them sleep'. The reader is instructed to 'Glance aside' and not to become involved with the romantic, escapist fantasy of the past, that of the Arthurian legend of 'white hart' and 'lance'. This is not where to look for spiritual fulfilment. The central quotation from an old play, 'Gently dip, but not too deep', pushes the reader away from delving into the magical, mythological past and instead points the way forward with the following Old Testament command: 'Lift your eyes'. The last four lines of the poem advise that we should look for fulfilment of our spiritual journey by turning to the mysteries of the Christian faith. The poem concludes with two simple symbols of Christianity, the 'hermit's chapel' and the 'pilgrim's prayer'. This sacred destination can be found where the 'grey light meets the green air', almost at the horizon, the world's end. I thought Eliot cleverly used a poem, which sounds like an incantation with its repetition, alliteration and strong rhyme, particularly the insistent end-rhymes of 'there', 'air' and 'prayer', to give an emphatic warning against becoming immersed in old superstitions and fantasy when seeking spiritual answers. 'Usk' clearly demonstrates the significance for Eliot of the spiritual journey.

Examiner's Comment

A clearly focused and well-organised paragraph showing close engagement with the text. Suitable quotes are used very effectively to trace the progress of thought through the poem. There are impressive references to the writing style, particularly Eliot's use of forceful rhyme, to emphasise his Christian viewpoint. Grade A.

CLASS/HOMEWORK EXERCISES

1. 'Eliot makes considerable use of visual imagery and varied sound effects in his poetry.' Discuss this statement in relation to the poem 'Usk'.

2. Copy the table below into your own notes and fill in critical comments about the last two quotations.

Key Quotes

Do not suddenly break the branch	The strong commanding tone of this opening line sets the mood of ominous warning in the poem.
Where the roads dip and where the roads rise	Insistent repetition and the undulating movement of the line effectively mimic the rolling hills of the Welsh countryside.
Seek only there	
Where the grey light meets the green air	

7 *FROM* LANDSCAPES: IV. RANNOCH, BY GLENCOE

Here the crow starves, here the patient stag
Breeds for the rifle. Between the soft moor
And the soft sky, scarcely room
To leap or soar. Substance crumbles, in the thin air
Moon cold or moon hot. The road winds in   5
Listlessness of ancient war,
Langour of broken steel,
Clamour of confused wrong, apt
In silence. Memory is strong
Beyond the bone. Pride snapped,   10
Shadow of pride is long, in the long pass
No concurrence of bone.

'Substance crumbles, in the thin air'

GLOSSARY

Rannoch: a moor in the Scottish Highlands, near the valley of Glencoe. It was the location of a terrible battle in 1692 when the Campbell clan massacred the MacDonalds.

4   *Substance*: material, solidity.

6   *Listlessness*: without energy or enthusiasm.

7   *Languor*: tiredness; pain.

8   *Clamour*: loud noise, outcry.

8   *apt*: appropriate, suitable.

11   *pass*: gap, route over mountains.

12   *concurrence*: agreement, co-operation.

EXPLORATIONS

1. In your opinion, what do the animal images of the first two lines contribute to the impression of Rannoch being presented by Eliot?

2. Trace how the poet presents his message that the present is weighed down by the past. Support your answer with suitable quotation from the text.

3. How effective are the poem's sound effects in conveying the atmosphere of Glencoe? Illustrate your response using accurate quotation from the poem.

STUDY NOTES

'Rannoch, by Glencoe' is the fourth poem in T.S. Eliot's five-part series, 'Landscapes' (1935). After visiting the Scottish Highlands, he composed this poem evoking the essence of the remote moor in condensed images, and its geography provides a compelling backdrop to the poet's message. Eliot was struck by Rannoch's pervading atmosphere, which he felt was a consequence of a 17th-century battle between two Scottish clans, the Campbells and the MacDonalds. Set during the winter season, this marvellously compressed poem captures the eerie sense of dislocation that is often found on old battlefields.

The **opening lines** convey an uninviting image of death. Rannoch's barren terrain presents nature at its worst: even 'the crow starves'. The long-suffering deer is fodder for the hunter's 'rifle'. This is a place of brooding menace and extreme harshness, both from nature and from man, captured in the startling death-in-life imagery. Eliot's dismal tone is in keeping with the slow-moving pace. Yet the insistent 's' alliteration hints at the rugged beauty of the bleak surroundings: 'Between the soft moor/And the soft sky'. But **it is a claustrophobic and oppressive place**. The cloudy sky hangs so low near the landscape that there is no room for the stag to leap or the crow to fly. Strangely, the references to softness appear negative, almost tyrannical. Nothing can be relied on in this place – the moon is changeable ('cold' or 'hot') and the rock is being eroded ('Substance crumbles, in the thin air').

Even the lazy description of the winding road in **lines 5–6** is misleading. Unlike the routeways symbolising salvation in Eliot's poem 'Usk', there is only 'Listlessness' and 'Languor' here. The countryside is weighed down and **haunted by disturbing memories of the past**, the notorious massacre of 1692. The 'broken steel' of an 'ancient war' still remains in the landscape. This locality is devoid of hope, rooted in the endless cycles of past violence. For Eliot, the silence of the place resonates with memories of the 'Clamour' of battle, which occurred due to transgressions on both sides ('confused wrong'). The alliterative sharp 'c' effect emphasises the uproar of battle.

In the poem's **closing lines**, Eliot captures the closeness of the past. There is no underlying peace in this land. Instead, disharmony remains between the bones of the dead enemies. The Scottish hills are darkened by the 'Shadow of pride'. This clearly suggests that the descendants of both clans have never become truly reconciled. The repetition of 'long' (**line 11**) stresses the brutal consequence of such a terrible event that took place over three centuries ago. In contrast to the hard mountain rock, which can be broken down over time, pride and self-worth do not crumble. Like a shadow blighting the landscape, **memory discourages healing**. This is the stark truth about human pride that Eliot uncovers in the rugged terrain of Rannoch. There is no sign of hope and certainly no religious perspective here.

The poem ends on a discordant note that bristles with tension and the lines run on to finish abruptly: 'Memory is strong/Beyond the bone'. The insistent force of Eliot's monosyllables, 'Pride', 'pass' and 'bone', create a stumbling rhythm. Assonant sounds – particularly the long mournful 'o' within **line 12** ('in the long pass/No concurrence of bone') – highlight **the sadness that suffuses the beautiful landscape** damaged for all time by the cruelty of nature and man. Readers are left in no doubt about the poem's central theme – historical events and old conflicts become entrenched in the places where they once occurred.

ANALYSIS

'Landscape or setting is an important symbol that T.S. Eliot uses to reflect both the inner and outer worlds.' Discuss this statement in relation to Eliot's poem 'Rannoch, by Glencoe'.

Sample Paragraph

Eliot uses landscape to represent much more than local scenery. In fact, it is a means of defining emotional and moral states in man, the inner world. Eliot, for me, captures the spirit of Glencoe in dark, vivid imagery associated with death and the winter season: 'the crow starves' and the 'patient stag' destined 'for the rifle'. This cruel place offers no opportunity to escape. Eliot references the terrible battle of 1692, the Massacre of Glencoe, which took place between two rival Scottish clans over conflicting views of loyalty. There was no place for the MacDonalds to flee to as they were killed by the very guests whom they trusted. The poet senses that over the course of time, Rannoch's landscape retains the traumatic atmosphere of the past, the 'Listlessness' which lingers from that 'ancient war'. Memory keeps the wrongdoing alive and so this bleak place becomes a symbol of what happens when humans do not aspire to a better future. I found Eliot's description of the unchanged, winding road revealing, suggesting that there is no hope, only emotional and moral stagnation. The mournful mood of the Scottish wind echoes in the long 'o' of 'Shadow of pride is long, in the long pass/No concurrence of bone'. Eliot uses landscape to show the outer world's bleak beauty, with its crumbling stone and haunting moonlight. But he also captures the dark workings of the inner human heart, which won't let go of the past.

Examiner's Comment

A very assured A-grade response to the question, tracing the progress of thought in the poem. The connections between past and present are explored effectively, using suitable references and accurate quotations. Comments on the poet's style are also insightful, showing good personal engagement. Expression is clear and coherent throughout.

CLASS/HOMEWORK EXERCISES

1. 'The poetry of T.S. Eliot is depressing and anguished.' Discuss this statement in relation to 'Rannoch, by Glencoe'. Refer to both the poet's subject matter and style in your response, using suitable quotation from the poem to support your views.

2. Copy the table below into your own notes and fill in critical comments about the last two quotations.

Key Quotes

Substance crumbles, in the thin air	The onomatopoeic verb 'crumbles' accurately describes the breakdown of the rock into loose scree due to the harsh weather conditions. It may also refer to how trusted guests became murderers in 1692.
The road winds in/Listlessness of ancient war	The assonance of the long 'i' catches the atmosphere of horror and exhaustion on the road following the great battle.
Memory is strong/Beyond the bone	
Pride snapped	

8 *FROM* FOUR QUARTETS: EAST COKER IV

The wounded surgeon plies the steel
That questions the distempered part;
Beneath the bleeding hands we feel
The sharp compassion of the healer's art
Resolving the enigma of the fever chart.   5

Our only health is the disease
If we obey the dying nurse
Whose constant care is not to please
But to remind of our, and Adam's curse,
And that, to be restored, our sickness must grow worse.   10

The whole earth is our hospital
Endowed by the ruined millionaire,
Wherein, if we do well, we shall
Die of the absolute paternal care
That will not leave us, but prevents us everywhere.   15

The chill ascends from feet to knees,
The fever sings in mental wires.
If to be warmed, then I must freeze
And quake in frigid purgatorial fires
Of which the flame is roses, and the smoke is briars.   20

The dripping blood our only drink,
The bloody flesh our only food:
In spite of which we like to think
That we are sound, substantial flesh and blood –
Again, in spite of that, we call this Friday good.   25

'the flame is roses, and the smoke is briars'

GLOSSARY

East Coker: a village in Somerset, near Yeovil. It is Eliot's ancestral home. Family and family history feature in the poem. He had found information on his family from 'Sketch of the Eliot Family', which described how his family had lived in East Coker for 200 years. Andrew Eliot left in 1669, disrupting the family history. Eliot also broke away from his family in America. In the poem, Eliot stresses the need for a journey and the need for inward change.

1   **wounded surgeon**: Jesus Christ, the Son of God, who suffered for our sins.

1   **plies:** works steadily using a tool.

1   **steel**: scalpel, a knife with a small, sharp blade used by a surgeon.

2   **questions**: probes, cross-examines.

2   **distempered**: diseased.

3   **bleeding hands**: the hands of Jesus were nailed to the Cross.

5   **Resolving**: sorting out what man could only 'chart' and observe.

5   **enigma**: puzzle, mystery, problem.

7   **dying nurse**: Church.

9   **Adam's curse**: original sin. Adam disobeyed the commandment of God and was banished from the Garden of Eden and he and all his descendants were now prone to disease and death.

12   **Endowed**: provide, donate.

12   **ruined millionaire**: Adam.

14   **paternal care**: God's care.

15   **prevents**: leads on, stops.

17   **mental wires**: mind's torment.

19   **quake**: tremble, cower.

19   **frigid**: cold, icy.

19   **purgatorial fires**: the soul burns in purgatory to be cleansed from sin before ascending to heaven.

24   **substantial**: of considerable importance, strongly built.

EXPLORATIONS

1. 'East Coker IV' is full of metaphysical paradoxes: 'sharp compassion', 'Our only health is the disease', 'to be restored, our sickness must grow worse', 'if we do well, we shall/Die', etc. Choose two of these paradoxes that made an impact on you and explain why they impressed you.

2. What, in your opinion, is the tone of the poem: devotional, assured, searching, frightened, etc.? Support your views by accurate quotation from the poem.

3. Do you consider the final verse a satisfactory conclusion to the poem? Explain the reasons for your opinion, using accurate references from the poem.

STUDY NOTES

'East Coker' forms part of the cycle of four poems titled Four Quartets, *widely regarded as Eliot's masterpiece. The poems were first published individually with a place name: 'Burnt Norton' (1936), 'East Coker' (1940), 'The Dry Salvages' (1941) and 'Little Gidding' (1942). This sequence is loosely based on the four seasons and the four elements. The title, 'Four Quartets', suggests a musical quartet, where themes and images are repeated as the meanings accumulate through the different instrumentation used. Time, experience, purgation, prayer and unity are the themes that are common to each poem.*

There is an historical dimension to 'East Coker', as Sir Thomas Elyot was baptised in St Michael's Church in East Coker in 1627. Another ancestor, Andrew Eliot, left East Coker for America in 1669. Eliot visited this village in the 1930s and his ashes are buried in the same church with the inscription, 'In my beginning is my end. Of your kindness, pray for the soul of Thomas Stearns Eliot, poet. In my end is my beginning.' Critics have described 'East Coker' as a poem of late summer, earth and faith. It is also seen by some as signifying hope that the English communities would survive World War II. The village is an idyll of England at the start of the war. In Eliot's view, the end of all exploring is 'to arrive where we started/And know the place for the first time'.

The poem 'East Coker' is divided into five sections. 'East Coker IV' is a formal, elegant section that uses **elaborate paradoxes**. It is full of personal and collective despair paired with the gloom of Good Friday. This religious meditation focuses on the central Christian doctrines of original sin (humanity's state after the fall of Adam), redemption (salvation through the sacrifice of Jesus on the Cross) and atonement (penance undertaken to purge the sin). The poem is focused on the magnitude of Christ's death on the Cross as a way of securing salvation for mankind.

Eliot enjoyed the Metaphysical poets, such as Donne, who used intricate comparisons in their work. In this poem in **stanza one**, Eliot uses the hospital as a metaphor for the world. The suffering patients are mankind. The 'wounded surgeon' is Jesus Christ, who operates to save sinful/diseased man. Stern love is shown by the surgeon as he skilfully 'plies the steel' to cure the 'distempered part'. He is 'wounded' like Jesus was after being pierced when on the Cross. The surgeon's 'bleeding hands' recall how Christ's hands were nailed to the Cross.

Through his suffering the puzzle, 'enigma', of sin, denoted by the 'fever chart', is being sorted out, 'Resolving'. This 'sharp compassion' is needed to solve the mystery of our ailing, sinful existence. Metaphysical poetry had a real sense of **argument** running through it, as here: we need to reject the demands of the body and achieve salvation through curing the body's ills. Suffering leads to grace. Eliot saw a real similarity between the poetry of the 17th century and that of the 20th century – both saw the disintegration of old traditions and the arrival of new learning.

In **stanza two the comparison is extended**: 'Our only health is the disease'. This refers to a poem by Andrew Marvell where the soul speaks of being 'Constrained not only to endure/Diseases, but, what's worse, the cure'. According to the poet, we have to do what the 'dying nurse', the Church, says. Its role is to comfort, 'not to please', but to remind us of our morality. This is a direct consequence of 'our, and Adam's curse'. We have to recognise that **we are sinful and that we need to be redeemed** and then we can be spiritually healthy. This is inspired by 'Dark Night of the Soul' by Saint John of the Cross, which told of the journey of the soul from its bodily home to its union with God. Purification is needed for spiritual growth.

Stanza three continues the parallel as Adam is described as the 'ruined millionaire': he had it all, Paradise, and threw it all away. He provided the 'whole earth' as a 'hospital' where we can learn the value of suffering and can be cured of our sickness. 'Endowed' suggests something that is gifted or bestowed. Here, it is used paradoxically by Eliot, as **Adam left us with sin, but opened the way for salvation** ('if we do well'). Adam's fall precipitated Christ's sacrifice. One could not have happened without the other. We will be looked after by 'absolute paternal care/That will not leave us'. It 'prevents us everywhere', going before us as spiritual guidance and also stopping us through death.

Rich, sensuous images in **stanza four** describe the fever of sickness: 'The chill ascends from feet to knees'. We feel the icy coldness of death. We experience the shrill sound of mental anguish in the assonance of 'The fever sings in mental wires'. In order to triumph, 'If to be warmed', the individual must suffer, 'freeze/ And quake', as atonement is sought in the contradictory 'frigid purgatorial fires' as the disease of sin is purified through suffering. This results in the experience of **divine love**, 'Of which the flame is roses'. This was the sacrifice on the Cross of Jesus. The 'briars' suggest the crown of thorns placed on Christ's head as he was crucified. The emblems of martyrdom are 'roses' and 'briars'.

The **fifth stanza** concludes with sensational, vivid images of the **Eucharist**. 'The dripping blood' (the wine) and 'The bloody flesh' (the host) form the only sustenance we need for eternal life. Eliot criticises our blindness, 'In spite of which we like to think' that we are whole and complete without this 'sound, substantial flesh and blood'. Nevertheless, he acknowledges that we do realise the value of Jesus' suffering because 'we call this Friday good'.

The **tone** of this poem is one of calm, detached humility. Its **devotional, assured voice** is contained in five stanzas of five lines. Each stanza concludes with a full stop, a complete syntactical unit on its own. The rhyme scheme is regular *ababb*, *cdcdd*, etc. This polished, formal yet private voice expresses the concerns of an entire generation in the midst of war and doubt.

ANALYSIS

'T.S. Eliot's poem "East Coker IV" is a bitter poem concluding in resignation.' Discuss this statement, referring to both the content and style of the poem. Support your response with careful quotation from the poem.

Sample Paragraph

I do not agree that this is a bitter poem. I did not think it vicious or hostile. It is a carefully crafted poem consisting of five stanzas, each containing five lines, making individual syntactical units, not a nasty virulent rant. Instead Eliot sets out in a dazzling display of elaborate comparisons the reality of this violent, sinful world which needs healing by the 'wounded surgeon', Jesus Christ. When I consider that this poem was written in 1940, against the background of the horrors of the Second World War, I consider that Eliot was correct in describing man's condition as the 'enigma of the fever chart'. He regards 'The whole earth' as 'our hospital', a place where there is sickness and healing must take place with 'The sharp compassion of the healer's art'. How can this be construed as bitter? Fever has to get worse before the body can heal itself. Eliot believed in the Christian doctrine of penance and salvation. In my opinion, that is why he speaks of purging sin/sickness 'in frigid purgatorial fires'. I do not consider that the poem ends in resignation, as there is hope because of Jesus Christ's sacrifice on the Cross which won us our salvation. This is captured in the quite shocking images of the Eucharist's wine and host, 'The dripping blood' and 'The bloody flesh'. Eliot concludes his poem by acknowledging that man does appreciate the sacrifice as 'we call this Friday good', a very positive end note!

Examiner's Comment

This is a robust personal response to the question and presents a number of strong arguments that show close engagement with the poem. Accurate quotations and contextual references are used effectively throughout. The persuasive approach is a little mechanical at times and there is overuse of the verb 'consider'. A basic grade A.

CLASS/HOMEWORK EXERCISES

1. ' "East Coker IV" is a poem whose lines fail to come to life.' Do you agree or disagree with this view of Eliot's poem? Explain your views, illustrating them with reference to the poem.

2. Copy the table below into your own notes and fill in critical comments about the last two quotations.

Key Quotes

enigma of the fever chart	This paradox shows that man's sinful condition can only be observed and noted by man. It needs divine intervention to solve the puzzle.
if we do well, we shall/Die of the absolute paternal care/ That will not leave us	Another paradox is used to describe the comforting yet terrifying reality of the human condition. God will not abandon us, but we have to reject our sinful ways – 'Die', divorce ourselves from the world – in order to be saved.
the flame is roses, and the smoke is briars	
in spite of that, we call this Friday good	

'T.S. Eliot's distinctive poetry is concerned with the search for meaning in an uncertain world.' Discuss this statement, with suitable reference to the poems of Eliot on your course.

Marking Scheme Guidelines

Expect candidates to agree and/or disagree with the given statement, but they should engage with 'distinctive poetry' and 'search for meaning in an uncertain world' (though not necessarily equally) in Eliot's poetry. Allow that 'distinctive' and 'uncertain' may be addressed explicitly or implicitly.

Material might be drawn from the following:
- Poet's disillusioned vision of 20th-century urban life
- Original poetic style and powerful imagery
- Unsettling and disturbing themes of alienation and failure
- Compelling search for satisfying relationships and spiritual meaning
- Revealing literary allusions and complex and cultural references
- Dramatic use of multiple narrative voices/personae
- Evocative moods/atmosphere: ironic, poignant, despondent, satirical, etc.

Sample Essay

(T.S. Eliot's distinctive poetry is concerned with the search for meaning in an uncertain world)

1. *I found T.S. Eliot's poetry difficult to understand at first. Some poems, such as 'Preludes' and 'Prufrock', were strangely atmospheric and the writing style was very fragmented. However, his insightful observations on modern society were always thought-provoking. It's not surprising that his poetry has made such an impact since the earliest publication back in the early decade of the 20th century, a time of major social change and uncertainty.*

2. *It is clear that many Eliot poems reflect the poet's own spiritual search. 'Journey of the Magi', his dramatic account of the three kings who visited the infant Jesus in Bethlehem, symbolises every human being seeking spiritual meaning. Eliot's approach, however, is unlike the traditional Bible story. He focuses on the physical hardships the magi faced in 'The very dead of winter'. The elderly magus who*

narrates the story admits 'There were times we regretted' the journey – especially since they had given up the pleasures of 'The summer palaces on slopes' and 'silken girls bringing sherbet'. Eliot reminds readers that Christianity is not an easy path to follow. The poem is typically symbolic, with many familiar Christian images of renewal, including 'an old white horse', a metaphor for Christian rebirth and the end of paganism. 'Six hands at an open door dicing for pieces of silver' refers to the betrayal of Jesus by Judas. The magus describes their destination – 'Finding the place; it was (you may say) satisfactory'. Such a deliberate understatement reflects the troubled minds of the magi as a result of the clash of their old lives and a new religion.

3. The poem's final lines describe the psychological change in the magi, who remained less than convinced about Christianity: 'this Birth was/Hard and bitter agony for us, like Death'. The journey marked the end of their pagan religion but did not give them complete satisfaction of faith. I liked the fact that the poem was multi-layered: the actual journey of the magi, Eliot's personal journey from doubt to Anglican faith and the journey of any individual in search of God. For me, 'Journey of the Magi' highlighted the idea that religious faith can never be free of serious doubt – 'That this was all folly'. The poem is characteristic of Eliot's recurring themes of alienation and powerlessness in a world that is constantly changing.

4. The absence of spirituality in post-war 20th-century society provides the background to 'The Love Song of J. Alfred Prufrock'. The poem's insecure central figure is characterised by his inability to take control of his life, but it is his need for fulfilment and his anxiety towards watching his time disappear which makes him such a tragic case. Unfortunately, Prufrock's fear of being rejected due to his age stops him from obtaining a companion or any future hopes. In this dramatic monologue, Prufrock brings us with him on a journey to meet an unnamed lady. It seems as though he intends to ask her 'an overwhelming question' – perhaps a proposal of marriage.

5. It soon becomes clear that Prufrock is both frustrated and neurotic. As we hear his random thoughts, it becomes clear that he is trying to know himself and make some sense of his unhappy existence – 'I have measured out my life with coffee spoons'. Prufrock questions everything. Eliot breaks up the poem into numerous sub-sections, reflecting the speaker's unsettled mind. He also uses the stream of consciousness

narrative effectively to show Prufrock's private anxieties about failing to find a meaningful life. Obsessed by ageing – 'I grow old … I shall wear the bottoms of my trousers rolled'. He repeatedly voices his timidity – '"Do I dare?' and, 'Do I dare?"' as well as his hopeless inferiority – 'It is impossible to say just what I mean!' I found the ending quite moving, particularly the haunting image of Prufrock abandoning his dreams of finding female companionship. He imagines being near the ocean and hearing mermaids singing, but faces up to the tragic reality of his lonely life – 'I do not think that they will sing to me'.

6. Just as Prufrock represents the dilemma of the materialistic world's loss of meaning, Eliot's poem 'Preludes' explores the solitary, mundane existences of unhappy individuals as they play out against the backdrop of the drab modern city. The poet is particularly successful at creating unsettling moods. Dramatic images of 'grimy scraps/Of withered leaves', 'newspapers from vacant lots' and 'broken blinds and chimney-pots' evoke the anonymous lives of dingy back-streets. The nameless characters Eliot introduces reflect their grim setting, going through daily routines of silent desperation – 'With the other masquerades/That time resumes'. I thought the poem's outlook was particularly pessimistic and in keeping with Eliot's view that modern urban life is disappointing and often degrading.

7. Almost all of the Eliot poems I studied dealt with individuals seeking meaningful relationships – either human or spiritual – against the pressures of their day-to-day lives. What defines the poet's approach, however, is the fact that he takes such a devastatingly dark view of life, expressing the despair and desolation of his time. Nevertheless, I found his poetic style original and surprising. Some poems made me re-think my attitudes to how other people assess their lives – particularly as they weigh up their hopes and dreams alongside the reality of what they have actually achieved.   (approx. 880 words)

Examiner's Comment

An impressive personal answer showing clear engagement with Eliot's poetry. The poems chosen for discussion allowed for a sustained, coherent approach, focusing on recurring themes of alienation and spiritual searching. Most main points are developed effectively and make good use of relevant quotation, particularly on 'Prufrock'. The expression is very well controlled throughout.

GRADE: A1
P = 15/15
C = 13/15
L = 5/15
M = 5/5
Total = 48/50

(45/50 MINUTES)

1. 'The poetry of T.S. Eliot explores serious issues of universal significance in a fresh and innovative style.' Discuss this statement, supporting your answer with suitable reference to the poems by Eliot on your course.

2. 'T.S. Eliot can be a challenging poet to understand, both in terms of language use and central themes.' To what extent do you agree with this statement? Support your answer with suitable reference to the poems by Eliot that you have studied.

3. 'Eliot's pessimistic vision of life is conveyed in poems that are both interesting and atmospheric.' Discuss this view, supporting your answer with suitable reference to the poems by Eliot on your course.

Sample Essay Plan (Q2)

'T.S. Eliot can be a challenging poet to understand, both in terms of language use and central themes.' To what extent do you agree with this statement? Support your answer with suitable reference to the poems by Eliot that you have studied.

- Intro: Eliot's irregular writing style is innovative – always inviting the reader to explore the possibilities of language. The wide-ranging subject matter can be obscure at times, but this reflects the complexity of experience in the modern age.

- Point 1: Poems address ideas that have universal significance, often focusing on spiritual and philosophical questions confronting the modern secular world. 'Preludes' exemplifies such compelling issues.

- Point 2: Readers are engaged by the dramatic scenes and intriguing atmospheres in 'Prufrock'. In his alienation and insecurity, the forlorn protagonist raises interesting questions about contemporary urban society.

- Point 3: Some of the shorter poems, e.g. 'Aunt Helen', are relatively accessible. This gentle satire is critical of aspects of polite society.

- Point 4: While cultural allusions and literary references can be demanding, they broaden and enrich our understanding of important themes, such as the Christian experience in 'Journey of the Magi' and 'East Coker IV'.

- Conclusion: Eliot's original poetic voice extends the boundaries of language and his thought-provoking poems have much to interest the modern reader in a rapidly changing world.

Sample Essay Plan (Q2)

Develop one of the above points into a paragraph.

Sample Paragraph: Point 3

Not all of Eliot's poems are difficult to understand. In 'Aunt Helen', the poet paints a satirical pen portrait of a lonely woman, his 'maiden aunt', a 'fashionable' society lady whose fussy lifestyle is seen as being quite absurd. I thought he managed to show respect while at the same time suggesting she was out of touch with reality. The 'silence in heaven' summed her up well. In a way, she had been half-dead all along. Eliot is also quite daring in ways – especially as he doesn't seem to be taking death too seriously: 'the undertaker wiped his feet' when he visited, as if Helen would expect good manners even after she had died. This dry sense of humour and quiet tone of voice is also quite evident in the final part of the poem where all the aunt's puritanical rules are no longer having any effect on the servants who are enjoying their brand new freedom: 'the footman sat upon the dining-table/Holding the second housemaid on his knees'. The poet's writing is suggestive but down-to-earth. I think Eliot's point is absolutely clear. The two servants are lower class, but they are certainly enjoying life – quite unlike the lonely spinster who had been really crushed by social etiquette . Sadly, she missed out on having fun when she had the chance.

Examiner's Comment

A lively response as part of a full essay answer. The question is addressed directly and there is good personal engagement with the poem. Some of the references to the poet's satirical tone are insightful. In the main, expression is reasonably well managed – although 'quite' is over-used. Grade B.

LAST WORDS

'Although the idea of a life not fully lived is central to his poetry, T.S. Eliot was not the dry old stick of his self-caricature.'

Craig Raine

'As a schoolboy in a Catholic boarding school in Derry, I was daunted by T.S. Eliot and all that he stood for.'

Seamus Heaney

'Genuine poetry can communicate before it is understood.'

T.S. Eliot

PHILIP LARKIN

1922-85

'An event provides a lead into a poem.'

Philip Larkin was born in 1922 in Coventry, England. He did not enjoy his childhood: 'Get out as early as you can/And don't have any kids yourself'. Nor did he like school. He had a stammer and was short-sighted, although he read widely and contributed to the school magazine. After graduating from Oxford, he went on to become a librarian. Larkin became a great admirer of Thomas Hardy's poetry, learning from Hardy how to make the commonplace and often dreary details of his life the basis for extremely tough, unsparing and memorable poems. He published several collections of poetry, much of which reflect ordinary English life. His searing, often mocking wit rarely concealed the poet's dark vision and underlying obsession with universal themes of mortality, love and human solitude. Yet Larkin's poems face the trials of living and dying with an orderly elegance that always moves the reader. Philip Larkin believed poetry should come from personal experience: 'I write about experiences ... simple everyday experiences ... I hope other people will come upon this ... pickled in verse ... and it will mean something to them.'

Prescribed Poems

❶ WEDDING-WIND

The wind blew all my wedding-day,
And my wedding-night was the night of the high wind;
And a stable door was banging, again and again,
That he must go and shut it, leaving me
Stupid in candlelight, hearing rain,   5
Seeing my face in the twisted candlestick,
Yet seeing nothing. When he came back
He said the horses were restless, and I was sad
That any man or beast that night should lack
The happiness I had.   10

      Now in the day
All's ravelled under the sun by the wind's blowing.
He has gone to look at the floods, and I
Carry a chipped pail to the chicken-run,
Set it down, and stare. All is the wind   15
Hunting through clouds and forests, thrashing
My apron and the hanging cloths on the line.
Can it be borne, this bodying-forth by wind
Of joy my actions turn on, like a thread
Carrying beads? Shall I be let to sleep   20
Now this perpetual morning shares my bed?
Can even death dry up
These new delighted lakes, conclude
Our kneeling as cattle by all-generous waters?

'and the hanging cloths on the line'

GLOSSARY

12   *ravelled*: pulled apart and untangled.
16   *thrashing*: moving; beating violently.
18   *borne*: carried by, endured.

EXPLORATIONS

1. How realistic do you think Larkin's portrayal of marriage is? Support your views with reference to the text.

2. Trace the tone in this poem. Does it change? What is different in the attitude of the speaker in the second section?

3. In your opinion, why does the poem end with three questions?

STUDY NOTES

'Wedding-Wind' was published in 1946. This narrative poem (Larkin was also a novelist) records details of a wedding day, night and the morning after. Larkin adopts the persona of a young bride to tell the story. He said, 'I can imagine ... the emotions of a bride ... without ever having been a woman or married.' This poem is a celebration of the joy of passionate love.

This direct, personal poem's **opening section** begins with the young bride stating that 'The wind blew all my wedding-day'. This 'high wind' blew throughout her day and the wedding night. Is it a symbol for passion and change? Is the poem linking the energy of the natural world with the force of human love? The adjective 'high' for Larkin meant elevated and elevating experiences. People rise above the ordinary to experience a spiritual feeling. The restless atmosphere of the day and night is caught in the description of the stable door 'banging, again and again'. This mundane detail shows Larkin's ear for the ordinary. The young woman relates how her husband has to 'go and shut' the banging door. Larkin believed that life as it was lived by ordinary people should and could provide the subject for poetry. The young bride feels inadequate, 'Stupid in candlelight', 'seeing nothing'. Her new husband returns, saying 'the horses were restless'. She feels compassion for all living things that are not experiencing the happiness 'I had'.

The **second section** of the poem is an **interior monologue** by the bride as she observes the destruction caused by the 'wind's blowing'. 'All's ravelled under the sun': the debris of the storm is clear for everyone to see. Both the world and the bride have been changed by some huge elemental force. She is now a woman of responsibilities. She recognises the practicalities of farming. There is no honeymoon. 'He has gone to look at the floods' and she has gone to feed the chickens. The detail of her 'chipped pail' lends a human, imperfect note to the scene. She sets the pail down and begins to reflect ('stare').

Now, unlike last night, she is seeing. The wind, this powerful force of nature, was a predator, 'Hunting through clouds and forests' (**line 16**). The violent force of the wind is contained in the verb 'thrashing'. Does this have connotations of the violent passion of love? Again, an ordinary sight, clothes hanging on a washing line ('My apron and the hanging cloths on the line'), makes the poem accessible to all, academic and non-academic. There is no exclusive reference to classical mythology, but the common stuff of life. The **poem concludes with three questions**. The young woman wonders if she will survive the 'joy my actions turn on'. The compound word 'bodying-forth' and the verb 'borne' suggest pregnancy. The simile 'like a thread/Carrying beads' implies praying and the sacredness of the holy state of matrimony. Or this thread could refer to a necklace, a gift or symbol of love given between the young couple.

The second question poses the problem of sleep: 'Shall I be let to sleep' (**line 20**). The bride now feels that every day is 'perpetual morning', as life seems full of exciting possibilities, so it is impossible to rest. She feels so blessed by love that she has almost been made immortal: 'Can even death dry up' her joy? She believes that these 'new delighted lakes' can never be 'dry', even though the wind dries water from the land. She is compelled to make a sign, 'conclude/Our kneeling as cattle'. The **biblical tones** of the compound word 'all-generous' show an optimistic view that joy can outlive death.

Larkin wanted his readers to experience his poetry and say, 'I've never thought of it that way before, but that's how it is.' He believed poetry should come from personal experience. Larkin disliked the idea that poetry should come from other poems. He was opposed to Modernism, a poetry movement that is allusory and inaccessible to the ordinary person. It is interesting to note that this poem takes **a private, human experience and links it with nature**. Does this lend a note of danger to the experience of young, passionate love? Parallel to the poem, dramatic changes were taking place in English society. The Second World War had just ended, followed by the depression of the 1950s, the affluence and student unrest of the 1960s and the emergence of socialism and multiculturalism. This rural English experience of young love is preserved by Larkin, 'pickled as it were in verse', despite all the changes taking place.

ANALYSIS

Larkin believed that poetry should help us 'enjoy and endure'. Do you agree or disagree with this statement? Support your view with references from the poem.

Sample Paragraph

I believe that this poem helps us enjoy life, thanks to the beautiful, passionate narrative of this young bride. The wind represents change and dynamism in the natural world, as well as in the world of the young woman. It is 'sacred', a 'high wind', which both scatters and cleans, 'All's ravelled under the sun by the wind's blowing'. The human details of ordinary life shine under the craftsmanship of Larkin, 'chipped pail', 'stable door ... banging, again and again', 'hanging cloths on the line'. The ordinary, somewhat irksome chores which we all must endure become the basis of passionate poetry as the young bride wonders whether all this 'joy of action' can be 'borne'. We are elevated, as the woman is, by the optimistic, mystical vision that love cannot be dimmed by death. We kneel at the 'all-generous waters'. Larkin has helped us to enjoy and endure.

Examiner's Comment

This short paragraph addresses both aspects of the question (enjoy and endure). The response shows a real appreciation of Larkin's poetic beliefs. More detailed analysis and comment on the key quotations would have resulted in a higher grade. However, the style throughout is assured and vocabulary and expression are very good. Grade B.

CLASS/HOMEWORK EXERCISES

1. Write a paragraph on how effectively Larkin uses metaphors to communicate his message in this poem. Support your answer with reference to the text.

2. Copy the table below into your own notes and fill in critical comments about the last two quotations.

Key Quotes

And my wedding-night was the night of the high wind	The reflective tone and adjective 'high' suggest that the wind is a sacred force for change.
All is the wind/Hunting through clouds and forests	The entire scene is pervaded by the personification of the wind as a hunter, on the lookout for prey.
this bodying-forth by wind/ Of joy my actions turn on	This terse line conveys the swelling motion of the wind enmeshed in the happiness experienced by the young bride.
Now this perpetual morning shares my bed	
Our kneeling as cattle by all-generous waters	

2 AT GRASS

The eye can hardly pick them out
From the cold shade they shelter in,
Till wind distresses tail and mane;
Then one crops grass, and moves about
– The other seeming to look on –   5
And stands anonymous again.

Yet fifteen years ago, perhaps
Two dozen distances sufficed
To fable them: faint afternoons
Of Cups and Stakes and Handicaps,   10
Whereby their names were artificed
To inlay faded, classic Junes –

Silks at the start: against the sky
Numbers and parasols: outside,
Squadrons of empty cars, and heat,   15
And littered grass: then the long cry
Hanging unhushed till it subside
To stop-press columns on the street.

Do memories plague their ears like flies?
They shake their heads. Dusk brims the shadows.   20
Summer by summer all stole away,
The starting-gates, the crowds and cries –
All but the unmolesting meadows.
Almanacked, their names live; they

Have slipped their names, and stand at ease,   25
Or gallop for what must be joy,
And not a fieldglass sees them home,
Or curious stop-watch prophesies:
Only the groom, and the groom's boy,
With bridles in the evening come.   30

'The starting-gates, the crowds and cries'

GLOSSARY

At Grass: a reference to the retirement of old racehorses.

3   *mane*: the hair on the back of a horse's neck.

4   *crops*: eats, chews.

8   *Two dozen distances sufficed*: 24 races were enough.

9   *To fable*: to make famous.

10   *Cups and Stakes and Handicaps*: various types of horse races.

11   *artificed*: displayed (on trophies, etc.).

12   *inlay*: ornamental fabric.

12   *classic*: traditional, important June races.

13   *Silks*: shirts ('colours') worn by jockeys.

14   *Numbers*: betting numbers displayed by bookies.

14   *parasols*: ladies' umbrellas.

15   *Squadrons*: long lines (of parked cars).

18   *stop-press*: news update (latest racing results).

19   *plague*: irritate.

23   *unmolesting*: harmless, gentle.

24   *Almanacked*: listed in the racing records.

29   *groom*: worker who looks after the horses.

30   *bridles*: restraints placed on the heads of horses.

EXPLORATIONS

1. Using close reference to the text, describe the atmosphere/mood in the opening stanza.

2. How does Larkin convey the excitement of the racecourse in stanza three? Refer to the text in your answer.

3. Choose two memorable images from the poem and briefly explain their effectiveness.

STUDY NOTES

'At Grass' was written in 1950 after the poet had seen a documentary film about a retired racehorse. Larkin, himself a lover of horses, saw them as exploited during their racing careers. This strikingly reflective poem, exploring the changes brought about by the passage of time, has been interpreted as a criticism of the passing fashion of celebrity and as a requiem for a bygone age.

Stanza one begins with a short description of two horses sheltering in the distance. Larkin remarks that 'The eye can hardly pick them out' before he has even explained what there is to pick out. It is only when a slight breeze 'distresses tail and mane' that the horses come to life. Even then, the 'cold shade' setting has a vague suggestion that these forgotten ('anonymous') animals are close to death. There is an **evocative visual quality** within these early lines and a mood of wistful sadness dominates.

In contrast to this feeling of stillness, Larkin begins to imagine the racehorses in their prime 'fifteen years ago'. The nostalgic flashback in the **second and third stanzas** recalls their triumphs in 'Cups and Stakes and Handicaps', enough 'To fable them' and ensure their reputation in racing history. The thrill and glamour of 'classic Junes' is recreated through vibrant images of the jockeys' colours ('Silks') and the 'Numbers and parasols'. **Cinematic details** ('empty cars', 'littered grass') and the excited cheering ('the long cry') of the crowds all convey the joy of unforgettable race meetings.

Stanza four returns to the present as Larkin considers the conscious experiences of the horses themselves. The line 'They shake their heads' is playfully ambiguous, both a negative response to the earlier question ('Do memories plague their ears like flies?') and an actual movement which horses carry out naturally. Larkin's **elegant imagery** communicates the subtle advance of time: 'Summer by summer' as 'Dusk brims the shadows'. There is a strong sense that at the end of their lives, these once-famous horses deserve to take their ease in 'unmolesting meadows'. Interestingly, the most remarkable verbs in the poem – 'fabled', 'artificed', 'inlay', 'Almanacked' – are all concerned with the way people have seen and recorded these horses. They have become racecourse stories, names engraved into trophies and recorded in official histories.

The dignified language and slow rhythm of **stanza five** suggest both the tranquil freedom of these retired horses and the reality that they are nearing the end of their long lives. For the moment, though, they 'gallop for what must be joy' – a typical Larkin comment which throws doubt onto an assertion even while in the process of making it. The poem ends on a consolatory note. Now that the horses have 'slipped their names' and are no longer chasing fame or glory, they can 'stand at ease', enjoying the peace and quiet. Broad assonant effects emphasise their sense of quiet fulfilment: 'Only the groom, and the groom's boy,/With bridles in the evening come'. The inverted syntax and mellow tone add to the sense of finality. In completing the natural cycle of their lives, Larkin's racehorses offer a model for the human condition of youth, achievement and old age. Characteristically, the development of thought in the poem moves from observation to reflection, leaving us to appreciate the **blend of celebration and sadness** that mark this beautiful poem.

ANALYSIS

Using close reference to the text, comment on the poet's use of contrast in 'At Grass'.

Sample Paragraph

Philip Larkin uses two distinct settings in 'At Grass'. This is a very effective device to highlight the past and present lives of the racehorses. At the start of the poem, he describes two horses grazing – but they are 'anonymous'. There is a dreamy, timeless feeling to the picture Larkin paints. I thought that even the title of the poem was similar to the title used of a painting of racehorses. There is very little movement involved in the description of the retired horses – in complete contrast with the middle section of the poem, where Larkin brings us back to their glory days, winning 'Cups, Stakes and Handicaps'. The hustle and bustle of the busy racetracks is seen in the colourful images and lively rhythms – 'Silks at the start against the blue sky'. The scene is noisy, with race goers shouting and reporters rushing to write their 'stop-press columns' after the winners are announced. The two contrasting atmospheres are very different. At the end of the poem, we see the two old horses 'stand at ease' – even the gentle sibilant sounds are in contrast with the hectic description of 'littered grass' at the race meetings. The tone in the last lines of the poem as the grooms 'in the late evening come' is gentle and subdued, highlighting the final days of these champion horses. Overall, Larkin uses contrasts very effectively to show the dramatic changes in the lives of these great horses, who have swapped their past glory for a well-earned rest.

Examiner's Comment

This is a well-sustained and focused response that examines the poet's use of contrasting settings, moods and sound effects in some detail. The commentary is informed and interesting. However, the answer is less successful due to the inaccurate quotations. A basic grade B.

CLASS/HOMEWORK EXERCISES

1. Describe the tone of the poem. Is it celebratory, sorrowful, resigned or realistic, or a combination of these? Refer to the text in your answer.

2. Copy the table below into your own notes and fill in critical comments about the last two quotations.

Key Quotes

From the cold shade they shelter in	The description of sheltering horses in the shadows suggests the inevitability of impending death.
Two dozen distances sufficed/ To fable them	Alliteration echoes the energy and triumph of these great horses in their prime.
Summer by summer all stole away	The passing of time is a central theme in the poem, evoked in the bittersweet sibilance and fluent rhythm of this memorable image.
Almanacked, their names live	
Only the groom, and the groom's boy,/With bridles in the evening come	

❸   CHURCH GOING

Once I am sure there's nothing going on
I step inside, letting the door thud shut.
Another church: matting, seats, and stone,
And little books; sprawlings of flowers, cut
For Sunday, brownish now; some brass and stuff   5
Up at the holy end; the small neat organ;
And a tense, musty, unignorable silence,
Brewed God knows how long. Hatless, I take off
My cycle-clips in awkward reverence,

Move forward, run my hand around the font.   10
From where I stand, the roof looks almost new –
Cleaned, or restored? Someone would know: I don't.
Mounting the lectern, I peruse a few
Hectoring large-scale verses, and pronounce
'Here endeth' much more loudly than I'd meant.   15
The echoes snigger briefly. Back at the door
I sign the book, donate an Irish sixpence,
Reflect the place was not worth stopping for.

Yet stop I did: in fact I often do,
And always end much at a loss like this,   20
Wondering what to look for; wondering, too,
When churches fall completely out of use
What we shall turn them into, if we shall keep
A few cathedrals chronically on show,
Their parchment, plate and pyx in locked cases,   25
And let the rest rent-free to rain and sheep.
Shall we avoid them as unlucky places?

Or, after dark, will dubious women come
To make their children touch a particular stone;
Pick simples for a cancer; or on some   30
Advised night see walking a dead one?
Power of some sort or other will go on
In games, in riddles, seemingly at random;
But superstition, like belief, must die,
And what remains when disbelief has gone?   35

Grass, weedy pavement, brambles, buttress, sky,
A shape less recognisable each week,
A purpose more obscure. I wonder who
Will be the last, the very last, to seek
This place for what it was; one of the crew   40
That tap and jot and know what rood-lofts were?
Some ruin-bibber, randy for antique,
Or Christmas-addict, counting on a whiff
Of gowns-and-bands and organ-pipes and myrrh?
Or will he be my representative,   45

Bored, uninformed, knowing the ghostly silt
Dispersed, yet tending to this cross of ground
Through suburb scrub because it held unspilt
So long and equably what since is found
Only in separation - marriage, and birth,   50
And death, and thoughts of these - for which was built
This special shell? For, though I've no idea
What this accoutred frowsty barn is worth,
It pleases me to stand in silence here;

A serious house on serious earth it is,   55
In whose blent air all our compulsions meet,
Are recognised, and robed as destinies.
And that much never can be obsolete,
Since someone will forever be surprising
A hunger in himself to be more serious,   60
And gravitating with it to this ground,
Which, he once heard, was proper to grow wise in,
If only that so many dead lie round.

'Which, he once heard, was proper
to grow wise in,/If only that so
many dead lie round'

GLOSSARY

9 *cycle-clips*: old-fashioned clips that fasten a cyclist's trouser leg.

10 *font*: stone bowl in a church used to store holy water.

13 *lectern*: a tall stand from which a speaker can read.

13 *peruse*: read carefully.

14 *Hectoring*: bullying, blustering.

15 *'Here endeth'*: Church of England services end each reading with the phrase 'Here endeth the lesson'.

24 *chronically*: lasting a long time; very badly.

25 *parchment*: animal skin formerly used for writing on.

25 *plate*: bowls, cups, etc. made of gold or silver and used for religious ceremonies.

25 *pyx*: container in which the blessed bread of the Eucharist is kept.

28 *dubious*: doubtful.

30 *simples*: medicinal herbs.

30 *cancer*: malignant growth.

31 *Advised*: recommended.

36 *buttress*: support for a wall.

41 *rood-lofts*: galleries in the shape of a cross.

42 *ruin-bibber*: someone fond of old buildings.

42 *randy*: excited.

44 *gowns-and-bands*: clerical dress.

44 *myrrh*: sweet-smelling resin used in incense at a religious ceremony.

46 *silt*: deposit left behind.

49 *equably*: calm and even-tempered.

53 *accoutred*: dressed; equipped.

53 *frowsty*: stale smelling; musty.

56 *blent*: blended, mixed.

56 *compulsions*: irresistible urges to do something.

58 *obsolete*: out of date.

61 *gravitating*: attracted towards.

EXPLORATIONS

1. What impression do you have of the speaker in the first two stanzas of this poem? Support your answer with reference to the text.

2. List two images that you consider to be spiritual in 'Church Going'. Comment on their effectiveness.

3. How does this poem change after the first two stanzas? What are the main considerations of the poet? Refer closely to the poem in your response.

STUDY NOTES

'Church Going' was written in 1954 as part of Larkin's poetry collection The Less Deceived. *He adopts his famous persona of the self-deprecating, observant, conversational outsider. Larkin said he felt the need to be on 'the periphery of things'. The title is a pun, suggesting both the attendance of religious ceremonies (church-going) and also suggesting that religious practice/religion itself was on the way out, passé. The inspiration for the poem came from an actual event experienced by Larkin when he stopped to look at a church while on a cycling trip.*

In the **first stanza**, Larkin is an interloper/intruder who only enters the church when he's sure it's empty ('nothing going on'). The run-on line movement mirrors the poet popping inside ('I step inside'). The onomatopoeic closing of the door echoes in 'thud shut'. We hear what is happening. A **jaded tone** of one who has seen and done it all before sounds from the phrase 'Another church'. He now gives us a general view of the church from floor to wall: matting, wooden seats, stone walls. He then closes in for a detailed view: 'little books', flowers that are 'brownish now'. This telling detail suggests something is not fresh; it's dying. Is this similar to church-going? Larkin felt strongly that when you go into church, you get a feeling that something is over, derelict.

He now becomes dismissive as he describes the sacred objects as 'some brass and stuff'. He says it is 'Up at the holy end'. He is indifferent rather than ignorant: 'I don't bother about that kind of thing,' he once declared. The atmosphere is 'tense', not serene; the church is 'musty', stale smelling. The **silence is all pervasive**, 'unignorable'. The atmosphere has been stewing or fermenting a long time, like tea or beer – only 'God knows how long'. This fact makes him anxious to show respect. He had already removed his hat, but now he cuts a slightly ridiculous figure as he removes his cycle-clips 'in awkward reverence'.

He moves around in the **second stanza**, like an uninformed tourist, randomly touching things ('run my hand around the font'). The use of the present tense in the first two stanzas gives an immediacy to the description. A telling question, 'Cleaned, or restored?', shows the poet's mind at work. It also shows that there is a community at work, and therefore continuity. The roof is being preserved, just as Larkin is preserving the church in his poem. Yet the dismissive, casual, **conversational tone** returns when he says that he thinks 'the place was not worth stopping for'.

A more formal, serious voice now is heard as the poet's inner self comes into focus. He begins to meditate in **stanza three** on the importance of churches ('wondering, too,/When churches fall completely out of use/What we shall turn them into'). This knowledgeable voice knows the ecclesiastical vocabulary: 'parchment', 'pyx'. In the future, these will no longer be used for ceremonies, but stored 'in locked cases'. Larkin was fond of the traditions of the Anglican Church, but now the old world is fading. He imagines the future of these churches as 'rent-free', worth nothing, housing only 'rain and sheep'. Here is a **desolate outlook**. The use of the plural first person pronoun 'we' suggests that Larkin thinks we will all be confronted with what to do with these large empty buildings. The negative view continues as the churches are described as 'unlucky places'.

In **stanza four**, superstition is overtaking belief. This is 'dark', 'dubious'; Larkin doesn't approve. However, he feels the power will remain ('Power of some sort'), and eventually, as always happens, nature will reclaim it: 'Grass ... brambles ... sky'. This landscape recalls the opening view of the interior of the church. Now, in Larkin's imaginings, it lies open to the elements. The long sentence shows the **ruminative mood** of the poet, as he wonders, in **stanza five**, who will be the last to seek out this place for what it once was, a dynamic church. He dismisses the learned academics ('ruin-bibber'), someone mad for old buildings.

In **stanza six**, Larkin wonders if his 'representative', 'Bored', will be one who understood the church's role in marking the great human landmarks of a life: birth, marriage and death. The poet is happy to be part of this space: 'It pleases me to stand in silence here'. In the **seventh stanza**, the **contemplative voice** states, 'A serious house on serious earth it is'. He realises he will be someone who is drawn to this place, as it is a place 'to grow wise in' as he experiences the essence of life, being alone ('dead lie around').

Larkin uses a traditional form of English poetry, a formal stanza pattern of seven nine-line stanzas. The rhythm is iambic pentameter, the traditional rhythm of English verse. The large, spacious form of the poem echoes the cavernous space of the church. The **regular rhyme scheme** punctuates this ordered but disappearing world. This poem is reminiscent of Shakespeare's sonnet recording the ruins of England's monasteries: 'Bare ruined choirs, where late the sweet birds sang'. Both poems are shot through with melancholy for a disappeared world.

ANALYSIS

After reading 'Church Going', do you feel a sense of disappointment and depression or a feeling of optimism? Support your view with references from the poem.

Sample Paragraph

I feel I have gained insight from this poem, as the poet, although he is dismissive in the first stanzas, when he flippantly remarks that the place was 'not worth stopping for', and that he donated an 'Irish sixpence' (inferior coinage?). Nevertheless, he feels that this place merits reverence, however 'awkward'. This place has a 'Power of some sort'. When his more serious side emerges, at the end of the poem, he acknowledges, rather like the Communists, that people need religion/belief, 'A hunger in himself'. We cannot exist totally on the level of animals, or in the shallow state of the cynical, critical sneer. He uses the word, 'gravitating', as if he/we are pulled by an irresistible force 'to this ground'. He has been told, 'he once heard', that there is a 'proper' place 'to grow wise in'. 'If only that so many dead lie round' shows us that this place marks the reality and finality of life-death. We live our lives in the shadow of our death, our loved ones' deaths, and the death of all living things. The poem has given me a real insight into the pessimistic reality of human affairs.

Examiner's Comment

This general response does not focus directly on the question. While expression and vocabulary are good, a treatment of stylistic effects, such as tone, would have improved the answer. Grade C.

CLASS/HOMEWORK EXERCISES

1. Larkin stated that the 'impulse to preserve lies at the bottom of all art'. What is Larkin trying to preserve in the poem 'Church Going'? In your opinion, does he succeed or fail? Support your answer with reference to the text.

2. Copy the table below into your own notes and fill in critical comments about the last two quotations.

Key Quotes

Brewed God knows how long	The metaphor of brewing emphatically underlines the length of time the church has been here.
Yet stop I did: in fact I often do	The casual tone of this line shows the first voice of the poem, that of the disinterested tourist.
Pick simples for a cancer	Superstition will replace belief as the churches die. People are looking for miracle cures for their ailments.
knowing the ghostly silt/ Dispersed	
In whose blent air all our compulsions meet	

❹ AN ARUNDEL TOMB

Side by side, their faces blurred,
The earl and countess lie in stone,
Their proper habits vaguely shown
As jointed armour, stiffened pleat,
And that faint hint of the absurd –   5
The little dogs under their feet.

Such plainness of the pre-baroque
Hardly involves the eye, until
It meets his left-hand gauntlet, still
Clasped empty in the other; and   10
One sees, with a sharp tender shock,
His hand withdrawn, holding her hand.

They would not think to lie so long.
Such faithfulness in effigy
Was just a detail friends would see: 15
A sculptor's sweet commissioned grace
Thrown off in helping to prolong
The Latin names around the base.

They would not guess how early in
Their supine stationary voyage   20
The air would change to soundless damage,
Turn the old tenantry away;
How soon succeeding eyes begin
To look, not read. Rigidly they

Persisted, linked, through lengths and breadths   25
Of time. Snow fell, undated. Light
Each summer thronged the glass. A bright
Litter of birdcalls strewed the same
Bone-riddled ground. And up the paths
The endless altered people came,   30

Washing at their identity.
Now, helpless in the hollow of
An unarmorial age, a trough

Of smoke in slow suspended skeins
Above their scrap of history,   35
Only an attitude remains:

Time has transfigured them into
Untruth. The stone fidelity
They hardly meant has come to be
Their final blazon, and to prove   40
Our almost-instinct almost true:
What will survive of us is love.

'What will survive of us is love'

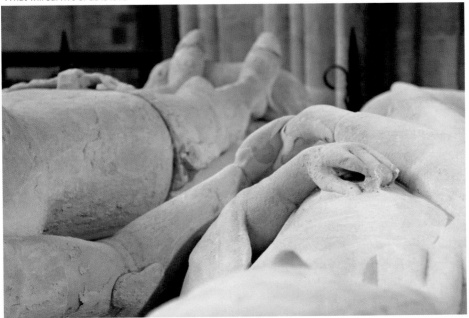

GLOSSARY

Title: The title refers to a 14th-century monument of the Earl of Arundel and his wife in Chichester Cathedral, West Sussex, England.

3   *proper habits*: appropriate burial clothes.
4   *pleat*: fold.
7   *pre-baroque*: plain, simple design (before the elaborate 17th-century baroque style).
9   *gauntlet*: glove.
14 *effigy*: figure, sculpted likeness.
20 *supine*: lying down.

22 *tenantry*: tenants living on a landlord's estate.
27 *thronged*: crowded.
28 *strewed*: spread across.
29 *Bone-riddled ground*: buried human remains.
33 *unarmorial*: unheroic.
33 *trough*: channel.
34 *skeins*: threads or coils (of smoke).
37 *transfigured*: transformed.
40 *blazon*: sign, symbol.

EXPLORATIONS

1. How would you describe the tone in the first stanza? Reverential? Intrigued? Superior?

2. Select two illustrations from the poem to show Larkin's keen eye for detail. Comment briefly on the effectiveness of each example.

3. Write a short personal response to this poem, highlighting the impact it made on you.

STUDY NOTES

'An Arundel Tomb' was written in 1956 after Larkin had visited Chichester Cathedral. He said that the effigies were unlike any he had ever seen before and that he found them 'extremely affecting'. The poem can be viewed in many ways – as a meditation on love and death, as a tribute to the power of art or even as a celebration of English history. Despite differences of interpretation, 'An Arundel Tomb' has always been a favourite of Larkin readers. It was read aloud at his memorial service held in London's Westminster Abbey in 1986.

In **stanza one**, we are immediately located before the stone statue of the Earl and Countess of Arundel. Larkin's description of the couple seems detached, the tone one of **ironic hesitation**. The couple's 'blurred' faces (eroded by time) are indistinct. Indeed, the earl's outdated armour and the 'little dogs under their feet' add a ludicrous dimension (a 'faint hint of the absurd') to the commemorative monument.

The poet continues to criticise the 'plainness' of the lifeless sculpture in **stanza two**. It is etched in an unappealingly dull 'pre-baroque' style. But he is suddenly taken by one particular detail. The earl's left hand has been withdrawn from its 'gauntlet' and is 'holding her hand'. This affectionate gesture between husband and wife has an immediate impact on Larkin – 'a sharp tender shock'. The image of 'His hand withdrawn, holding her hand' stops the poet in his tracks. We can sense Larkin's concentration in the **slow rhythm** and emphatic 'h' alliteration of **line 12**. Do the joined hands represent the triumph of love over time, or is that just wishful thinking?

In **stanza three**, Larkin reflects on the relationship between the earl and countess. **Line 13** is puzzling: 'They would not think to lie so long'. Is this an obvious reference to the couple's long rest in the tomb? Or have they failed to find a heavenly afterlife? Might there be a **pun on the word 'lie'**? Perhaps the loving hand-holding is an untrue representation? Larkin wonders if the sculptor invented this demonstrative touch to make the statue more interesting to the general public and to 'prolong' the earl's family name long after the Latin inscription would be understood.

Stanzas four and five focus particularly on the passing of time, a central theme in the poem. The earl and countess could not have imagined the effects of the damp cathedral air ('soundless damage') eroding their tomb. Great social change has also happened over the centuries; 'the old tenantry' and the use of Latin – and the importance of Christianity, presumably – have disappeared. Larkin's strikingly **sensory images** evoke the changing seasons: 'Snow fell, undated. Light/Each summer thronged the glass'. The signs of natural vitality and rejuvenation are in stark contrast to the 'Bone-riddled ground' over which modern-day visitors to the cathedral ('endless altered people') arrive to view the monument.

The countless tourists to the medieval couple's tomb have long been 'Washing at their identity' (**stanza six**). There is a suggestion of erosion (the earl and countess are no longer understood as they once were) and purification (the couple are idealised as romantic and artistic symbols). Larkin asserts that the effigies are 'helpless' in this 'unarmorial age'. The poet's **cynical tone** reflects his distaste for the vulgarity and ignorance around him. Today's generation has a shallow appreciation of love – 'Only an attitude remains'.

This idea is developed in **stanza seven**, where Larkin questions the public's misguided response to the statue. For him, the sentimental yearning to see the couple's 'fidelity' as a triumph of love over death is an 'Untruth', and something the earl and countess probably never intended. Nonetheless, the instinctual desire for enduring love may well be another admirable aspect of human behaviour. Many commentators view the final lines ('Our almost-instinct almost true:/What will survive of us is love') as a positive affirmation by Larkin. Others see in it a typically despondent statement of the opposite (namely, self-deluding hope in the face of reality). Like the rest of the poem, the ending is **typically paradoxical** and thought provoking, allowing us to decide for ourselves about Larkin's attitude concerning the power of love to transcend time.

ANALYSIS

Comment on Larkin's use of ambiguous language in 'An Arundel Tomb'.

Sample Paragraph

Philip Larkin's poem 'An Arundel Tomb' is noted for its ambiguity. The opening description of the rigid figures carved in stone is both sympathetic and satirical at the same time. Their expressions are described as 'blurred', suggesting that they are faceless and unreal. Larkin adds that there are 'little dogs under their feet'. He finds this ridiculous and might be hinting that this privileged earl and countess were used to being spoiled and pampered. On the other hand, the image makes the elderly pair seem human. The word 'lie' is used a number of times. The couple 'lie in stone'. This might simply refer to the position of the bodies, but it could also mean that they are sending out a false message that they are a loving couple whose love has conquered death. Yet the earl and his wife 'would not think to lie so long', suggesting that they never planned to give this false impression. Although Larkin's ambivalent approach engaged my interest in the poem, I am still not exactly sure about his own point of view as to the true relationship between the earl and countess. However, the effect of his wordplay is to produce a poem which is very rich and suggestive in meaning, encouraging us to think twice before judging by appearances.

Examiner's Comment

A well-illustrated personal response that examines Larkin's subtle use of language at various points in the poem. The expression throughout the paragraph is clear and varied. Grade-A standard.

CLASS/HOMEWORK EXERCISES

1. Outline the main theme presented in 'An Arundel Tomb'. In your answer, trace the way the poet develops his ideas during the course of the poem.

2. Copy the table below into your own notes and fill in critical comments about the last two quotations.

Key Quotes

The earl and countess lie in stone	The image conveys a sense of looking directly at the monument. Is the word 'lie' used ambiguously to suggest the illusion of the couple's love?
Their supine stationary voyage	Contrasting references to inactivity and action (death and life) are a distinctive feature of the poem.
A bright/Litter of birdcalls	Slender vowels and alliteration add to the vitality of this memorable image.
Washing at their identity	
What will survive of us is love	

5 THE WHITSUN WEDDINGS

That Whitsun, I was late getting away:
    Not till about
One-twenty on the sunlit Saturday
Did my three-quarters-empty train pull out,
All windows down, all cushions hot, all sense   5
Of being in a hurry gone. We ran
Behind the backs of houses, crossed a street
Of blinding windscreens, smelt the fish-dock; thence
The river's level drifting breadth began,
Where sky and Lincolnshire and water meet.   10

All afternoon, through the tall heat that slept
    For miles inland,
A slow and stopping curve southwards we kept.
Wide farms went by, short-shadowed cattle, and
Canals with floatings of industrial froth;   15
A hothouse flashed uniquely: hedges dipped
And rose: and now and then a smell of grass
Displaced the reek of buttoned carriage-cloth
Until the next town, new and nondescript,
Approached with acres of dismantled cars.   20

At first, I didn't notice what a noise
    The weddings made
Each station that we stopped at: sun destroys
The interest of what's happening in the shade,
And down the long cool platforms whoops and skirls   25
I took for porters larking with the mails,
And went on reading. Once we started, though,
We passed them, grinning and pomaded, girls
In parodies of fashion, heels and veils,
All posed irresolutely, watching us go,   30

As if out on the end of an event
    Waving goodbye
To something that survived it. Struck, I leant
More promptly out next time, more curiously,
And saw it all again in different terms: 35

The fathers with broad belts under their suits
And seamy foreheads; mothers loud and fat;
An uncle shouting smut; and then the perms,
The nylon gloves and jewellery-substitutes,
The lemons, mauves, and olive-ochres that   40

Marked off the girls unreally from the rest.
        Yes, from cafés
And banquet-halls up yards, and bunting-dressed
Coach-party annexes, the wedding-days
Were coming to an end. All down the line   45
Fresh couples climbed aboard: the rest stood round;
The last confetti and advice were thrown,
And, as we moved, each face seemed to define
Just what it saw departing: children frowned
At something dull; fathers had never known   50

Success so huge and wholly farcical;
        The women shared
The secret like a happy funeral;
While girls, gripping their handbags tighter, stared
At a religious wounding. Free at last,   55
And loaded with the sum of all they saw,
We hurried towards London, shuffling gouts of steam.
Now fields were building-plots, and poplars cast
Long shadows over major roads, and for
Some fifty minutes, that in time would seem   60

Just long enough to settle hats and say
        I nearly died,
A dozen marriages got under way.
They watched the landscape, sitting side by side
– An Odeon went past, a cooling tower,   65
And someone running up to bowl – and none
Thought of the others they would never meet
Or how their lives would all contain this hour.
I thought of London spread out in the sun,
Its postal districts packed like squares of wheat: 70

There we were aimed. And as we raced across
    Bright knots of rail
Past standing Pullmans, walls of blackened moss
Came close, and it was nearly done, this frail
Travelling coincidence; and what it held   75
Stood ready to be loosed with all the power
That being changed can give. We slowed again,
And as the tightened brakes took hold, there swelled
A sense of falling, like an arrow-shower
Sent out of sight, somewhere becoming rain.   80

'now and then a smell of grass'

GLOSSARY

Title: Whit (Pentecost) Sunday, the seventh after Easter, was a popular time for weddings.

19 *nondescript*: ordinary.
25 *skirls*: high-pitched cries.
26 *larking*: joking, carrying on.
28 *pomaded*: perfumed.
29 *parodies*: imitations.
30 *irresolutely*: hesitantly.
37 *seamy*: lined.
38 *smut*: rude or suggestive comments.

38 *perms*: waved hairstyles popular at the time.
40 *olive-ochres*: green and gold colours.
41 *unreally*: falsely.
44 *annexes*: reserved areas.
57 *gouts*: great spurts.
65 *Odeon*: popular cinema name.
73 *Pullmans*: luxury rail carriages (sleeping cars).
79 *arrow-shower*: short outburst of rain.

EXPLORATIONS

1. What is Larkin's attitude to the wedding parties that he describes in stanzas three and four? Refer to the text in your answer.

2. Select two visual images from the poem to show Larkin's eye for observational detail. Comment briefly on the effectiveness of each example.

3. Write a short personal response to 'The Whitsun Weddings', highlighting the impact it made on you.

STUDY NOTES

Larkin began writing 'The Whitsun Weddings' in 1957, and spent over a year drafting it. He said, 'You couldn't be on that train without feeling the young lives all starting off, and that just for a moment you were touching them. Doncaster, Retford, Grantham, Newark, Peterborough, and at every station more wedding parties. It was wonderful, a marvellous afternoon.' While the poem is lengthy by Larkin's standards, it moves typically from specific observation to an insightful reflection of love and marriage.

The poem's positive **title** immediately suggests celebration. Larkin's personal narrative makes use of everyday colloquial speech ('I was late getting away') to introduce this seemingly ordinary account of his afternoon journey from Hull to London. The **opening lines** of **stanza one** build to a steady rhythm, like a train leaving a railway station. At first, the poet's senses are engaged but not fully absorbed in his surroundings. However, his language ('The river's level drifting breadth') conveys the numbing drowsiness of a warm summer day. Larkin's characteristic eye for detail evokes the **claustrophobic atmosphere** inside the carriage: 'All windows down, all cushions hot'. The panoramic picture of the outside view 'Where sky and Lincolnshire and water meet' reveals his appreciation of nature and an enthusiasm for the English landscape.

Although the poet seems somewhat removed from the rest of society, his sense of place and expressive description continue into **stanza two**: 'Wide farms went by, short-shadowed cattle'. The June weather is personified ('the tall heat that slept'), adding to an already oppressive mood. Occasional run-through phrasing ('hedges dipped/And rose') echoes the movement of the train on its 'curve southwards'. Always a realist, Larkin includes a number of **unappealing images** associated with the industrial age: 'floatings of industrial froth' and 'acres of dismantled cars'. This convincing sense of the familiar is characteristic of a poet who is known for vividly recording life in post-war England.

Stanza three focuses on the various wedding groups arriving on the station platforms. Larkin gradually realises that the 'whoops and skirls' he hears on the platforms are the animated voices of 'grinning and pomaded' girls who are seeing off the honeymooners. The **poet's tone wavers** between derision of the guests' style ('parodies of fashion') and admiration of their glamorous 'heels and veils'.

Despite his ironic detachment, Larkin cannot help but be increasingly attracted ('more curiously') to the **small dramas** taking place around him. He observes the various groups – 'fathers with broad belts under their suits', 'mothers loud and fat'. For much of **stanza four**, his attitude is condescending, referring to one vulgar uncle 'shouting smut'. He is equally disdainful of the clothes on show ('lemons, mauves and olive-ochres') and the cheap 'jewellery-substitutes'.

The poet's apparent class superiority is also evident in **stanza five** as he begins to wonder about the tawdry wedding receptions that have been taking place in 'cafés' and 'banquet-halls up yards'. Despite all this derision, Larkin detects a more important undertone beneath the brash celebrations. All the newlywed couples are about to leave their familiar lives behind. The **inherent sadness** and inevitability of the moment are summed up as 'The last confetti and advice were thrown'. Meanwhile, real life resumes for the children after the enjoyment of the day, while proud fathers feel relieved that all the fuss is over. For Larkin himself, however, the occasion has brought him closer to the people he has been observing and criticising.

Stanza six marks a change in the poet's outlook. More sensitive than before, he imagines how the older, more realistic wives view married life pragmatically as 'a happy funeral', likely to bring both joy and sorrow. This 'secret' is not yet understood by the impressionable younger girls carefully 'gripping their handbags tighter' and who presumably have more romantic notions about marriage. Larkin sees them as facing 'a religious wounding', a typically ambiguous comment, suggesting both the wedding ritual and the likely hurt that lies ahead. From this moment, the poet associates himself more closely with the newlywed couples aboard the train ('Free at last'). He is no longer merely a detached observer as 'We hurried towards London'. The poem's **rhythm gathers pace**, perhaps reflecting his growing mood of optimism.

The lines maintain their momentum in **stanza seven** as Larkin's fellow-passengers relive the excitement of the day ('I nearly died'). The train journey has let the poet realise that the people he has seen are all interconnected ('their lives would all contain this hour'). This is coupled with the poignant understanding that it is only Larkin himself who is conscious of this fact ('none/Thought of the others they would never meet'). This overview of how the random lives of individuals form a greater pattern is teased out further as he uses an **inventive rural simile** to describe London's numerous 'postal districts packed like squares of wheat'.

At the start of **stanza eight**, there is little doubt that Larkin is aware of the full significance of this weekend outing. The 'dozen marriages' have made a lasting impact on the poet. As the train arrives at its destination, he reflects on 'this frail/Travelling coincidence'. Is he simply saying that all of life can be viewed as a journey where we meet people by chance, and that some of these encounters have the power to change us? The **last lines** reach a high point 'as the tightened brakes took hold' and the poem ends on a **dramatic note** ('A sense of falling'), suggesting both danger and adventure. The final image of the distant 'arrow-shower ... becoming rain' is an exciting one, hinting at romance, beauty and even sadness. Elusive to the end, Larkin's poem invites us to consider the wonderful experience of life in all its richness.

ANALYSIS

It has been said that Philip Larkin's poetry is gloomy and pessimistic. In your opinion, is this true of 'The Whitsun Weddings'? Refer to the poem in your answer.

Sample Paragraph

Larkin is more of a realistic poet than a pessimistic one. In my opinion, he celebrated traditional English life in 'The Whitsun Weddings'. He has a love for the English landscape. Even the fish-dock in Hull get his attention. His description of the horizon 'where the sky over Lincolnshire and the water meet' is evidence of his love of his native land. He seems obsessed by the young wedding couples and their families when he sees them at the rail stations. He might be poking fun at them here and there, but it is all good-natured, never mean. Larkin laughs at the 'nylon gloves and the jewellery substitutes' and at the 'uncle shouting out smut' at the honeymooners. This is all very good-natured. And certainly not gloomy. I think the speaking tone he uses shows that he admires these happy wedding guests. He's almost envious of their enjoyment. Philip hears the 'whoops' of the 'mothers loud and very fat', but he seems to be just smiling at their sense of fun. Not that Larkin is a complete bundle of laughs. There are some serious bits, of course. However, he is just being real when he describes the secret comments of the experienced wives who see married life as 'a happy funeral'. Overall, I think Larkin is upbeat and celebrates working-class life.

Examiner's Comment

While this lively paragraph makes a reasonable attempt to address the question in a focused way, some points lack development and the expression isn't always controlled. Some of the quotations are also incorrect. Grade-C standard.

CLASS/HOMEWORK EXERCISES

1. It has been said of Larkin that he observes 'ordinary people doing ordinary things'. To what extent do you agree with this statement in light of your reading of 'The Whitsun Weddings'?

2. Copy the table below into your own notes and fill in critical comments about the last two quotations.

Key Quotes

That Whitsun, I was late getting away	From the outset, Larkin's colloquial style and personal narrative approach draw in the reader.
I leant/More promptly out next time	The image illustrates the poet's increasing fascination with the lives of the wedding parties.
The women shared/The secret like a happy funeral	Larkin contrasts different reactions to the newlyweds. Does the realism of the older women reflect his own sceptical attitude towards marriage?
and none/Thought of the others they would never meet	
like an arrow-shower/Sent out of sight, somewhere becoming rain	

6   ## MCMXIV

Those long uneven lines
Standing as patiently
As if they were stretched outside
The Oval or Villa Park,
The crowns of hats, the sun   5
On moustached archaic faces
Grinning as if it were all
An August Bank Holiday lark;

And the shut shops, the bleached
Established names on the sunblinds,   10
The farthings and sovereigns,
And dark-clothed children at play
Called after kings and queens,
The tin advertisements
For cocoa and twist, and the pubs   15
Wide open all day;

And the countryside not caring:
The place names all hazed over
With flowering grasses, and fields
Shadowing Domesday lines   20
Under wheat's restless silence;
The differently-dressed servants
With tiny rooms in huge houses,
The dust behind limousines;

Never such innocence,   25
Never before or since,
As changed itself to past
Without a word – the men
Leaving the gardens tidy,
The thousands of marriages   30
Lasting a little while longer:
Never such innocence again.

'Those long uneven lines'

GLOSSARY

Title: The title refers to the Roman numerals for 1914, the year that World War I began. It became known as the Great War, a landmark event in the 20th century.

4 *The Oval:* famous cricket ground near London.

4 *Villa Park:* Birmingham home ground of Aston Villa football club.

6 *archaic:* dated, old-fashioned.

8 *lark:* celebration, spree.

11 *farthings and sovereigns:* currency used at the time. The copper farthing was just a quarter of a penny, while the gold sovereign coin was worth £1.

15 *twist:* probably refers to a small piece of tobacco.

20 *Domesday:* medieval spelling of Doomsday (or Judgement Day); in 1086, William the Conqueror compiled a record of English land ownership in the Domesday Book.

24 *limousines:* luxury cars.

EXPLORATIONS

1. Suggest a reason to explain why the poet chose to write the title in Roman numerals. (Where else might the letters MCMXIV be seen?)

2. In your opinion, is Larkin's view of the past accurate and realistic or is it sentimental and idealised? Refer to the text in your answer.

3. What do you think is meant by the final line, 'Never such innocence again'? Briefly explain your answer.

STUDY NOTES

This elegiac poem, written in 1960, has often been read as a nostalgic account of a vanished English way of life. The Roman numerals of the title evoke war memorials and the detailed descriptions seem to suggest old photographs. The whole poem consists of one long sentence, giving a sense of timelessness and connecting readers with the men lining up for army service.

Larkin's meditation begins with a description of an old photograph of 'uneven lines' of British volunteers outside an army recruiting office at the start of World War I. In **stanza one**, the poet observes that the men are queuing happily, as if for a game of cricket or football. The **tragic irony** of their fate is suggested by the image of the sun shining on their 'moustached archaic faces' and their carefree expressions, 'Grinning' as if it was all just a 'lark'. Larkin's tone seems unclear. Does he admire the men's idealism and courage or is there a sense that these raw recruits are naïvely seeking adventure?

The holiday atmosphere continues in **stanza two** with a wistful celebration of pre-war English life. Larkin lists some of the hallmarks of a bygone era: 'farthings and sovereigns', 'children at play', 'cocoa and twist'. Trusted shops ('Established names') and public houses ('Wide open all day') add to this **relaxed feeling** of security. Overall, this idealised image of a long-lost England is one of innocence, freedom and stability.

The poet swaps the familiar town setting for the open countryside in **stanza three**. At first, the mood seems untroubled ('not caring'). The alliterative effect and soft sibilant sounds of 'flowering grasses, and fields' evoke England's green and pleasant land. But the positive mood is suddenly overshadowed by the reference to 'Domesday lines' – a chilling echo of the earlier 'uneven lines' of men whose lives are likely to end on the battlefield. The reality of mass war graves is further stressed by the unsettling image of the 'wheat's restless silence'. Larkin's **tone becomes increasingly critical** as he focuses on the class divisions ('differently-dressed servants') prevalent within English society. Images of 'tiny rooms in huge houses' and 'dust behind limousines' suggest that social inequality was hidden away hypocritically.

The powerfully emotive force of **stanza four** emphasises the passing of an innocent age: 'Never before or since'. Purposeful rhythm and repetition ('never' is used three times) reflect Larkin's shocking realisation that the war would mark a turning point in our understanding of man's inhumanity to man. The compelling image of countless naïve volunteers leaving their homes, unaware that their marriages would only last 'a little while longer', is undeniably poignant. Rather than being a hymn of sentimental nostalgia, the **poem is dark** with the shadow of unexpected death and we are left with an enduring sense of the human tragedy involved.

ANALYSIS

In your view, how well does Larkin's poem 'MCMXIV' convey the innocence of pre-war England?

Sample Paragraph

Many of Philip Larkin's poems on our course, e.g. 'Ambulances' and 'The Whitsun Weddings', give me a good insight into the past and ordinary English life. This is certainly true of his war poem 'MCMXIV'. The poem begins with a series of images showing long lines of young men signing up to enlist in the war. They are 'Grinning' and have no notion of the horrors before them. Their innocence is very well seen in the way Larkin shows them standing 'patiently' as though they were waiting to enter a football stadium. There is a photographic quality to his descriptions. Life seems simple, carefree. The poet suggests this with images of bank holidays, familiar shop advertisements, young children playing and the pubs 'Wide open all day'. But there is another, darker side to pre-war society – social division. Larkin reminds us of the 'differently-dressed servants' who are slaving away in 'tiny rooms' for the upper classes. By the end of the poem, he suggests that the innocent pre-war years were about to be replaced with a horrifying time of conflict, mass destruction and death. I found the final verse very effective, repeating the awful truth – 'Never such innocence again'. The peace and harmony of the past would be shattered for all time.

Examiner's Comment

An assured personal response, focused throughout and well illustrated. Quotations are integrated effectively and the answer ranges widely over the positive and negative aspects of English life presented in the poem. Grade A.

> ## CLASS/HOMEWORK EXERCISES

1. How does Larkin establish the underlying sense of death that pervades the poem? Refer closely to the text in your answer.

2. Copy the table below into your own notes and fill in critical comments about the last two quotations.

Key Quotes

Those long uneven lines	The description of the enlisting men, as yet undisciplined, is in contrast to the grim reality of what lies ahead.
An August Bank Holiday lark	The archaic word 'lark' (meaning fun) exposes the innocence of the volunteers. How much sympathy does Larkin have for them?
Under wheat's restless silence	This subtle image foreshadows the mass war graves of Europe. Sibilance adds to the poignant mood.
tiny rooms in huge houses	
Never such innocence again	

⑦ AMBULANCES

Closed like confessionals, they thread
Loud noons of cities, giving back
None of the glances they absorb.
Light glossy grey, arms on a plaque,
They come to rest at any kerb: 5
All streets in time are visited.

Then children strewn on steps or road,
Or women coming from the shops
Past smells of different dinners, see
A wild white face that overtops   10
Red stretcher-blankets momently
As it is carried in and stowed,

And sense the solving emptiness
That lies just under all we do,
And for a second get it whole,   15
So permanent and blank and true.
The fastened doors recede. *Poor soul*,
They whisper at their own distress;

For borne away in deadened air
May go the sudden shut of loss   20
Round something nearly at an end,
And what cohered in it across
The years, the unique random blend
Of families and fashions, there

At last begin to loosen. Far   25
From the exchange of love to lie
Unreachable inside a room
The traffic parts to let go by
Brings closer what is left to come,
And dulls to distance all we are.   30

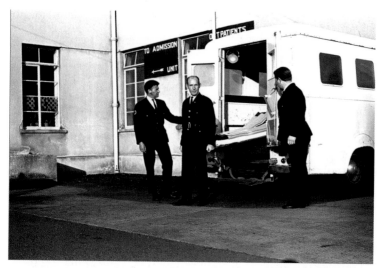

'They come to rest at any kerb'

GLOSSARY

1   *confessionals*: small, box-like rooms used by Catholic priests to hear confessions.
4   *plaque*: shiny metal sign on the side of the ambulance.
7   *strewn*: scattered around.

12   *stowed*: stored.
17   *recede*: move away.
22   *cohered*: brought together.

EXPLORATIONS

1. How does Larkin present the ambulances in stanza one? Are they mysterious? Comforting? Disturbing? Refer to the text in your answer.

2. From your reading of the second stanza, what evidence can you find of the poet's superb eye for interesting detail?

3. Critics have said that Philip Larkin's poems are more realistic than pessimistic. In your opinion, is this the case in 'Ambulances'? Give reasons for your answer.

'Ambulances' is a reflection on life and mortality, written in the early 1960s when an ambulance was usually associated with bad news. Larkin once remarked that every-thing he wrote had 'the consciousness of approaching death in the background'.

What do you think of when you see an ambulance? A serious road accident or some other emergency? Do you feel a sense of fear or of hope? People usually become apprehensive when they hear an ambulance siren. Are they genuinely concerned or are they just being inquisitive and voyeuristic?

From the outset of 'Ambulances', the **tone is uneasy**. There is an immediate sense of threat from these anonymous 'grey' vans that prowl around 'Loud noons of cities'. Even in the hustle and bustle of urban life, nobody escapes. Larkin sees these vehicles as symbols of death. An ambulance can take anyone away at any time. The patient is confined and vulnerable in much the same way as everyone is unable to escape dying: 'All streets in times are visited'. The dramatic **opening line** of the **first stanza** compares the ambulance van to a confessional – a place where people experience spiritual rebirth and make their peace with God. This religious image forces readers to face up to the inevitability of death. The poet personifies the vehicles, but they are as unresponsive as a corpse, 'giving back/None of the glances they absorb'. Bystanders glance nervously at passing ambulances, perhaps hoping deep down that their time has not yet come. However, the randomness of death is starkly emphasised by the line 'They come to rest at any kerb'. We are all powerless against the stark reality of our mortality.

Stanza two demonstrates Larkin's **keen eye for vivid detail** as he describes the reaction of onlookers when an ambulance arrives and disturbs a quiet neighbourhood. The street is suddenly transformed. Normal life stops for a moment as people consider the significance of what is happening. Simple, colloquial language illustrates the sharp contrast between everyday life ('children strewn on steps or road') and the hidden terror of death as the patient (now an unknown body described as 'it') is carried out to the ambulance. The colour images highlight the anguish of life-threatening illness ('A wild white face') and danger ('Red stretcher-blankets').

Larkin's tone is much more reflective in **stanza three**. This is typical of his writing. The crowd of spectators watching the small drama taking place 'sense the solving emptiness/That lies just under all we do'. They have been forced to confront the one underlying truth that all life ends with the mystery of dying. The poet himself was an atheist who could only believe in the 'emptiness' of oblivion after death. Unlike the earlier third-person description in the opening stanzas, the introduction of the pronoun 'we' gives the poem a universal significance. Death is our common fate and, in Larkin's belief, makes life meaningless. This seems to be the central moment of truth, or **epiphany**, in the poem – the morbid discovery that human existence is futile. Modern secular society avoids death. It is a taboo subject that we only think about when we are forced to.

For Larkin, all of our daily concerns – cooking, playing, etc. – are merely ways of filling time until death transports us to a state of 'permanent and blank' nothingness. As the ambulance pulls away, the poet suggests that people's whispered sympathy ('Poor soul') for the patient is really a selfish expression of 'their own distress'. Such irony is a common feature of Larkin's cynical observations of everyday life.

In the **final two stanzas**, the mood of depression deepens as Larkin considers the dying patient experiencing 'the sudden shut of loss'. **Stark imagery** and a deliberate rhythm combine to suggest the great change that death will bring, separating the individual from family and identity. The sensation of being isolated inside the ambulance ('Unreachable inside a room') echoes the earlier alienation of the confessional and adds to the growing sense of panic. Death will eventually alter ('loosen') everything.

Although the syntax (order of words) is complex at the end, Larkin manages to give a clear impression of his own sombre philosophy. As with much of his work, he is able to take a particular circumstance and find a general truth in it. The poem ends on a sweetly serene note of disillusion. Although ambulances try to save lives, they are actually the messengers of unavoidable death. The final disarming image leaves a **lingering sense of bleakness**. As the traffic parts and the ambulance siren quickly fades away, death also 'dulls to distance all we are'. For Larkin, there is no higher purpose to human existence, no comforting afterlife.

ANALYSIS

Write a paragraph on Larkin's use of vivid and realistic images in 'Ambulances'.

Sample Paragraph

The opening lines of 'Ambulances' contain many authentic images of the vans weaving in and out of traffic as they 'thread' their way through a busy city. We are given an immediate sense of the everyday setting and the noisy street: 'Loud noons of cities'. This condensed image effectively conveys a realistic impression of the city-centre sounds at midday. Larkin adds drama to the scene by describing one 'Light glossy grey' ambulance suddenly coming to a 'rest at any kerb'. It is the immediate focus of attention. The poet fills in the dramatic scene with precise pictures of the various spectators. Women coming from the shops stop and stare. There is realistic detailed description of the 'smells of different dinners' and of the children who are innocently playing, 'strewn on steps or road'. However, Larkin's picture of the sick patient is the most convincing of all. 'A wild white face' staring up from the 'Red stretcher-blankets' suggests pain and fear. The vivid images create a compelling sense of the seriousness of what is happening.

Examiner's Comment

As part of a full essay answer, this A-grade paragraph is firmly focused on how Larkin selects vibrant and energetic images to convey meaning and reinforce his themes. The quotations are effectively used to illustrate the poet's skill in creating key moments of drama surrounding the sudden arrival of the ambulance.

CLASS/HOMEWORK EXERCISES

1. How would you describe the dominant mood of 'Ambulances'? Using evidence from the poem, write a paragraph showing how Larkin creates this mood. (Model your answer on the sample paragraph above.)

2. Copy the table below into your own notes and fill in critical comments about the last two quotations.

Key Quotes

They come to rest at any kerb	The ambulance (representing death) can come at any time. This is a central theme in the poem.
children strewn on steps…/A wild white face	Typically, Larkin's evocative and detailed imagery is taken from everyday life.
the solving emptiness	Everyone must eventually face up to the reality of death. Assonant and sibilant effects add poignancy to the phrase.
They whisper at their own distress	
Unreachable inside a room	

⑧ THE TREES

The trees are coming into leaf
Like something almost being said;
The recent buds relax and spread,
Their greennesss is a kind of grief.

Is it they are born again   5
And we grow old? No, they die too.
Their yearly trick of looking new
Is written down in rings of grain.

Yet still the unresting castles thresh
In fullgrown thickness every May.   10
Last year is dead, they seem to say,
Begin afresh, afresh, afresh.

'The recent buds relax and spread'

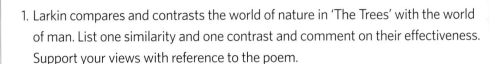

EXPLORATIONS

1. Larkin compares and contrasts the world of nature in 'The Trees' with the world of man. List one similarity and one contrast and comment on their effectiveness. Support your views with reference to the poem.

2. 'Like something almost being said'. In your opinion, what is almost being said? To whom and by whom is it being said?

3. 'Begin afresh, afresh, afresh.' Do you think this line is optimistic or full of false hope?

STUDY NOTES

'The Trees' was written in 1967 and forms part of the High Windows *collection. At this point, Larkin's personal life had become complicated. His mother was suffering from the early stages of Alzheimer's. This adds a special resonance to the last line of the poem. Do you think that people often long to 'Begin afresh, afresh, afresh'?*

Larkin deals with the classic theme of transience (passing time) in this lyric poem. The language in the **opening stanza** is harmonious and sombre, as long vowel sounds ('a', 'o' and 'u') announce the arrival of spring. The event is seen as inevitable; Larkin conveys the feeling that this has happened so often before. The mystery of the leaves' tentative arrival is suggested in the simile 'Like something almost being said'. We know it's going to happen, but we don't know how or why. It just does. Note the use of 'we' – this is a message for all of us. The verbs 'relax and spread' vividly convey the abundant covering of leaves on the former bare branches. But this **rejuvenation of nature** is not greeted warmly by the poet, who states that it is 'a kind of grief'. For whom is there sorrow? Man is unable to renew himself. Is the poet perhaps thinking of lost opportunities, what might have been? Or perhaps he is thinking of loved ones who are sick. The slow three-beat rhythm (iambic tetrameter) perfectly suits this lyrical meditation on the theme of decay and death.

In the **second stanza**, Larkin asks a **rhetorical question** to explore this thought further: 'Is it that they are born again/And we grow old?' The stark answer comes in the broken line 'No, they die too'. He does not flinch from the unpalatable reality of the finality of all living things. Time passes relentlessly and mercilessly, and the passage through time is recorded 'in rings of grain' in the tree trunks. The trees' appearance of renewal is just that – appearance, a 'trick'. The rhyme here (*cddc*) is pertinent: 'born again' rhymes with 'rings of grain', emphasising that their trick of renewal is exposed in the tree trunk.

Larkin's tone changes abruptly in the **third stanza**. The energy and life of the blossoming trees is celebrated in the metaphor 'unresting castles'. Spring's dynamic growth is shown in the compound word 'fullgrown' and in the assonance of 'unresting' and 'thresh'. Life springs back 'every May'. The trees, symbols of courage, are giving a message of hope to mankind as they seem to say, 'Last year is dead'. There is no use grieving over what is gone; concentrate on the future. The trees' exhortation is charged with urgency in the appeal 'Begin afresh, afresh, afresh'. Is this what was hinted at in the earlier phrase, 'Like something almost being said'? The **vibrant rhetoric** of spring demands that we seize the day. The life-force of the trees is sending out the hope-filled message: don't give up. Is this longing for life attractive but false? Which is the abiding message of the poem: the vitality of life or the inevitability of death? Could it be both?

ANALYSIS

Larkin was dismissive of his insights in this poem. He mocked 'The Trees' as 'awful tripe'. Do you agree or disagree with this view? Support your opinion with references from the poem.

Sample Paragraph

Larkin wrote of his 'astounded delight at the renewal of the natural world'. This lyric, with its theme of transience, emphasises this view, but also brings it a step further. Here is no attractive, false idea of renewal. The poet realises that the trees will, after renewing themselves year after year (unlike humans), eventually die. The abrupt broken line 'No, they die too' boldly states this fact. He calls their rejuvenation a 'trick', as if there is something false or deceitful in what they do. The passage of inexorable time is marked in the material, decaying world in 'rings of grain'. This is definitely not 'tripe', but genuine insight into the nature of things, however unsavoury. I feel his imagination is caught by the vitality and dynamism of the growing trees, which he describes as 'unresting castles'. The onomatopoeic 'thresh' captures this swaying movement and sense of being vibrantly alive. The concluding line, with its repetitive appeal to 'Begin afresh, afresh, afresh', seems to me to be a plea for hope. Life should be lived to the brim. So the voice of the trees/the poet is telling us to seize the day. I believe that Larkin was very wrong to be so dismissive of this lyric. Each new day brings with it the possibility of wonder.

Examiner's Comment

This focused paragraph eloquently argues the merits of Larkin's poem. A clear viewpoint is established, detailing a range of points. Expression and vocabulary are impressive. The judicious use of quotation adds weight to the response. Grade A.

CLASS/HOMEWORK EXERCISES

1. Larkin said, 'When you've read a poem, that's it, it's all quite clear what it means.' Having read 'The Trees', would you agree or disagree with this view? Support your answer with reference to the text.

2. Copy the table below into your own notes and fill in critical comments about the last two quotations.

Key Quotes

The trees are coming into leaf/Like something almost being said	This simile vividly shows the tentative arrival of the new growth on the trees and hints at the mystery of life.
Is it that they are born again/ And we grow old?	Larkin poses a rhetorical question, teasing out the difference between the fate of the trees and humans.
Their yearly trick of looking new	The word 'trick' suggests deception and double-dealing on the part of the trees, as they 'seem' to be rejuvenated each year. They appear to be defeating time.
Yet still the unresting castles thresh	
Begin afresh, afresh, afresh	

❾ THE EXPLOSION

On the day of the explosion
Shadows pointed towards the pithead:
In the sun the slagheap slept.

Down the lane came men in pitboots
Coughing oath-edged talk and pipe-smoke,   5
Shouldering off the freshened silence.

One chased after rabbits; lost them;
Came back with a nest of lark's eggs;
Showed them; lodged them in the grasses.

So they passed in beards and moleskins,   10
Fathers, brothers, nicknames, laughter,
Through the tall gates standing open.

At noon there came a tremor; cows
Stopped chewing for a second; sun,
Scarfed as in a heat-haze, dimmed.   15

The dead go on before us, they
Are sitting in God's house in comfort,
We shall see them face to face –

Plain as lettering in the chapels
It was said, and for a second   20
Wives saw men of the explosion

Larger than in life they managed –
Gold as on a coin, or walking
Somehow from the sun towards them,

One showing the eggs unbroken.   25

'Fathers, brothers, nicknames, laughter'

GLOSSARY

2   *pithead*: the top part of a mine.
3   *slagheap*: man-made hill formed from the waste of coal mining.
4   *pitboots*: heavy boots worn by miners.
8   *lark's eggs*: the eggs of the skylark, a native bird of England and Ireland.

10   *moleskins*: heavy material worn by working men.
15   *Scarfed*: wrapped up.

EXPLORATIONS

1. Does Larkin give a realistic picture of the working men? Choose two realistic details (images) that you found effective.

2. Would you consider this poem a religious poem? Why or why not?

3. Comment on the concluding image as a symbol of redemption.

STUDY NOTES

'The Explosion' documents a tragedy that can randomly happen to a community, but it offers a consolation that is not present in Larkin's other poems. The word 'explosion' brings to mind a loud bang, destruction, dead bodies. What other words do you associate with the word 'explosion'?

The source of this poem was a documentary Larkin watched on the coal-mining industry. The poem gives an account of an underground accident in which a number of miners lost their lives. Many of the miners' wives were supposed to have seen visions of their husbands at the moment of the explosion. Larkin also said, 'I heard a song about a mine disaster ... it made me want to write the same thing, a mine disaster with a vision of immortality at the end ... that's the point of the eggs.'

The poem opens quietly as the scene is observed in **stanza one** and we are gently led into the drama: 'On the day of the explosion'. Notice the word 'the'. This is a specific event that will affect specific people. The details give a premonition of disaster: 'Shadows pointed towards the pithead'. The alliteration of the explosive letter 'p' adds to the menace, as does the personification: 'slagheap slept'. The image of a sleeping monster that will wreak havoc if awoken is suggested. The alliteration of 's' emphasises the **uneasy peace**.

In contrast, along come the noisy miners, swearing and coughing in **stanza two**. An impression of proud, ordinary, strong young men from the tough world of the mines is given in a few well-chosen details: 'pitboots', 'Coughing oath-edged talk and pipe-smoke'. The **onomatopoeia** in the line 'Shouldering off the freshened silence' gives an idea of their rough strength. They walk unknowing, but we know and this adds to the growing tension and suspense in the poem. We are brought closer to the miners in **stanza three** as we observe them playing about. One chases rabbits, but comes back with a 'nest of lark's eggs'. He 'shows' the eggs. These are men who are interested in and deeply respectful of nature. He 'lodged' the eggs in the grasses, where the mother bird could find them. We see the sensitivity in these tough men.

The miners are part of a close-knit community, as we learn in **stanza four**: 'Fathers, brothers, nicknames, laughter'. The poignancy is becoming unbearable for the reader as we realise all will be blown apart by the event that is about to occur. The 'tall gates' are waiting, 'standing open', almost like the gates of the underworld, inescapable. These men meet their fate in **stanza five** ('So they passed'). The **language is almost biblical**. The ending is becoming inevitable. Larkin records the accident calmly, without melodrama. Instead we are presented with the ripple effects of the explosion on nature: 'cows/Stopped chewing' and the sun 'dimmed' as it was supposed to have done at the crucifixion of Christ. Time stands still. The explosion only registered for a 'second'. This is in contrast with the world of the men, where nothing will ever be the same again. But the rescue and the grief are unmentioned. We are left to imagine the horror.

In the final part of the poem (**stanzas six to nine**), the focus is changed. Now we are looking at the wives and their reactions to the deaths. The passage from the Bible is in italics, words of comfort, a certainty of resurrection: 'We shall see them face to face'. The wives believe this so strongly that they have a glimpse of their husbands and sons 'for a second'. Notice the difference of the reaction of the wives and the animals. The women's lives are irrevocably changed, but the animals resume their grazing. This terrible tragedy is of no consequence to the world of nature. They are unable to explain this vision 'Somehow'. These men are as they were and also are now transformed, 'Larger than in life'. They are walking in brilliant light. The sun is now the blazing sun of eternity. They are 'Gold as on a coin', a pure and enduring metal. The **rhythm is stately and formal**, which suits the religious viewpoint.

The poem ends on a note of affirmation, with the **potent image** of the unbroken eggs suggesting the hope of resurrection, the continuity of life and the strength of the ties of love. The **last line** stands alone, separated from the eight other three-line stanzas. Larkin's scepticism is absent. He is moved by sympathy for these men and their families. As the poet has said (in 'An Arundel Tomb'), 'What will survive of us is love'. This is the last poem in his last collection of poetry. Is it being suggested that love triumphs over death? Is this a modern religious poem?

ANALYSIS

Write a paragraph on Larkin's use of memorable images in 'The Explosion'.

Sample Paragraph

Larkin captures the scene on the day of the explosion with a few well-chosen visual details. He alerts the reader to the possibility of disaster with the sinister image of the 'shadows' which 'pointed towards the pithead', almost as if they were arrows of destiny marking the target of the miners. The air of menace is further emphasised with the memorable image of the slagheap as it 'slept' in the sun. The personification suggests a sleeping monster that will cause chaos if woken up. The image of the 'tall gates standing open' appealed to me, as it suggested the entry of the men into death's kingdom. The long vowel sounds slow the line. Death does not know time. These vowels, 'a' and 'o', lend a stately, solemn rhythm to the phrase, which reminds me of a ceremonial funeral march. The final image, contained in the floating last line, 'One showing the eggs unbroken', is full of optimism and hope, as it reminds me of Easter and the Resurrection of Christ. The image reflects a rare moment when Larkin has a positive attitude towards a Christian afterlife. The little eggs suggest renewal, the beginning of a new era. Larkin has laid aside his cynicism. The poem ends on this memorable image of transcendence, making the poem a beautiful religious credo.

Examiner's Comment

This is a succinct and well-controlled paragraph. The student has a close knowledge of the text and has clearly understood the task. The writing is fluent throughout and makes effective use of pertinent quotation. Grade A.

CLASS/HOMEWORK EXERCISES

1. Write a paragraph on how the structure of the poem helps Larkin communicate his theme effectively. (Look at the arrangement of the stanzas scene by scene on the page, the use of run-on lines, the placement of key words, the use of italics and the separate last line.)

2. Copy the table below into your own notes and fill in critical comments about the last two quotations.

Key Quotes

So they passed in beards and moleskins	The use of detailed images adds a strong visual quality and realism to the description of the miners.
Fathers, brothers, nicknames, laughter	Larkin recognises and admires the ordinary lives of this hardworking mining community.
At noon, there came a tremor	There are no details about the actual explosion. The tone is detached and the poet seems stunned by the event.
We shall see them face to face	
the eggs unbroken	

⑩ CUT GRASS

Cut grass lies frail:
Brief is the breath
Mown stalks exhale.
Long, long the death

It dies in the white hours   5
Of young-leafed June
With chestnut flowers,
With hedges snowlike strewn,

White lilac bowed,
Lost lanes of Queen Anne's lace,   10
And that high-builded cloud
Moving at summer's pace.

'Lost lanes of Queen Anne's lace'

GLOSSARY

2   *Brief is the breath*: life is short (the Bible says: 'all the glory of man is as flowers of grass').

8   *strewn*: covered untidily.

10   *Queen Anne's lace*: cow parsley, a white wild flower with lace-like blooms.

EXPLORATIONS

1. This poem gives a picture of a rural landscape. What colour predominates? List three examples. What is the colour white usually associated with? (Innocence, weddings, funeral flowers, purity, etc.) In your opinion, why does Larkin use this colour?

2. In your opinion, what is the mood of the poem? Does it change or not? Give evidence from the text to support your view.

3. Write a paragraph giving your own personal response to this poem. Refer closely to the text in your answer.

STUDY NOTES

'Cut Grass' is a lyric dealing with a recurring theme in Larkin's poetry: passing time and death. Written in 1971, it appeared in his collection High Windows. It is a calm poem that Larkin saw as a 'succession of images'. His verdict was, 'I like it all right'. Yet it was written at the end of Larkin's life, when he was very bitter about the state of England ('what an end to a great country'). He was critical of socialism and immigrants: 'I have always been right wing ... I identify with certain virtues (thrift, hard work, reverence, desire to preserve).'

The Bible states that 'All flesh is grass'. The title of 'Cut Grass' echoes this classic theme implicitly as we are reminded of the figure of Father Time/Death with his scythe. All living things are mown down. The setting of this poem is a meadow that has been recently mown. 'Cut grass lies frail' suggests the fragility and brevity of life against the relentless approach of inescapable death. The word 'frail' almost seems to expire as its sound drifts away at the end of the **first line** of **stanza one**. The short, unpredictable life of the grass is eloquently captured in the alliterative phrase 'Brief is the breath'. Explosive 'b' sounds reflect the action of breathing in and out. This **personification**, continued in the verb 'exhale', implies the parallel between our tenuous hold on life and that of all living things. The full stop at the end of this line underscores the reality of death and its finality. In contrast to this, the first stanza runs on into the next stanza to emphasise the fact that death is endless; it is not subject to time: 'Long, long the death'.

Stanza two tells us when the grass in the meadow dies, just at the moment when all other things are growing profusely. The trees are beginning to come into leaf and the hedges are covered in foaming whitethorn, like snow ('snowlike strewn'). The alliteration and **run-on lines** suggest the abundance of nature. Nature has the ability to renew itself, as the compound word 'young-leafed' suggests. We wonder: can man renew himself? The assonance ('hours', 'flowers') adds a poignant, melancholy note to this stanza, as in the midst of life is death.

In the **third stanza**, this abundance continues as the succession of beautiful white images mirror each other: 'White lilac bowed' flows into frothy 'lanes of Queen Anne's lace'. This wild flower appears every summer in out-of-the way lanes throughout rural England. Is this poem also an elegy for a disappearing England? The **alliteration** of 'l' suggests the meandering, winding lanes of the countryside. Towering white clouds add to this picture of rural serenity, as they glide effortlessly by, 'Moving at summer's pace'. But all will die in their own time. This elegy is like a lament or requiem, its long vowel sounds suggesting the lingering of the bereaved, unwilling to let the dead go. The poet's tone is sympathetic, resigned to the inevitable.

Here is no Christian consolation, no exhortation to live life passionately. The two-sentence poem is divided into short, abrupt sentences at the start which showcase the harsh finality of death. The poem then moves into the long run-on lines of the second sentence, which is stately and dignified and is suitable for a lament. The **regular rhyme scheme** (*abab, cdcd, efef*) underpins the fact that time passes and death comes; it is unavoidable. Larkin clearly valued traditional English poetry forms, as he valued England.

ANALYSIS

Larkin said he wrote two kinds of poems, 'the beautiful and true'. Discuss this statement, referring to the poem 'Cut Grass'. Support your view with references from the poem.

Sample Paragraph

In my opinion, Larkin has indeed written a poem that resonates with truth. There is no escaping the sad finality of all human existence, 'Brief is the breath'. The poet does not give us any consolation either in this elegy. The real truth of human mortality floats in our consciousness as timeless and as inevitable as the 'high-builded cloud' floats in the sky on a summer's day. I also think this poem is beautiful, as the succession of idyllic images which are truly English are presented to us. The smell of cut grass is suggested in the evocative line 'Mown stalks exhale'. The abundance and generosity of nature is shown in the alliterative phrase 'hedges snowlike strewn'. But for me the real beauty of the poem lies in the musical writing. It reminds me of a song lyric. The assonance of long vowel sounds ('Long, long') and slender vowels ('White lilac') evoke long, lazy summer evenings that are quintessentially English. The melancholic phrase 'Lost lanes' seems to be lamenting a lost way of life, as well as death, as the 'l' sound lingers on the ear. Larkin is a superb craftsman. The gentle fading sounds of the words 'frail' and 'exhale' both disappear, as all individual existence does into the inevitability of death. The finality of death is punctuated sternly by the full stop after 'exhale'. The compound words 'young-leafed', 'high-builded' show the beauty of life. The regular rhyme scheme (*abab, cdcd, efef*) moves as effortlessly as the clouds 'at summer's pace'. Larkin expresses a classic, true theme in a beautiful way. Like him, I like this poem 'all right'.

Examiner's Comment

This paragraph addresses the two elements of the question (beautiful and true). It shows a real appreciation of poetic technique. Fluent and varied expression, particularly the impressive vocabulary, merits a grade A.

CLASS/HOMEWORK EXERCISES

1. Larkin's poems show 'loneliness, emptiness and mortality'. Do you agree that this is true of 'Cut Grass'? Refer to the text in your answer.

2. Copy the table below into your own notes and fill in critical comments about the last two quotations.

Key Quotes

Cut grass lies frail	Life is short for all living things.
Mown stalks exhale	The long vowel sounds ('a' and 'o') slow the pace of the line, emphasising the inevitability of passing time.
It dies in the white hours/Of young-leafed June	Contrast adds a poignant tone. The rest of nature is very much alive, as referenced by the compound word 'young-leafed'.
Lost lanes of Queen Anne's lace	
And that high-builded cloud/ Moving at summer's pace	

'Philip Larkin explores the darker side of life, but with a warm, compassionate voice.'
Discuss this statement, supporting the points you make with suitable reference to the
poems by Larkin on your course.

Marking Scheme Guidelines

Candidates are free to agree and/or disagree with the given statement. However,
they should show clear evidence of personal engagement with the poetry of
Philip Larkin. The key terms ('darker side of life' and 'warm, compassionate voice')
should be addressed either implicitly or explicitly. Allow for a wide range of
approaches in the answering.

Material might be drawn from the following:

- Ambivalent attitude to love, death, religion
- Larkin projects a misleading/enigmatic persona
- Widely varying tones and atmospheres
- Can be seen to celebrate/criticise ordinary English life
- Ambiguous interpretation of his imagery
- Fatalistic/pessimistic attitude, etc.

Sample Essay

(Larkin explores the darker side of life with a warm, compassionate voice)

1. *Philip Larkin seems to enjoy adopting a morose persona. His subject matter can be*
   dark and he can be a very critical poetic voice. Larkin often reflects on the futility
   of life and the inevitability of death e.g. in his poem, 'Ambulances'. Elsewhere,
   he addresses random tragedy in a sympathetic way ('The Explosion'). His tone
   is sometimes filled with gloom and melancholy, 'Brief is the breath'. He can be
   critical, 'differently-dressed servants'. Yet I like Larkin's poetry because he celebrates
   the healing power of love and marriage ('Wedding Wind'). Many of his poems
   reveal an affection for English communities and ordinary people. He explores how
   love transcends time ('An Arundel Tomb'). At times, his imagery is beautiful and
   affirmative and I enjoy his dry sense of humour.

2. I don't know of a more touchingly tender moment than that described in 'An Arundel Tomb'. At first, the poet seems detached at the sight of the tomb of the Earl of Arundel and his wife. Their faces are 'blurred', worn by time. The 'little dogs under their feet' are that 'faint hint of the absurd'. But the poet draws the reader's attention 'with a sharp tender shock' to this detail of affection. The Earl's 'hand is withdrawn, holding her hand'. The alliteration of 'h' and the stately rhythm emphasise the importance of close human relationships. Can love transcend time in this 'stone fidelity'? The poem's last line states 'What will survive of us is love'. Even if 'Only an attitude remains', I am comforted that the message is one of lasting love.

3. Love is also the subject of 'Wedding Wind'. Larkin adopts the persona of a young bride, 'I can imagine … the emotions of a bride'. I found it interesting that life lived by ordinary people should be a subject for poetry. The imperfect detail, 'I/Carry a chipped pail to the chicken run' and mundane sight of 'My apron and the hanging cloths on the line' glow due to the skill of the poet. Irritating jobs may have to be endured, but they are transfigured by the joy of the young woman, 'this bodying forth by wind/Of joy my actions turn on'. These actions are 'like a thread carrying beads'. The sacrament of marriage is vividly evoked by this simile. I realised that these ordinary actions form part of the state of holy matrimony. The young woman feels so blessed she wonders 'Can even death dry up/These new delighted lakes'. Larkin has celebrated passionate young love in the English countryside.

4. 'Ambulances' reflect Larkin's view of life's futility. An ambulance arrives, a common experience in modern life. But Larkin adds 'They come to rest at any kerb'. Suddenly the perspective has changed. The reader and the bystanders all hope that their time will not come soon. I found the way the poet allowed the second last stanza rush into the last one very interesting as I now became aware that it was mimicking what was happening. All ties were unravelling for the sick person. All that was familiar was receding, 'the unique random blend/Of families and fashions, there/At last begin to loosen'. Here is a poet who is compassionate, who understands what it means to be human, and how terrifying it must be as sickness 'dulls to distance all we are'.

5. Philip Larkin can also be dryly humorous. In his affectionate account of a summer train journey, 'The Whitsun Weddings', I enjoyed the seaside postcard sketches of 'mothers loud and fat;/An uncle shouting smut; and then the perms,/The nylon gloves and jewellery-substitutes'. But he also made me think about the reality of

families parting and changing as children set off on their new lives and parents are left behind, 'The last confetti and advice were thrown'. The sheer richness of the experience of life is described.

6. *Larkin explores death, the banal every day, sickness and the vulgarity of ordinary life. In my opinion, the reason Philip Larkin is popular is not because of his exploration of cruelty and fear, but because the warm voice of the poet emerges. The detail of the held hand, the image of the 'thread carrying beads', the compassion for the aloneness of the sick, 'Far from the exchange of love to lie', the heightened exciting distant 'arrow shower ... becoming rain' all remain in my memory. For me the sympathetic voice of the poet in the midst of life's traumas is the reason for Larkin's enduring popularity.*

(approx. 740 words)

Examiner's Comment

A well-organised essay, confidently written and showing some close personal engagement with Larkin's poetry. Some points deserve fuller discussion in longer paragraphs, e.g. there is a superficial treatment of 'The Whitsun Weddings'. However, there is effective use of quotations and the expression throughout is impressive.

GRADE: A2

P = 13/15

C = 12/15

L = 13/15

M = 5/5

Total = 43/50

SAMPLE LEAVING CERT QUESTIONS ON LARKIN'S POETRY

(45/50 MINUTES)

1. 'Philip Larkin speaks intimately to the reader about love and loss through visual images, metaphors and sound effects.' Do you agree with this assessment of his poetry? Your answer should focus on his themes and the way he expresses them. Support the points you make with suitable reference to the poems by Larkin on your course.

2. 'A dark ironic wit energises Larkin's realistic reflections on mortality and immortality.' Discuss this statement, supporting your answer with suitable reference to the poetry by Larkin on your course.

3. 'Larkin presents insightful reflections as he surveys the ordinary sights of life in 20th-century England.' Write a response to this view, supporting your points with reference to the poems by Larkin on your course.

Sample Essay Plan (Q1)

'Philip Larkin speaks intimately to the reader about love and loss through visual images, metaphors and sound effects.' Do you agree with this assessment of his poetry? Your answer should focus on his themes and the way he expresses them. Support the points you make with suitable reference to the poems by Larkin on your course.

- Intro: Identify the elements of the question to be addressed ('intimately', themes of mortality and love, using the techniques of 'visual images, metaphors and sound effects'). The observant eyes of Larkin compassionately view relevant and recurring themes of transience, death and love. He faces up to universal fears honestly while maintaining compassion for the ordinary individual.

- Point 1: 'Wedding Wind' – by adopting the persona of a young bride, Larkin celebrates the joy of passionate love and also its everyday irritants through vivid imagery ('All's ravelled under the sun') and powerful similes ('like a thread/ Carrying beads').

- Point 2: 'Cut Grass' – quiet exploration of the fragility and brevity of life through the predominance of the colour white ('hedges snowlike strewn'), explosive sound effects ('Brief is the breath') and effective personification ('Mown stalks exhale').

- Point 3: 'The Explosion' – captures the random nature of disastrous events. Menace of impending doom shown through personification: 'the slagheap slept'. Uplifting, affirming images: 'Gold as on a coin', 'showing the eggs unbroken'.

- Point 4: 'The Trees' – celebration of human resilience and courage in the face of certain death. Use of present continuous tense, sibilance and an even rhyme scheme gently give a positive outlook.

- Point 5: 'Ambulances' – indiscriminate nature of disaster in human affairs graphically described through evocative imagery ('Closed like confessionals') and sound effects ('A wild white face').

- Conclusion: Larkin speaks quietly about the terrifying aspects of life, transience, disaster and death, sometimes offering comfort, sometimes accepting what cannot be changed. He celebrates love by showing ordinary people doing ordinary things.

Sample Essay Plan (Q1)

Develop one of the above points into a paragraph.

Sample Paragraph: Point 2

In the calm elegy 'Cut Grass', Larkin conjures up an idealised image of rural England that was fast disappearing: 'White lilac bowed,/Lost lanes of Queen Anne's lace'. The long vowel sounds 'a' and 'o' convey the reluctance of letting go of something precious. The poet does not offer comfort in this lyrical exploration of the finality of death, starkly stating 'Brief is the breath'. The explosive 'b' sounds mimic the in-and-out motion of inhaling and exhaling, a true sign of life. Through personification, 'Cut grass lies frail', 'Mown stalks exhale', the finality of death is presented. Here the reader comes face to face with the tenuous hold on life and the finality of death. The full stop emphasises the reality from which there is no escape while the run-on line stresses limitless death: 'Long, long the death /It dies'. The dignified tone of the poem brought home clearly to me the chilling message that time cuts down all living things. In the regular rhyme scheme ('frail', 'exhale'; 'breath', 'death'), Larkin effortlessly captures the unavoidable fact that we all disappear into the inevitable unknown after death. Confidentially, as if speaking to a child, this poet allows us to look at the reality of his human existence and experience the still, sad music of humanity.

Examiner's Comment

As part of a full essay, this is a very good personal response that addresses the question with confidence. The focus on Larkin's language use is impressive. A range of accurate quotations are used effectively to support discussion points. Clear and fluent expression add to the quality of the answer. Grade A.

LAST WORDS

'Larkin's poems are melancholy, melodious, disenchanted, bewitching, perfectly written and perfectly approachable.'

Seamus Heaney

'People marvelled that a poet they had never met could have spoken to them so intimately.'

Andrew Motion

'I want readers to feel yes, I've never thought of it that way, but that's how it is.'

Philip Larkin

'I chose poetry because it was different. '

E iléan Ní Chuilleanáin is regarded by many as one of the most important contemporary Irish women poets. Her subject matter ranges from social commentary and considerations of religious issues to quiet, introspective poems about human nature. She has also translated poetry from a number of languages. Ní Chuilleanáin is noted for being mysterious and complex; her poems usually have subtle messages that unfold only through multiple readings. She is well read in history and a strong sense of connection between past and present characterises her work, in which she often draws interesting parallels between historical events and modern situations. Many of her poems highlight the contrast between fluidity and stillness, life and death, and of the undeniable passing of time and humanity's attempts to stop change. They are usually intricately layered, often subtle half-revelations, but always both carefully controlled and even startling. She herself has frequently referred to the importance of secrecy in her poetry. Most critics agree that Ní Chuilleanáin's poems resist easy explanations and variously show her interest in explorations of transition, the sacred, women's experience and history.

Prescribed Poems HIGHER LEVEL

① LUCINA SCHYNNING IN SILENCE OF THE NICHT

Moon shining in silence of the night
The heaven being all full of stars
I was reading my book in a ruin
By a sour candle, without roast meat or music
Strong drink or a shield from the air   5
Blowing in the crazed window, and I felt
Moonlight on my head, clear after three days' rain.

I washed in cold water; it was orange, channelled down bogs
Dipped between cresses.
The bats flew through my room where I slept safely.   10
Sheep stared at me when I woke.

Behind me the waves of darkness lay, the plague
Of mice, plague of beetles
Crawling out of the spines of books,
Plague shadowing pale faces with clay   15
The disease of the moon gone astray.

In the desert I relaxed, amazed
As the mosaic beasts on the chapel floor
When Cromwell had departed and they saw
The sky growing through the hole in the roof.   20

Sheepdogs embraced me; the grasshopper
Returned with a lark and bee.
I looked down between hedges of high thorn and saw
The hare, absorbed, sitting still
In the middle of the track; I heard   25
Again the chirp of the stream running.

'shining in silence of the night'

GLOSSARY

Title: Lucina is another name for Diana, the moon goddess. In Roman mythology, Lucina was the goddess of childbirth. Ní Chuilleanáin's title comes from the opening line of 'The Antichrist', a satirical poem by the Scottish poet William Dunbar (c. 1460–1517).

9   *cresses*: small strongly flavoured leaves.
12   *plague*: curse, diseased group.
14   *spines*: inner parts, backs.
16   *astray*: off course.

18   *mosaic*: mixed, assorted.
19   *Cromwell*: Oliver Cromwell (1599–1658), controversial English military and political leader who led an army of invasion in 1649–50, which conquered most of Ireland. Cromwell is still regarded largely as a figure of hatred in the Irish Republic, his name being associated with massacre, religious persecution and mass dispossession of the Catholic community.
26   *chirp*: lively sound, twitter.

EXPLORATIONS

1. How would you describe the atmosphere in the poem's opening stanza? Refer to the text in your answer.

2. Choose one image taken from the natural world that you found particularly interesting. Comment briefly on its effectiveness.

3. Based on your reading of this poem, do you think Ní Chuilleanáin presents a realistic view of Irish history? Give reasons for your response.

STUDY NOTES

Eiléan Ní Chuilleanáin takes her title from a Middle Scots poem by William Dunbar. 'Lucina Schynning in Silence of the Nicht' is set in a ruin somewhere in Ireland, after Oliver Cromwell had devastated the country in 1649. However, Ní Chuilleanáin's beautiful and haunting poem is much more than a meditation on an historical event. The poet achieves immediacy by means of a dramatic monologue that recreates the whisperings of desolation in the aftermath of Cromwell's march through Ireland.

As in so many of her poems, Ní Chuilleanáin invites readers into a **strangely compelling setting**. The poet personifies the moon, creating an uneasy atmosphere. Silence enhances the dramatic effect: 'The heaven being all full of stars'. This eerie scene is described in a series of random details. The language – with its archaic Scottish dialect – is note-like and seemingly timeless. There is a notable absence of punctuation and a stilted rhythm as the unknown speaker's voice is introduced: 'I was reading my book in a ruin' (line 3). The series of fragmentary images – 'a sour candle', 'the crazed window' – are immediately unsettling, drawing us back to a darker age in Ireland's troubled history.

Characteristically, Ní Chuilleanáin leaves readers to unravel the poem's veiled meanings and the identity of the dispossessed narrator is never made known. Instead, this forlorn figure 'without roast meat or music' is associated with material and cultural deprivation – **a likely symbol of an oppressed Ireland**? Does the absence of 'Strong drink or a shield' add to the notion of a defeated people? Despite the obvious indications of almost incomprehensible suffering, some respite can still be found: 'I felt/Moonlight on my head, clear after three days' rain' (line 7). This simple image of nature – illuminating and refreshing – suggests comforting signs of recovery.

Ní Chuilleanáin's startling drama moves into the wild Irish landscape: 'I washed in cold water; it was orange'. The sense of native Irish resistance against foreign invasion is clearly evident in the reference to Dutch-born Protestant William of Orange, who defeated the army of Catholic James II at the Battle of the Boyne in 1690. But the poet focuses on the speaker's experience of displacement, illustrating the **alienation which existed within nationalist Ireland**. The narrator, surrounded by animal life and the open sky, becomes an extension of animate and inanimate nature: 'The bats flew through my room ... Sheep stared at me' (line 10).

In an increasingly surreal atmosphere, the mood becomes much more disturbed. The poet's apocalyptic dream-vision highlights the 'waves of darkness' in an uninterrupted nightmarish sequence of repulsive images: 'plague/Of mice, plague of beetles/Crawling'. The **emphatic repetition of 'plague' resonates with images of widespread misery, disease and famine**. Nor does the poet ignore the distorted history of Ireland that has resulted from prejudice, propaganda and vested interest 'Crawling out of the spines of books' (line 14). What stands out, however, is Ní Chuilleanáin's ability to suggest distressing glimpses of our island's dark past, poignantly depicted in her heart-rending language describing innocent death: 'Plague shadowing pale faces with clay/The disease of the moon gone astray'.

There is a distinctive change of mood in **lines 17–20** as the speaker reflects on the aching aftermath in the period after 'Cromwell had departed'. References to Christian retreat and renewal indicate the **consolation provided by religious faith**: 'In the desert I relaxed, amazed/As the mosaic beasts on the chapel floor'. This sense of wonder through the possibility of spiritual fulfilment is developed in the metaphorical image of 'The sky growing through the hole in the roof'. As always, landscape and nature are features of Ní Chuilleanáin's poem, allowing readers access to her subtle thinking.

In sharp contrast to the earlier trauma, the final tone is remarkably composed and harmonious. The language – which has been somewhat archaic throughout much of the poem – is noticeably biblical: 'Sheepdogs embraced me; the grasshopper/Returned with a lark and bee'. **There is an unmistakable sense of survival and newfound confidence** in **line 23**: 'I looked down between hedges of high thorn'. Ní Chuilleanáin's recognition of 'The hare, absorbed, sitting still' (a cross-reference to her poem 'On Lacking the Killer Instinct') reinforces the feeling of quiet resignation. Is she alluding to the maturity and relative peace of the present Irish state? At any rate, the poem ends on a hopeful note of vigorous resilience, with one of nature's liveliest sounds, 'the chirp of the stream running'.

Throughout this elusive poem, Ní Chuilleanáin has explored fascinating aspects of Irish history – a story that has been often lost in the 'silence of the night'. So much of Ireland's past is marked by exploitation and resistance. The poem has deep undercurrents of countless conflicts springing from both without and within. The moon has long been associated with love, beauty, loneliness, lunacy and death. Some critics have suggested that Ní Chuilleanáin's poem uses the moon to symbolise the struggle of women through the centuries. As usual, readers are free to judge for themselves. However, there is little doubt that 'Lucina Schynning in Silence of the Nicht' presents us with **an intense, self-enclosed world** – but one where the tensions and aspirations of Ireland's complex story are imaginatively encapsulated.

ANALYSIS

'Eiléan Ní Chuilleanáin's poems offer rich rewards to the perceptive reader.' Discuss this view, with particular reference to 'Lucina Schynning in Silence of the Nicht'.

Sample Paragraph

While I first found Ní Chuilleanáin's poetry obscure and quite difficult, I really enjoyed reading 'Lucina Schynning'. The strange title and eerie atmosphere under the moonlight is typical of a poet who makes us, the reader, imagine the 'world' of the poem. I found it all very dramatic. The narrative voice seemed very traumatised and was convincing as it represented Ireland's troubled history – 'I washed myself in cold water', 'Behind me, waves of darkness'. What I really liked about the poet was that she suggested, rather than explained. The description of Irish people starving and dying was very moving – especially because of the word 'plague'. Ní Chuilleanáin's images of suffering were balanced by the positive ending. The character in the poem was at one with nature – 'sheep embraced me'. The poem asked many questions about how people today look at the past. I thought the final lines were really encouraging. The poet used many simple nature images of the hare 'sitting still' and the 'chirp of the stream' to show a present-day Ireland where there is peace and contentment – unlike the war-torn past of the history books. Overall, I did enjoy 'Lucina Schynning' as it reminded me that there is still meaning in the beauty of nature.

Examiner's Comment

This is a reasonably good response to a general question on the poem. There is evidence of personal engagement and some worthwhile discussion points which show an appreciation of Ní Chuilleanáin's poetic voice. Some of the quotations are slightly inaccurate and the adverb 'really' is overused. Grade C.

CLASS/HOMEWORK EXERCISES

1. 'Ní Chuilleanáin's distinctive poetry is filled with subtle messages.' Discuss this statement, with particular reference to 'Lucina Schynning in Silence of the Nicht'.

2. Copy the table below into your own notes and fill in critical comments about the last two quotations.

Key Quotes

Blowing in the crazed window	Ní Chuilleanáin's central character is depicted as being overwhelmed by forces which cannot be controlled. The adjective 'crazed' emphasises the feeling of an absurd and dangerous world.
Plague shadowing pale faces with clay	The poem has many powerful images of Ireland's past – in this case, there are harrowing traces of terrified victims facing death.
The sky growing through the hole in the roof	
the chirp of the stream running	

2 ## THE SECOND VOYAGE

Odysseus rested on his oar and saw
The ruffled foreheads of the waves
Crocodiling and mincing past: he rammed
The oar between their jaws and looked down
 In the simmering sea where scribbles of weed defined   5
 Uncertain depth, and the slim fishes progressed
 In fatal formation, and thought
                              If there was a single
Streak of decency in these waves now, they'd be ridged
Pocked and dented with the battering they've had,   10
And we could name them as Adam named the beasts,
Saluting a new one with dismay, or a notorious one
With admiration; they'd notice us passing
And rejoice at our shipwreck, but these
Have less character than sheep and need more patience.   15

I know what I'll do he said;
I'll park my ship in the crook of a long pier
(And I'll take you with me he said to the oar)
I'll face the rising ground and walk away
From tidal waters, up riverbeds   20
Where herons parcel out the miles of stream,
Over gaps in the hills, through warm
Silent valleys, and when I meet a farmer
Bold enough to look me in the eye
With 'where are you off to with that long   25
Winnowing fan over your shoulder?'
There I will stand still
And I'll plant you for a gatepost or a hitching-post
And leave you as a tidemark. I can go back
And organise my house then.   30
                              But the profound
Unfenced valleys of the ocean still held him;
He had only the oar to make them keep their distance;
The sea was still frying under the ship's side.

He considered the water-lilies, and thought about fountains   35
Spraying as wide as willows in empty squares,

The sugarstick of water clattering into the kettle,
The flat lakes bisecting the rushes. He remembered spiders and frogs
Housekeeping at the roadside in brown trickles floored with mud,
Horsetroughs, the black canal, pale swans at dark;   40
His face grew damp with tears that tasted
Like his own sweat or the insults of the sea.

'the simmering sea'

GLOSSARY

1	*Odysseus*: Greek mythic king and warrior. He is also the literary hero of Homer's epic tale, *The Odyssey*, which tells of Odysseus's 10-year struggle to return home from the Trojan War.	3	*mincing*: moving daintily.
		10	*Pocked*: disfigured.
		12	*notorious*: infamous.
		21	*herons*: long-necked wading birds.
		21	*parcel*: mark, measure.
2	*ruffled*: wrinkled, tangled.	26	*Winnowing*: probing.
3	*Crocodiling*: gliding.	38	*bisecting*: cutting through.

EXPLORATIONS

1. From your reading of the first stanza (lines 1–15), describe Odysseus's relationship with the sea. Refer to the text in your response.

2. Select two interesting images from the poem and comment on the effectiveness of each.

3. Write your own personal response to 'The Second Voyage', supporting the points you make with reference to the text.

STUDY NOTES

The relationship between past and present is one of Eiléan Ní Chuilleanáin's recurring themes. In addressing the present within the context of history, she often explores contrasts, such as life and death, motion and stillness, and the inevitable tension between time passing and people's desire to resist change. 'The Second Voyage' refers to the Greek hero Odysseus, whose first epic journey was a relentless battle with the treacherous ocean. But growing frustrated by the endless struggle against nature, he decides that his next voyage will be on land and therefore less demanding.

From the outset, Odysseus is presented as a slightly bemused and ridiculous figure. There is a cartoon-like quality to the exaggerated ocean setting as Ní Chuilleanáin immediately portrays this legendary hero resting on his oar and watching the 'ruffled foreheads of the waves/Crocodiling and mincing past' (**line 3**). The poet expands this metaphor, describing the waves as great beasts to be challenged: 'he rammed/The oar between their jaws'. **Ní Chuilleanáin's derisive humour mocks the great wanderer's inflated sense of his own masculinity.** But there is no denying that Odysseus is still excited by the 'Uncertain depth' beneath him. For him, anything is possible at sea, where he is truly in his element. The personification is childlike, suggesting his peevish annoyance at being unable to conquer the ocean waves, which don't possess 'a single/Streak of decency' (**line 9**).

Ní Chuilleanáin's tone is playfully critical. As always, the poet's skill lies in her vigorous images, such as the 'slim fishes' beneath 'scribbles of weeds'. Odysseus's powerful physicality is contrasted with the seemingly pretty waves, which somehow resist the 'battering they've had'. Lording over this surreal scene and filled with disappointment, the egotistical Greek warrior thinks about the Garden of Eden. He is soon envying Adam, who was given God-given control over all living things and had 'named the beasts' of the earth. Completely unaware of the irony of his excessive pride, Odysseus is overwhelmed by self-pity and resorts to ridiculing these foolish waves, which fail to 'rejoice at our shipwreck' (**line 14**).

Ní Chuilleanáin develops the whimsical drama by letting us hear Odysseus's petulant voice as he prepares to seek recognition onshore. Armed with renewed confidence and his trusty oar – ('I'll take you with me he said to the oar') – he sets out to 'face the rising ground' and seek affirmation far away 'From tidal waters'. But despite the purposeful rhythm and self-assured tone, there is a strong underlying sense that he is deluding himself. The landscape might be serenely beautiful, but it is confined. Unlike the boundless sea, birds define it: 'herons parcel out the miles of stream' (**line 21**). Yet the brave warrior is eager to boast of his exploits in the outside world and hopes to tell his story to the first farmer he meets who is 'Bold enough to look me in the eye'. **Odysseus even tries to convince himself that it is time to put down roots**, to plant his oar as 'a gatepost or a hitching-post'. Then he will be ready to return home and 'organise my house'. However, the laboured rhythm and imposing multi-syllabic language convey his half-heartedness about settling down.

Indeed, there are already signs that Odysseus will never surrender the freedom and adventure of dangerous ocean voyages. The powerful oar, which once signified dynamism and exhilaration, is now seen as a decorative symbol of stillness, a 'Winnowing fan'. Unable to deny his true destiny any longer, **he accepts that he cannot ignore his urge to control the sea**: the 'Unfenced valleys of the ocean still held him' (**line 32**). But his ironic situation remains; while the freedom he yearns for is unattainable on land, he is still unable to conquer the seemingly infinite sea.

The poem's final section is sympathetic to Odysseus's dilemma. Ní Chuilleanáin replaces the pompous first-person pronouns with her own measured narrative account: 'He considered the water-lilies, and thought about fountains' (**line 35**). The poet makes extensive use of **contrasting water images to highlight land and sea**. Unlike the water 'frying under the ship's side', settled life appears controlled, but unattractive ('Horsetroughs, the black canal'). His uneasy memories of home ('water clattering', 'pale swans at dark') are ominous. For Odysseus, his second excursion into landlocked civilisation offers so little fulfillment that 'His face grew damp with tears'. The hero is forever drawn to that first epic voyage and the wonderful experience of ocean living, with which he is inextricably bound: 'Like his own sweat or the insults of the sea'.

The fluctuating water images – another familiar feature of Eiléan Ní Chuilleanáin's writing – reflect the complex narrative threads throughout the poem. Transitions of various kinds are central to her work. The poet has also been very involved in translating texts, and believes that because of the limits imposed by the translator, the process can never be completely true to the original language. Some literary critics see 'The Second Voyage' as an **extended metaphor exploring how language and culture resist translation**, but like so many of Ní Chuilleanáin's enigmatic poems, the ultimate interpretation is left to individual readers themselves.

ANALYSIS

'Ní Chuilleanáin's poetry makes effective use of contrasts to illuminate her themes.' Discuss this view, with particular reference to 'The Second Voyage'.

Sample Paragraph

Contrasting themes, such as life and death, permanence and transience, and motion and stillness are all prominent within Eiléan Ní Chuilleanáin's 'The Second Voyage'. Such contrasts make it easier to understand her poetic world. The opening description of arrogant Odysseus who 'rammed' his oar against the waves shows a macho larger-than-life character whose extrovert behaviour could not be more unlike the silent sea with its 'Uncertain depth' which he will never tame. Momentarily, the irritated hero makes up his mind to undertake a new 'voyage' by seeking glory on land. But the reality of settled life disappoints him. Revealing images of fixed landmarks – 'a gatepost', 'hitching-post', 'tidemark' – all convey the sense of motionless disinterest. Odysseus is immediately aware of the contrasting dynamic qualities of the sea's 'Unfenced valleys'. Throughout the last stanza, Odysseus debates the relative attractions of land and sea. I found it interesting that the man-made images were all water-based – 'fountains', 'brown trickles', 'the black canal' – and all lacking the mystery and danger of the open sea which Odysseus longs for. The ending of the poem rounds off the choices facing Odysseus. Once again, Ní Chuilleanáin succeeds in juxtaposing his love-hate obsession with the mysterious ocean as his tears taste 'Like his own sweat or the insults of the sea'.

Examiner's Comment

The introductory overview established a very good basis for exploring interesting contrasts within the poem. There is some well-focused and worthwhile personal engagement with the text and suitable quotations provide valuable support. Diction and expression are also excellent throughout. Grade A.

CLASS/HOMEWORK EXERCISES

1. 'Eiléan Ní Chuilleanáin presents readers with unsettling scenes, both real and otherworldly.' Discuss this statement, with particular reference to 'The Second Voyage'. Refer to the text in your answer.

2. Copy the table below into your own notes and fill in critical comments about the last two quotations.

Key Quotes

The ruffled foreheads of the waves/ Crocodiling and mincing past	Ní Chuilleanáin's sardonic humour personifies the sea to reflect Odysseus's irritation that it ignores him and is beyond his control.
In the simmering sea where scribbles of weed defined/Uncertain depth	Alliterative sibilant effects add to this vivid image of the inscrutable ocean that Odysseus finds so challenging and mysterious.
herons parcel out the miles of stream,/ Over gaps in the hills, through warm/ Silent valleys	
But the profound/Unfenced valleys of the ocean still held him	

main subject: life and death.

3 DEATHS AND ENGINES

We came down above the houses *feeling uneasy about landing.*
In a stiff curve, and
At the edge of Paris airport
Saw an empty tunnel *Comparing her father's death to the accident.*
– The back half of a plane, black *Adds to the chill of the experience.*
On the snow, nobody near it, *black on the snow: contrast.*
Tubular, burnt-out and frozen. *A sense of death and devestation*

When we faced again *assonance in use.*
The snow-white runways in the dark *continues the story of the plane*
No sound came over *adds a sense of being more eerie*
The loudspeakers, except the sighs
Of the lonely pilot. *despair, loneliness, worry. May be linked to father's death.*

The cold of metal wings is contagious: *internal rhyme + alliteration*
Soon you will need wings of your own, *"You" making it universal.*
Cornered in the angle where *Planes metal wings being cold,*
Time and life like a knife and fork *eventually we will experience*
Cross, and the lifeline in your palm *the coldness of death.*
Breaks, and the curve of an aeroplane's track *"wings" = angels.*
Meets the straight skyline. *brings death.* *Knife and fork: part of our lives, death is too.*

The images of relief: *Change of tone, more upbeat. Sometimes we can flee death*
Hospital pyjamas, screens round a bed *Happy cheerful mood.*
A man with a bloody face
Sitting up in bed, conversing cheerfully
Through cut lips: *alliteration.*
These will fail you some time. *mood change, we all won't be as lucky.*

You will find yourself alone *The final stanze offers a harsh*
Accelerating down a blind *truth that death will, after*
Alley, too late to stop *everything get us.*
And know how light your death is; *Metaphor: compares experience of death to driving down a dark alley.*
You will be scattered like wreckage, *run on lines to focus on the speed of death*
The pieces every one a different shape
Will spin and lodge in the hearts *We will cease to feel anything,*
Of all who love you. *it will impact the people that love us. we will live in the people that love us.*

'snow-white runways'

ends on a realistic yet hopeful way.

GLOSSARY

7   *Tubular*: cylindrical, tube shaped.
13   *contagious*: catching.
23   *conversing*: chatting.

27   *Accelerating*: speeding.
32   *lodge*: settle.

EXPLORATIONS

1. Describe the atmosphere at the airport in the first two stanzas. Refer to the text in your response.

2. Based on your reading of lines 13–25, choose one image that you found particularly memorable and comment on its effectiveness.

3. Write your personal response to 'Deaths and Engines', referring closely to the poem in your answer.

STUDY NOTES

'Deaths and Engines' contextualises Eiléan Ní Chuilleanáin's experience of death – and particularly her father's death – within the setting of another 'burnt-out' ruin: the abandoned wreckage of an aircraft engine. Characteristically, the poet's metaphorical sense is so complete that at times it dominates the poem, constantly inviting readers to tease out meaningful connections within the language.

As with so many of her poems, Ní Chuilleanáin begins mid-narrative – as dreams often do – with an aeroplane coming in to land in Paris. The sense of danger as the plane descends in 'a stiff curve' is typical of the edgy imagery found in **stanza one**. **The memory immediately suggests a moment of insight – of coming down to earth**: 'We came down above the houses/In a stiff curve'. Details are stark – particularly the absorbing description of the 'empty tunnel' and the peculiar sight of the 'back half of a plane' that has been 'burnt-out and frozen' against the wintry landscape. The contrast of the deserted 'black' wreckage 'On the snow' accentuates the visual effect, adding drama to the memory.

Stanza two emphasises the surreal nature of the hushed 'snow-white runways in the dark'. The poet continues to construct a dreamlike sense of uneasy silence and chilling alienation. The only sounds coming over the loudspeakers are the unsettling 'sighs/Of the lonely pilot'. There is an underlying suggestion of a weary individual – perhaps facing death. This is given a wider relevance by the unnerving opening of **stanza three**: 'The cold of metal wings is contagious'. For the poet, this insightful moment marks a changing perspective: 'Soon you will need wings of your own'. The 'you' might refer to Ní Chuilleanáin's dying father or the poet herself or possibly the reader. From this point onwards, the metaphor of the wrecked aircraft is central to the fragmentary memories of her father's illness and death. **The poet interweaves two narratives**: the trajectory of the plane as it 'Meets the straight skyline' and the mark of her father's natural life span ('the lifeline in your palm'). Ní Chuilleanáin uses the memorable image of the crossed knife and fork to suggest the inescapable destiny that confronts the dying.

The poet's familiar preoccupations of tension and mystery are even more obvious in **stanza four**. Disjointed scenes of 'Hospital pyjamas, screens round a bed' are introduced as 'images of relief'– at least temporarily. **But the prevailing mood is of inevitable death** – 'These will fail you some time'. The poet expresses the final reality of every human being in **stanza five**: 'You will find yourself alone'. Ní Chuilleanáin conveys the nightmarish realisation of irreversible death through recognisable images of losing control: 'Accelerating down a blind/Alley, too late to stop'. Run-on lines and a persistent rhythm add to the sense of powerlessness. Once again, there are echoes of the 'empty tunnel' and the 'burnt-out' plane. Nevertheless, in imagining her father's final moments, the poet can relate to his experience of dying as a release, so that they both understood 'how light your death is'.

The resigned tone of **stanza six** reflects Ní Chuilleanáin's deeper understanding of mortality. In celebrating her father's life within a context of enduring love, the poet is able to simultaneously dismantle and preserve the relationship she has had with her father. She returns to the image of the wrecked aeroplane, accepting that in death, 'You will be scattered like wreckage'. However, far from feeling sadness for her father's loss, **Ní Chuilleanáin takes comfort in knowing that he will live 'in the hearts/Of all who love you'**. The sentiment is subdued and poignant, and all the more powerful since it comes from a poet who rarely expresses her feelings directly.

To a great extent, the poem is about families and how they process their personal tragedies. As always, Ní Chuilleanáin's oblique approach is open to many interpretations. But she seems to be suggesting that it takes the sudden shock of death to acknowledge the closeness of relationships in our lives. Typically, in dealing with such emotional subjects as separation, grief and the death of a loved one, **the poet never lapses into sentimentality**. 'Deaths and Engines' was written during the escalation of violence in Northern Ireland, and some critics have understood the poem as a commentary on the human cost of conflict. In the end, readers are left to make up their own minds.

ANALYSIS

'Ní Chuilleanáin's poems of separation and estrangement transcend the limits of personal experience.' Discuss this view, with particular reference to 'Deaths and Engines'.

Sample Paragraph

One of the most interesting aspects of Eiléan Ní Chuilleanáin's poetry is her focus on the natural life cycle. Even though she deals with the distressing subject of her father's death in 'Deaths and Engines', I found the poem to be more uplifting than depressing. In closely comparing his death to the wrecked plane she saw in Paris, 'Tubular, burnt-out and frozen', she eventually realises that all the 'pieces' of the wreckage 'Will spin and lodge in the hearts/Of all who love you'. Just because death has separated her from her father physically does not mean the end of their love. The poem also shows Ní Chuilleanáin empathising with her father and stressing the individual experience of death for every human being: 'You will find yourself alone/Accelerating down a blind/ Alley, too late to stop'. Her message is simple – every individual must face death unaccompanied. In her poems, Ní Chuilleanáin can really accept the natural cycle – and this has meaning for every reader. In 'Fireman's Lift', for example, she also came to terms with a close family death – that of her mother by comparing her passing to the glorious Assumption of the Virgin Mary. I believe that such poems transcend the individual and emphasise the naturalness of separation and loss.

Examiner's Comment

This is a well-focused response to the question and shows a close understanding of the poem. Accurate quotations are used effectively to support key points. Expression is clear and there is some good personal engagement. The cross-reference is also welcome. Grade A.

CLASS/HOMEWORK EXERCISES

1. 'What defines Eiléan Ní Chuilleanáin's poetry is its imaginative power and precision of language.' Discuss this statement, with particular reference to 'Deaths and Engines'.

2. Copy the table below into your own notes and fill in critical comments about the last two quotations.

Key Quotes

The back half of a plane, black/On the snow, nobody near it	Ní Chuilleanáin's graphic description of the abandoned aircraft – associating it with disaster and violent death – is surreal and unnerving. Like so much of her writing, it transports readers into states of refreshed perception.
The cold of metal wings is contagious:/Soon you will need wings of your own	The frozen wings of the wrecked plane make an immediate impact on the poet, who connects the image to her father. There is an underlying sense of realisation and the suggestion of angels leading the dying soul to heaven.
The images of relief:/ Hospital pyjamas, screens round a bed	
And know how light your death is	

ordinary title.

4   STREET *explores edges and boundaries*
poem creates a dream like situation

Run on lines: adds to his excitement
when seeing her + the blood.   *(Narrative)*

He fell in love with the butcher's daughter *Opens with an unidentified*
                                                man falling in
When he saw her passing by in her white trousers *love with an unidentified*
Butcher's   *woman.*
daughter, Dangling a knife on a ring at her belt. *Connected with her*
makes it   *job*
more. He stared at the dark shining drops on the paving-stones. *Tease*
sinister *He is fascinated by her, he is staring at the blood from the*
and   *blood is attracting* *knife.*
eerie. One day he followed her *build of tension.*   *him*   5.
                                                         picturing him *creating*
Half open or, Down the slanting lane at the back of the shambles. *around* *sense of*
closed?   *unease.*
Is only A door stood half-open *Has she left it open*
half the   *on purpose?*
story being And the stairs were brushed and clean, *feminine qualities. "slanting journey"*
told? Her shoes paired on the bottom step, *keeping in touch with feminine*
Mystery.   *side.*
Each tread marked with the red crescent *concrete images* 10 *contrast to*
                                          but obscure   *the*
Her bare heels left, fading to faintest at the top.   *butchers'.*
                     alliteration.
an enigma at the end. Created suspense + tension,
"red crescent", referring to blood.   'And the stairs were brushed and clean'

GLOSSARY

3   *Dangling*: hanging freely, displaying.
6   *shambles*: untidy market scene; place
     of slaughter.
10   *tread*: undersole of a shoe; top
     surface of a step in a staircase.

10   *crescent*: half-moon; sickle shape.
11   *fading*: dwindling, perishing.
11   *faintest*: weakest, exhausted.

EXPLORATIONS

1. Why do you think Ní Chuilleanáin chose to name her poem 'Street' and yet gives the street no name? Give reasons for your response.

2. Which image did you find most intriguing in the poem? Refer closely to the text in your answer.

3. Were you satisfied by the poem's conclusion? Briefly explain your response.

STUDY NOTES

'Street' is a short lyric poem from Ní Chuilleanáin's collection The Magdalene Sermon *(1989). Mary Magdalene was the first person to witness the Resurrection of Christ and these poems reflect on women's religious experiences. The poems also depict edges, borders and crossings between different kinds of worlds as though passing through thresholds and intersections from one realm of experience to another, just as Christ rose from the dead. Characteristically, the poet reveals and conceals women and their strange responsibilities in a graceful, luminous voice.*

Ní Chuilleanáin believed in the importance of the ordinary and the domestic as new metaphors for human experience. In the **first section** of the poem, she quietly tells a somewhat unusual tale, giving readers a memorable glimpse into another reality. It is the story of a man falling in love with a woman, 'the butcher's daughter'. Flowing run-on lines depict the rising emotions of the man as he catches sight of her 'in her white trousers'. This colour is often associated with purity and innocence, but it is also the traditional colour butchers wear in their work. **A close-up shot captures a disturbing detail.** 'Dangling' describes the careless movement of the knife as it sways from the 'ring at her belt'. The verb is carefully positioned at the beginning of the line, as it tantalises and entices like a piece of shining jewellery; yet this knife has a deadly purpose. The man is captivated: 'He stared at the dark shining drops on the paving-stones'. Has this knife recently been used? Has blood just been spilled? Is he, as if in a fairytale, suddenly enthralled by the glittering yet lethal trade of the slaughterer?

In the **second section**, the narrative continues, becoming increasingly menacing: 'One day he followed her'. The assonant 'ow' sound disquietly enhances his journey. Ní Chuilleanáin specialises in the 'poetic of descriptive places'. The man's journey takes him 'Down the slanting lane at the back of the shambles'. **Varying line lengths add to the growing tension.** The adjective 'slanting' suggests a sinister backstreet where everything is oblique, tilted, half-concealed. The 'shambles' is a rough market where meat is carved and animals are slaughtered. To the outside world, it is a place of violence and mayhem. Is Ní Chuilleanáin making a hidden reference to the slaughter of Christ on the cross? 'A door stood half-open'. Does the door admit or shut out? Is this a symbol of the threshold between life and death which Christ breached? As always, the poet invites the reader to make sense of the clues. A secret is being half-revealed, a mystery is being highlighted. Where does the door lead?

Eiléan Ní Chuilleanáin often peoples her poems with women who studiously attend to their chores. (Mary Magdalene attended to Jesus, washing his feet with her tears and drying them with her hair.) Here 'the stairs were brushed and clean'. Are they awaiting a visit or is this the attention to hygiene which is normal in the butchering trade? This poet's population of silent figures disclose little information. The 'butcher's daughter' had left 'shoes paired on the bottom step'. Yet even this tangible detail reveals only mystery. The full narrative is missing. Is there a suggestion that the man and woman will soon be a pair as well? An inviting flight of stairs leads to all sorts of possibilities. **Ní Chuilleanáin has created a typically ambivalent scenario** filled with underlying danger and excitement. This dreamlike encounter is imbued with an unforgettable atmosphere of edgy anticipation as profound silence echoes.

The poem concludes with a defined image. The girl's 'bare heels' have left traces which become more indistinct as they ascend the stairs. This is emphasised by the alliterative phrase 'fading to faintest'. These are 'marked with the red crescent', like a secret sign beckoning through the enjambed lines. **The mystery resonates.** What really is marked with the bow shapes? The stairs? Her shoes? The heels? Readers are kept wondering. What does the future hold for this couple? Detailed close-ups have been presented, yet there are tantalising gaps in the narrative as we are left like the man who was enticed by the 'Dangling' knife, lured into this ominous atmosphere. As in so many of her elusive dramas, disrupting patterns of communication allows the poet to draw attention to the problem of communication itself. Is this the rounded insight to be glimpsed in the poem?

ANALYSIS

'Poems of waiting, dramatic and incident rich, are told quietly by Ní Chuilleanáin.' Discuss this statement in relation to the poem 'Street'.

Sample Paragraph

I felt that the poem 'Street' inveigled me into its dreamlike, surreal yet tangible world rather like the man is lured by the 'butcher's daughter'. I was caught as if in a dream, that state of consciousness which shimmers between sleep and wakefulness, where details are clearly recognisable, 'the dark shining drops', 'the red crescent/her bare heels left', yet their meaning is shrouded in mystery. Just as the 'half-open' door both invites and repels, this poem reveals and conceals as the reader wonders what is about to happen. Will the encounter take place between the man and the woman? Will he disappear at the top of the steps? Is she waiting for him there or has she disappeared? What has she been doing? What will she do? The reader has been brought like the man on a 'slanting' journey. The full view of the lane was obscured from him, the full story is hidden from the reader by the obliqueness of the poem. Yet just like a dream the atmosphere is unforgettable, the waiting is palpably ominous. The poem disappears at its conclusion as the 'red crescent' marks flow 'fading to faintest at the top'. Suspense and tension reverberate. As in life nobody knows what will happen next. This tale is told calmly as the poet carefully positions the instrument of allure at the edge of the line 'Dangling' to highlight its swaying inviting movement. The reader is led like the man, by well-realised signs, 'drops', a 'lane', a 'door', 'stairs' and footprints as if following a trail in a fairytale. Yet the poet does not release the dramatic tensions at the poem's conclusion leaving it to resonate in the reader's consciousness.

Examiner's Comment

This response shows a remarkably close reading of the poem, using suitable reference and quotation to address the question throughout. Discussion points are clear and there is good engagement with the text. Expression is impressive – fluent, varied and well controlled. Grade A.

> ## CLASS/HOMEWORK EXERCISES

1. 'Ní Chuilleanáin's poetry is oblique, yet concrete.' Discuss this statement in relation to 'Street'.

2. Copy the table below into your own notes and fill in critical comments about the last two quotations.

Key Quotes

He fell in love with the butcher's daughter	This poem opens in the manner of a fairytale with clear, uncluttered narrative. Neither the people nor the street are named, giving the poem a universal significance and the mystery of myth.
dark shining drops on the paving-stones	The evidence of the butcher's trade lies on the ground, yet the attraction of the blood stains is pinpointed by the focus on their lurid, glistening appearance.
A door stood half-open	
Each tread marked with the red crescent	

This poem represents a persons →
dying journey they have to go through
in order to pass onto another world.
Closes with a sense of love and loss.

(handwritten top margin): struggle that the angels have to lift Mary into heaven. The skill needed by nurses in looking after sick/powerless people. Struggle behind labour + the wonder of a woman giving birth.

5 **FIREMAN'S LIFT** *(handwritten: ordinary title, supporting the full weight of a person on your shoulders, linked to angels heaving Mary to heaven.)*

I was standing beside you looking up *(handwritten: narrative style opening, recalling a shared memory)*
Through the big tree of the cupola *(handwritten: captures the beauty of the dome shaped, dome if opening up, painting.)*
Where the church splits wide open to admit *(handwritten: The brightness seems intense.)*
(handwritten: alliteration) Celestial choirs, the fall-out of brightness. *(handwritten: Heavenly touch – "celestial" adds to the splendor and awe. Intimate moment shared between mother and daughter.)*

The Virgin was spiralling to heaven,
Hauled up in stages. Past mist and shining, *(handwritten: sense their determination)*
Teams of angelic arms were heaving, *(handwritten: sense the protective loving side to the angels. Reflects energy from)*
Supporting, crowding her, and we stepped *(handwritten: the firemen to haul people to safety)*

(handwritten left margin: filled with energy and busyness. reflects sorts of labour / birth.)

Back, as the painter longed to *(handwritten: recalls them taking in its totality. Very active, the whole time (painting))*
While his arm swept in the large strokes.
We saw the work entire, and how light 10

Melted and faded bodies so that *(handwritten: The architecture + art come together as one to create)*
Loose feet and elbows and staring eyes *(handwritten: this illusion, its a masterpiece.)*
Floated in the wide stone petticoat
Clear and free as weeds. *(handwritten: Simile, to tell us about the floating sensation)* 15

This is what love sees, that angle: *(handwritten: Her mother's womb bared her, like Mary's womb bared Jesus.)*
The crick in the branch loaded with fruit,
A jaw defining itself, a shoulder yoked, *(handwritten: Images of determination.)*

The back making itself a roof *(handwritten: Crane lifting her up and)*
The legs a bridge, the hands *(handwritten: also cradling the body.)* 20
A crane and a cradle. *(handwritten: Nurses look after sick people, minding them every step of the way. love and affection so relevant)*

Their heads bowed over to reflect on her *(handwritten: Contradictory statement. (paradox))*
Fair face and hair so like their own *(handwritten: Poet reflects the gentleness of the angels.)*
As she passed through their hands. We saw them *(handwritten: Could be her mother passing her)*
Lifting her, the pillars of their arms *(handwritten: power/strength from one world to another. support system, on angels behalf/nurses.)* 25
(handwritten left margin: The Virgin) (Her face a capital leaning into an arch) *(handwritten: She needs the support.)*
As the muscles clung and shifted
For a final purchase together
Under her weight as she came to the edge of the cloud. *(handwritten: A quiet kind of triumph, sense of achievement.)*
(handwritten: The Virgin Mary has reached heaven + her mother has passed on to the next life.)
Parma 1963 – Dublin 1994

(handwritten: 'spiralling to heaven')

GLOSSARY

Fireman's Lift: The term refers to a technique commonly used by emergency service workers to carry someone to safety by placing the carried person across the shoulders of the carrier.

The Assumption of the Virgin: Roman Catholic Church teaching states that the Virgin Mary, having completed the course of her earthly life, was assumed (or elevated) body and soul into heavenly glory.

Antonio Allegri da Correggio (1489–1534), usually known as Correggio, was the foremost painter of the Parma school of the Italian Renaissance. One of his best-known works, *The Assumption of the Virgin*, is a fresco which decorates the dome of the Duomo (Cathedral) of Parma, in northern Italy.

2   *cupola*: dome-shaped roof.
4   *Celestial*: heavenly, divine.
5   *spiralling*: whirling, twisting.
17 *crick*: arch, strain.
18 *yoked*: forced, strained.
26 *capital*: upper section of a column supporting a ceiling or arch.

EXPLORATIONS

1. Based on your reading of the poem, comment on the appropriateness of the title, 'Fireman's Lift'.

2. Choose one visual image from the poem which you consider particularly effective. Briefly explain your choice.

3. Write your own short personal response to the poem.

STUDY NOTES

This extraordinary poem describes the scene depicted in the painter Correggio's masterpiece, Assumption of the Virgin. In 1963 Eiléan Ní Chuilleanáin and her mother had visited Parma Cathedral. Following her mother's death in 1994, the poet used the visit as the setting for 'Fireman's Lift', describing it as a 'cheering-up poem, when my mother was dying because I absolutely knew that she would want me to write a poem about her dying...'

The poem begins with Ní Chuilleanáin's vivid memory of the moment when she and her mother were looking up at Corregio's celebrated ceiling mural. In the **opening stanza**, she invites readers into the Italian setting: 'I was standing beside you looking up/Through the big tree of the cupola'. There is an **immediate dreamlike sense of intimacy and closeness between mother and daughter**, as though they were both aware that something significant was happening. From the outset, the focus is on the majestic painting's mystery and symbolism, reaching heavenwards to imagined 'Celestial choirs'.

Stanza two emphasises the struggle of the angels to lift Mary into the heavens, and the awkwardness and wonder of being pushed in such a similar manner to birth. We are encouraged to become part of the dynamic scene within the reality of this great spectacle. The dynamic verbs 'spiralling' and 'heaving' suggest **the physical effort involved in raising the Virgin from her earthly life**. Line breaks and frequent commas are used to create a sluggish pace. Ní Chuilleanáin is drawn to the collective energy which becomes a fireman's lift of 'Teams of angelic arms', and the effort to raise Mary 'Past mist and shining' is relentless.

Ní Chuilleanáin then considers the overwhelming effect of Corregio's 'work entire', designed to give the illusion of real and simulated architecture within the painted fresco. This awe-inspiring achievement is reflected in the pulsating run-through rhythms and hushed tones of **stanzas three** and **four**. **Dramatic images of the angelic figures and saints assisting Mary's Assumption give expression to the artist's powerful vision**: 'Melted and faded bodies' are intermingled with 'elbows and staring eyes'. Within the dome/petticoat image, Ní Chuilleanáin describes Correggio's Virgin passing into another glorious life. All the time, this vortex of bodies and faces around her are fully engaged in assisting Mary to reach the waiting Christ.

Stanza five defines an important turning point for the poet, who can now make sense of her mother's death through a fresh understanding of Corregio's perspective: 'This is what love sees, that angle'. **The assured tone marks a coming-to-terms with deep personal loss.** Ní Chuilleanáin's renewed appreciation of the painting enables her to accept the burden of letting the dead go. Her resignation is evident in the poignant image of a 'branch loaded with fruit', an obvious symbol of the natural cycle.

Stanzas six and **seven** return to **Corregio's mesmerising skill in his interaction of art and architecture** within the cathedral dome. This intricate collusion is seen in sharper focus, providing a context for Ní Chuilleanáin to reassert her changing relationship with her mother. The restless limbs of the painted angels are in perfect harmony with the great Duomo ceiling: 'The back making itself a roof/The legs a bridge'. This intriguingly harmonious composition merging paint and plaster adds to the urgency of ensuring that the dying soul achieves its ultimate ascension to heaven.

The **final stanzas** observe the figures attending on Mary, 'heads bowed over to reflect on her/Fair face'. Their tenderness is evident in both sound and tone. The poet has said that, on one level, 'Fireman's Lift' is about the nurses who looked after her mother when she was dying. Typically, the poet broadens our understanding of suffering, showing people caring and concerned. The concluding lines, however, acknowledge **the strength of spirit which Ní Chuilleanáin singles out as the hallmark of her mother's life and death**. This is reflected in the purposeful expression on the Virgin's face: 'As the muscles clung and shifted/For a final purchase'. Tactile 'u' sounds ('usc', 'ung', 'urch', etc.) and the drawn-out rhythms emphasise that body goes with soul in the movement across this threshold: 'to the edge of the cloud'.

Death and rebirth are recurring themes in Ní Chuilleanáin's work. But in honouring her mother's life and associating her passing with the Assumption of the Virgin, the poet has brought together Italian art, religion and a deep sense of sorrow. Essentially, however, **'Fireman's Lift' is a moving expression of the poet's enduring love** for her mother. It is not unusual for readers of Ní Chuilleanáin's poetry to encounter beautiful images which leave them searching. Nevertheless, this poem has a universal significance. It is infused with an astounding sense of love, loss and triumph as the ascending figure disappears into the clouds. Poised on the edge of this unknowable boundary, the rest is mystery.

ANALYSIS

'For Eiléan Ní Chuilleanáin, boundaries and transitions are central concerns.' Discuss this view with particular reference to 'Fireman's Lift'.

Sample Paragraph

I found 'Fireman's Lift' both puzzling and interesting. Ní Chuilleanáin managed to link her mother's death with the famous painting by Antonio Correggio, *The Assumption of the Virgin*. In describing her memory of a holiday visit to Parma Cathedral, the poet seemed to enter the reality of the mural and see her own relationship with her mother in a new way – almost like one of the angels who desperately tries to raise Mary to heaven, 'Teams of angelic arms were heaving'. The transition is shown in terms of brute strength – the Virgin is 'Hauled up in stages'. But the poet also reflects the transition between this life and the next in the optical illusions painted on the dome's structure. Everything appears to be integrated – for example, the hands of angels act as a 'crane and a cradle' supporting Mary. She leans on the 'pillars of their arms'. This metaphor blurs the distinction between stonework and painted figures. The poet sees no difference between her own prayers for her mother's soul and the work of the saints who raise the Virgin. To me, Ní Chuilleanáin is absorbed in the art work. I found this typical of her poetry in that she wanders beyond borders and margins, just as Correggio did within his celebrated painting.

Examiner's Comment

This is a very well-written response which addresses the question directly and uses references effectively. There is good engagement with the poem throughout. Clear points explore the poet's emphasis on the blurred lines within the Correggio painting, and between it and Ní Chuilleanáin's own attitude. Grade-A standard.

CLASS/HOMEWORK EXERCISES

1. 'Eiléan Ní Chuilleanáin's poems explore the persistence of memory in a highly distinctive style.' Discuss this statement with particular reference to 'Fireman's Lift'.

2. Copy the table below into your own notes and fill in critical comments about the last two quotations.

Key Quotes

I was standing beside you looking up	Ní Chuilleanáin's simple opening image is not only applicable to a shared moment in Parma Cathedral, but suggests the tender memories of children and the lasting influence of parents.
Teams of angelic arms were heaving	The energetic language and forceful alliteration reflect the enormous collective effort to ensure the Virgin Mary's ascension to heaven.
As she passed through their hands the muscles clung and shifted	

❻ ALL FOR YOU

Once beyond the gate of the strange stableyard, we dismount.
The donkey walks on, straight in at a wide door
And sticks his head in a manger.

The great staircase of the hall slouches back,
Sprawling between warm wings. It is for you.   5
As the steps wind and warp
Among the vaults, their thick ribs part; the doors
Of guardroom, chapel, storeroom
Swing wide and the breath of ovens
Flows out, the rage of brushwood,   10
The roots torn and butchered.

It is for you, the dry fragrance of tea-chests
The tins shining in ranks, the ten-pound jars
Rich with shrivelled fruit. Where better to lie down
And sleep, along the labelled shelves,   15
With the key still in your pocket?

'steps wind and warp/Among the vaults'

GLOSSARY

6   *wind*: curve, meander.
6   *warp*: bend, buckle.
7   *vaults*: large rooms often used for storage; chambers beneath a church.

7   *ribs*: curved structures that support a vault.
10 *brushwood*: undergrowth, small twigs and branches.

EXPLORATIONS

1. Based on your reading of the poem, comment on the appropriateness of the title, 'All for You'.

2. Choose one memorable image from the poem and briefly explain its effectiveness.

3. Write your own individual response to the poem, referring closely to the text in your answer.

STUDY NOTES

'All for You' comes from Eiléan Ní Chuilleanáin's The Brazen Serpent *(1994). The book's title refers to the biblical story of Moses and the Israelites in the desert. God had become angry with his people, as they had spoken against their leader, Moses, and He let fierce snakes crawl among them and bite them. Moses prayed for the people and God instructed Moses to make a bronze serpent and place it upon a pole in public view. Anyone who was bitten could then look on the brazen snake and they would be cured. This foreshadows the raising onto the cross of Jesus Christ, who died to save sinners. Therefore, God made this sacrifice 'All for You'. Ní Chuilleanáin's collection of poems brings the possibility of hope, of getting through bad times, of being redeemed.*

Ní Chuilleanáin **collapses time and distinctions betweeen places** in 'All for You'. Line by line, the reader is drawn into deeper water until the bottom can no longer be touched, a recurring feature of this poet's complex work. The **first three lines** describe a scene that resonates with detail from the Bible story of the birth of Jesus: 'the strange stableyard', 'The donkey', the 'manger'. Why is the stableyard 'strange'? In the biblical account, Joseph and Mary had to leave their home town and travel to Bethlehem to be listed for a tax census. As is often the case with Ní Chuilleanáin's dramatic presentations, the reader must piece together a bare minimum of narrative sense. However, there is a sense of inevitability about the journey being described.

In **lines 4–11**, a noticeably different time and space is realised. What follows is **a series of evocative images and metaphors relating to a transitional experience**. Personification brings a staircase vividly to life as it 'slouches back', lolling and slumping – 'Sprawling' almost like a reclining animal as it sits between the 'warm wings' of the hall. Is it ominous or welcoming? It is waiting, as the bronze serpent awaited the Israelites, like a gift 'for you'. Ní Chuilleanáin does not determine the identity of 'you', instead leaving it open to speculation so that 'you' could have a universal application and refer to anyone. Is this gift for all? The poet's descriptive talent engages the reader as the grand staircase is depicted with great clarity, yet its full significance is never defined. Alliteration ('wind and warp') conveys the stairs' sinuous movement, curling like an uncoiling animal through the 'thick ribs' of the intimidating vaults.

The architectural metaphor is a strong element in Ní Chuilleanáin's poetry, which is full of mysterious crannies and alcoves. Could this imposing building be a convent waiting to welcome a young woman as its doors open, revealing the imposing interior of 'guardroom, chapel' and 'storeroom'? The poet's three aunts were nuns and she has commented, 'One is constantly made aware of the fact that the past does not go away, that it is walking around the place causing trouble at every moment.' Is this reference therefore autobiographical or does it encompass a wider significance? Could the staircase lead to salvation and heaven?

A rush of heat from the nearby ovens is suddenly palpable – again conveyed through the poet's effective working of personification: 'the breath of ovens/Flows out'. Ní Chuilleanáin uses a violent image to describe the fierce temperature: 'the rage of brushwood'. This is continued in the savagery with which the kindling has been collected: 'roots torn out and butchered'. Is there an echo of the biblical tale of the burning bush from the **Book of Exodus**, where God directed Moses to the Promised Land? This story teaches that we should be able to obey God whenever he calls us. Is the poet also referencing the story of Christ, 'butchered' on the cross for the sins of the world? The forceful rhythm of these dramatic lines creates an intensity, a climax of dread, almost like an ecstatic spiritual experience.

There is a marked **change of tone** in the **last five lines**. All the tension eases within the ordered space of the building's provisions store. Readers are now immersed in the moment, smelling the 'dry fragrance of tea-chests', observing 'tins shining in ranks, the ten-pound jars'. Repetition of the rich 'r' sound suggests the store's abundance of goods. Yet there is also an unease secreted in this image of confined order. The fruit is 'shrivelled', the fragrance is 'dry'. Is there a life withering, unable to reproduce? Is this another central dimension of religious life? The poem concludes with a rhetorical question intimating that there is nowhere better to take rest, just as Joseph and Mary did long ago in that 'strange stable yard', than here 'along the labelled shelves'. The body's surrender and submission to God's will enables it to act.

Another biblical reference is suggested in the final detail of the 'key still in your pocket'. In Isaiah 33:6, faith is the key to salvation: 'He will be the sure foundation of your times, a rich store of salvation and wisdom and knowledge; the fear of the Lord is the key to this treasure.' Ní Chuilleanáin's poem focuses on the experience of Christian faith as imagined through the imposing challenge and triumph of religious vocations. The 'key' image is typically contradictory – symbolising both confinement and freedom. Is the poet presenting the central paradox of Christian belief? Can the soul's redemption only be achieved through submission to God's will? Characteristically, Ní Chuilleanáin's multi-layered narrative has been subtly woven, offering a glimpse, perhaps, of salvation and hope.

ANALYSIS

'Eiléan Ní Chuilleanáin's poetry is an unshaped fire demanding to be organised into a sequence of words and images.' Discuss this statement in relation to 'All for You'.

Sample Paragraph

'All for You' is an unsettling poem which seems to emerge from the subconscious like an unformed fire. This poet's work resists containment as she wanders beyond borders. The poem springs from the idea of a gift which is 'All for You'. This can be the reward of spiritual salvation as the continuous references to the Bible – the story of Christ's birth is interwoven with references to Old Testament scenes, such as 'the rage of brushwood'. Like an 'unshaped fire', the poem's religious theme 'Flows out' like the heat from the ovens. Yet it is carefully layered. Fragmentary narratives are overlaid and remain long after the poem is read. I thought the image of the writhing staircase which 'slouches back' was very effective as it suggested the brazen serpent which Moses erected to gain salvation for his own people. The image also symbolised the harsh ladder of life which Christians must climb to reach salvation. Ní Chuilleanáin's use of alliteration, 'wind and warp', emphasised the twisting turns life takes and also called to mind the uncoiling serpent – the devil, perhaps. The poet has often written about nuns and she includes several interesting images relating to the enclosed life of a convent. I got the sense of being in a strange building with old-fashioned rooms and vaults. The storeroom imagery reflected the enclosed religious world, with 'the dry fragrance of tea-chests' and 'shrivelled fruit'. The sense of routine and order was also present: 'The tins shining in ranks'. Ironically, this strict religious life of submission represented the 'key' to salvation. The repetition of 'It is for you' suggests a generous God wishing to give a precious gift and what gift could be more important than the gift of hope? All the poet's ideas are expressed in patterns of visionary and spiritual language which can be seen as a powerful 'unshaped fire'.

Examiner's Comment

A clear personal response to a challenging question. Key discussion points are effectively illustrated, showing a good understanding of this complex poem – and particularly the poet's use of dense symbols and overlapping images. Expression throughout is varied, fluent and well controlled. Grade A.

CLASS/HOMEWORK EXERCISES

1. 'Ní Chuilleanáin's language is supple and acute enough to undertake its most difficult subject: how we perceive and understand the world.' Discuss this statement in relation to the prescribed work of the poet on your course.

2. Copy the table below into your own notes and fill in critical comments about the last two quotations.

Key Quotes

The donkey walks on, straight in at a wide door/ And sticks his head in a manger	This scene is echoed in the following image of the hall where doors 'Swing wide'. The donkey does not hesitate to follow its instincts to take sustenance at its trough. Is it equally natural for someone entering a religious order to accept the gift being offered?
the steps wind and warp	Alliteration vividly conveys the twisting movement of the great staircase. The image could also be seen as a metaphor for the difficulties encountered in the Christian journey to salvation.
guardroom, chapel, storeroom	
the ten-pound jars/Rich with shrivelled fruit	

❼ FOLLOWING

So she follows the trail of her father's coat through the fair
Shouldering past beasts packed solid as books,
And the dealing men nearly as slow to give way –
A block of a belly, a back like a mountain,
A shifting elbow like a plumber's bend –   5
When she catches a glimpse of a shirt-cuff, a handkerchief,
Then the hard brim of his hat, skimming along,

Until she is tracing light footsteps
Across the shivering bog by starlight,
The dead corpse risen from the wakehouse   10
Gliding before her in a white habit.
The ground is forested with gesturing trunks,
Hands of women dragging needles,
Half-choked heads in the water of cuttings,
Mouths that roar like the noise of the fair day.   15

She comes to where he is seated
With whiskey poured in two glasses
In a library where the light is clean,
His clothes all finely laundered,
Ironed facings and linings.   20
The smooth foxed leaf has been hidden
In a forest of fine shufflings,
The square of white linen
That held three drops
Of her heart's blood is shelved   25
Between the gatherings
That go to make a book –
The crushed flowers among the pages crack
The spine open, push the bindings apart.

'And the dealing men nearly as slow to give way'

GLOSSARY

Following: coming after in time or sequence, people about to be mentioned or listed; those who admire or support somebody.

2 *beasts*: animals at an Irish mart.

3 *dealing men*: dealers, men who bargain as they buy and sell animals at an Irish fair.

5 *plumber's bend*: length of 18 inches from the bend of the elbow to the tip of the middle finger.

7 *brim*: edge.

10 *wakehouse*: house, particularly in Ireland, where a dead person is laid out; people come to console the grieving relatives and to pay their respects to the deceased.

14 *cuttings*: small pieces of plants.

20 *facings*: strengthening linings; collar, cuffs and trimmings on a uniform coat.

20 *linings*: layers of material used to cover and protect.

21 *foxed*: soiled; marked with fox-like reddish spots and stains, often found on old books and documents.

21 *leaf*: single sheet of paper.

22 *shufflings*: walking slowly and awkwardly.

29 *spine*: vertical back of book to which pages are attached.

29 *bindings*: material which holds pages together.

EXPLORATIONS

1. Based on your reading of the poem, show how Eiléan Ní Chuilleanáin conjures up the atmosphere of an Irish fair day. Refer closely to the text in your response.

2. In your opinion, how many settings are there in this poem? Which one did you prefer? Give reasons for your choice, quoting to support your answer.

3. Choose one vivid image from the third stanza of the poem and briefly explain its effectiveness.

STUDY NOTES

Eiléan Ní Chuilleanáin often assumes a storytelling role in her poems as she relates memories from the past. She readjusts the perspective of readers by taking us into the lives of ordinary people who literally and physically made history. In her collection The Brazen Serpent, *Ní Chuilleanáin highlights family and women as makers of history.*

She hints at the untold through her use of characters, silences and secrets. These
confidential witnesses, like the poet herself, reconstruct subtle revelations of family
unease and discontentment. Female imagery expresses what is silenced. The poet
frequently explores religious themes as well as death and rebirth. Quietly and precisely,
she offers us the comfort that the past does not go away.

In the **opening section**, the poet begins her story in her usual oblique,
non-confessional style, yet deeply engages the reader despite her seeming
detachment. A vividly realised journey by a girl through the hurly-burly of an
Irish fair day catapults the reader into the story. She is trying to follow her father
through the dense crowds: 'the trail of her father's coat through the fair'. Long
run-on lines and broad vowels convey the difficulty of negotiating the route as
she attempts to push past 'beasts packed as solid as books'. This unusual simile
illustrates the tightly packed rows of animals. Nor could she easily make her way
through the dealers, men caught up in the very serious business of buying and
selling, making a deal. Their thick-set bodies, bulky like their animals, are described
through a tumbling list of similes and metaphors to highlight their immobile
weight: 'A block of a belly, a back like a mountain'. A 'shifting elbow' is like the
measure used in plumbing. All these images reinforce the **tough, masculine world
of the fair**. Ní Chuilleanáin has pushed the reader, through her unwavering gaze,
into the poem's self-enclosed world.

Suddenly, in **line 6**, the girl catches a glimpse of her father. This is shown by
a list of his clothing: 'a shirt-cuff, a handkerchief,/Then the hard brim of his hat'.
His progress is swift and effortless. He moves as swiftly as the punctuation (a
series of fast-moving commas) accelerates the motion of the line. Sharp contrast
in the verbs used to describe the progress of the girl and her father **highlight
their different rates of success in moving through the fair**. The girl is struggling,
'Shouldering past', while the father moves with ease, 'skimming along'. Is Ní
Chuilleanáin suggesting that a woman finds it difficult to negotiate a man's world?
The poet has hypnotically caught the excitement as well as the danger of the fair
day.

Distance and time blur in the **second section**. Ní Chuilleanáin shifts the scene
and time frame from the noise and physical bulk of the fair to the **'shivering
bog'**. Personification and slender vowels effectively convey the cold 'starlight'
scene as she is revisiting, 'tracing light footsteps', mapping faint prints. **A surreal,
nightmarish world is presented**, as 'The dead corpse risen from the wakehouse'

appears 'before her in a white habit'. Whose corpse is this? The effortless sense of 'Gliding' suggests the agile movement of the father. Momentarily, the packed animals of the fair have given way to the ground 'forested with gesturing trunks'. Now the heavy trees are highlighting her way, as she will ultimately follow her father into death. Thin waving rushes are evocatively described as 'Hands of women dragging needles'. Their slow cumbersome movement is presented in visionary terms. Is this a reference to the story from the Bible when the Pharaoh of Egypt decreed that because of the increasing numbers of Israelites, all first-born boys were to be drowned in the River Nile? Are these the half-choked heads? Is this the wail of Israelite women and children as they cry and 'roar' like the beasts in the fair, aware of their fate? Or is it a reference to the subordination of women as they work?

In the poem's **concluding section**, the girl meets her father in a much more hospitable setting with 'whiskey poured in two glasses', 'His clothes all finely laundered'. Within these domestic interiors of the poet's imagination lies the remote **possibility of utopia**. The 'square of white linen', redolent of the survivor's suffering, shrunk and stained by the body's signifiers of hurt, becomes a relic of love and loss. Ní Chuilleanáin has commented, 'A relic is something you enclose, and then you enclose the reliquary in something else. In the The Book of Kells exhibition, the book satchel is in leather, which is meant to protect, and there is a shrine which in turn is meant to protect the book'. A relic is associated with people seeking comfort in difficult times. The past is beautifully evoked in the phrase 'The smooth foxed leaf has been hidden', with its haunting image of time-stained pages. Inside the book are 'crushed flowers', reminders that love was violated, yet something of it remains. These memories have tremendous power; they 'crack' and push apart as if being reborn. Living and dead touch each other through such memories. The dust and noise of the cattle market, the cold starry bog have all evaporated to be replaced by this interior where the 'light is clean', making it easy to see. Comfort and hope are being offered as the poem suggests that the past is not dead.

ANALYSIS

'Ní Chuilleanáin's poems explore how the most basic legends – family stories – fragment and alter in each individual's memory.' Discuss this statement with particular reference to the poem 'Following'.

Sample Paragraph

I think we tell ourselves stories about the past and I wonder do we need to revisit them in order to see the past differently, to assimilate it and move on in hope? Ní Chuilleanáin's poem, 'Following', dredges up fragments of uniquely Irish family stories (the fair day, a wake, women sewing) and rearranges them, as cards are moved in 'shufflings'. This reconstructs and transforms the past so that we can see and understand from a new perspective. We are brought as followers, just like the girl in the fair, on a journey to discover that the past is not dead, but resonates through the present by means of relics, 'The square of white linen', and so gives hope and comfort to those left behind. The title suggests to me that we are all following one another on the same journey through life, but at different paces, as the girl and the father in the fair. In the masculine world of the fair, 'beasts packed solid as books' the girl found it hard to negotiate her way. The poet has identified the difficult role women have in life, 'dragging needles', employed in repetitive domestic drudgery. These women are unable to express their opinions and concerns, 'Half-choked'. The legends become 'crushed flowers' yet the poet suggests that they are so potent that they can 'crack' open and push apart the book in which they are enclosed. I felt that she was communicating the message of hope that the past does not stay in the past but reverberates and pulses through the present. Our memories do not remain 'shelved' but live again in the present through the power of relics.

Examiner's Comment

This is an assured response, focused throughout and very well illustrated. Quotations are integrated effectively and the answer ranges widely. There is clear evidence of good engagement with the poet's central theme of memory. Expression is also varied and well controlled. Grade A.

CLASS/HOMEWORK EXERCISES

1. 'The mysterious writing style of Ní Chuilleanáin allows the reader to explore the poems on many levels, each tracking a different aspect of the cycle of life.' Discuss this statement in relation to the prescribed poems of this poet on your course.

2. Copy the table below into your own notes and fill in critical comments about the last two quotations.

Key Quotes

Following	This title not only refers to the girl's efforts to follow her father, but also to her admiration of him and how he was about to be remembered. It also suggests that she is following her father as he moves through life to death.
Half-choked heads in the water of cuttings	Two stories merge: the biblical account of the drowned children of the Jews and the contemporary story of women's subordination in the sharp world of dominant men. Their lack of opportunity and importance is graphically conveyed in the compound word 'Half-choked'.
In a forest of fine shufflings	
The square of white linen	

8 KILCASH

From the Irish, c.1800

What will we do now for timber,
With the last of the woods laid low –
No word of Kilcash nor its household,
Their bell is silenced now,
Where the lady lived with such honour,   5
No woman so heaped with praise,
Earls came across oceans to see her
And heard the sweet words of Mass.

It's the cause of my long affliction
To see your neat gates knocked down,   10
The long walks affording no shade now
And the avenue overgrown,
The fine house that kept out the weather,
Its people depressed and tamed;
And their names with the faithful departed,   15
The Bishop and Lady Iveagh!

The geese and the ducks' commotion,
The eagle's shout, are no more,
The roar of the bees gone silent,
Their wax and their honey store   20
Deserted. Now at evening
The musical birds are stilled
And the cuckoo is dumb in the treetops
That sang lullaby to the world.

Even the deer and the hunters   25
That follow the mountain way
Look down upon us with pity,
The house that was famed in its day;
The smooth wide lawn is all broken,
No shelter from wind and rain;   30
The paddock has turned to a dairy
Where the fine creatures grazed.

Mist hangs low on the branches
No sunlight can sweep aside,
Darkness falls among daylight   35
And the streams are all run dry;
No hazel, no holly, no berry,
Bare naked rocks and cold;
The forest park is leafless
And all the game gone wild.   40

And now the worst of our troubles:
She has followed the prince of the Gaels –
He has borne off the gentle maiden,
Summoned to France and to Spain.
Her company laments her   45
That she fed with silver and gold:
One who never preyed on the people
But was the poor souls' friend.

My prayer to Mary and Jesus
She may come safe home to us here   50
To dancing and rejoicing
To fiddling and bonfire
That our ancestors' house will rise up,
Kilcash built up anew
And from now to the end of the story   55
May it never again be laid low.

'long walks affording no shade now'

GLOSSARY

Title: Eiléan Ní Chuilleanáin's translation of the early 19th-century ballad *Caoine Cill Chais* (The Lament for Kilcash), an anonymous lament that the castle of Cill Chais stood empty, its woods cut down and all its old grandeur disappeared. Kilcash was one of the great houses of a branch of the Butler family near Clonmel, Co. Tipperary, until well into the 18th century. Ní Chuilleanáin's poem encompasses several generations of the Butler family, but the presiding spirit is that of Margaret Butler, Viscountess Iveagh (who died in 1744).

2   *the last of the woods*: a reference to the mass clearance of native Irish forests by plantation settlers to create agricultural land and to fuel the colonial economy. The woodland belonging to the Butlers of Kilcash were sold in 1797 and 1801.

5   *the lady*: Margaret Butler, Viscountess Iveagh, a staunch Catholic (d.1744).

16   *The Bishop*: Catholic clergy – including Lady Iveagh's brother-in-law – were often given shelter in Kilcash.

17   *commotion*: noise, clamour.

24   *lullaby*: soothing song.

31   *paddock*: enclosure.

42   *prince of the Gaels*: probably a reference to the 18th Earl of Ormonde.

43   *the gentle maiden*: Countess, wife of the 18th Earl.

47   *preyed*: harmed, took advantage of.

EXPLORATIONS

1. From your reading of the poem, what is your impression of Lady Iveagh? Refer to the text in your answer.

2. Choose one interesting image from 'Kilcash' that you consider particularly effective. Give reasons to explain why this image appealed to you.

3. Write your own individual response to the poem, referring closely to the text in your answer.

STUDY NOTES

'Kilcash' comes from Eiléan Ní Chuilleanáin's The Girl Who Married the Reindeer *(2001). Many of the poems in this collection deal with outsiders and the dispossessed. Kilcash was the great house of one of the branches of the Butler family near Clonmel, Co. Tipperary, until the 18th century. The Butlers were Catholic landed gentry who*

had come to Ireland as part of an Anglo-Norman invasion during the 12th century and had taken over vast amounts of land. Over time, the family became absorbed into Irish ways. Ní Chuilleanáin's version of the traditional Irish elegy, Caoine Cill Chais, *mourns the death of Margaret Butler, Viscountess Iveagh.*

Stanza one opens with a plaintive voice lamenting 'What will we do now for timber'. The ballad was originally composed in the early 1800s following the demise of the Butlers of Kilcash and the eventual clearing of the family's extensive woodlands, which had supplied timber for local people. **The early tone typifies the entire poem's sense of hopelessness now that the woods are 'laid low'.** The systematic felling of trees is symbolic of the decline of this aristocratic Catholic family. Following colonisation, the Irish were consigned to Nature as a symbol of their barbarity. In some British circles, they were referred to as the 'natural wild Irish' because the country's remote boglands and forests offered shelter to Irish rebels. The poem emphasises the uneasy silence around Kilcash and the speaker pays extravagant tribute to 'the lady' of the house, who is immediately associated with Ireland's Catholic resistance: 'Earls came across oceans to see her'.

As always, Ní Chuilleanáin's approach is layered, recognising the genuine feelings of loss while suggesting a misplaced dependence on all those who exploited the native population. For the most part, however, the poem's anonymous narrator appears to express the desolation ('long affliction') felt by the impoverished and leaderless Irish of the time. There is no shortage of evidence to illustrate what has happened to the 'fine house'. Throughout **stanzas two** and **three**, broad assonant sounds add to the maudlin sentiments. **The 'neat gates knocked down' and the 'avenue overgrown' reflect the dramatic turnaround in fortunes.** But is Ní Chuilleanáin's translation of the old song also unearthing an underlying sense of delight in the sudden fall of the mighty? There is 'no shade now' for the once powerful gentry as well as the impoverished community. Many of the references to the 'stilled' birds and animals can also be seen as both a loss and a possible release from an unhappy phase of oppression and dependence.

Images of hardship taken from nature dominate **stanzas four** and **five**. The abandoned peasants are depicted as pitiable. The atmosphere becomes increasingly disturbing as the natural world order is transformed: 'Darkness falls among daylight/And the streams are all run dry'. **As in so many other Irish legends, the landscape reflects the terms of the Butlers' exile**: 'The forest park is leafless'. Negative language patterns – 'No sunlight', 'No hazel, no holly' – highlight the sense of mordant despondency resulting from abandonment. Relentlessly, the regular lines and ponderous rhythm work together to create a monotonous trance-like effect. The extravagant praise for 'the gentle maiden' (a likely reference to the wife of the 18th Earl) dominates **stanza six**. As a representative of the Butler dynasty, her absence is seen as 'the worst of our troubles' and she is glorified as someone 'who never preyed on the people' despite her privileged lifestyle.

The prayer-like tone of the **final stanza** is in keeping with the deep yearning for a return to the old ways in Kilcash. The Catholic allusion also reinforces the central importance of religion in expressing political and cultural identity. In wishing to restore the former Gaelic order, the speaker imagines lively scenes of communal celebration: 'fiddling and bonfire'. **The aspiration that the castle will be 'built up anew' offers a clear symbol of recovery.** This rallying call is in keeping with traditional laments and is characteristic of the poet's sympathies for the oppressed. Ní Chuilleanáin has retained the rhetorical style of Gaelic poetry throughout, revealing the experience of isolated communities through numerous images of restless desolation and uncomfortable silences.

'Kilcash' marks a significant transition in Irish history. As the old native aristocracy suffered military and political defeat and, in many cases, exile, the world order that had supported the bardic poets disappeared. In these circumstances, it is hardly surprising that much Irish poetry of this period laments these changes and the poet's plight. However, **Ní Chuilleanáin's translation of the old ballad differs from other versions in being more ambivalent towards Viscountess Iveagh and what she represented**. Is the poem a poignant expression of loss and a genuine tribute to those landlords who were seen as humane? Does the poet satirise the subservient native Irish who had been conditioned to accept some convenient generosity from the Catholic gentry? To what extent did the original lament present a romantic distortion of Ireland's history? Readers are left to decide for themselves.

ANALYSIS

'Eiléan Ní Chuilleanáin's poems retain the power to connect past and present in ways that never cease to fascinate.' Discuss this statement, with particular reference to 'Kilcash'.

Sample Paragraph

On a first reading, I thought that 'Kilcash' was a simple adaptation of the old Gaelic ballad, 'Caoine Cill Chais'. After studying the poem, however, I feel that Eiléan Ní Chuilleanáin has raised many interesting questions about Irish history. For a start, the poem is a translation and the original bard's view of the 18th century Butler line is buried beneath Ní Chuilleanáin's. The opening lament of the deprived peasants seems self-pitying – 'What will we do now for timber'. The compliments paid to Lady Iveagh (Margaret Butler) are lavish and focus on her Catholic faith and support for the old Gaelic culture – 'Earls came across oceans to see her'. As a young person looking back on this period of upheaval, I could appreciate the way disposed Irish people had become dependent on the Catholic gentry as symbols of freedom. The poem repeatedly places 'the lady' as the epitome of hope – 'the poor souls' friend'. It was interesting to see how the flight of the Butlers reduced people to complete dependence, so that all they could do was pray for a miraculous reversal of history 'that our ancestors' house will rise up'. The main insight I gained from the poem was that colonisation – whether by Catholic or Protestant landlords – had broken the Irish spirit. Ní Chuilleanáin manages to link past and present very subtly, broadening our view of the complex relationships between powerful interests and a conquered population.

Examiner's Comment

An assured personal response, focused throughout and very well illustrated with suitable quotations. The paragraph carefully highlights Ní Chuilleanáin's exploration of the plight of the native Irish community in various ways. Points are clearly expressed throughout. Grade A.

CLASS/HOMEWORK EXERCISES

1. 'Ní Chuilleanáin's distinctive poetic world provides an accessible platform for voices from the margin.' Discuss this view, with particular reference to 'Kilcash'.

2. Copy the table below into your own notes and fill in critical comments about the last two quotations.

Key Quotes

What will we do now for timber,/With the last of the woods laid low	The opening admission of loss and dependence sets the nostalgic tone for the rest of this traditional ballad.
the sweet words of Mass	Ní Chuilleanáin emphasises the 'sweet words' of Catholicism as being of crucial importance to native Irish communities in expressing their cultural identity.
Darkness falls among daylight	
Her company laments her/ That she fed with silver and gold	

9 TRANSLATION *—reburial*
— voices of women
— conveys lonely image.

for the reburial of the Magdalenes
suggests respect.

The soil frayed and sifted evens the score — *colloquial language*
all the same despite different
There are women here from every county, *united in a shared background.*
injustice.
Just as there were in the laundry.   *↓ extent of suffering.*

esthetic language
White light blinded and bleached out   *change in language*
The high relief of a glance, where steam danced   *alliteration + personification*   5
Around stone drains and giggled and slipped across water.
emphasis broken sad lives.   *endless amount of laundry.*
not allowed look at each other.
Assist them now, ridges under the veil, shifting,   *prayer like*
spirits set spirits free through
Searching for their parents, their names,   *poignant, lost identities. death.*
The edges of words grinding against nature,   *restless spirits*
voices played   *(not happy)*
no part.
As if, when water sank between the rotten teeth   10
Of soap, and every grasp seemed melted, one voice   *physical imagery*
Had begun, rising above the shuffle and hum   *sense of struggle*
contrast: voice gaining power   *(hopelessness)*
Until every pocket in her skull blared with the note — *determined voice will*
be heard
Allow us now to hear it, sharp as an infant's cry   *— similes → comparing*   *voice*
While the grass takes root, while the steam rises: *adds*   15
(life goes on)   *poignancy.*

Washed clean of idiom · the baked crust   *— brings poem to conclusion*
Of words that made my temporary name ·   *— unusual punctuation*
A parasite that grew in me · that spell   *— rhyming scheme.*
Lifted · I lie in earth sifted to dust ·
Let the bunched keys I bore slacken and fall ·   20
I rise and forget · a cloud over my time.

'Washed clean of idiom'

✱ note at the back.
also.

GLOSSARY

Subtitle: The Magdalenes refers to Irish women, particularly unmarried mothers, who were separated from their children and forced to work in convent laundries. Inmates were required to undertake hard physical labour, including washing and needlework. They also endured a daily regime that included long periods of prayer and enforced silence. In Ireland, such institutions were known as Magdalene laundries. It has been estimated that up to 30,000 women passed through such laundries in Ireland, the last one of which (in Waterford) closed on 25 September 1996.

1   *frayed*: ragged.
1   *sifted*: sorted, examined.
3   *the laundry*: clothes washing area.
13 *blared*: rang out, resounded.
16 *idiom*: language, misinterpretation.
18 *parasite*: bloodsucker.

EXPLORATIONS

1. Comment on the effectiveness of the poem's title, 'Translation', in relation to the themes that Ní Chuilleanáin addresses in the poem.

2. Choose one image from the poem that you found particularly interesting. Briefly explain your choice.

3. How does the poem make you feel? Give reasons for your response, supporting the points you make with reference to the text.

STUDY NOTES

During the early 1990s, the remains of more than 150 women were discovered at several Dublin religious institutions as the properties were being excavated. The bones, from women buried over a very long period, were cremated and reburied in Glasnevin Cemetery. Eiléan Ní Chuilleanáin's poem was read at the reburial ceremony to commemorate Magdalene laundry women from all over Ireland. 'Translation' links the writer's work with the belated acknowledgement, in the late 20th century, of the stolen lives and hidden deaths of generations of Irishwomen incarcerated in Magdalene convents.

The poem begins with a macabre description of the Glasnevin grave where the reburial is taking place: 'The soil frayed and sifted evens the score'. Ní Chuilleanáin expresses the feelings of the mourners ('here from every county') who are **united by a shared sense of injustice**. This dramatic ceremony represents a formal acknowledgement of a dark period in Ireland's social history. **Line 4** takes readers back in time behind convent walls and imagines the grim laundry rooms in which the Magdelene women worked: 'White light blinded and bleached out/The high relief of a glance'.

The poet's delicate and precise language contrasts the grinding oppression of routine manual labour with the young women's natural playfulness. **Their stolen youth and lost gaiety are poignantly conveyed through familiar images of the laundry,** 'where steam danced/Around stone drains and giggled and slipped across water' (**line 6**). Vigorous verbs and a jaunty rhythm add emphasis to the sad irony of their broken lives. The relentless scrubbing was intended to wash away the women's sins. However, no matter how much the women washed, they were considered dirty and sinful throughout their lives.

All through the poem, Ní Chuilleanáin focuses on the importance of words and naming as though she herself is aiming to make sense of the shocking Magdalene story. But how is she to respond to the women who have come to the graveyard, 'Searching for their parents, their names'? Typically, the language is dense and multi-layered. In death, these former laundry workers are mere 'ridges under the veil' of the anonymous earth. The metaphor in **line 7** also evokes images of the stern Magdalene nuns. **Ní Chuilleanáin sees all these women as victims of less enlightened times**, ironically recalled in the prayer-like note of invocation: 'Assist them now'.

The poem's title becomes clear as we recognise **Ní Chuilleanáin's intention to communicate ('translate') decades of silence into meaningful expression on behalf of the Magdalene laundry inmates**. Their relentless efforts to eventually become a 'voice' is compared to the almost impossible challenge of 'rising above the shuffle and hum' within the noisy laundry itself. In **line 9**, Ní Chuilleanáin visualises the women setting 'The edges of words grinding against nature' until their misrepresentation is overcome as it is turned to dust along with their bodies.

From **line 13**, much of the **focus is placed on exploring the experience of one of the nuns who managed the laundries**. As the true history emerges, she is also being cleansed of 'the baked crust/Of words that made my temporary name'. The 'temporary name' is her name in religion, that is, the saint's name she chose upon entering strict convent life, which, as Ní Chuilleanáin notes, involved relinquishing her previous identity as an individual. She too has been exploited and the poet's generous tone reflects an understanding of this woman, who is caught between conflicting influences of duty, care, indoctrination and doubt, 'Until every pocket in her skull blared'. The evocative reference to the 'infant's cry' echoes the enduring sense of loss felt by young mothers who were forced to give up their babies shortly after birth.

In the poem's **final lines**, we hear the voice of a convent reverend mother, whose role is defined by 'the bunched keys I bore'. The reburial ceremony has also cleansed her from 'that spell' which maintained the cruel system she once served. Almost overwhelmed, she now recognises the 'parasite' power 'that grew in me' and only now can the keys she carries, an obvious symbol of her role as gaoler, 'slacken and fall'. **Bleak, disturbing images and broken rhythms have an unnerving, timeless effect.** This woman's punitive authority over others has haunted her beyond the grave.

In the end, Ní Chuilleanáin's measured and balanced approach shows genuine compassion for all institutionalised victims, drawing together the countless young women and those in charge in their common confinement. In addition to their time spent in convents, they are now reunited, sifting the earth that they have all become. **The tragic legacy of these institutions involves women at many levels.** Nevertheless, the poem itself is a faithful translation, as these victims have been raised from their graves by the poet's response to their collective dead voice. Ní Chuilleanáin relates their compelling story to 'Allow us now to hear it'. She also tenderly acknowledges the complete silencing of the Irish Magdalenes as they did their enforced and, in some cases, lifelong penance.

Although Eiléan Ní Chuilleanáin's mournful 'translation' reveals glimpses of their true history, **none of these Magdalene women can ever be given back the lives they had before they entered the laundries**. The poem stops short of pretending to even the score in terms of power between those in authority and the totally subservient and permanently disgraced women under their control. At best, their small voices rise up together like 'steam' and form a 'cloud over my time' (**line 21**). This metaphor of the cloud can be construed as a shadow of shame over Irish society, but it can also be seen as a warning that the cycle of abuse is likely to be repeated.

ANALYSIS

'Ní Chuilleanáin's poems often address important aspects of women's experiences in an insightful fashion.' Discuss this view, with particular reference to 'Translations'.

Sample Paragraph

I would completely agree that 'Translations' deals with an issue which is important to Irish women. The scandal of what happened to the unfortunate girls who were locked up in Magdalene convents deserves to be publicised. Eiléan Ní Chuilleanáin's poem certainly gave me a deeper understanding of their disturbing story. The dramatic opening description of the reburial service was attended by relatives 'from every county', suggesting the scale of the mistreatment. The details of the cold laundries – where 'White light blinded' seemed a subtle way of symbolising the misguided actions of those religious orders who punished young girls. I admired the poet's fair treatment of those nuns who are also presented as being imprisoned, even replacing their own natural identities with 'temporary' saints' names. The poem's last stanza was revealing as it envisaged one of the severe nuns who was still confused by her part in the cruelty. She only recognises the 'parasite' of heartless authority within her when it is too late. The poet makes it clear that she was a product of an oppressive Catholic Ireland and under the 'spell' of misguided power. In my opinion, 'Translation' succeeds in explaining the true story of the Magdalene women. It is all the more powerful because Ní Chuilleanáin avoids being over-emotional. Her quiet tone conveys sensitivity and sadness for this dreadful period in Irish history which still lingers like 'a cloud over my time'.

Examiner's Comment

This succinct and focused response shows a clear understanding of the poem and of Ní Chuilleanáin's considered approach to her theme. Short quotations are well integrated and the discussion points range over much of the poem. There is also some very good personal interaction. Grade A.

CLASS/HOMEWORK EXERCISES

1. 'Eiléan Ní Chuilleanáin's poetry offers a variety of interesting perspectives that vividly convey themes of universal relevance.' Discuss this statement with particular reference to 'Translation'.

2. Copy the table below into your own notes and fill in critical comments about the last two quotations.

Key Quotes

The soil frayed and sifted evens the score	Ní Chuilleanáin's opening line sets the reburial scene in Glasnevin Cemetery. The description of the soil being spread evenly on the graves conveys a sense of finality, of coming to terms with the past.
White light blinded and bleached out/The high relief of a glance	Revealing details of conditions within the laundry are unsettlingly poignant. The sharply alliterative verbs are suggestive of how the Magdalene story was covered up for such a long time.
Assist them now, ridges under the veil	
Allow us now to hear it, sharp as an infant's cry	

Memory poem.

metaphorically: life journey, don't know what's ahead. we have to accept what's to come.

10 THE BEND IN THE ROAD *holds memory and it evokes past events. linking the past and the present.*

literal side: child getting sick.

This is the place where the child *starts off simplistic, conversational tone. run on lines captures the activity.* *distances herself from the situation*

Felt sick in the car and they pulled over *"the" = universal.*

And waited in the shadow of a house.

simile = / personification A tall tree like a cat's tail waited too. *Fairy tale like, changes the tone to mysterious.*

They opened the windows and breathed   5

Easily, while nothing moved. Then he was better. *captures the stillness + anticipation. journey resumes.*

Over twelve years it has become the place *tone becomes more personal.*

Where you were sick one day on the way to the lake. *She's letting us become a part of her memory*

You are taller now than us. *she notes the changes from the past 12 years.*

The tree is taller, the house is quite covered in   10

With green creeper, and the bend *The bend + silence is still there.*

In the road is as silent as ever it was on that day. *Nature imagery: green creeper. idea of nature being alive adds mystery.*

Piled high, wrapped lightly, like the one cumulus cloud *starting off with 2 similes.*

In a perfect sky, softly packed like the air, *past memories in this stanza are piled high and the cloud becomes a store house for the*

Is all that went on in those years, the absences,   15 *her lost loved ones (father, mother, sister)*

The faces never long absent from thought,

The bodies alive then and the airy space they took up *she poignantly recalls her loved ones.*

When we saw them wrapped and sealed by sickness *Remembers the sickness.*

Guessing the piled weight of sleep *Death casted shadows over her memories.*

We knew they could not carry for long; *They couldn't carry on any longer.*   20

This is the place of their presence: in the tree, in the air. *It's become the basis of memory for lost family members.*

she remembers them fondly
For her, they now live in this area (universal)

'This is the place'

GLOSSARY

11 *creeper*: climbing plant.

13 *cumulus*: rounded, fluffy.

EXPLORATIONS

1. Based on your reading of the poem, comment on the appropriateness of the title, 'The Bend in the Road'.

2. Choose one image from 'The Bend in the Road' that you consider effective. Give reasons why this image appealed to you.

3. How would you describe the poem's conclusion? Is it mysterious? Hopeful? Comforting? Bitter? Briefly explain your response.

STUDY NOTES

'The Bend in the Road' is part of Eiléan Ní Chuilleanáin's poetry collection The Girl Who Married the Reindeer. In many of these poems, the autobiographical becomes transformed as Ní Chuilleanáin takes a moment in time and fills it with arresting images, exact description, stillness and secrecy, linking together selected memories from various times and places. This poem's title suggests that the road will go on even though it is not visible at the moment.

Stanza one opens with Ní Chuilleanáin pointing to the exact place where 'the child/Felt sick in the car and they pulled over'. The memory of such a familiar occurrence is given significance by the use of the demonstrative pronoun, 'This'. Run-on lines catch the flurry of activity as concerned adults attend to the sick child. Everything is still as they 'waited' for the sickness to pass. This suspended moment resonates as they linger 'in the shadow of a house'. **For a split second, an ominous – almost surreal – atmosphere begins to develop.** The poet introduces a slightly sinister simile, 'A tall tree like a cat's tail', peeking in from the world of fairytale. Then the tree is personified: it 'waited too' as people and landscape merge in the moment of hush. Suddenly, a simple action ('They opened the windows') relieves the tension and everyone 'breathed/Easily'. The position of the adverb at the beginning of the line captures the relief at the recovery of the child. Yet the stationary atmosphere remained: 'while nothing moved'. However, the routine narrative of everyday life quickly resumes: 'Then he was better'.

In the **second stanza**, this roadside location takes on the shared resonance of memory: 'Over twelve years'. Readers are left imagining how the adults and child, when passing 'the place', would point it out as 'Where you were sick one day on the way to the lake'. The length of the line mirrors the long car journey. There is a sense of time being concentrated. Ní Chuilleanáin marvels at how the child has grown to adulthood: 'You are taller now than us'. The place has also changed – and even the tree is 'taller'. Assonance pinpoints how the nearby house is becoming yet more mysterious, 'quite covered in/With green creeper'. The insidious 'ee' sound mimics the silent takeover of the house by nature, as it recedes more and more into the shadows. Nature is alive. Creepings and rustlings stir, dispersing solidity and sureness. The poet cleverly places the line as if on a bend at the turn of a line: 'the bend/In the road is as silent as ever it was on that day'. Everything seems focused on the serenity of the place. **A bend in a road prevents seeing what is coming next. Is this an obvious symbol of the human experience?** No one knows what lies ahead. The tone of this reflective stanza is introspective as Ní Chuilleanáin considers the undeniable passing of time and the human condition.

In the **final stanza**, memory and place interplay with other recollections. The poet's attention turns towards the sky, which she imagines 'Piled high' with past experiences. A lifetime's memories now tower 'like the one cumulus cloud/In a perfect sky'. The alliteration of the hard 'c' successfully captures the billowing cloud as it sails through the sky. **Similarly, the recollections of 'all that went on in those years' heave and surge as they drift through the poet's consciousness.** Naturally, they flow from the exact description of 'the bend/In the road'. They are now visible as feelings of loss expand into the present: 'The faces never long absent from thought'. Ní Chuilleanáin had lost not only her father and mother, but also her sister. But she remembers them **similarly** as they were, 'bodies alive then and the airy space they took up', just as the cloud in the sky. Poignantly, the poet also recalls them in their final sickness, 'wrapped and sealed by sickness', as if they had been parcelled for dispatch away from the ordinary routine of life by the ordeal of suffering.

[handwritten annotation: their deaths to clouds releasing rain. Comparing The people will eventually let go of their lives.]

However, the harsh reality of sickness and old age is also recognised: 'We knew they could not carry for long'. Just as the cloud grows bigger as it absorbs moisture, finally dissolving into rain, so did the poet's loved ones buckle beneath the weight of their illness, under the 'piled weight of sleep'. **Ní Chuilleanáin finds constant reminders of her family's past in the natural world.** She uses a simple image of cloud-like shapes of pillows and bed-covers as they surrender to sickness. Characteristically, the thinking within the poem has progressed considerably. The poet has widened its scope, its spatial dimension, to include those external experiences to which she so eloquently pays witness. Indeed, the poem now stands as a monument to silence and time, absence and presence, past and present. The moment of stillness is invoked. This roadside location takes on a special importance. It marks the place where lost family members now reside. Ní Chuilleanáin's alliterative language is emphatic: 'This is the place of their presence'. They belong 'in the tree, in the air'. As in so many of her poems, Ní Chuilleanáin honours the invisible, unseen presence of other thoughts and feelings that – just like the bend in the road – lie waiting in silence to be discovered and brought to life again.

ANALYSIS

'Eiléan Ní Chuilleanáin's poetry illuminates ephemeral moments of perception in exact description.' Discuss this view in relation to 'The Bend in the Road'. Use suitable reference and quotation to support the points you make.

Sample Paragraph

I agree that Ní Chuilleanáin's poem, 'The Bend in the Road' is filled with meticulously accurate description. The opening lines pinpoint the exact place where 'the child/Felt sick in the car' and they 'pulled over'. The ordinary conversational language, 'They opened the windows', 'Then he was better', brings me into this precise moment in time and place. I can see the dark, cool shadow of the house. I experience the tree as if a child through the almost cartoon-like simile, 'A tall tree like a cat's tail'. Yet, an otherworldly experience hovers as personification transforms the tree into a living being; it 'waited too'. The poet reveals that 'nothing moved' as if all was in suspense awaiting some dramatic revelation. And it is displayed. The place has become a metaphor for the reality of being human. Everything in life changes. The poet suddenly realises that the child has now grown into a man, 'You are taller than us now'. Nothing has remained the same, 'The tree is taller'. Assonance subtly illustrates the changed house now overgrown with 'green creeper'. Another layer is added with the perception that the place has become suffused with the 'presence' of those 'faces never long absent from thought'. This still, silent moment has allowed boundaries to be crossed as memories float 'Piled high, wrapped lightly, like the one cumulus cloud/In a perfect sky'. I now began to understand that in a static moment, the conventional distinctions between life and death, being and memory, all recede and become blurred. The past now lives again, 'in the tree, in the air'. Through carefully observed, precise description of material things, this poet transports readers into a different place to an understanding that many experiences, 'all that went on in those years', can be savoured in various forms, 'softly packed like the air'.

Examiner's Comment

This is a very successful personal response to the question. Accurate and apt quotes provide good support for discussion points which range through the poem effectively. There is evidence of genuine engagement with the poem and expression is also impressive throughout. Grade A.

CLASS/HOMEWORK EXERCISES

1. 'Space in Ní Chuilleanáin's poetry is used as an expression of one's experience of the world and is a metaphor for the linking together of self and the world, within and without.' Discuss this statement, with particular reference to 'The Bend in the Road'.

2. Copy the table below into your own notes and fill in critical comments about the last two quotations.

Key Quotes

A tall tree like a cat's tail waited too	The repetition of the hard 't' sound and the somewhat surreal comparison are reminiscent of a young child's story.
the bend/In the road is as silent as ever it was on that day	The mystery and suspense of what might be lurking around the corner is caught by a careful positioning of the line break and the emphasis on the silence of the day.
like the one cumulus cloud/ In a perfect sky	
wrapped and sealed by sickness	

guilt, fear and excitement, what do you think is
the dominant emotion in this poem?

[handwritten: Begins and ends with a silent image of a hare.]

11 ON LACKING THE KILLER INSTINCT

[handwritten: ruthless determination to succeed]

[handwritten: blending past + present]

[handwritten top right: At the end she's come to terms with her father's death.]

[handwritten: captures the motionless Hare, calm and at ease.]

One hare, absorbed, sitting still,
Right in the grassy middle of the track,
I met when I fled up into the hills, that time *[handwritten: running away from reality]*
My father was dying in a hospital –
I see her suddenly again, borne back *[handwritten: alliteration]*   5
By the morning paper's prize photograph:
Two greyhounds tumbling over, absurdly gross,
While the hare shoots off to the left, her bright eye
Full not only of speed and fear *[handwritten: vivid imagery and run on lines that mimic the chase of the hare.]*
But surely in the moment a glad power *[handwritten: captures the fear of the hare. thrill survival is captured.]*   10

Like my father's, running from a lorry-load of soldiers
In nineteen twenty-one, nineteen years old, never
Such gladness, he said, cornering in the narrow road *[handwritten: Comparing him to the hare (glad)]*
Between high hedges, in summer dusk. *[handwritten: imagery]*
                              The hare *[handwritten: Inhumane that the hare is being hunted and the british should never hunted her father.]*   15
Like him should never have been coursed,
But, clever, she gets off; another day
She'll fool the stupid dogs, double back *[handwritten: Referring to cleverness of hare.]*
On her own scent, downhill, and choose her time
To spring away out of the frame, all while   20
The pack is labouring up.
                  The lorry was growling *[handwritten: incorporates the dog imagery personification]*
And he was clever, he saw a house *[handwritten: comparison of father and hare (clever)]*
And risked an open kitchen door. The soldiers
Found six people in a country kitchen, one   25
Drying his face, dazed-looking, the towel *[handwritten: The father like the hare had both near death experiences. Both were determined to live.]*
Half covering his face. The lorry left,
The people let him sleep there, he came out
Into a blissful dawn. Should he have chanced that door? *[handwritten: glad power] [handwritten: Questions his decisions. Risks involved on opening the door.]*
If the sheltering house had been burned down, what good   30
Could all his bright running have done
For those that harboured him?
                  And I should not *[handwritten: Thinking about her father's death and she eventually went back.]*
Have run away, but I went back to the city *[handwritten: symbolic of her cleansing her soul, removing her guilt.]*
Next morning, washed in brown bog water,   35
And I thought about the hare, in her hour of ease. *[handwritten: in his hour of need] [handwritten: Dogs and soldiers haven't the killer instinct]*

[handwritten bottom left: Father + Hare have killer instinct.]

[handwritten bottom: 'While the hare shoots off to the left']

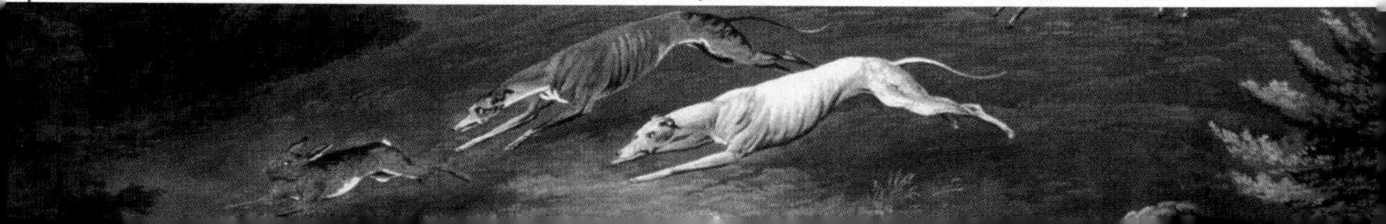

GLOSSARY

1	*hare*: mammal resembling a large rabbit.	7	*gross*: disgusting, outrageous.
1	*absorbed*: engrossed, immersed, preoccupied.	16	*coursed*: hunted with greyhounds.
		20	*frame*: picture, enclosure.
7	*absurdly*: ridiculously, nonsensically.	21	*labouring*: moving with difficulty.

EXPLORATIONS

1. Who, in your opinion, lacked the killer instinct in this poem? Was it the hare, the soldiers, the greyhounds, the father, the poet? Refer closely to the text in your response.

2. The poet alters time and place frequently in this poem. With the aid of quotations, trace these changes as the poem develops.

3. Did you find the poem's conclusion satisfying or mystifying? Give reasons for your response, referring closely to the text.

STUDY NOTES

'On Lacking the Killer Instinct' is part of Eiléan Ní Chuilleanáin's The Sun-fish *collection. A sunfish is so-called due to its habit of basking on the water's surface. Ní Chuilleanáin often presents daily life with a sense of mystery and otherworldliness as the poems move between various realms of experience. Each scene lies open to another version of the narrative. She blurs the distance between past and present in this three-part poem. History, which is something of an Irish obsession, always informs the present. This poet discovers and remembers. As she herself has said, 'In order for the poem to get written, something has to happen.'*

The title of the poem immediately intrigues and unsettles. The **opening lines** focus on a stationary hare, silent, engrossed, 'absorbed', at rest. It is a vivid picture. Why is this hare preoccupied? The sibilant alliterative phrase, 'sitting still', captures the motionless animal in 'the middle of the track'. This **naturalistic**

setting and image is brought into high resolution as the poet recounts that her own journey 'up into the hills' caused her to meet this creature. Ní Chuilleanáin juxtaposes the stillness of the wild hare with her own headlong flight from the awful reality, 'that time/My father was dying in a hospital'. In describing this terrible experience, her tone is remarkably controlled – detached, yet compassionate.

Another narrative thread is introduced in **line 6** when the poet recalls the 'morning paper's prize photograph'. Here the predators are presented as ungainly, almost comical characters incapable of purposeful action: 'Two greyhounds tumbling over, absurdly gross'. The broad vowels and repetition of 'r' highlight the hounds' unattractively large appearance. Irish coursing is a competitive sport where dogs are tested on their ability to run and overtake the hare, turning it without capturing it. It is often regarded as a cruel activity that causes pain and suffering to the pursued creature. From the start of the poem, **readers are left wondering who exactly lacks the killer instinct**. Do the dogs not have the urge to pounce and kill? Has the hare got the killer instinct, running for its life, showing the strong will to survive against all odds? The rapid run-on lines mimic the speed and agility of the hare exulting in 'glad power'.

In **line 11**, the **reader is taken into another realm** – a common feature of Ní Chuilleanáin's interconnected narratives. In this case, she recalls another pursuit. Her father was a combatant in the Irish Civil War in 1922 and was on the run. Like the hare, he fled, 'cornering in the narrow road/Between high hedges, in summer dusk'. Both are linked through 'gladness' as they exult in their capacity to outrun their pursuers. For her father, this was a 'lorry-load of soldiers' – the compound word emphasising the unequal odds against which the poet's father struggled. This is similar to the hare's predicament against the 'Two greyhounds'. The precise placing of 'The hare' tucked away at the end of **line 15** suggests the animal's escape. Ní Chuilleanáin comments that neither the hare nor her father should ever have 'been coursed'. She is happy to think that on some other occasion, the hare is likely to outwit the 'stupid dogs' and will 'spring away out of the frame', nimbly escaping her pursuers. In Irish coursing, the hare is not run on open land but in a secure enclosure over a set distance. The heavy, panting exertions of the pursuing dogs is illustrated in the run-through line, 'all while/The pack is labouring up'.

Ní Chuilleanáin returns to her father's story in **line 22**, imagining a moment of danger from his time as a fugitive. The scene is dominated by the threatening sound of a lorry, 'growling' like a pursuing hound. The repetition of the adjective 'clever' links her father and the hare as he too made his escape. Intent on surviving, 'he saw a house/And risked an open kitchen door'. The **enemy soldiers go through the motions of pursuit cursorily, seemingly lacking the killer instinct** when they 'Found six people in a country kitchen'. Ní Chuilleanáin is characteristically ambivalent about why the rebels were not challenged, reminding us of the contradictory attitudes among the various combatants of the Civil War. For whatever reason, the fugitives ('one/Drying his face, dazed-looking') were not arrested and their deception worked. The poet's father is allowed refuge: 'The people let him sleep there'. Throughout Ireland's troubled history, 'safe houses' existed that sheltered those on the run. In her mind's eye, the poet pictures her father emerging in triumph the next day 'Into a blissful dawn' (**line 29**). In a series of questions, she considers his crucial decision to stand his ground and feign innocence. In retrospect, anything might have happened to affect the outcome at 'the sheltering house'. Ní Chuilleanáin emphasises how chance has played such a significant role – not just in her father's life, but in Ireland's history.

The poet concludes by returning to the opening scene. Having observed the hare and remembered her father's encounter during the Civil War, she now realises that she should never have run away from her dying father. Her decision to return is seen as a mature one – almost like a religious ritual in which the poet cleanses herself, 'washed in brown bog water'. Is this a form of absolution to remove her guilt for running away? Typically, she uses this unifying symbol to gently draw the poem's three narratives together. After the common experience of the turbulence of the run, all three (the hare, the father and the poet herself) have entered a new state of being – calm composure. Ní Chuilleanáin reflects on 'the hare, in her hour of ease', the soft monosyllabic final word gently conveying a sense of peace and reconciliation. The poem closes as it began, with the **beautiful silent image of the hare**, self-possessed and serene after all the turmoil of the chase.

ANALYSIS

'Eiléan Ní Chuilleanáin is a quiet, introspective, enigmatic poet.' Discuss this statement with particular reference to 'On Lacking the Killer Instinct'.

Sample Paragraph

I thought the poem, 'On Lacking the Killer Instinct', moved effortlessly, mysteriously weaving three different narratives: the intently observed story of the hare and greyhounds, the quietly detached family history of her father's escape in 1921 and her own headlong flight from the city. Ní Chuilleanáin creates small clear windows into the narratives and the reader can then glimpse multi-views of human experience and discord, 'One hare ... I met ... that time/ My father was dying in a hospital'. She celebrates resilience, the hare's 'bright eye' is full of 'a glad power'. Similarly, her father exulted in his cleverness, 'never/Such gladness' as he out-manoeuvred the 'lorry-load of soldiers'. The poet also faced up to the unpalatable fact of death and 'went back to the city/ Next morning'. Her impressionistic style is similar to watching a photograph as it slowly develops before our eyes. At first there are vague unconnected shapes, but as the order establishes itself, the meaning becomes clear. Ní Chuilleanáin gazes intently on a familiar sight, the still hare, which becomes more strange under her spellbound observation and she links it to the flight and survival contest which underpins all of life. The reader is effortlessly guided through different times and places as the focus of the poet's gaze shifts from the hunt of the hare in coursing to the hunt of her father in his role in the Civil War, 'In nineteen twenty-one, nineteen years old'. She then quietly reflects on her own flight and concludes that running does not solve problems, 'what good/Could all his bright running have done/For those that harboured him?' In the end, this poet poses questions that resonate. Does she too lack the killer instinct, the capacity to seize and capture rather than suggest? The long monosyllabic word 'ease' suggests that staying calm and still is more effective than running. Yet who lacked the killer instinct, the hare, the greyhounds, the father, the soldiers, the poet? Is the killer instinct worth having? This enigmatic, introspective poet leaves us with an image of quiet stillness to ponder.

Examiner's Comment

This is a very clear and focused response to a testing question. Interesting critical points – aptly illustrated by accurate quotations – range widely, tracing the subtle development of the poem's various narrative threads. The questions posed at the end round off the discussion effectively. Grade A.

CLASS/HOMEWORK EXERCISES

1. 'Eiléan Ní Chuilleanáin's poems elude categories and invite and challenge the reader in equal measure.' Discuss this statement with particular reference to 'On Lacking the Killer Instinct'.

2. Copy the table below into your own notes and fill in critical comments about the last two quotations.

Key Quotes

I see her suddenly again, borne back	Ní Chuilleanáin's effortless movement between settings and time is clearly conveyed by the alliterative explosive phrase.
While the hare shoots off to the left	The dramatic verb captures the sudden darting movement of the elusive fleeing hare as she seeks to escape the pursuing hounds. The detailed direction conveys the poet's close observation.
cornering in the narrow road/Between high hedges	
Should he have chanced that door?	

12 TO NIALL WOODS AND XENYA OSTROVSKIA, MARRIED IN DUBLIN ON 9 SEPTEMBER 2009

When you look out across the fields
And you both see the same star
Pitching its tent on the point of the steeple –
That is the time to set out on your journey,
With half a loaf and your mother's blessing.   5

Leave behind the places that you knew:
All that you leave behind you will find once more,
You will find it in the stories;
The sleeping beauty in her high tower
With her talking cat asleep   10
Solid beside her feet – you will see her again.

When the cat wakes up he will speak in Irish and Russian
And every night he will tell you a different tale
About the firebird that stole the golden apples,
Gone every morning out of the emperor's garden,   15
And about the King of Ireland's Son and the Enchanter's Daughter.

The story the cat does not know is the Book of Ruth
And I have no time to tell you how she fared
When she went out at night and she was afraid,
In the beginning of the barley harvest,   20
Or how she trusted to strangers, and stood by her word:

You will have to trust me, she lived happily ever after.

'the firebird that stole the golden apples'

GLOSSARY

Title: An epithalamium is a poem (or song) in celebration of a wedding. Eiléan Ní Chuilleanáin has included this poem (to her son Niall and his bride, Xenya) as the introductory dedication in her poetry collection *The Sun-fish*.

9   *sleeping beauty*: European fairytale from 'La Belle au bois dormant' (Beauty of the sleeping wood) by Charles Perrault and 'Dornroschen' (Little Briar Rose) by the Brothers Grimm.

14   *the firebird*: Russian fairytale; 'Tsarevitch Ivan, the Fire Bird and the Gray Wolf' by Alexander Afanasyev.

16   *the King of Ireland's Son*: Irish fairytale; 'The King of Ireland's Son' by Padraic Colum.

17   *Book of Ruth*: religious story from the Old Testament.

21   *Or how she trusted to strangers*: In the Bible story, Boaz owned the field Ruth harvested. He was a relative of the family and by law could 'redeem' her if he married her now that she was a widow. He wished to do so because he admired how she had stood by her mother-in-law, 'For wherever you go, I will go'.

EXPLORATIONS

1. Do you think the references to fairytales are appropriate on the occasion of Eiléan Ní Chuilleanáin's son's marriage? Give one reason for your answer.

2. In your opinion, what is the dominant tone of voice in the poem? Is it one of warning, reassurance, hope, consolation? Briefly explain your response with reference to the poem.

3. Why do you think the poet placed the last line apart from the rest of the poem? Give one reason for your opinion.

STUDY NOTES

'I write poems that mean a lot to me.' (Eiléan Ní Chuilleanáin) This particular poem is dedicated to her son, Niall, and his new bride, Xenya, on the happy occasion of their marriage. Folklore is central to this poet's work. Her mother, Eilis Dillon, was a famous writer of children's stories. Fairytales allow Ní Chuilleanáin the opportunity to approach a subject from an oblique, non-confessional perspective. It gives distance. Story-tellers

rarely comment on or explain what happens. They simply tell the tale. In this poem, Ní Chuilleanáin refers to folklore and a well-known Bible story as she addresses the young couple.

The **first stanza** opens with **warm advice** from a loving mother as she gives the young man leave to set out on his own journey through life with his new partner. Run-on lines contain a beautiful, romantic image of a harmonious vision: 'you both see the same star'. Personification and alliteration bring this natural image to radiant life, 'Pitching its tent on the point of the steeple', suggesting the new home which the young couple are about to set up for themselves. **Ní Chuilleanáin's gaze is one of relentless clarity and attentiveness. She illuminates details.** She also counsels that it is the right time to go, 'to set out on your journey' when you are prepared ('With half a loaf') and with good wishes ('and your mother's blessing'). She combines colloquial and fairytale language. The tone is warm, but also pragmatic – offering practical advice to the newlyweds to make the most of whatever they have to start with: 'half a loaf is better than none'.

Stanza two begins with the imperative warning: 'Leave behind'. The mother is advising the couple to forget 'the places that you knew'. Is 'places' a metaphor for their actual homes or their cultural environments? Or does it refer to values the young people hold sacred? She consoles them that past experiences can still be found 'in the stories'. Ní Chuilleanáin now weaves an intricate web of such stories from many different sources. The first tale is that of 'sleeping beauty in her high tower'. This classic folk story involves a beautiful princess, enchantment and a handsome prince who has to brave the obstacles of tall trees that surround the castle and its sleeping princess. **Is Ní Chuilleanáin illustrating that the path to true love is filled with difficulties and that only the brave will be successful?** The extended run-on lines suggest the hundred years' sleep of the spellbound princess, who can only be awakened by a kiss. The poet also makes use of another familiar element of fairytales – talking animals. In this case, the 'talking cat' probably refers to Irish folklore, and the King of Cats, a renowned teller of tales. Ní Chuilleanáin is able to link the basic characteristics of the animal with human behaviour. The cat slumbers with the princess, 'Solid', stable and dependable, beside her feet. Despite the poet's realism, however, this fairytale allusion is primarily optimistic.

In **stanza three**, Ní Chuilleanáin imagines the cat awakening and telling stories in both 'Irish and Russian', a likely reference to the young couple's **two cultural backgrounds**. The poet has said that in her work she is trying 'to suggest, to phrase, to find a way to make it possible for somebody to pick up certain suggestions ... They might not be seeing what I am seeing'. The poet continues to set her personal wishes for Niall and Xenya within the context of folktales, turning to the Russian tradition: 'Tsarevitch, the Fire Bird and the Gray Wolf'. Again, the hero of this story is on a challenging mission, as he attempts to catch the 'firebird that stole the golden apples ... out of the emperor's garden'. The assonance of the broad vowel 'o' emphasises the exasperation of the repeated theft. As always in folklore, courage and determination are required before the hero can overcome many ordeals and find true happiness.

Ní Chuilleanáin introduces the Irish tradition with the story of the King of Ireland's son, who must pluck three hairs from the Enchanter's beard in order to save his own life. On his quest, he gains the hand of Fedelma, the Enchanter's youngest daughter. But he falls asleep and loses her to the King of the Land of Mist. **Is the poet simply advising her son and daughter-in-law that love must be cherished and never taken for granted?** Throughout the poem, she draws heavily on stories where heroes have to fight for what they believe in. All of these tales convey the same central meaning – that lasting love has to be won through daring, determination and sacrifice.

In the playful link into **stanza four**, Ní Chuilleanáin remarks that 'the story the cat does not know is the Book of Ruth'. This final story is not from the world of folklore, but from the Bible, (although the poet has commented that 'a lot of religious narrative is very folkloric'). The Book of Ruth teaches that **genuine love can require uncompromising sacrifice**, and that such unselfish love will be well rewarded. This particular tale of inclusivity shows two different cultures coming together. The Israelites (sons of Naomi) marry women from the Moab tribe, one of whom is Ruth. She embraces Naomi's people, land, culture and God. This is very pertinent to the newly married couple, as they are also from different lands and cultures. Not surprisingly, the biblical tale is one of loving kindness – but it also includes a realistic message. After her husband's death, Ruth chooses to stay with her mother-in-law and undertakes the backbreaking farm work of gleaning to support the family. This involves lifting the grain and stalks left behind after the harvesting of barley. The metaphor of the harvest is another reminder that married couples will reap what they sow, depending on the effort and commitment made to their relationship.

The poem's last line is placed apart to emphasise its significance. Ní Chuilleanáin tells the newlyweds that they 'will have to trust me' – presumably just as Ruth trusted her mother-in-law, Naomi. For doing this, she was rewarded with living 'happily ever after', as in the best tales. The poet's quietly light-hearted approach, however, does not lessen her own deeply felt hopes for Niall and Xenya. **All the stories she has used are concerned with the essential qualities of a loving relationship** – and share a common thread of courage, faithfulness and honesty as the couple journey to a happy future. Tales and dreams are the shadow-truths that will endure. Ní Chuilleanáin's final tone is clearly sincere, upbeat and forward looking.

ANALYSIS

'The imagination is not the refuge but the true site of authority.' Comment on this statement in relation to the poem 'To Niall Woods and Xenya Ostrovskia, Married in Dublin on 9 September 2009'.

Sample Paragraph

I feel that Ní Chuilleanáin's poem has subtle messages which only become clear after several readings. I think the poet is counselling her son and his new bride, Xenya, that stories, 'the imagination' are where truth, 'the true site of authority' lies. Stories are not escapism, although we may scoff in this modern age at 'Once upon a time'. The stories she chooses, 'sleeping beauty in her high tower', 'the firebird that stole the golden apples' and the 'King of Ireland's Son and the Enchanter's Daughter' all suggest that perseverance and sincerity win the day. I believe that this is a good message to give to the couple as they 'set out' on their journey. Nothing worthwhile is won easily. This is not escapism, but reality. While the language, 'half a loaf and your mother's blessing', and imagery (even the beautiful lines which describe the 'star/Pitching its tent on the point of the steeple') seem to be from the land of children's fiction, they resound with good sense. I thought the inclusion of the story of Ruth was very apt as it involved two cultures which is relevant to the couple's Irish and Russian origins, but also to many other situations in this time of immigration. People in this new era will have to 'trust to strangers'. But if integrity and loving kindness is shown, as Ruth's story demonstrated long ago, the prize of a happy future can be won. 'You will have to trust me, she lived happily ever after.' I understood that Ní Chuilleanáin is showing that no matter where these imaginative tales come from, Europe, Russia, Ireland or the Bible, obstacles have to be overcome in life through resolution and perseverance. This is a tough message, there is no hiding here. I thought the poet was clever because by putting this insight into the realm of a fairy story, it does not sound like preaching which the young couple might resent, yet the message rings true throughout time from this 'site of authority' the kingdom of story-telling.

Examiner's Comment

A well-supported and sustained personal response showing genuine engagement with the poem. The focused opening tackles the discussion question directly. This is followed by several clear points tracing the development of thought throughout the poem. Accurate quotations and clear expression are also commendable features of the paragraph. Grade A.

CLASS/HOMEWORK EXERCISES

1. What impression of Ní Chuilleanáin do you get from reading 'To Niall Woods and Xenya Ostrovskia, Married in Dublin on 9 September 2009'? Write at least one paragraph in response, illustrating your views with reference to the text of the poem.

2. Use the blank spaces to fill in critical comments about the last two quotations.

Key Quotes

When you look out across the fields/And you both see the same star	The poet is acknowledging that the time has come for the young couple to strike out on their own as they look at what the world has to offer. The simple, romantic image of the star conveys vividly that they share the same vision of the future.
You will find it in the stories	Ní Chuilleanáin offers strong support and advice to the newlyweds. The truths that the young couple have known will not be lost because they are moving on. The spirit and value of these old tales will always be available in folklore.
About the firebird that stole the golden apples	
the King of Ireland's Son and the Enchanter's Daughter	

LEAVING CERT SAMPLE ESSAY

'Eiléan Ní Chuilleanáin's extraordinary poetic world reveals compelling narratives which never cease to captivate readers.' Discuss this view, supporting your answer with suitable reference to the poems on your course.

Marking Scheme Guidelines

Candidates are free to agree and/or disagree with the given statement. The poet's treatment of themes and subject matter should be addressed, as well as her individual approach, distinctive writing style, etc. Reward responses that show clear evidence of genuine engagement with the poems. Expect discussion on how Ní Chuilleanáin's poetry appeals/does not appeal to readers.

Material might be drawn from the following:

- Poet's views on life/relationships.
- Recurring optimistic themes on life and rebirth; the continuous past
- Fragmented narrative; innovative narrative blending
- Collapse of time and place
- Atmospheric detail; artistic and architectural references
- Dispassionate, detached tone of storyteller
- Focus on uniquely Irish phenomena
- Biblical, historical and mythical references
- Mystical/spiritual experience
- Layered and interwoven nuances challenge the reader, etc.

Sample Essay

(Ní Chuilleanáin's extraordinary poetic world reveals compelling narratives which captivate readers)

1. *To me, Eiléan Ní Chuilleanáin's lyrical world thrives on the creeping rustlings and barely noticed stirrings of life. Enthralling stories are quietly let slip to bewitch and enchant her readers in a wide range of variety, from hopeful poems such as 'All for You' to the family stories of 'Fireman's Lift' and 'To Niall Woods and Xenya.'*

2. *'The Bend in the Road' takes a normal event, a child becoming car-sick, and transforms it with arresting images from the surreal, ominous world of the fairytale,*

'A tall tree like a cat's tail'. The poet links together selected memories from various times and places and so mesmerises the reader with the resonance from this 'bend/In the road'. The family all point, on subsequent journeys to 'Where you were sick on the way to the lake'. Ní Chuilleanáin's intent gaze reminds us that a bend in the road, which is cleverly emphasised by its line placement, prevents seeing what is around the corner. Now the poet interjects another memory into the story, the death of loved ones 'Piled high, wrapped lightly, like the one cumulus cloud/In a perfect sky'. This place now becomes 'the place of their presence'. They live now 'in the tree, in the air' because this is where they are remembered. Ní Chuilleanáin fuses parallel narratives, the ill child, the revisited bend in the road, the sick and dying relatives to uncover the mystical truth, the past shines through the present.

3. The driving narrative of the young girl in 'Following' as she attempts to keep up with her father on a hectic fair day holds the readers who are pulled into this world by the unusual description of 'beasts packed solid as books'. The explosive 'b' links 'beasts' and 'books' and I can really picture the crammed animals standing in lines as they await sale. Other stories are woven into the poem, as the image of the dead father appears, not 'skimming' as before but 'Gliding' as the girl crosses the 'shivering bog'. He is now sitting in 'the library where the light is clear'. The poet is tantalising readers, challenging us to engage and 'push ... open' the poem, just as the 'crushed flowers', an evocative image for past shared memories, force the book open. Once more the reader is comforted by the message that the past is not dead. The girl's suffering is represented by 'The square of white linen'. It is not 'shelved', never to be thought of or experienced again. It will emerge, 'crack/The spine open'.

4. Ní Chuilleanáin has remarked that she has been 'captivated by history'. She recounts a story in the poem, 'On Lacking the Killer Instinct', which her father had told her about running away from the Black and Tans when he was a young man. The reader is submerged into the Ireland of 1922 as the soldiers hunt her father. He seeks refuge in a 'safe house'. The blessed relief of the escape is graphically conveyed in the detail, 'he came out/Into a blissful dawn'. In my opinion, the reader is delighted at the father's breath-taking escape. It is similar to the escape of the hare, recounted in the earlier part of the poem, 'her bright eye/Full not only of speed and fear/But surely in the moment a glad power'. Narratives are blended

together seamlessly as the poet relates her own flight from the awful reality of her father's final illness, 'I fled up into the hills, that time/My father was dying a in hospital'.

5. 'Fireman's Lift' also deals with the harsh truth of her mother's death. They had both visited Parma Cathedral once and their close relationship is clearly caught. 'I was standing beside you looking up/Through the big tree of the cupola'. The strong verbs, 'spiralling' and 'heaving' capture the huge effort of the angels as they lifted Mary in to the heavens from her earthly life. The hands of the angels act as a 'crane and support' for Mary. 'Their heads bowed to reflect on her/Fair face' reminded the poet of the nurses who tended her mother in her final illness. Readers become immersed in the poem's storyline when the poet comments, 'This is what love sees, that angle'. The poet is coming to terms with the harsh reality that life has a natural cycle, 'The crick in the branch loaded with fruit'. The reader stands with mother and daughter marvelling as 'The Virgin was spiralling to heaven'. Now it is time for the poet's mother to go too.

6. Although Ní Chuilleanáin tells a story from an oblique, non-confessional perspective, this detachment does not prevent her engaging her reader. In the epithalamium, 'To Niall Woods and Xenya' she intricately weaves Russian ('the firebird') and Irish ('the Enchanter's Daughter') stories as she celebrates the two diverse cultures of the young couple. She also uses the story to gently pass on her thoughts and advice on their new life together. I thought the phrase, 'you both see the same star', showed how she understood that the young couple had a shared vision of life. But Ruth's story from the Bible was most fascinating. She had to show courage to succeed as she trusted to strangers. The young people will also need these qualities if they are to succeed in the best tradition of the fairytale to 'live happily ever after'. This, of course, is what every reader dreams of.

7. For me, Ní Chuilleanáin has opened a poetic world in which she intertwines stories from the fabric of her own family life, 'poems that mean a lot to me', with those from many other varied sources. The reader stands fascinated and delighted by a bend in the road, a hare 'sitting still', 'The sleeping beauty in her high tower', the Virgin Mary as 'she came to the edge of the cloud', a 'key still in your pocket', all thanks to the gaze and skill of a remarkable poet.

(approx. 990 words)

Examiner's Comment

This is a well-sustained personal response that shows clear engagement with several of Ní Chuilleanáin's poems. Effective use is made of accurate quotations and reference to support the critical discussion. While some points could benefit from further development, the essay is organised effectively and is written confidently.

GRADE: A1

P = 15/15

C = 13/15

L = 13/15

M = 5/5

Total = 46/50

SAMPLE LEAVING CERT QUESTIONS ON NÍ CHUILLEANÁIN'S POETRY

(45/50 MINUTES)

1. 'Ní Chuilleanáin's beguiling poems emerge from an intense but insightful imagination.' Do you agree with this assessment of her poetry? Write a response, supporting your points with reference to the poems on your course.

2. 'Eiléan Ní Chuilleanáin is a truly original poet who leads us into altered landscapes and enhances our understanding of the world around us.' To what extent would you agree with this statement? In your response, refer to the poems on your course.

3 'Ní Chuilleanáin's subject matter can be challenging at times, but her writing style is always highly impressive.' Write a response to this view, supporting the points you make with suitable reference to the poetry on your course.

Sample Essay Plan (Q1)

'Ní Chuilleanáin's beguiling poems emerge from an intense but insightful imagination.' Do you agree with this assessment of her poetry? Write a response, supporting your points with reference to the poems on your course.

- Intro: Ní Chuilleanáin's innovative treatment of a broad thematic range – Irish history, myth, transience, memory, relationships, loss, religious life, the dispossessed, etc.

- Point 1: 'Fireman's Lift' – compelling treatment of her mother's death. Importance of dramatic setting as a context for personal experiences/ memories. Poet's sympathetic tone, atmospheric detail, artistic references.

- Point 2: 'Translation' – perceptive account of the Magdalene laundry workers. Sensitive approach to women victims. Use of effective symbols. Collapse of time. Silence and understated meanings. Imaginative and interwoven nuances affect readers.

- Point 3: Dispassionate, detached tone of storyteller – 'Deaths and Engines', 'Kilcash'. Underlying sense of the poet's compassion. Interlinked layered narrative threads entice the reader.

- Conclusion: Poetry can challenge/excite responses – Ní Chuilleanáin's mesmeric exploration of universal themes invites readers to unravel the secrets of her work.

Sample Essay Plan (Q1)

Develop one of the above points into a paragraph.

Sample Paragraph: Point 2

'Translation' offers an intriguing account of a dark period in recent Irish history. Ní Chuilleanáin's quiet dramatisation of the Magdalene laundry victims begins in Glasnevin Cemetery, with an unnerving description: 'soil frayed and sifted evens the score'. This image is typical of the poet, suggesting both the surface of the communal grave and the horrifying injustice that has happened over the years. In death, these women have become 'ridges under the veil' of the earth. The reference also conveys a sense of the strict Magdalene nuns who are also viewed as victims of an unchristian era. Time and places blend throughout the poem. The poet's concentrated vision of the laundries is associated with their exploitation – 'where steam danced/Around stone drains and giggled and slipped across water'. She contrasts the girls' youthful spirit with the cold conditions around them. I could make sense of the poem's title as Ní Chuilleanáin's aim was to reveal (or 'translate') the true Magdalene story. Without a trace of sentimentality, 'Translation' movingly recalls a whole generation of women whose lives were ruined. Generously, the ending focuses on the authoritarian figure of an unnamed nun who is envisioned in death and who finally understands the tragedy – 'Allow us now to hear it, sharp as an infant's cry'. This line suggested the communal suffering shared by the nuns and the unmarried mothers who were separated from their babies. The poet's intense depiction of the Magdalene experience is highly compelling, allowing me to relate to this truly regrettable 'cloud over my time'.

Examiner's Comment

As part of a full essay, this is a focused and competent A-grade paragraph that offers clear personal engagement with the poem. The discussion relating to Ní Chuilleanáin's dense imagery is impressive. Apt – and accurate – quotes are used effectively throughout and expression is fluent.

LAST WORDS

'There is something second-sighted about Eiléan Ní Chuilleanáin's work. Her poems see things anew, in a rinsed and dreamstruck light.'

Seamus Heaney

'Ní Chuilleanáin's eccentric poems uncover hidden dramas in many guises, and she continually holds us captive by her luminous voice.'

Molly Bendall

'Her voice and technique are so solid, so secure, and contain deep echoes of older poetry, as Irish verse tends to do.'

Robert Hudson

SYLVIA PLATH

1932-63

‘Out of the ash
I rise with my red hair
And I eat men like air.’

Born in Boston, Massachusetts, in 1932, Sylvia Plath is a writer whose best-known poems are noted for their intense focus and vibrant, personal imagery. Her writing talent – and ambition to succeed – was evident from an early age. She kept a journal during childhood and published her early poems in literary magazines and newspapers. After studying Art and English at college, Plath moved to Cambridge, England, in the mid-1950s. Here she met and later married the poet Ted Hughes. The couple had two children, Frieda and Nicholas, but the marriage was not to last. Plath continued to write through the late 1950s and early 1960s. During the final years of her life, she produced numerous confessional poems of stark revelation, channelling her long-standing anxiety and doubt into poetic verses of great power and pathos. At her creative peak, Sylvia Plath took her own life on 11 February 1963.

Prescribed Poems   HIGHER LEVEL

❶ BLACK ROOK IN RAINY WEATHER

On the stiff twig up there
Hunches a wet black rook
Arranging and rearranging its feathers in the rain.
I do not expect a miracle
Or an accident   5

To set the sight on fire
In my eye, nor seek
Any more in the desultory weather some design,
But let spotted leaves fall as they fall,
Without ceremony, or portent.   10

Although, I admit, I desire,
Occasionally, some backtalk
From the mute sky, I can't honestly complain:
A certain minor light may still
Lean incandescent   15

Out of kitchen table or chair
As if a celestial burning took
Possession of the most obtuse objects now and then –
Thus hallowing an interval
Otherwise inconsequent   20

By bestowing largesse, honour,
One might say love. At any rate, I now walk
Wary (for it could happen
Even in this dull ruinous landscape); skeptical,
Yet politic; ignorant   25

Of whatever angel may choose to flare
Suddenly at my elbow. I only know that a rook
Ordering its black feathers can so shine
As to seize my senses, haul
My eyelids up, and grant   30

A brief respite from fear
Of total neutrality. With luck,
Trekking stubborn through this season
Of fatigue, I shall
Patch together a content   35

Of sorts. Miracles occur,
If you care to call those spasmodic
Tricks of radiance miracles. The wait's begun again,
The long wait for the angel,
For that rare, random descent.   40

'Hunches a wet black rook'

GLOSSARY

8	*desultory*: unexceptional, oppressive.	21	*largesse*: generous, giving.
10	*portent*: omen.	24	*skeptical*: wary, suspicious.
15	*incandescent*: glowing.	25	*politic*: wise and likely to prove advantageous.
19	*hallowing*: making holy.		
20	*inconsequent*: of no importance.	37	*spasmodic*: occurring in bursts.

EXPLORATIONS

1. What is the mood of the poet? How does the weather described in the poem reflect this mood?

2. In your opinion, why do you think Plath sees light coming from ordinary household objects such as kitchen tables and chairs?

3. What do you think the final stanza means? Consider the phrase 'The wait's begun again'. What is the poet waiting for?

STUDY NOTES

'Black Rook in Rainy Weather' was written while Plath was studying in Cambridge in 1956. It contains many of her trademarks, including the exploration of emotions, the use of weather, colour and natural objects as symbols, and the dreamlike world. She explores a number of themes: fear of the future, lack of identity and poetic inspiration.

   Stanza one begins with the straightforward description of a bird grooming itself, which the poet observes on a rainy day. But on closer inspection, the mood of the poem is set with the words 'stiff' and 'Hunches'. The bird is at the mercy of the elements ('wet') and there is no easy movement ('stiff'). **This atmospheric opening is dull and low key.** The black rook is a bird of ill omen. But the bird is presenting its best image to the world as it sits 'Arranging and rearranging its feathers'. Plath longed to excel in both life and art. If she were inspired, the rook would take on a new light as if on fire. But she doesn't see this happening. Even the weather is 'desultory' in the fading season of autumn. Poetic inspiration is miraculous; it is not ordinary. The world is experienced in a heightened way. Notice the long line, which seems out of proportion with the rest as she declares that she doesn't expect any order or 'design' in the haphazard weather. The decaying leaves will fall with no ritual, without any organisation, just as they will. **This is a chaotic world**, a random place with no design, just as poetic inspiration happens by chance. It is also accidental, like the falling leaves. We cannot seek it, we receive it. It is active, we are passive.

After this low-key opening, the poem starts to take flight in **stanzas three** and **four** when the poet states: 'I desire'. Plath employs a witty metaphor as she looks for 'some backtalk' from the 'mute sky'. **She would like to connect with it.** It could happen on her walk, or even at home if she were to experience a 'certain minor light' shining from an ordinary, everyday object like a chair. The association of fire and light makes an ordinary moment special. It is 'hallowing'; it is giving generously ('largesse'). She is hoping against hope. Plath may be sceptical, but she is going forward carefully in case she misses the magic moment. **She must stay alert and watchful.** She must be 'politic', wise.

Stanzas six, **seven** and **eight** discuss poetic inspiration. Plath doesn't know if it will happen to her or how it will happen. Two contrasting attitudes are at loggerheads: hope and despair. The rook might inspire her: '**Miracles occur**'. If she were motivated, it would relieve 'total neutrality', this nothingness she feels when living uninspired. Although she is tired, she is insistent, 'stubborn'. The poet will have to 'Patch' something together. She shows human vulnerability, but she is trying. This determination is a different tone from the negative one at the beginning.

Literature was as important to Plath as friends and family. What she can't live without, therefore, is inspiration – a dark, passionless existence. **Depression** is an empty state with no feeling or direction, yet her view of creativity is romantic. It is miraculous, available only to a chosen few. 'The long wait for the angel' has begun. Notice the constant use of the personal pronoun 'I'. This is a poet who is very aware of self and her own personal responses to events and feelings. The outside world becomes a metaphor for her own interior world.

Plath uses both archaic language and slang, as if reinforcing the randomness of the world. This is also mirrored in the run-on lines. All is haphazard, but carefully arranged, so even the extended **third-to-last line** stretches out as it waits for the 'random descent' of inspiration. In this **carefully arranged disorder**, two worlds are seen. One is negative: 'desultory', 'spotted', 'mute', 'dull', 'ruinous', stubborn', 'fatigue'. This is indicative of her own bleak mood. The other world is positive: 'fire', 'light', 'incandescent', 'celestial', 'hallowing', 'largesse', 'honour', 'love', 'shine'. Here is the possibility of radiance.

ANALYSIS

'Plath's poems are carefully composed and beautifully phrased.' Write a paragraph in response to this statement, illustrating your answer with close reference to the poem 'Black Rook in Rainy Weather'.

Sample Paragraph

Just like the rook, Plath 'arranges and rearranges' her words with infinite care to communicate the contrast between the dull life of 'total neutrality' which occurs when she is not inspired, when nothing sets 'the sight on fire'. I particularly admire how she artfully arranges disorder in the poem. This mirrors the chance of poetic inspiration. Long lines poke untidily out of the first three stanzas, seeking the 'minor light' to 'Lean incandescent' upon them. I also like how the lines run in a seemingly untidy way into each other, as do some stanzas. Stanza three goes into four, as it describes the chance of a light coming from an ordinary object, such as a kitchen chair, which is seen only if the poet is inspired. The alliteration of 'rare, random' in the last line mirrors the gift of poetic technique which will be given to the poet if she can receive the blessed benediction of poetic inspiration. 'Miracles occur'.

Examiner's Comment

Close reading of the poem is evident in this brief, original response to Plath's poetic technique. Quotations are very well used here to highlight Plath's ability to create disordered order. Grade-A standard.

CLASS/HOMEWORK EXERCISES

1. In your opinion, has the poet given up hope of being inspired? Use reference to the poem in your answer.

2. Copy the table below into your own notes and fill in critical comments about the last two quotations.

Key Quotes

But let spotted leaves fall as they fall	Decaying leaves drop as they will, without ceremony or any ritual to mark the event.
As if a celestial burning took/Possession of the most obtuse objects now and then	Poetic inspiration allows Plath to see the most ordinary things in a state of heightened awareness. They appear transformed into objects of beauty.
If you care to call those spasmodic/Tricks of radiance miracles	
that rare, random descent	

❷ THE TIMES ARE TIDY

Unlucky the hero born
In this province of the stuck record
Where the most watchful cooks go jobless
And the mayor's rôtisserie turns
Round of its own accord.   5

There's no career in the venture
Of riding against the lizard,
Himself withered these latter-days
To leaf-size from lack of action:
History's beaten the hazard.   10

The last crone got burnt up
More than eight decades back
With the love-hot herb, the talking cat,
But the children are better for it,
The cow milk's cream an inch thick.   15

'riding against the lizard'

GLOSSARY

2   *province*: a remote place.
2   *stuck record*: the needle would sometimes
    get jammed on a vinyl music album.

4   *rôtisserie*: meat on a rotating skewer.
7   *lizard*: dragon.
11 *crone*: old witch.

EXPLORATIONS

1. What is suggested by the poem's title? Is Plath being cynical about modern life? Develop your response in a short paragraph.

2. Select one image from the poem that suggests that the past was much more dangerous and exciting than the present. Comment on its effectiveness.

3. Do you agree or disagree with the speaker's view of modern life? Give reasons for your answer.

STUDY NOTES

'The Times Are Tidy' was written in 1958. In this short poem, Plath casts a cold eye on contemporary life and culture, which she sees as bland and unadventurous. The poem's ironic title clearly suggests Plath's dissatisfaction with the over-regulated society of her day. Do you think you are living in an heroic age or do you believe that most people have lost their sense of wonder? Is there anyone in public life whom you really admire? Perhaps you despair of politicians, particularly when their promises sound like a 'stuck record'.

Stanza one is dominated by hard-hitting images reflecting how the world of fairytale excitement has disappeared. From the outset, **the tone is scornful and dismissive**. Plath believes that any hero would be totally out of place amid the mediocrity of our times. True talent ('the most watchful cooks') is largely unrewarded. The unexpected imagery of the 'stuck record' and the mayor's rotating spit symbolise complacent monotony and lack of progress, particularly during the late 1950s, when Plath wrote the poem. Both images convey a sense of purposeless circling, of people going nowhere. It seems as though the poet is seething with frustration at the inertia and conformity of her own life and times.

Plath's **darkly embittered sense of humour** becomes evident in **stanza two**. She laments the current lack of honour and courage – something which once existed in the world of fairytales. Unlike the past, contemporary society is compromised. There are no idealistic dragon-slayers any more. The worker who dares to stand up and criticise ('riding against the lizard') is risking demotion. The modern dragon – a metaphor for the challenges we face – has even been reduced to a mere lizard. Despite this, we are afraid of confrontation and prefer to retreat. The verb 'withered' suggests the weakness and decay of our safe, modern world. The poet openly complains that 'History's beaten the hazard'. Over time, we have somehow defeated all sense of adventure and daring. These qualities belong in the distant past.

In **stanza three**, Plath continues to contrast past and present. Witches are no longer burned at the stake. This might well suggest that superstition has disappeared, and with it, all imagination. The last two lines are ironic in tone, reflecting the poet's deep **disenchantment with the excesses of our consumer society**. The final image – 'the cow milk's cream an inch thick' – signifies overindulgence. At one time, it was thought that supernatural forces could reduce the milk yield from cows.

The poet clearly accepts that **society has changed for the worse**. Children may have everything they want nowadays, but they have lost their sense of wonder and excitement. She laments the loss of legendary heroism. Medieval dragons and wicked witches (complete with magic potions and talking cats) no longer exist. Her conclusion is that life today is decidedly less interesting than it used to be. Unlike so much of Plath's work, the personal pronoun 'I' is not used in this poem. However, the views expressed are highly contemptuous and the weary, frustrated tone clearly suggests that Plath herself feels unfulfilled.

ANALYSIS

Write a paragraph on Plath's critical tone in 'The Times Are Tidy'.

Sample Paragraph

The tone of voice in 'The Times Are Tidy' is almost irrationally critical of modern life. Plath has nothing good to say about today's world as she sees it. The poem's title is glib and self-satisfied, just like the neatly organised society that Plath seems to despise. The opening comment – 'Unlucky the hero born/ In this province' – emphasises this negative tone. The poet's mocking attitude becomes increasingly disparaging as she rails against the unproductive images of easy living – 'the stuck record' and 'the mayor's rôtisserie'. Plath goes on to contrast today's apathetic society with the more spirited medieval era, when knights in armour existed. The poet deliberately omits all the positive aspects of modern life and chooses to give a very one-sided view of the world. Plath ends on a sarcastic note, sneering at the advances of our world of plenty – 'cream an inch thick'. The voice here – and indeed, throughout the entire poem – is both sardonic and superior.

Examiner's Comment

This A-grade paragraph demonstrates strong analytical skills and is firmly focused on Plath's judgmental tone. The supporting references range widely and effectively illustrate the poet's critical attitude. Quotations are particularly well integrated and the management of language is assured throughout.

CLASS/HOMEWORK EXERCISES

1. Outline the main theme in 'The Times Are Tidy'. In your answer, trace the way the poet develops her ideas during the course of the poem.

2. Copy the table below into your own notes and fill in critical comments about the last two quotations.

Key Quotes

Unlucky the hero born/In this province	Plath is clearly disillusioned with the unheroic world in which she lives.
the mayor's rôtisserie turns/ Round of its own accord	The image of automation suggests how complacent and predictable life has become. Nothing seems to change.
But the children are better for it	
The cow milk's cream an inch thick	

❸ MORNING SONG

Love set you going like a fat gold watch.
The midwife slapped your footsoles, and your bald cry
Took its place among the elements.

Our voices echo, magnifying your arrival. New statue.
In a drafty museum, your nakedness   5
Shadows our safety. We stand round blankly as walls.

I'm no more your mother
Than the cloud that distils a mirror to reflect its own slow
Effacement at the wind's hand.

All night your moth-breath   10
Flickers among the flat pink roses. I wake to listen:
A far sea moves in my ear.

One cry, and I stumble from bed, cow-heavy and floral
In my Victorian nightgown.
Your mouth opens clean as a cat's. The window square   15

Whitens and swallows its dull stars. And now you try
Your handful of notes;
The clear vowels rise like balloons.

'The clear vowels rise like balloons'

GLOSSARY

2   *midwife*: a person trained to assist at childbirth.

3   *elements*: primitive, natural, atmospheric forces.

9   *Effacement*: gradual disappearance.

11   *pink roses*: images on the wallpaper.

18   *vowels*: speech sounds made without stopping the flow of the breath.

EXPLORATIONS

1. Comment on the suitability and effectiveness of the simile in line 1.

2. What is the attitude of the mother to the new arrival? Does her attitude change in the course of the poem? Refer to the text in your answer.

3. A metaphor links two things so that one idea explains or gives a new viewpoint about the other. Choose one metaphor from the poem and comment on its effectiveness.

STUDY NOTES

'Morning Song' was written in 1961. Plath explores the complex issues of the relationship between a mother and a child, celebrating the birth of the infant but also touching on deep feelings of loss and separation.

Do all mothers immediately welcome and fall in love with a new baby? Are some of them overwhelmed or even depressed after giving birth? Are parents often anxious about the new responsibilities a baby brings? Plath wrote this poem after two intensely personal experiences, celebrating the birth of her daughter, Frieda, who was 10 months old when she wrote the poem, and shortly after a miscarriage. The poem is realistic and never strays into sentimentality or cliché. The title 'Morning' suggests a new beginning and 'Song' a celebration.

Stanza one describes the arrival of the child into the world in a strong, confident, rhythmic sentence announcing the act of creation: 'Love set you going'.

The simile comparing the child to a 'fat gold watch' suggests a plump baby, a rich and precious object. The broad vowel effects emphasise the physical presence of the baby. The 'ticking' sound conveys action and dynamism, but also the passage of time. The child is now part of the mortal world where change and death are inevitable. At this moment of birth, the baby is the centre of attention as the midwife and parents surround her. But this is a cruel world, as we see from the words 'slapped' and 'bald'. The child is now part of the universe as she takes her place among the 'elements'. The verbs in this stanza are in the past tense – **the mother is looking back at the event**. The rest of the poem is written in the present tense, which adds to the immediacy of the experience.

Stanza two has a feeling of disorientation, as if the mother feels separated from the child now that she has left the womb. There is a nightmarish, surreal quality to the lines 'Our voices echo, magnifying your arrival'. Plath sees the child as a new exhibit ('New statue') in a museum. Commas and full stops break up the flow of the lines and **the tone becomes more stilted and detached**. The child as a work of art is special and unique, but the museum is 'drafty', again a reference to the harshness of the world. The baby's vulnerability is stressed by its 'nakedness'. The midwife's and parents' frozen response is caught in the phrase 'blankly as walls'. They anxiously observe, unsure about their ability to protect. This baby also represents a threat to their relationship as she 'Shadows' their safety. The child is perceived as having a negative impact on the parents, perhaps driving them apart rather than uniting them.

Stanza three catches the **complex relationship between child and mother**. Plath feels she can't be maternal ('no more your mother'). This is vividly shown in the image of the cloud that rains, creating a puddle. **But in the act of creation, it destroys itself and its destruction is reflected in the pool of water.** Throughout her life, the poet was haunted by a fear of her own personal disintegration and annihilation. Does she see a conflict between becoming a mother and remaining a writer? She also realises as the child grows and matures that she will age, moving closer to death, and this will be reflected in the child's gaze. The mood of this stanza is one of dislocation, estrangement and powerlessness. Notice how the three lines of the stanza run into each other as the cloud disappears.

In **stanza four**, the tone changes to one of intimate, maternal love as the caring mother becomes alert to her child's needs. The situation described is warm and homely – the 'flat pink roses' are very different to the chill 'museum' of a previous stanza. The fragile breathing of the little child is beautifully described as 'your moth-breath/Flickers'. **Onomatopoeia in 'Flickers' mimics the tiny breathing noises of the child.** The mother is anticipating her baby's needs as she wakes ('listen'). The breathing child evokes happy memories of Plath's seaside childhood ('A far sea moves in my ear'). The infant cries and the attentive mother springs into action. She laughs at herself as she describes the comical figure she makes, 'cow-heavy and floral'. She feels awkward as she 'stumble[s]' to tend her child, whose eager mouth is shown by a startling image ('clean as a cat's') as it opens wide to receive the night feed of milk. The stanza flows smoothly over into **stanza five**, just as nature flows to its own rhythm and does not obey clocks or any other man-made rules. Night becomes morning as the child swallows the milk and the window swallows the stars.

Children demand a parent's time and energy. **The child now defines herself** with her unique collection of sounds ('Your handful of notes'). This poem opened with the instinctive, elemental 'bald' cry of a newborn, but closes on a lovely, happy image of music and colour, as the baby's song's notes 'rise like balloons'.

ANALYSIS

The poem opens with the word 'Love'. Is this poem about parental love or parental anxiety?

Sample Paragraph

'Morning Song' contains both as the tone varies from the confident assertion that 'Love' was the source of the child to the curiously disengaged tone of the second stanza, where the parents 'stand round blankly as walls'. The enormity of the event of the birth of their child into a harsh world, 'drafty museum', seems to overwhelm them, particularly the mother. In the third stanza, she declares that she is not the child's mother, and explores her feelings of annihilation through the complex image of the disintegrating cloud, which creates only to be destroyed in the act of creation. However, the poem ends on a positive, loving note as the attentive mother feeds her child on demand, listening to her baby's song 'rise like balloons'. This poem realistically deals with the conflicting emotions new parents experience at a birth.

Examiner's Comment

> The short paragraph deals confidently with both attitudes in a well-sustained
> argument effectively using pertinent quotes. These references range widely
> over much of the poem and the expression is very well controlled. Grade B.

CLASS/HOMEWORK EXERCISES

1. Look at the different sounds described in the poem, such as 'slapped', 'bald cry',
   'A far sea moves', 'The clear vowels rise', and comment on their effectiveness.

2. Copy the table below into your own notes and fill in critical comments about the
   last two quotations.

Key Quotes

The midwife slapped your footsoles	After a birth, the nurse slaps the child to make it cry and clear the mucus from its mouth and nose.
your nakedness/Shadows our safety	The baby's vulnerability is a threat to the parents' relationship.
Our voices echo, magnifying your arrival	
And now you try/Your handful of notes	

4   FINISTERRE

This was the land's end: the last fingers, knuckled and rheumatic,
Cramped on nothing. Black
Admonitory cliffs, and the sea exploding
With no bottom, or anything on the other side of it,
Whitened by the faces of the drowned.   5
Now it is only gloomy, a dump of rocks –
Leftover soldiers from old, messy wars.
The sea cannons into their ear, but they don't budge.
Other rocks hide their grudges under the water.

The cliffs are edged with trefoils, stars and bells   10
Such as fingers might embroider, close to death,
Almost too small for the mists to bother with.
The mists are part of the ancient paraphernalia –
Souls, rolled in the doom-noise of the sea.
They bruise the rocks out of existence, then resurrect them.   15
They go up without hope, like sighs.
I walk among them, and they stuff my mouth with cotton.
When they free me, I am beaded with tears.

Our Lady of the Shipwrecked is striding toward the horizon,
Her marble skirts blown back in two pink wings.   20
A marble sailor kneels at her foot distractedly, and at his foot
A peasant woman in black
Is praying to the monument of the sailor praying.
Our Lady of the Shipwrecked is three times life size,
Her lips sweet with divinity.   25
She does not hear what the sailor or the peasant is saying –
She is in love with the beautiful formlessness of the sea.

Gull-colored laces flap in the sea drafts
Beside the postcard stalls.
The peasants anchor them with conches. One is told: 30
'These are the pretty trinkets the sea hides,
Little shells made up into necklaces and toy ladies.
They do not come from the Bay of the Dead down there,
But from another place, tropical and blue,
We have never been to.   35
These are our crêpes. Eat them before they blow cold.'

'and the sea exploding'

GLOSSARY

1	*land's end*: literally 'Finisterre'; the western tip of Brittany.
3	*Admonitory*: warning.
10	*trefoils*: three-leaved plants.
13	*paraphernalia*: discarded items.
14	*doom-noise*: hopeless sounds.
19	*Our Lady of the Shipwrecked*: the mother of Christ prayed for sailors.
30	*conches*: shells.
31	*trinkets*: cheap jewellery.
36	*crêpes*: light pancakes.

EXPLORATIONS

1. Would you agree that this is a disquieting poem that is likely to disturb readers? Refer to the text in your answer.

2. There are several changes of tone in this poem. Describe two contrasting tones, using close reference to the text.

3. What does the poem reveal to you about Sylvia Plath's own state of mind? Use reference to the text in your response.

STUDY NOTES

'Finisterre' was written in 1960 following Plath's visit to Brittany, France. As with many of her poems, the description of the place can be interpreted both literally and metaphorically.

The sea has always inspired poets and artists. It is at times welcoming, menacing, beautiful, peaceful and mysterious. Throughout her short life, Sylvia Plath loved the ocean. She spent her childhood years on the Atlantic coast just north of Boston. This setting provides a source for many of her poetic ideas. Terror and death loom large in her descriptive poem 'Finisterre', in which the pounding rhythm of storm waves off the Breton coast represents **Plath's inner turmoil**.

Stanza one opens dramatically and immediately creates a disturbing atmosphere. Plath describes the rocky headland as being 'knuckled and rheumatic'. In a series of powerful images ('the last fingers', 'Black/Admonitory cliffs', 'and the sea exploding'), the poet recreates the uproar and commotion of the scene. The **grisly personification** is startling, linking the shoreline with suffering and decay. There is a real sense of conflict between sea and land. Both are closely associated with death ('the faces of the drowned'). The jagged rocks are compared to 'Leftover soldiers' who 'hide their grudges under the water'. There is a noticeable tone of regret and protest against the futility of conflict, which is denounced as 'old, messy wars'.

Plath's **negative imagery** is relentless, with harsh consonant sounds ('knuckled', 'Cramped', 'exploding') emphasising the force of raging storm waves. The use of contrasting colours intensifies the imagery. As the 'sea cannons' against the headland, the atmosphere is 'only gloomy'. It is hard not to see the bleak seascape as a reflection of Plath's own unhappy state.

In **stanza two**, the poet turns away from the cruel sea and focuses momentarily on the small plants clinging to the cliff edge. However, these 'trefoils, stars and bells' are also 'close to death'. If anything, they reinforce the **unsettling mood** and draw the poet back to the ocean mists, which she thinks of as symbolising the souls of the dead, lost in 'the doom-noise of the sea'. Plath imagines the heavy mists transforming the rocks, destroying them 'out of existence' before managing to 'resurrect them' again. In a **surreal sequence**, the poet enters the water ('I walk among them') and joins the wretched souls who lie there. Her growing sense of panic is suggested by the stark admission: 'they stuff my mouth with cotton'. The experience is agonising and leaves her 'beaded with tears'.

Plath's thoughts turn to a marble statue of 'Our Lady of the Shipwrecked' in **stanza three**. Once again, in her imagination, she creates a **dramatic narrative** around the religious figure. This monument to the patron saint of the ocean should offer some consolation to the kneeling sailor and a grieving peasant woman who pray to the mother of God. Ironically, their pleas are completely ignored – 'She does not hear' their prayers because 'She is in love with the beautiful formlessness of the sea'. The feeling of hopelessness is all pervading. Is the poet expressing her own **feelings of failure and despondency** here? Or is she also attacking the ineffectiveness of religion? The description of the statue is certainly unflattering. The figure is flighty and self-centred: 'Her marble skirts blown back in two pink wings'. In contrast, the powerful ocean remains fascinating.

In the **fourth stanza**, Plath describes the local Bretons who sell souvenirs to tourists. Unlike the previous three stanzas, **the mood appears to be much lighter** as the poet describes the friendly stall-keepers going about their business. It is another irony that their livelihood (selling 'pretty trinkets') is dependent on the sea and its beauty. Like the statue, the locals seem unconcerned by the tragic history of the ocean. Indeed, they are keen to play down 'the Bay of the Dead' and explain that what they sell is imported 'from another place, tropical and blue'. In the final line, a stall-holder advises the poet to enjoy the pancakes she has bought: 'Eat them before they blow cold'. Although the immediate mood is untroubled, the final phrase brings us back to the earlier – and more disturbing – parts of the poem where Plath described the raging storms and the nameless lost souls who have perished at sea.

ANALYSIS

Write a paragraph on Sylvia Plath's use of detailed description in 'Finisterre'.

Sample Paragraph

The opening images of the rocks – 'the last fingers, knuckled and rheumatic' – are of decrepit old age. The strong visual impact is a regular feature of Sylvia Plath's writing. The first half of the poem is filled with memorable details of the windswept coastline. In her careful choice of descriptive terms, Plath uses broad vowels to evoke a pervading feeling of dejection. Words such as 'drowned', 'gloomy', 'rolled' and 'doom' help to create this dismal effect. The dramatic aural image, 'The sea cannons', echoes the roar of turbulent waves crashing onto the rocks. Plath's eye for close observation is also seen in her portrait of the holy statue – 'Her lips sweet with divinity'. The poem ends with a painstaking sketch of the Breton traders selling postcards and 'Little shells made up into necklaces and toy ladies'. The local people seem to have come to terms with 'the Bay of the Dead' and are getting on with life. Overall, the use of details throughout the poem leaves readers with a strong sense of place and community.

Examiner's Comment

Quotations are very well used here to highlight Plath's ability to create specific scenes and moods through precise description. The examples range over much of the poem and the writing is both varied and controlled throughout. Grade-A standard.

CLASS/HOMEWORK EXERCISES

1. It has been said that vivid, startling imagery gives a surreal quality to 'Finisterre'. Using reference to the poem, write a paragraph responding to this statement.

2. Copy the table below into your own notes and fill in critical comments about the last two quotations.

Key Quotes

Admonitory cliffs, and the sea exploding/With no bottom	Striking and dramatic images are a recurring feature throughout the poem.
Souls, rolled in the doom-noise of the sea	The poem is dominated by the underlying themes of fear, hopelessness and death.
Now it is only gloomy, a dump of rocks	
These are our crêpes. Eat them before they blow cold	

⑤ MIRROR

I am silver and exact. I have no preconceptions.
Whatever I see I swallow immediately
Just as it is, unmisted by love or dislike.
I am not cruel, only truthful –
The eye of a little god, four-cornered.   5
Most of the time I meditate on the opposite wall.
It is pink, with speckles. I have looked at it so long
I think it is part of my heart. But it flickers.
Faces and darkness separate us over and over.

Now I am a lake. A woman bends over me,   10
Searching my reaches for what she really is.
Then she turns to those liars, the candles or the moon.
I see her back, and reflect it faithfully.
She rewards me with tears and an agitation of hands.
I am important to her. She comes and goes.   15
Each morning it is her face that replaces the darkness.
In me she has drowned a young girl, and in me an old woman
Rises toward her day after day, like a terrible fish.

'The eye of a little god, four-cornered'

GLOSSARY

1   *exact*: accurate, giving all details; to insist on payment.

1   *preconceptions*: thoughts already formed.

11   *reaches*: range of distance or depth.

14   *agitation*: shaking, anxious.

EXPLORATIONS

1. Select two images that suggest the dark, sinister side of the mirror. Would you consider that these images show an unforgiving way of viewing oneself?

2. What are the parallels and contrasts between a mirror and a lake? Develop your response in a written paragraph.

3. Write your own personal response to this poem, referring closely to the text in your answer.

STUDY NOTES

'Mirror' was written in 1961 as Sylvia Plath approached her twenty-ninth birthday. In this dark poem, Plath views the inevitability of old age and death, our preoccupation with image and our search for an identity.

Do you think everyone looks at themselves in a mirror? Would you consider that people are fascinated, disappointed or even obsessed by what they see? Does a mirror accurately reflect the truth? Do people actually see what is reflected or is it distorted by notions and ideals they or society have? Consider the use of mirrors in fairytales: 'Mirror, mirror on the wall, who's the fairest of them all?' Mirrors are also used in myths, such as the story of Narcissus, who drowned having fallen in love with his reflection, and *Through the Looking Glass* is a famous children's book. Mirrors are also used in horror films as the dividing line between fantasy and reality.

In this poem, Plath often gives us a startling new angle on an everyday object. The function of a mirror is to reflect whatever is put in front of it. **Stanza one** opens with a ringing declaration by the mirror: 'I am silver and exact'. This **personification has a sinister effect** in the poem as the mirror describes an almost claustrophobic relationship with a particular woman. The voice of the mirror is clear, direct and precise. It announces that it reports exactly what there is without any alteration. We have to decide if the mirror is telling the truth, as it says it has no bias ('no preconceptions'). It does not judge; it reflects the image received. The mirror adopts the position of an impartial observer, but it is active, almost ruthless ('I swallow'). It is not cruel, but truthful.

Yet how truthful is a mirror image, as it flattens a three-dimensional object into two dimensions? The image sent out has no depth. The voice of the mirror becomes smug as it sees itself as the ruler of those reflected ('The eye of a little god'). Our obsession with ourselves causes us to worship at the mirror that reflects our image. In the modern world, people are often disappointed with their reflections, wishing they were thinner, younger, better looking. But **the mirror insists it tells the truth**; it doesn't flatter or hurt. The mirror explains how it spends its day gazing at the opposite wall, which is carefully described as 'pink, with speckles'. It feels as if the wall is part of itself. This reflection is disturbed by the faces of people and the dying light. The passage of time is evoked in the phrase 'over and over'.

In **stanza two**, the mirror now announces that it is 'a lake'. Both are flat surfaces that reflect. However, a lake is another dimension, it has depth. **There is danger.** The image is now drawn into its murky depths. The woman is looking in and down, not just at. It is as if she is struggling to find who she really is, what her true path in life is. Plath frequently questioned who she was. Expectations for young women in the 1950s were limiting. Appearance was important, as were the roles of wife, mother and homemaker. But Plath also wanted to write: 'Will I submerge my embarrassing desires and aspirations, refuse to face myself?' The mirror becomes irritated and jealous of the woman as she turns to the deceptive soft light of 'those liars, the candles or the moon'. The mirror remains faithful, reflecting her back. **The woman is dissatisfied with her image.** In her insecurity, she weeps and wrings her hands. Plath always tried to do her best, to be a model student, almost desperate to excel and be affirmed. Is there a danger in seeking perfection? Do we need to be kind to ourselves? Do we need to love ourselves? Again, the mirror pompously announces 'I am important to her'.

The march of time passing is emphasised by 'comes and goes', 'Each morning' and 'day after day'. The woman keeps coming back. The mirror's sense of its importance is shown by the frequent use of 'I' and the repetition of 'in me'. As time passes, the woman is facing the truth of her human condition as her reflection changes and ages in the mirror. Her youth is 'drowned', to be replaced by a monstrous vision of an old woman 'like a terrible fish'. **The lonely drama of living and dying is recorded with a dreamlike, nightmarish quality.** There is no comforting rhyme in the poem, only the controlled rhythm of time. The mirror does not give what a human being desires: comfort and warmth. Instead, it impersonally reminds us of our mortality.

ANALYSIS

What is your personal response to the relationship between the mirror and the woman? Support your views with reference to the poem.

Sample Paragraph

I feel the mirror is like an alter ego, which is coolly appraising the woman in an unforgiving way. The mirror is 'silver'. This cold metal object is heartless. Although the mirror repeatedly states that it does not judge, 'I have no preconceptions', the woman feels judged and wanting: 'She rewards me with tears and an agitation of hands.' I think the relationship between the woman and the mirror is dangerous and poisonous. She does indeed 'drown' in the mirror, as she never feels good enough. Is this the payment the mirror exacts? The complacent mirror rules her like a tyrannical 'little god, four-cornered'. It reminds me of how today we are never satisfied with our image, always wanting something else, more perfect. Plath also strove to be perfect. This obsessive relationship shows a troubled self, a lack of self-love. Who is saying that the older woman is 'like a terrible fish'? I think the mirror has become the voice of a society which values women only for their looks and youth, rather than what they are capable of achieving.

Examiner's Comment

In this fluent and personal response, the candidate has given a distinctive and well-supported account of the uneasy relationship between the mirror and the woman. Grade-A answer.

CLASS/HOMEWORK EXERCISES

1. How are the qualities of terror and despair shown in the imagery of the poem?

2. Copy the table below into your own notes and fill in critical comments about the last two quotations.

Key Quotes

I have no preconceptions	The mirror states that it objectively reflects reality.
The eye of a little god, four-cornered	Plath's metaphor emphasises how this rectangular mirror considers itself very important.
I am silver and exact	
in me an old woman/Rises toward her day after day, like a terrible fish	

6   # PHEASANT

You said you would kill it this morning.
Do not kill it. It startles me still,
The jut of that odd, dark head, pacing

Through the uncut grass on the elm's hill.
It is something to own a pheasant,   5
Or just to be visited at all.

I am not mystical: it isn't
As if I thought it had a spirit.
It is simply in its element.

That gives it a kingliness, a right.   10
The print of its big foot last winter,
The tail-track, on the snow in our court –

The wonder of it, in that pallor,
Through crosshatch of sparrow and starling.
Is it its rareness, then? It is rare.   15

But a dozen would be worth having,
A hundred, on that hill – green and red,
Crossing and recrossing: a fine thing!

It is such a good shape, so vivid.
It's a little cornucopia.   20
It unclaps, brown as a leaf, and loud,

Settles in the elm, and is easy.
It was sunning in the narcissi.
I trespass stupidly. Let be, let be.

'in its element'

GLOSSARY

1   *You*: probably addressed to Plath's
    husband.
3   *jut*: extending outwards.
7   *mystical*: spiritual, supernatural.
13 *pallor*: pale colour.

14 *crosshatch*: criss-cross trail.
20 *cornucopia*: unexpected treasure.
23 *narcissi*: bright spring flowers.

EXPLORATIONS

1. Explain Sylvia Plath's attitude to nature based on your reading of 'Pheasant'.

2. Compile a list of the poet's arguments for not killing the pheasant.

3. Write a paragraph on the effectiveness of Plath's imagery in the poem.

STUDY NOTES

'Pheasant' was written in 1962 and reflects Plath's deep appreciation of the natural world. Its enthusiastic mood contrasts with much of her more disturbing work. The poem is structured in eight tercets (three-line stanzas) with a subtle, interlocking rhyming pattern (known as terza rima).

The poem opens with an urgent plea by Plath to spare the pheasant's life: 'Do not kill it'. In the **first two stanzas**, the tone is tense as the poet offers a variety of reasons for sparing this impressive game bird. She is both shocked and excited by the pheasant: 'It startles me still'. Plath admits to feeling honoured in the presence of the bird: 'It is something to own a pheasant'. The broken rhythm of the early lines adds an abruptness that heightens the sense of urgency. **Plath seems spellbound by the bird's beauty** ('The jut of that odd, dark head') now that it is under threat. But the poet is also keen to play down any sentimentality in her attitude to the pheasant. **Stanza three** opens with a straightforward explanation of her attitude: 'it isn't/As if I thought it had a spirit'. Instead, **she values the bird for its graceful beauty and naturalness**: 'It is simply in its element.' Plath is keen to show her recognition of the pheasant's right to exist because it possesses a certain majestic quality, 'a kingliness'. In **stanza four**, the poet recalls an earlier winter scene when she marvelled at the pheasant's distinctive footprint in the snow. The bird has made an even greater impression on Plath, summed up in the key phrase 'The wonder of it', at the start of **stanza five**. She remembers **the colourful pheasant's distinguishing marks against the pale snow**, so unlike the 'crosshatch' pattern of smaller birds, such as the sparrow and starling. This makes the pheasant particularly 'rare' and valuable in Plath's eyes.

The poet can hardly contain her regard for the pheasant and her tone becomes increasingly enthusiastic in **stanza six** as she dreams of having first a 'dozen' and then a 'hundred' of the birds. In a few **well-chosen details**, she highlights their colour and energy ('green and red,/Crossing and recrossing') and adds an emphatic compliment: 'a fine thing!' Her delight continues into **stanza seven**, where Plath proclaims her ceaseless admiration for the pheasant: 'It's a little cornucopia', an inspirational source of joy and surprise.

Throughout the poem, Plath has emphasised that the pheasant rightly belongs in its natural surroundings, and this is also true of the final lines. **Stanza eight** is considered and assured. From the poet's point of view, **the pheasant's right to live is beyond dispute**. While the bird is 'sunning in the narcissi', she herself has become the unwelcome intruder: 'I trespass stupidly'. Plath ends by echoing the opening appeal to spare the pheasant's life: 'Let be, let be.' The quietly insistent repetition and the underlying tone of unease are a final reminder of the need to respect nature.

It has been suggested that the pheasant symbolises Plath's insecure relationship with Ted Hughes. For various reasons, their marriage was under severe strain in 1962 and Plath feared that Hughes was intent on ending it. This interpretation adds a greater poignancy to the poem.

ANALYSIS

There are several mood changes in 'Pheasant'. What do you consider to be the dominant mood in the poem? Refer to the text in your answer.

Sample Paragraph

The mood at the beginning of 'Pheasant' is nervous and really uptight. Plath seems to have given up hope about the pheasant. It is facing death. She repeats the word 'kill' and admits to being shocked at the very thought of what the bird is facing. She herself seems desperate and fearful. This is shown by the short sentence, 'Do not kill it'. But the outlook soon changes. Plath describes the pheasant 'pacing' and 'in its element'. But she seems less stressed as she describes the 'kingliness' of the pheasant. But the mood soon settles down as Plath celebrates the life of this really beautiful bird. The mood becomes calmer and ends in almost a whisper, 'Let be, let be'. The dominant mood is calm and considered in the poem.

Examiner's Comment

This is a reasonably well-focused response to the question. The candidate points out the change of mood following the first stanza. Some worthwhile references are used to show the poem's principal mood. The expression, however, is flawed in places (e.g. using 'but' to start sentences). The standard is C-grade overall.

CLASS/HOMEWORK EXERCISES

1. Plath sets out to convince the reader of the pheasant's right to life. Does she succeed in her aim? Give reasons for your answer.

2. Copy the table below into your own notes and fill in critical comments about the last two quotations.

Key Quotes

pacing/Through the uncut grass on the elm's hill	Plath is a keen observer of the pheasant and uses details to capture its steady movement.
That gives it a kingliness, a right	Man's relationship with the world of nature is central to 'Pheasant'.
I am not mystical	
It unclaps, brown as a leaf	

❼ ELM

For Ruth Fainlight

I know the bottom, she says. I know it with my great tap root;
It is what you fear.
I do not fear it: I have been there.

Is it the sea you hear in me,
Its dissatisfactions?   5
Or the voice of nothing, that was your madness?

Love is a shadow.
How you lie and cry after it
Listen: these are its hooves: it has gone off, like a horse.

All night I shall gallop thus, impetuously,   10
Till your head is a stone, your pillow a little turf,
Echoing, echoing.

Or shall I bring you the sound of poisons?
This is rain now, this big hush.
And this is the fruit of it: tin-white, like arsenic.   15

I have suffered the atrocity of sunsets.
Scorched to the root
My red filaments burn and stand, a hand of wires.

Now I break up in pieces that fly about like clubs.
A wind of such violence   20
Will tolerate no bystanding: I must shriek.

The moon, also, is merciless: she would drag me
Cruelly, being barren.
Her radiance scathes me. Or perhaps I have caught her.

I let her go. I let her go   25
Diminished and flat, as after radical surgery.
How your bad dreams possess and endow me.

I am inhabited by a cry.
Nightly it flaps out
Looking, with its hooks, for something to love.   30

I am terrified by this dark thing
That sleeps in me;
All day I feel its soft, feathery turnings, its malignity.

Clouds pass and disperse.
Are those the faces of love, those pale irretrievables?   35
Is it for such I agitate my heart?

I am incapable of more knowledge.
What is this, this face
So murderous in its strangle of branches? –

Its snaky acids hiss.   40
It petrifies the will. These are the isolate, slow faults
That kill, that kill, that kill.

'I am terrified by this dark thing'

GLOSSARY

Title: The wych elm is a large deciduous tree, with a massive straight trunk and tangled branches. It was once a favourite timber of coffin makers. Plath dedicated the poem to a close friend, Ruth Fainlight, another American poet.

1   *the bottom:* lowest depths.
1   *tap root:* the main root.

15   *arsenic:* poison.
18   *filaments:* fibres, nerves.
24   *scathes:* injures, scalds.
33   *malignity:* evil.
34   *disperse:* scatter widely.
35   *irretrievables:* things lost forever.
40   *snaky acids:* deceptive poisons.
41   *petrifies:* terrifies.

EXPLORATIONS

1. There are many sinister nature images in this poem. Select two that you find particularly unsettling and comment on their effectiveness.

2. Trace and examine how love is presented and viewed by the poet. Support the points you make with reference to the text.

3. Write your own individual response to this poem, referring closely to the text in your answer.

STUDY NOTES

Written in April 1962, 'Elm' is one of Sylvia Plath's most challenging and intensely dramatic poems. Plath personifies the elm tree to create a surreal scene. It 'speaks' in a traumatic voice to someone else, the 'you' of line 2, the poet herself – or the reader, perhaps. Both voices interact throughout the poem, almost always expressing pain and anguish. Critics often associate these powerful emotions with the poet's own personal problems – Plath had experienced electric shock treatment for depression. However, this may well limit our understanding of what is a complex exploration of many emotions.

The **opening stanza** is unnerving. The poet appears to be dramatising an exchange between herself and the elm by imagining what the tree might say to her. The immediate effect is eerily surreal. From the start, **the narrative voice is obsessed with instability and despair**: 'I know the bottom'. The tree is described in both physical terms ('my great tap root' penetrating far into the ground) and also as a state of mind ('I do not fear it'). The depth of depression imagined is reinforced by the repetition of 'I know' and the stark simplicity of the chilling comment 'It is what you fear'.

The bizarre exchange between the two 'speakers' continues in **stanza two**. The elm questions the poet about the nature of her **mental state**. Does the wind blowing through its branches remind her of the haunting sound of the sea? Or even 'the voice of nothing' – the numbing experience of madness?

Stanzas three and **four** focus on the dangers and disappointments of love – 'a shadow'. The tone is wary, emphasised by the comparison of a wild horse that has 'gone off'. The relentless sounds of the wind in the elm will be a bitter reminder, 'echoing' this loss of love 'Till your head is a stone'. **Assonance** is effectively used here to heighten the sense of hurt and abandonment. For much of the middle section of the poem (**stanzas five** to **nine**), the elm's intimidating voice continues to dramatise a series of horrifying experiences associated with madness. The tree has endured extreme elements – rain ('the sound of poisons'), sunshine ('Scorched to the root'), wind ('of such violence') and also the moon ('Her radiance scathes me'). **The harsh imagery and frenzied language** ('burn', 'shriek', 'merciless') combine to create a sense of shocking destructiveness.

Stanzas 10 and **11** mark a turning point where the voices of the tree and the poet become indistinguishable. This is achieved by the seemingly harmless image of an owl inhabiting the branches, searching for 'something to love'. The speaker is haunted by 'this dark thing'. The **poet's vulnerability** is particularly evident in her stark admission: 'I feel its soft, feathery turnings, its malignity'. Plath has come to relate her unknown demons to a deadly tumour.

In the **last three stanzas**, the poet's voice seems more distant and calm before the final storm. The image of the passing clouds ('the faces of love') highlight the notion of rejection as the root cause of Plath's depression. The poem ends on a visionary note when she imagines being confronted by a 'murderous' snake that appears in the branches: 'It petrifies the will'. The scene of **growing terror builds to a hideous climax** until her own mental and emotional states (her 'slow faults') end up destroying her. The intensity of the final line, 'That kill, that kill, that kill', leaves readers with a harrowing understanding of Plath's paralysis of despair.

ANALYSIS

Do you think that 'Elm' has a surreal, nightmarish quality? In your response, refer to the text to support your views.

Sample Paragraph

I would agree that Sylvia Plath has created a very disturbing mood in the poem, 'Elm'. Giving the tree a speaking voice of its own is like something from a child's fairy story. Plath compares love to a galloping horse. The poem is mainly about depression and madness. So it's bound to be out of the ordinary. The speaker in the poem is confused and asks weird questions, such as 'Is it the sea you hear inside me?' She is obsessive and totally paranoid. Everything is against her, as far as she imagines it. The weather is seen as an enemy even, 'the rain is like arsenic' and 'sounds like poisons'. The end is as if she is having a bad dream with imagining a fierce hissing snake in the tree coming after her. This represents Plath's deepest nightmare, the fear of loneliness. The whole poem is surreal and confusing – especially the images.

Examiner's Comment

This short paragraph includes some worthwhile references to the poem's disturbing aspects. The points are note-like, however, and the writing style lacks control. Some of the quotations are also inaccurate. C-grade standard.

CLASS/HOMEWORK EXERCISES

1. What evidence of Plath's deep depression and hypersensitivity is revealed in the poem 'Elm'? Refer closely to the text in your answer.

2. Copy the table below into your own notes and fill in critical comments about the last two quotations.

Key Quotes

I know it with my great tap root	Through the 'voice' of the elm, Plath uses the tree metaphor to suggest her own depths of despair.
My red filaments burn and stand, a hand of wires	This image of suffering may relate to the poet's own experience of electric shock treatment for depression.
the atrocity of sunsets	
Its snaky acids hiss	

8 POETRY IN JULY *Sounds like a nice poem, quite the opposite*

sentimental

Her head was in emotional turmoil

Little poppies, little hell flames, *Metaphor, comparing poppies to flames*
Do you do no harm? *Questioning the poppies as if she wants hell then to do her harm.*

personification

You flicker. I cannot touch you. *Is she disappointed or relieved th*
I put my hands among the flames. Nothing burns. *they don't burn.*

And it exhausts me to watch you *Image became more unattractive*
Flickering like that, wrinkly and clear red, like the skin of a mouth.

smile

A mouth just bloodied. *Metaphor Repetition of blood suggest.*
Little bloody skirts! *danger, shows there's something not right in her mind.*

There are fumes that I cannot touch. *She wants to be drugged*
Where are your opiates, your nauseous capsules? *by the poppies.*   10
She wants to be realeased.

If I could bleed, or sleep! – *Intended violence / alienation / death*
If my mouth could marry a hurt like that! *wants to be connected to her own pain*

Or your liquors seep to me, in this glass capsule, *She wants the fumes*
Dulling and stilling. *She wants them to*   *to seep into that*
seep in until her senses stop.   *capsule.*

wants to
be numbed
on earth.

But colorless. Colorless. *She wants*   *She wants*
except nothingness.   *oblivion.*   15

'You flicker. I cannot touch you' *longing for escape.*

GLOSSARY

1	*hell flames*: most poppies are red, flame-like.
9	*fumes*: the effects of drugs.
10	*opiates*: sleep-inducing narcotics.

10	*nauseous*: causing sickness.
13	*liquors*: drug vapours.
13	*capsule*: small container.
15	*colorless*: drained, lifeless.

EXPLORATIONS

1. Examine the title, 'Poppies in July', in light of the main subject matter in the poem. Is the title misleading? Explain your answer.

2. What evidence can you find in 'Poppies in July' that the speaker is yearning to escape?

3. Colour imagery plays a significant role in the poem. Comment on how effectively colour is used.

STUDY NOTES

Like most confessional writers, Sylvia Plath's work reflects her own personal experiences, without filtering any of the painful emotions. She wrote 'Poppies in July' in the summer of 1962, during the break-up of her marriage.

The **first stanza** is marked by an uneasy sense of foreboding. The speaker (almost certainly Plath herself) compares the blazing red poppies to 'little hell flames' before directly confronting them: 'Do you do no harm?' **Her distress is obvious** from the start. The poem's title may well have led readers to expect a more conventional nature poem. Instead, the flowers are presented as being highly treacherous, and all the more deceptive because they are 'little'.

Plath develops the fire image in **lines 3–6**. However, even though she places her hands 'among the flames', she finds that 'Nothing burns' and she is forced to watch them 'Flickering'. It almost seems as though she is so tired and numb that **she has transcended pain** and can experience nothing: 'it exhausts me to watch you'. Ironically, the more vivid the poppies are, the more lethargic she feels.

The uncomfortable and disturbed mood increases in the **fourth stanza** with two **startling images**, both personifying the flowers. Comparing the poppy to 'A mouth just bloodied' suggests recent violence and physical suffering. The 'bloody skirts' metaphor is equally harrowing. There is further evidence of the poet's overpowering weariness in the prominent use of broad vowel sounds, for example in 'exhausts', 'mouth' and 'bloodied'.

In the **fifth stanza**, Plath's disorientated state turns to a distracted longing for escape. Having failed to use the vibrancy of the poppies to distract her from her pain, she now craves the feeling of oblivion or unconsciousness. But although she desires the dulling effects of drugs derived from the poppies, her **tone is hopelessly cynical** as she describes the 'fumes that I cannot touch'.

The mood becomes even more distraught in **lines 11–12**, with the poet begging for any alternative to her anguished state. 'If I could bleed, or sleep!' is an emphatic plea for release. It is her final attempt to retain some control of her life in the face of an overwhelming sense of powerlessness. Plath's **growing alienation** seems so unbearably intense at this point that it directly draws the reader's sympathy.

The **last three lines** record the poet's surrender, perhaps a kind of death wish. Worn down by her inner demons and the bright colours of the poppies, Plath lets herself become resigned to a 'colorless' world of nothingness. Her **complete passivity** and helplessness are emphasised by the dreamlike quality of the phrase 'Dulling and stilling'. As she drifts into a death-like 'colorless' private hell, there remains a terrible sense of betrayal, as if she is still being haunted by the bright red flowers. The ending of 'Poppies in July' is so dark and joyless that it is easy to see why the poem is often seen as a desperate cry for help.

ANALYSIS

'Poppies in July' is one of Plath's most disturbing poems. What aspects of the poem affected you most?

Sample Paragraph

'Poppies in July' was written at a time when Plath was struggling with the fact that her husband had deserted her. This affected her deeply and it is clear that the poppies are a symbol of this excruciating time. Everything about the poem is negative. The images of the poppies are nearly all associated with fire and blood. Plath's language is alarming when she compares the poppies to 'little hell flames' and also 'the skin of a mouth'. The most disturbing aspect is Plath's own unstable mind. She seems to be in a kind of trance, obsessed by the red colours of the poppies, which remind her of blood. I got the impression that she was nearly going insane in the end. She seems suicidal – 'If I could bleed'. For me, this is the most disturbing moment in the poem. I can get some idea of her troubled mind. Plath cannot stand reality and seeks a way out through drugs or death. The last image is of Plath sinking into a dull state of drowsiness, unable to cope with the world around her.

Examiner's Comment

Overall, a solid B-grade response which responds personally to the question. While the candidate dealt well with the disturbing thought in the poem, there could have been a more thorough exploration of Plath's style and how it enhances her theme of depression.

► CLASS/HOMEWORK EXERCISES

1. Would you agree that loneliness and pain are the central themes of 'Poppies in July'? Refer to the text of the poem when writing your response.

2. Copy the table below into your own notes and fill in critical comments about the last two quotations.

Key Quotes

You flicker. I cannot touch you	The contrast between the poppies' energy and Plath's own passive state is a memorable feature of the poem.
And it exhausts me to watch you	Plath's overwhelming sense of despair is central to the poem.
Where are your opiates, your nauseous capsules?	
If my mouth could marry a hurt like that!	

9 THE ARRIVAL OF THE BEE BOX

I ordered this, this clean wood box
Square as a chair and almost too heavy to lift.
I would say it was the coffin of a midget
Or a square baby
Were there not such a din in it.   5

The box is locked, it is dangerous.
I have to live with it overnight
And I can't keep away from it.
There are no windows, so I can't see what is in there.
There is only a little grid, no exit.   10

I put my eye to the grid.
It is dark, dark,
With the swarmy feeling of African hands
Minute and shrunk for export,
Black on black, angrily clambering.   15

How can I let them out?
It is the noise that appalls me most of all, *the noise scares her.*
The unintelligible syllables. *Reflect her mind. Doesn't understand.*
It is like a Roman mob, *If they are let loose they will create*
danger.
Small, taken one by one, but my god, together! *She's awestruck*   20

I lay my ear to furious Latin. *Unknown language*
Metaphor I am not a Caesar.
I have simply ordered a box of maniacs. *Situation is under control.*
They can be sent back.
They can die, I need feed them nothing, I am the owner.   25
She realises the power she has

I wonder how hungry they are. *Concerned about the bees.*
I wonder if they would forget me *The idea of loosing her identity by*
turning into a tree.
If I just undid the locks and stood back and turned into a tree.
There is the laburnum, its blond colonnades, *Comparing the branches*
And the petticoats of the cherry.   *to blonde*   30
                                                                   ringlets

They might ignore me immediately
In my moon suit and funeral veil.
I am no source of honey
So why should they turn on me?
Tomorrow I will be sweet God, I will set them free.   *She has the 35*
control to set them free.

The box is only temporary.
Her state of mind is only temporary.

'It is the noise that appalls me'

GLOSSARY

10 *grid*: wire network.
13 *swarmy*: like a large group of bees.
22 *Caesar*: famous Roman ruler.
29 *laburnum*: tree with yellow hanging flowers.

29 *colonnades*: long groups of flowers arranged in a row of columns.
32 *moon suit*: protective clothing worn by beekeepers; all-in-one suit.

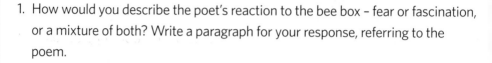

EXPLORATIONS

1. How would you describe the poet's reaction to the bee box – fear or fascination, or a mixture of both? Write a paragraph for your response, referring to the poem.

2. Select two surreal images from the poem and comment on the effectiveness of each.

3. Would you describe this poem as exploring and overcoming one's fears and anxieties? Is the ending optimistic or pessimistic, in your opinion?

STUDY NOTES

'The Arrival of the Bee Box' was written in 1962, shortly after Plath's separation from her husband. Her father, who died when she was a child, had been a bee expert and Plath and her husband had recently taken up beekeeping. She explores order, power, control, confinement and freedom in this deeply personal poem.

The poem opens with a simple statement: 'I ordered this'. Straightaway, the emphasis is on order and control. The poet's tone in **stanza one** seems both matter-of-fact and surprised, as if thinking: 'Yes, I was the one who ordered this' and also 'Did I really order this?' **This drama has only one character, Plath herself.** We observe her responses and reactions to the arrival of the bee box. Notice the extensive use of the personal pronoun 'I'. We both see and hear the event.

The box is described as being made of 'clean wood' and given a homely quality with the simile 'Square as a chair'. But then a surreal, dreamlike metaphor, 'the coffin of a midget/Or a square baby', brings us into a **nightmare world**. The abnormal is suggested by the use of 'midget' and deformity by 'square baby'. The coffin conveys not only death, but also entrapment and confinement, preoccupations of the poet. The box has now become a sinister object. A witty sound effect closes the first stanza, as 'din in it' mimics the sound of the bees. They are like badly behaved children.

Stanza two explores the **poet's ambivalent attitude to the box**. She is fascinated by it, as she is curious to see inside ('I can't keep away from it'). Yet she is also frightened by it, as she describes the box as 'dangerous'. She peers in. The **third stanza** becomes claustrophobic and oppressive with the repetition of 'dark' and the grotesque image of 'the swarmy feeling of African hands/ Minute and shrunk for export'. The milling of the bees/slaves is vividly captured as they heave around in the heat in an atmosphere of menace and oppression, hopelessly desperate. We hear the bees in **stanza four**. The metaphor of a Roman mob is used to show how if they are let loose they will create **chaos and danger**. The assonance of 'appalls' and 'all' underlines the poet's terror. The phrase 'unintelligible syllables', with its onomatopoeia and its difficult pronunciation, lets us hear the angry buzzing. Plath is awestruck at their collective force and energy: 'but my god, together!' Notice the use of the exclamation mark.

The poet tries to listen, but only hears 'furious Latin' she does not understand. She doubts her capacity to control them, stating that she is 'not a Caesar', the powerful ruler of the Romans, in **stanza five**. She regards them as 'maniacs'. Then she realises that if she has ordered them, she can return them: 'They can be sent back'. **She has some control of this situation.** Plath can even decide their fate, whether they live or die: 'I need feed them nothing'. She has now redefined the situation as she realises that she is 'the owner'. They belong to her.

The feminine, nurturing side of her now emerges as she wonders 'how hungry they are'. The stereotype of the pretty woman surfaces in the description of the bees' natural habitat of trees in **stanza six**. Plath thinks if she releases them, they would go back to the trees, 'laburnum' and 'cherry'. She herself would then merge into the landscape and become a tree. This is a reference to a Greek myth where Daphne was being pursued by Apollo. After begging the gods to be saved, they turned her into a tree.

Now she refers to herself in her beekeeping outfit of veil and boiler suit in **stanza seven**. She rhetorically asks why they would attack her, as she is not a source of sustenance ('I am no source of honey'). **She decides to be compassionate**: 'Tomorrow I will be sweet God, I will set them free'. She realises that they are imprisoned only for now: 'The box is only temporary'.

This poem can also be read on another level. The box could represent the poet's attempt to be what others expect, the typical 1950s woman – pretty, compliant, nurturing. The bees could represent the dark side of her personality, which both fascinated and terrified Plath. She has to accept this: 'I have to live with it overnight'. **The box is like Pandora's box**: safe when locked, but full of danger when opened. Although she finds this disturbing, she also feels she must explore it in the interests of developing as a poet. The references to the doomed character of Daphne and the 'funeral veil' echo chillingly. Would these dark thoughts, if given their freedom, drive her to suicide? The form of this poem is seven stanzas of five lines. One line stands alone, free like the bees or her dark thoughts. If the box represents Plath's outside appearance or body, it is mortal, it is temporary. Will the thoughts, if freed from the body, stop?

ANALYSIS

How does this poem address the themes of order and power? Write a paragraph in response. Support your views with reference to the text.

Sample Paragraph

The poem opens with a reference to order, 'I ordered this'. It is an assertion of power, a deliberate act by 'I'. Throughout the poem the repetition of 'I' suggests a person who consciously chooses to act in a certain way. 'I put my eye to the grid', 'I lay my ear to furious Latin'. It is as if the poet wishes to confront and control her fears over the contents of the box. This box contains live, buzzing bees, whose wellbeing lies in the hands of the poet. 'I need feed them nothing, I am the owner'. Although she realises that she is not 'Caesar', the mighty Roman ruler, she can choose to be 'sweet God'. She alone has the power to release the bees, 'The box is only temporary'. This poem can also be read as referring to the control a person exercises when confronting their innermost fears and desires. These thoughts can be ignored or faced. The person owns these thoughts and can choose to contain them or confront them. Plath feared her own dark side, but felt it should be explored to enable her to progress as a poet. For her 'The box is only temporary'.

Examiner's Comment

This note-like response summarises parts of the poem that allude to order and power. However, it fails to address the question about the poet's approach to the central themes. There is little discussion about Plath's attitude to power. Grade C.

CLASS/HOMEWORK EXERCISES

1. How does Plath create a dramatic atmosphere in 'The Arrival of the Bee Box'?

2. Copy the table below into your own notes and fill in critical comments about the last two quotations.

Key Quotes

Key Quotes	
I have to live with it overnight/And I can't keep away from it	The poet refers to the intense relationship she has with the box, from which she cannot escape.
With the swarmy feeling of African hands/Minute and shrunk for export	The bees are described as miniature African slaves who are imprisoned as they are sent off to another country.
Tomorrow I will be sweet God	
The box is only temporary	

Explain the different tone changes throughout the poem.

Theme of motherhood.

Huge tone changes throughout.

10 CHILD

statement implies not everything in her world is beautif

Your clear eye is the one absolutely beautiful thing.
I want to fill it with color and ducks,
The zoo of the new

She longs to give her child beautiful positive images

evokes childh images + the sense of wonder.

Whose name you meditate –
April snowdrop, Indian pipe,
Little

Flower imagery, suggests spring, which suggest hope.

metaphors describing the child

hasn't been effected by life & unblemished

Stalk without wrinkle,
Pool in which images
Should be grand and classical

suggests childs potential to blossom. Without wrinkles, his pure

She longs for her childs innocent eyes to see only beautiful and classical sights.

metaphors for his eyes

Not this troublous
Wringing of hands, this dark
Ceiling without a star.

He sees what his mother is going through. Doubts her abilities to show him happiness, emotionally unable. He witnesses her emotional trauma

change of tone to quite gloomy.

metaphor for her own life no brightness

'The zoo of the new' portrays a sense of oppression very poignant.

She felt inadequate but still loved her children.

✱ Notes at the back also.

GLOSSARY

4	*meditate*: reflect.
5	*Indian pipe*: American woodland flower.
7	*Stalk*: plant stem.
9	*classical*: impressive, enduring.
10	*troublous*: disturbed.

EXPLORATIONS

1. What was your own immediate reaction after reading 'Child'? Refer to the text in your answer.

2. Which images in the poem are most effective in contrasting the world of the child and the world of the adult?

3. Plath uses various sound effects to enhance her themes in 'Child'. Comment briefly on two interesting examples.

STUDY NOTES

Sylvia Plath's son was born in January 1962. A year later, not long before the poet's own death, she wrote 'Child', a short poem that reflects her intense feelings about motherhood.

The first line of **stanza one** shows the **poet's emphatic appreciation of childhood** innocence: 'Your clear eye is the one absolutely beautiful thing'. The tone at first is hopeful. Her love for the new child is generous and unconditional: 'I want to fill it with color'. The childlike language is lively and playful. Plath plans to give her child the happiest of times, filled with 'color and ducks'. The vigorous rhythm and animated internal rhyme in the phrase 'The zoo of the new' are imaginative, capturing the sense of **youthful wonder**.

In **stanza two**, the poet continues to associate her child with all that is best about the natural world. The baby is like the most fragile of flowers, the 'April snowdrop'. The assonance in this phrase has a musical effect, like a soft lullaby. Yet her own fascination appears to mask a deeper concern. Plath feels that such a perfect childhood experience is unlikely to last very long. Despite all her positive sentiments, what she wants for **the vulnerable child** seems directly at odds with what is possible in a **flawed world**.

Run-on lines are a recurring feature of the poem and these add to the feeling of freedom and innocent intensity. **Stanza three** includes two **effective comparisons**, again taken from nature. Plath sees the child as an unblemished 'Stalk' that should grow perfectly. A second quality of childhood's pure innocence is found in the 'Pool' metaphor. We are reminded of the opening image – the child's 'clear eye', always trusting and sincere.

The poet would love to provide a magical future for her young child, so that the pool would reflect 'grand and classical' images. However, as a loving mother, she is trapped between her **idealism** – the joy she wants for her child – and a **distressing reality** – an awareness that the child's life will not be perfectly happy. This shocking realisation becomes clear in **stanza four** and overshadows her hopes completely. The final images are stark and powerful – the pathetic 'Wringing of hands' giving emphasis to her helplessness. The last line poignantly portrays the paradox of the tension between Plath's dreams for the child in the face of the despair she feels about the oppressive world: this 'Ceiling without a star'. This dark mood is in sharp contrast with the rest of the poem. The early celebration has been replaced by anguish and an overwhelming sense of failure.

ANALYSIS

Do you think 'Child' is a positive or negative poem? Refer to the text in explaining your response.

Sample Paragraph

I think Plath's poem, 'Child', is essentially about a mother's inadequacy. The poet wants the best for her innocent son. Although the first half of the poem focuses on her wishes to protect him, this changes at the end. Plath starts off by wanting to fill the boy's life with happy experiences (bright colours and toys) and keep him close to nature. There are numerous references to nature right through the poem and Plath compares her son to an 'April snowdrop'. This tender image gave me a very positive feeling. Everything about the child is wonderful at first. He is 'absolutely beautiful'. This all changes at the end of the poem. The mood turns negative. Plath talks of being confined in a darkened room which has a 'Ceiling without a star'. This is in total contrast with the images early on which were of the bright outdoors. The poet was positive at the start. This has been replaced with negative feelings. The ending is dark and 'troublous' because Plath knows that her child will grow up and experience pain just as she has.

Examiner's Comment

This paragraph addresses the question well and offers a clear response. The candidate effectively illustrates the changing mood from optimism to pessimism and uses apt quotations in support. The style of writing is a little note-like and pedestrian. A basic B-grade standard.

CLASS/HOMEWORK EXERCISES

1. Write a paragraph comparing 'Child' with 'Morning Song'. Refer to theme and style in both poems.

2. Copy the table below into your own notes and fill in critical comments about the last two quotations.

Key Quotes

Your clear eye	The newborn child is innocent and is still unaffected by the corrupt world.
I want to fill it with color and ducks	The childlike language reflects the mother's desire to be part of her child's innocent world.
Not this troublous/Wringing of hands	
this dark/Ceiling without a star	

LEAVING CERT SAMPLE ESSAY

'The intensity of Sylvia Plath's poetic world can often be an uncomfortable experience for readers.' Discuss this view, supporting your response with suitable reference to the poems by Plath on your course.

Marking Scheme Guidelines

Candidates are free to agree and/or disagree with the statement. They may choose to focus on the positive aspects of Plath's poetry. However, the key terms ('intensity of Sylvia Plath's poetic world' and 'uncomfortable experience') should be addressed implicitly or explicitly. Reward responses that show clear evidence of personal engagement with the poems. Allow for a wide range of approaches in the answering.

Material might be drawn from the following:

• Complexity of mother–child relationships
• Preoccupation with life's darker side
• Striking images and unsettling tones
• The poet's experiences and their impact on her poetry
• Powerful themes of nature, disillusionment, transience, etc.

Sample Essay

(Reading Sylvia Plath's poetry)

1. *The poetry of Sylvia Plath tends to create deep responses, many of them disquieting. Plath's engulfing depression led her to take a view of the world which is alarming and sometimes perverse. However, her great understanding of life and love for her children led her to write some uplifting poems that can bring joy to readers.*

2. *Motherhood had a highly potent effect on Plath as a person. This is clearly evident in 'Morning Song' which is addressed to her daughter. At the start of the poem, she uses an interesting metaphor to describe her newborn child: 'fat, gold watch'. This image suggests that the baby is something valuable, to be treasured and praised. However, the watch may also symbolise the dark undercurrent that time is passing, it is slipping away for both mother and daughter. This ambiguity exists in much of Plath's work and, when examined may be a cause for distress and discomfort for the reader. Plath is also conscious of the sheer magnitude of her daughter's birth,*

remarking how her 'cry took its place among the elements'. The poet chooses to present the notion that her daughter is a work of art with the words 'new statue in a draughty museum'. The use of the word 'draughty' seems to represent her view of the world as both cold and isolated. It is into this harsh new reality that her child will venture, a disconcerting thought for both the poet and the reader.

3. I found the poem's final image particularly effective – describing the birth of the baby herself trying out a 'handful of notes'. Plath develops the metaphor, referring to the 'vowel sounds' as they 'rise like balloons'. While the tone seems to be celebratory, the image of a balloon suggests something fragile, flimsy and transient. Throughout this poem, I could detect the underlying urgency – a mother's fears for her child facing an unknown future. Her feelings of deep uncertainty – 'I'm no more your mother/Than the cloud that distils a mirror' – reflect a tragic insecurity. It is as though she feels guilty for bringing her daughter into the world and eventually abandoning her. Even in her more upbeat poems, Plath subtly presents distressing thoughts to the reader.

4. To some extent, 'Black Rook in Rainy Weather' arises from the poet's feelings of contentment with life. She expresses this with the words: 'I do not expect a miracle or an accident'. This inner peace leads the poet to rejoice in the mundane and urge us 'to let spotted leaves fall as they fall, without ceremony'. In considering the mystery of poetic inspiration, Plath becomes aware that 'miracles occur' even if they are only 'spasmodic tricks of radiance'. However, even this poem is punctuated by an implicit sense of loneliness as Plath professes to 'desire some back-talk from the mute sky'. The poet's feelings of isolation seem to be ever present, even in her moments of relative calm.

5. 'Poppies in July' is undoubtedly one of the most disturbing poems by Plath. It deals with the horrors of her depression. The title seems to suggest a joyful image, but this could not be further from the truth. She refers to the poppies as 'little hell flames', seeing them as instruments which add to her suffering. The imagery is both intense and dramatic. There are repeated references to blood – 'clear red', 'A mouth just bloodied'. However, Plath would rather feel pain than feel nothing at all. She is horrified when she puts her 'hand among the flames and nothing burns'. The poet longs to find the poppies 'dulling and stilling' and for everything to be 'colorless'. The word is repeated in the poem's final line, clearly emphasising her alienation. This poem gave me a vivid description of how Plath feels choked by her destructive feelings. The depth of her despair is evident throughout.

6. The poet explores a similar experience in 'Elm', which starts with the words 'I know the bottom, I know it with my great tap root'. The reference to a root suggests that she not only knew the depths of despair, but draws her entire existence from that dark, hopeless place. We are told that Plath has 'suffered the atrocity of sunsets'. This hatred of something generally considered to be beautiful is a startling indication of her depression. Plath sees her sorrow as something that exists within herself and reveals that 'all day she feels its dark, feathery turnings, its malignity'. This horrifying image portrays the utter helplessness of the poet, the fact that she is entirely at the mercy of her own desolation. It is an image that fills the reader with dread and fear, as Plath herself must have felt when she wrote the poem. I thought the ending was extremely upsetting, reflecting the terrible enduring effects of her own destructive feelings –'That kill, that kill, that kill'.

7. The explicit nature of Plath's darker poetic world affects the reader deeply, revealing the horrors and terrible reality of utter despair. Few people could read Plath's poetry and remain unchanged by it.

(approx. 845 words)

Examiner's Comment

This answer clearly shows close engagement with Plath's poetry. The emphasis on the effect of vivid imagery and varying tones is sustained throughout. Judicious use of apt quotations allows for some good development of key points (e.g. in paragraphs 2 and 5). Overall, expression is generally fluent, varied and well managed.

GRADE: A2

P = 13/15
C = 13/15
L = 12/15
M = 5/5
Total = 43/50

SAMPLE LEAVING CERT QUESTIONS ON PLATH'S POETRY

(45/50 MINUTES)

1. 'Sylvia Plath's poetry reflects a wide range of powerful emotions conveyed through thought-provoking imagery.' Discuss this statement, supporting your response with suitable reference to the poems by Plath on your course.

2. 'Although elements of Plath's poetry can sometimes be challenging, her skill with language ensures that she is always in control of her subject matter.' Discuss this

view, supporting your points with suitable reference to the poems by Plath on your course.

3. 'The vitality of Sylvia Plath's personality is evident in poems that are both atmospheric and insightful.' Write a response to this statement, supporting your points with reference to the poems by Plath on your course.

Sample Essay Plan (Q2)

'Although elements of Plath's poetry can sometimes be challenging, her skill with language ensures that she is always in control of her subject matter.' Discuss this view, supporting your points with suitable reference to the poems by Plath on your course.

- Intro: Identify the elements of the question to be addressed. Introduce Plath's intensely disturbing themes and her innovative use of language.

- Point 1: Inner torment of 'Elm' presented through complex imagery and unsettling symbolism, allowing the reader to appreciate a nightmare world.

- Point 2: Contrast is effectively used in 'Poppies in July'. The speaker's deep yearning to escape is highlighted by the startling imagery of the flowers.

- Point 3: The depression in 'Black Rook in Rainy Weather' is also emphasised by varying tones and conflicting images from nature and religion.

- Point 4: 'Child' and 'Morning Song' both express strong themes about relationships through the poet's mastery of language. Tones vary from anguish and depression to celebration and realism.

- Conclusion: Many poems deal with extreme emotional states while Plath's poetic control and confident technique never lapse.

Sample Essay Plan (Q2)

Develop one of the above points into a paragraph.

Sample Paragraph: Point 2

'Poppies in July' is an intense poem about Plath's desperation to escape from her unhappy world. It begins on a disturbing note. The speaker is troubled by the sight of poppies she calls 'little hell flames'. The references to hell and fire are developed through the rest of the poem, suggesting an extremely disturbed mind. The image of the red flames is both dramatic and terrifying – and typical of Plath's intense poetry. Readers can sense a stand-off between the poppies and Plath herself. The flowers almost seem to mock the poet: 'You flicker. I cannot touch you'. Other images in the poem add to our understanding of the poet's deep pain: 'A mouth just bloodied' and 'fumes that I cannot touch'. Plath describes the poppies in a way that reveals her own troubled mental state. She is exhausted, almost beyond despair. We see her control of language when she contrasts the colour of the poppies with her own lifeless mood. The reader is left with a genuine sense of Plath's anguish. Unlike the blazing red flowers, the poet herself is hopelessly 'colorless'.

Examiner's Comment

Although short, this is a well-focused paragraph that concentrates on Plath's ability to use language in an inventive and controlled fashion. The contrast between the vivid appearance of the poppies and the poet's own bleak mood is effectively illustrated. There is also a good sense of engagement with the feelings expressed in the poem. Grade-A standard.

LAST WORDS

'Her poems have that heart-breaking quality about them.'

Joyce Carol Oates

'Artists are a special breed. They are passionate and temperamental. Their feelings flow into the work they create.'

J. Timothy King

'I am a genius of a writer; I have it in me. I am writing the best poems of my life.'

Sylvia Plath

W. B. YEATS

1865-1939

'I have spread my
dreams under your feet.'

W illiam Butler Yeats was born in Dublin in 1865.
The son of a well-known Irish painter, John Butler
Yeats, he spent much of his childhood in Co. Sligo.
As a young writer, Yeats became involved with
the Celtic Revival, a movement against the cultural influences
of English rule in Ireland that sought to promote the spirit of
our native heritage. His writing drew extensively from Irish
mythology and folklore. Another great influence was the
Irish revolutionary Maud Gonne, a woman as famous for her
passionate nationalist politics as for her beauty. She rejected
Yeats, who eventually married another woman, Georgie Hyde
Lees. However, Maud Gonne remained a powerful figure in
Yeats's writing. Over the years, Yeats became deeply involved in
Irish politics and despite independence from England, his work
reflected a pessimism about the political situation here. He also
had a lifelong interest in mysticism and the occult. Appointed
a senator of the Irish Free State in 1922, he is remembered as
an important cultural leader, as a major playwright (he was one
of the founders of Dublin's Abbey Theatre) and as one of the
greatest 20th-century poets. Yeats was awarded the Nobel Prize
in 1923 and died in 1939 at the age of 73.

Prescribed Poems

[handwritten annotations in top margin:] rene: juss...nativeised mossalgic yearning for his native countryside - quest for wisdom, deep internal traths - an attempt to see into the heart of things.

[handwritten left margin:] Nature poem.

① THE LAKE ISLE OF INNISFREE

[handwritten:] uses traditional rural building material ie g "wattles" "clay".

[handwritten right:] 1st line biblical allusion almost like the intro of a ceremony. written in 1st person, scene shows a rustic imagery man + garden

I will arise and go now, and go to Innisfree,

And a small cabin build there, of clay and wattles made: *[handwritten: planning to build]*

Nine bean-rows will I have there, a hive for the honey-bee, *[handwritten: simple sweetne + richness of li]*

And live alone in the bee-loud glade. *[handwritten: as well as a musical ambience - overall vision is one of rustic rural primitiveness with a hint of hermitage.]*

[handwritten left margin: Repetition]

[handwritten left margin: The continued use reinforces the strange + magical atmosphere]

And I shall have some peace there, for peace comes dropping slow, *[handwritten: A the 5 romantic]*

Dropping from the veils of the morning to where the cricket sings; *[handwritten: B view of the human]*

[handwritten left margin: (Metaphor through nature + wildlife of the area.]

There midnight's all a glimmer, and noon a purple glow, *[handwritten: A being alone with nature + perfect harmon]*

And evening full of the linnet's wings. *[handwritten: soothing effect B with its sights + sounds is here. the alluring picture of morning dro in veils and the whimsical but beautiful imagery of midnight + noon.]*

[handwritten left margin: Alliteration the calming sounds of the water lapping continues the atmosphere]

I will arise and go now, for always night and day *[handwritten: A]*

I hear lake water lapping with low sounds by the shore; *[handwritten: B sibilance]* 10

While I stand on the roadway, or on the pavements grey, *[handwritten: A change of]*

I hear it in the deep heart's core. *[handwritten: B him. part of him. tense, the sound bring him back to Innisfree.]*

[handwritten: contrast to his present environment - cold, colour less + lifeless "grey pavements" even in this contemporary environment his longing is so strong that he can hear it deep in his heart]

'I hear lake water lapping with low sounds by the shore'

GLOSSARY

Innisfree: island of heather.

2 *clay and wattles*: rods and mud were used to build small houses.

7 *midnight's all a glimmer*: stars are shining very brightly in the countryside.

8 *linnet*: songbird.

10 *lapping*: gentle sounds made by water at the edge of a shore.

12 *heart's core*: essential part; the centre of the poet's being.

EXPLORATIONS

1. This poem was voted number one in a recent *Irish Times* poll of the top 100 poems. Why do you think it appeals to so many readers?

2. What does the poem reveal to you about Yeats's own state of mind? Use reference to the text in your response.

3. How does the second stanza describe the rhythm of the passing day? Use quotations to illustrate your response.

STUDY NOTES

'The Lake Isle of Innisfree' was written in 1890. Yeats was in London, looking in a shop window at a little toy fountain. He was feeling very homesick. He said the sound of the 'tinkle of water' reminded him of 'lake water'. He was longing to escape from the grind of everyday life and he wrote an 'old daydream of mine'.

This timeless poem has long been a favourite with exiles everywhere, as it **expresses a longing for a place of deep peace**. The tone in **stanza one** is deliberate, not casual, as the poet announces his decision to go. There are biblical overtones here: 'I will arise and go to my father,' the prodigal son announces. This lends the occasion solemnity. Then the poet describes the idyllic life of self-sufficiency: 'Nine bean-rows' and 'a hive for the honey-bee'. These details give the poem a timeless quality as the poet lives 'alone in the beeloud glade'.

Stanza two describes Innisfree so vividly that the future tense of 'I will arise' gives way to the present: 'There midnight's all a glimmer'. The **repetition** of 'peace' and 'dropping' suits the subject, as it lulls us into this tranquil place to which we all aspire to go at some point in our lives. Beautiful imagery brings us through the day, from the gentle white mists of the morning that lie like carelessly thrown veils over the lake to the blazing purple of the heather under the midday sun. The starry night, which can only be seen in the clear skies of the countryside, is vividly described as 'midnight's all a glimmer', with slender vowel sounds suggesting the sharp light of the stars. The soft 'l', 'm' and 'p' sounds in this stanza create a gentle and magical mood.

The **third stanza** repeats the opening, giving the air of a solemn ritual taking place. The **verbal music** in this stanza is striking, as the broad vowel sounds slow down the line 'I hear lake water lapping with low sounds by the shore', emphasising peace and tranquility. Notice the alliteration of 'l' and the assonance of 'o' all adding to the serene calm of the scene. The only **contemporary detail** in the poem is 'pavements grey', suggesting the relentless concrete of the city. The exile's awareness of what he loves is eloquently expressed as he declares he hears the sound 'in the deep heart's core'. Notice the monosyllabic ending, which drums home how much he longs for this place. Regular end rhyme (*abab*) and the regular four beats in each fourth line reinforce the harmony of this peaceful place.

ANALYSIS

What musical sounds did you find effective in this poem? Write a paragraph, illustrating your answer with references to the text.

Sample Paragraph

Yeats said that this poem was his 'first lyric with anything in its rhythm of my own music'. 'The Lake Isle of Innisfree' has a solemn, deliberate tone. It even has biblical overtones. The steady end rhyme ('Innisfree', 'honeybee') adds to this stately music. The poet uses broad vowels to slow down the pace of the poem. This is an idyllic place where time almost stands still, 'alone in the bee-loud glade'. The repetition of 'peace' and 'dropping' creates a dreamy, soporific effect in this 'old daydream' of Yeats's. The brightly shining stars and the rapid movement of the bird's wings provide contrast as busy slender vowels in 'midnight's all a glimmer' and 'linnet's wings' tremble on the page. The soft 'l' sounds and alliteration in the line 'I hear lake water lapping with low sounds by the shore' bring us back to the calm, magical scene. I thought the consonance of 'la' and 'lo' also added to this effect. The final line beats out its message with five strong monosyllabic words: 'In the deep heart's core'. The phrase underlines the longing of the emigrant. This contrasts wonderfully with the slipping away of reality in 'pavements grey' as the exile relives his heart's desire.

Examiner's Comment

A good understanding of the techniques used by a poet to create music and the effect this has on the poem is displayed in the answer. Quotations are very well used here to back up this personal response. Grade-A standard.

▶ CLASS/HOMEWORK EXERCISES

1. Pick out two images from the poem that appeal to you and discuss the reasons for their appeal.

2. Copy the table below into your own notes and fill in critical comments about the last two quotations.

Key Quotes

Nine bean-rows will I have there	Throughout the poem, Yeats is nostalgic for his homeland. He is yearning to return to the simple life he once enjoyed.
Dropping from the veils of the morning	The use of assonance emphasises the serene atmosphere of this magical place as the white mist lies over the lake.
peace comes dropping slow	
I hear it in the deep heart's core	

[handwritten top margin:] Theme - bitter disillusion with recent social changes - the central impulse behind the poem is the disparagement of the present by setting it in opposition with the romanticised past. ... expressing a personal opinion in public.

❷ SEPTEMBER 1913

[handwritten:] Opening stanza is very scath- — the people he is addressing are without dignity + beauty - these

[left margin handwritten:] Tone: Bitter + dismissive

[handwritten:] A merchant whose lives he suggests are focused on have... occupations. - praying + saving

What need you, being come to sense,
But fumble in a greasy till *B*
And add the halfpence to the pence *A*
And prayer to shivering prayer, until *B*

[left margin:] Rhetorical q's

You have dried the marrow from the bone? *C*
For men were born to pray and save: *A*

[left margin:] Repitition

Romantic Ireland's dead and gone, *C*
It's with O'Leary in the grave. *D*

[handwritten right:] They have no love for their count... and have made Ireland a selfish materialistic society. The image of the "greasy till" conveys the right note of contempt for the whole class he represents, making its activities appear sordid + mean. The refrain against all of the above — Yeats offers a nobler vision of Irel...

[left margin handwritten:] The colloquial 3rd last line highlights, Yeats simile, ... those who died were giving so much they were incapable. Repitition of saving themselves.

Yet they were of a different kind, *A*
The names that stilled your childish play, *B*
They have gone about the world like wind, *A*
But little time had they to pray *B*
For whom the hangman's rope was spun, *C*
And what, God help us, could they save? *D*
Romantic Ireland's dead and gone, *C*
It's with O'Leary in the grave. *D*

[handwritten right:] A "yet" signals a different tone. There is a contrast - the unselfish, patriotic acts of the pas... who have little thought of saving/praying but were prepared to die for the freedom of their country. Their mere names were enough to bring little children's play to a halt - people were in awe of them... The image of the wind catches the power and force of their commitment + the image of the rope gives the sense of inevitability, their destiny + sacrifice.

Was it for this the wild geese spread
The grey wing upon every tide;
For this that all that blood was shed,
For this Edward Fitzgerald died,   20
And Robert Emmet and Wolfe Tone,
All that delirium of the brave?
Romantic Ireland's dead and gone,
It's with O'Leary in the grave.

[left margin:] Repitition

Yet could we turn the years again,   25
And call those exiles as they were
In all their loneliness and pain,
You'd cry, 'Some woman's yellow hair
Has maddened every mother's son':
They weighed so lightly what they gave.   30
But let them be, they're dead and gone,
They're with O'Leary in the grave.

'Romantic Ireland's dead and gone'

GLOSSARY

1   *you*: merchants and business people.
8   *O'Leary*: John O'Leary, Fenian leader, one of
    Yeats's heroes.   *IRB*
9   *they*: the selfless Irish patriots.
17 *the wild geese*: Irish Independence soldiers
    forced into exile in Europe after 1690.

20 *Edward Fitzgerald*: 18th-century Irish
    aristocrat and revolutionary.
21 *Robert Emmet and Wolfe Tone*: Irish rebel
    leaders. Emmet was hanged in 1803. Tone
    committed suicide in prison after being
    sentenced to death in 1798.

EXPLORATIONS

1. Comment on the effectiveness of the images used in the first five lines of the
   poem.

2. How would you describe the tone of this poem? Is it bitter, sad, ironic, angry,
   etc.? Refer closely to the text in your answer.

3. Were the patriots named in the poem heroes or fools? Write a paragraph in
   response to Yeats's views.

STUDY NOTES

'September 1913' is typical of Yeats's hard-hitting political poems. Both the content and
tone are harsh as the poet airs his views on public issues, contrasting the idealism of
Ireland's heroic past with the uncultured present.

Yeats had been a great supporter of Sir Hugh Lane, who had offered his extensive art collection to the city of Dublin, provided the paintings would be on show in a suitable gallery. When the authorities failed to arrange this, Lane withdrew his offer. The controversy infuriated Yeats, who criticised Dublin Corporation for being miserly and anti-cultural. For him, it represented **a new low in the country's drift into vulgarity and crass commercialism**. The year 1913 was also a year of great hardship, partly because of a general strike and lock-out of workers. Poverty and deprivation were widespread at the time, particularly in Dublin's tenements.

The **first stanza** begins with a derisive **attack on a materialistic society** that Yeats sees as being both greedy and hypocritical. Ireland's middle classes are preoccupied with making money and slavish religious devotion. The rhetorical opening is sharply sarcastic, as the poet depicts the petty, penny-pinching shopkeepers who 'fumble in a greasy till'. Yeats's tone is as angry as it is ironic: 'For men were born to pray and save'. Images of the dried bone and 'shivering prayer' are equally forceful – the poor are exploited by ruthless employers and a domineering Church. This disturbing picture leads the poet to regret the loss of 'Romantic Ireland' in the concluding refrain.

Stanza two develops the contrast between past and present as Yeats considers the **heroism and generosity of an earlier era**. Ireland's patriots – 'names that stilled' earlier generations of children – could hardly have been more unlike the present middle class. Yeats clearly relates to the self-sacrifice of idealistic Irish freedom fighters: 'And what, God help us, could they save?' These disdainful words echo the fearful prayers referred to at the start of the poem. The heroes of the past were so selfless that they did not even concern themselves with saving their own lives.

The wistful and nostalgic tone of **stanza three** is obvious in the rhetorical question about all those Irish soldiers who had been exiled in the late 17th century. Yeats's high regard for these men is evoked by comparing them to 'wild geese', a plaintive metaphor reflecting their nobility. Yet the poet's admiration for past idealism is diminished by the fact that **such heroic dedication was all for nothing**. The repetition of 'for this' hammers home Yeats's contempt for the pious materialists of his own imperfect age. In listing a roll of honour, he singles out the most impressive patriots of his own class, the Anglo-Irish Ascendancy. For the poet, Fitzgerald, Emmet and Tone are among the most admirable Irishmen.

In using the phrase 'All that delirium of the brave', Yeats suggests that their passionate dedication to Irish freedom bordered on a frenzied or misplaced sense of daring.

This romanticised appreciation continues into the **final stanza**, where the poet imagines the 'loneliness and pain' of the heroic dead. His empathy towards them is underpinned by an **even more vicious portrayal of the new middle class**. He argues that the establishment figures of his own time would be unable to comprehend anything about the values and dreams of 'Romantic Ireland'. At best, they would be confused by the ludicrous self-sacrifice of the past. At worst, the present generation would accuse the patriots of being insane or of trying to impress friends or lovers. Perhaps Yeats is illustrating the cynical thinking of his time, when many politicians courted national popularity. 'Some woman's yellow hair' might well refer to the traditional symbol of Ireland as a beautiful woman.

The poet's disgust on behalf of the patriots is rounded off in the last two lines: 'But let them be, they're dead and gone'. The refrain has been changed slightly, adding further emphasis and a **sense of finality**. After reading this savage satire, we are left with a deep sense of Yeats's bitter disillusionment towards his contemporaries. The extreme feelings expressed in the poem offer a dispirited vision of an unworthy country. It isn't surprising that some critics have accused Yeats of over-romanticising the heroism of Ireland's past, of being narrow minded and even elitist. At any rate, the poem challenges us to examine the values of the state we are in, our understanding of Irish history and the meaning of heroism.

ANALYSIS

'September 1913' is based on contrasting images of meanness and generosity. Which set of images makes the greater impact? Write your response in a paragraph, referring closely to the text in your answer.

Sample Paragraph

Although W. B. Yeats ridicules the greedy shopkeepers and landlords of Dublin, he makes a much greater impression in describing the patriots of old Ireland – 'names that stilled your childish play'. The image stops us in our tracks. We can imagine how children used to hold men like Wolfe Tone and Robert Emmet in such great respect. Yeats uses the beautiful image of the wild geese spreading 'The grey wing upon every tide' to describe the dignified flight of Irish soldiers who refused to accept colonial rule. The poet's simple imagery is taken from the world of nature and has a vivid quality that makes us aware of the poet's high opinion of those heroes who were prepared to die for their beliefs.

Examiner's Comment

Clearly written and well supported, this C-grade response addresses the question directly. There is evidence of close engagement with the poem. In addition, the expression is varied, fluent and controlled throughout. However, further development of key contrast points would be expected for a top grade.

CLASS/HOMEWORK EXERCISES

1. How relevant is 'September 1913' to present-day Ireland? Refer to the text of the poem when writing your response.

2. Copy the table below into your own notes and fill in critical comments about the last two quotations.

Key Quotes

What need you, being come to sense	Rhetorical questions satirise those smug people who knew how to exploit situations to their advantage.
Romantic Ireland's dead and gone	In his refrain, Yeats is caught between deep disillusionment towards his contemporaries and admiration for a more idealistic age.
You have dried the marrow from the bone	
For this that all that blood was shed	

mention contrast throughout

[handwritten annotations:] Theme = ageing passion/love.
tone = sadness/ melancholy nostalgic
impersonal
dignified meditative state

3 THE WILD SWANS AT COOLE

The trees are in their autumn beauty,
The woodland paths are dry,
Under the October twilight the water
Mirrors a still sky; — *sense of peace*
Upon the brimming water among the stones
Are nine-and-fifty swans. — *prompt an emotional indirect sadness.*

[handwritten:] Sad at the passing of time
beautiful imagery of October
prompt an emotional response

The nineteenth autumn has come upon me — *personification — conscious of his advancing age becomes personal (p).*
Since I first made my count;
I saw, before I had well finished,
All suddenly mount   *metaphor*
And scatter wheeling in great broken rings
Upon their clamorous wings. — *symbolises freedom from the constraint of time*

10

I have looked upon those brilliant creatures,
And now my heart is sore.
All's changed since I, hearing at twilight, 15
The first time on this shore,   *metaphor + alliteration*
The bell-beat of their wings above my head, — *swans beating wings*
Trod with a lighter tread.   *his heart is sore*

[handwritten:] at his most personal
Realisation brings about sorrow.

Unwearied still, lover by lover,   *repetition*
They paddle in the cold   *contrast*   20
Companionable streams or climb the air;
Their hearts have not grown old;   *personification + emotions.*
Passion or conquest, wander where they will,
Attend upon them still.

[handwritten:] yeats jealousy of swans for mating for life
swans symbol for continuity
contrast between himself + swans.

But now they drift on the still water,   25
Mysterious, beautiful;
Among what rushes will they build,
By what lake's edge or pool
Delight men's eyes when I awake some day
To find they have flown away?   30

[handwritten:] Contrast. Change in the birds energy.
optimistic note
swans beauty, love, youth
Also pessimistic. when swans desert him he will lose his creativity as they are a symbol of this

'The bell-beat of their wings above my head'

GLOSSARY

5	*brimming*: filled to the very top or edge.
12	*clamorous*: loud, confused noise.
18	*Trod ... tread*: walked lightly; carefree.

19	*lover by lover*: swans mate for life; this highlights Yeats's loneliness.
21	*Companionable*: friendly.
24	*Attend upon them still*: waits on them yet.

EXPLORATIONS

1. Why do you think the poet chose the season of autumn as his setting? What changes occur at this time of year? Where are these referred to in the poem?

2. In your opinion, what are the main contrasts between the swans and the poet? Describe two, using close reference to the text.

3. What do you think the final stanza means? Consider the phrase 'I awake'. What does the poet awake from?

STUDY NOTES

'The Wild Swans at Coole' was written in 1916. Yeats loved spending time in the West, especially at Coole, the home of Lady Gregory, his friend and patron. He was 51 when he wrote this poem, which contrasts the swans' beauty and apparent seeming immortality with Yeats's ageing, mortal self.

The poem opens with a tranquil, serene scene of **autumnal beauty** in the park of Lady Gregory's home in Galway. This romantic image is described in great detail: the 'woodland paths are dry'. It is evening, 'October twilight'. The water is 'brimming'. The swans are carefully counted, 'nine-and-fifty'. The use of the soft letters 'l', 'm' and 's' emphasise the calm of the scene in **stanza one**.

In **stanza two**, the poem moves to the personal as he recalls that it is 19 years since he first counted the swans. The word 'count' links the two stanzas. The poet's counting is interrupted as these mysterious creatures all suddenly rise into the sky. Run-through lines suggest the flowing movement of the rising swans.

Strong verbs ('mount', 'scatter') reinforce this elemental action. The great beating wings of the swans are captured in the onomatopoeic 'clamorous wings'. They are independent and refuse to be restrained. The ring is a symbol of eternity. The swans are making the same patterns as they have always made; they are unchanging. **Stanza two** is linked to **stanza three** by the phrases 'I saw' and 'I have looked'. Now the poet tells us his 'heart is sore'. He has taken stock and is **dissatisfied with his emotional situation**. He is 51, alone and unmarried and concerned that his poetic powers are lessening: '**All's changed**'. All humans want things to remain as they are, but life is full of change. He has lost the great love of his life, the beautiful Irish activist, Maud Gonne. He also laments the loss of his youth, when he 'Trod with a lighter tread'. Nineteen years earlier, he was much more carefree. The noise of the beating wings of the swans is effectively captured in the compound word 'bell-beat'. The alliterative 'b' reinforces the steady, flapping sound. The poet is using his intense personal experiences to express universal truths.

The swans in **stanza four** are **symbols of eternity**, ageless, 'Unwearied still'. They are united, 'lover by lover'. They experience life together ('Companionable streams'), not on their own, like the poet. He envies them their defiance of time: 'Their hearts have not grown old'. They do what they want, when they want. They are full of 'Passion or conquest'. By contrast, he is indirectly telling us, he feels old and worn out. The **spiral imagery** of the 'great broken rings' is reminiscent of the spirals seen in ancient carvings representing eternity. Yeats believed there was a cyclical pattern behind all things. The swans can live in two elements, water and air, thus linking these elements together. They are living, vital, immortal, unlike their surroundings. The trees are yellowing ('autumn beauty') and the dry 'woodland paths' suggest the lack of creative force which the poet is experiencing. Yeats is heartbroken and weary. Only the swans transcend time.

Stanza five explores a **philosophy of life**, linked to the previous stanza by the repetition of 'still'. The swans have returned to the water, 'Mysterious, beautiful'. The poem ends on a speculative note as the poet asks where they will 'Delight men's eyes'. Is he referring to the fact that **they will continue to be a source of pleasure to someone else** long after he is dead? The swans appear immortal, a continuing source of happiness as they practise their patterns, whereas the poet is not able to continue improving his own writing, as he is mortal. The poet is slipping into the cruel season of winter while the swans infinitely 'drift on the still water'.

ANALYSIS

Poets use patterns to communicate their message. With reference to 'The Wild Swans at Coole', write a paragraph on Yeats's use of pattern, referring to imagery, sound effects, rhyme, etc.

Sample Paragraph

The rhyme scheme in 'The Wild Swans at Coole' is *abcbdd*. When I look at the words which these rhymes stress, I see another layer in this poem. The marked contrast between the dry woodland paths, which are so suggestive of the drying up of creativity, and the water which 'Mirrors a still sky' is very effective. The water is teeming with life. In the second stanza the poet is anchored to the land as he makes his 'count', while the swans are free to fly at a moment's notice, 'All suddenly mount'. When Yeats first went to Coole, he was suffering from a broken heart and this is echoed in the rhyming lines 'And now my heart is sore', 'The first time on this shore'. Although the swans are in the 'cold', they have not 'grown old'. Finally, he wonders where these 'Mysterious and beautiful' creatures will be: 'By what lake's edge or pool'. Similarly, another layer of meaning is created by the rhyme of the last two lines of each stanza. I particularly liked the rhyme in the last stanza: 'when I awake some day/To find they have flown away'. This sums up for me the sadness of the poet as he realises he is mortal, whereas they are immortal. It may even suggest his dread that his poetic inspiration, which is as mysterious and beautiful as the swans, may suddenly desert him too. I think examining the carefully worked patterns of the poem increases both our enjoyment of the poem as well as our understanding of the poet's message.

Examiner's Comment

The student has engaged in a personal way to answer this question. Detailed attention has been given to the poet's use of rhyme. An effective, well-developed discussion that makes good use of quotations to sustain the argument. Confident expression adds to the A-grade standard.

CLASS/HOMEWORK EXERCISES

1. Is the poem more concerned with the poet than the swans? Write a paragraph responding to this statement, referring to the text.

2. Copy the table below into your own notes and fill in critical comments about the last two quotations.

Key Quotes

The woodland paths are dry	Using symbolism, Yeats expresses his fears of ageing and the loss of his poetic imagination.
And now my heart is sore	Yeats admits to being dissatisfied with his life. The assonance adds to the poignancy.
Unwearied still, lover by lover	
Mysterious, beautiful	

④ AN IRISH AIRMAN FORESEES HIS DEATH

I know that I shall meet my fate
Somewhere among the clouds above;
Those that I fight I do not hate,
Those that I guard I do not love;
My country is Kiltartan Cross,   5
My countrymen Kiltartan's poor,
No likely end could bring them loss
Or leave them happier than before.
Nor law, nor duty bade me fight,
Nor public men, nor cheering crowds,   10
A lonely impulse of delight
Drove to this tumult in the clouds;
I balanced all, brought all to mind,
The years to come seemed waste of breath,
A waste of breath the years behind   15
In balance with this life, this death.

'I balanced all'

GLOSSARY

The Irish airman in this poem is Major Robert Gregory (1881–1918), son of Yeats's close friend, Lady Gregory. He was shot down and killed while on service in northern Italy.

3   *Those that I fight*: the Germans.

4   *Those that I guard*: Allied countries, such as England and France.

5   *Kiltartan*: townland near the Gregory estate in Co. Galway.

7   *likely end*: outcome.

12 *tumult:* turmoil; confusion.

EXPLORATIONS

1. 'This poem is not just an elegy or lament in memory of the dead airman. It is also an insight into the excitement and exhilaration of warfare.' Write your response to this statement, using close reference to the text.

2. Write a paragraph on Yeats's use of repetition throughout the poem. Refer to the text in your answer.

3. Imagine you are Robert Gregory. Write a short diary entry reflecting your thoughts and feelings about becoming a fighter pilot. Base your comments on the text of the poem.

STUDY NOTES

Thousands of Irishmen fought and died in the British armed forces during the First World War. Robert Gregory was killed in Italy at the age of 37. The airman's death had a lasting effect on Yeats, who wrote several poems about him.

Is it right to assume anything about young men who fight for their countries? Why do they enlist? Do they always know what they are fighting for? In this poem, Yeats expresses what he believes is the airman's viewpoint as he comes face to face with death. This **fatalistic attitude** is prevalent in the emphatic **opening line**. The poem's title also leads us to believe that the speaker has an intuitive sense that his death is about to happen. But despite this premonition, he seems strangely resigned to risking his life.

In **lines 3-4**, he makes it clear that he neither hates his German enemies nor loves the British and their allies. His thoughts are with the people he knows best back in Kiltartan, Co. Galway. Major Gregory recognises the irony of their detachment from the war. The ordinary people of his homeland are unlikely to be affected at all by whatever happens on the killing fields of mainland Europe. Does he feel that he is abandoning his fellow countrymen? What is the dominant tone of **lines 7-8**? Is there an underlying bitterness?

In **line 9**, the speaker takes time to reflect on why he joined the air force and immediately dismisses the obvious reasons of conscription ('law') or patriotism ('duty'). As a volunteer, Gregory is more openly cynical of the 'public men' and 'cheering crowds' he mentions in **line 10**. Like many in the military who have experienced the realities of warfare, **he is suspicious of hollow patriotism** and has no time for political leaders and popular adulation. So why did Robert Gregory choose to endanger his life by going to war? The answer lies in the key comments 'A lonely impulse of delight' (**line 11**) and 'I balanced all' (**line 13**). The first phrase is paradoxical. The airman experiences not just the excitement, but also the isolation of flying. At the same time, his 'impulse' to enlist as a fighter pilot reflects both his **desire for adventure** as well as his regret.

The **last four lines** explain the real reason behind his decision. It was neither rash nor emotional, but simply a question of balance. Having examined his life closely, Gregory has chosen the heroism of a self-sacrificing death. It is as though he only feels truly alive during the 'tumult' of battle. Yeats's language is particularly evocative at this point. Awesome air battles are effectively echoed in such dynamic phrasing as 'impulse of delight' and 'tumult in the clouds'. This **sense of freedom and power** is repeatedly contrasted with the dreary and predictable security of life away from the war – dismissed out of hand as a 'waste of breath'. From the airman's perspective, as a man of action, dying in battle is in keeping with 'this life' that he has chosen. Such a death would be his final adventurous exploit.

Some commentators have criticised Yeats's poem for glorifying war and pointless risk-taking. Others have suggested that the poet successfully highlights Anglo-Irish attitudes, neither exclusively Irish nor English. The poet certainly raises interesting questions about national identity and ways of thinking about war. However, in elegising Robert Gregory, he emphasises the **airman's daring solitude**. Perhaps this same thrill lies at the heart of other important choices in life, including the creative activity of artists. Is there a sense that the poet and the pilot are alike, both of them taking calculated risks in what they do?

ANALYSIS

What do you think is the poem's dominant or central mood? Write your response in a paragraph, referring closely to the text in your answer.

Sample Paragraph

The title itself suggests fear. However, the airman accepts his impending death as if it is a natural result. 'Fate' suggests destiny, the unavoidable. The rest of the poem is dominated by a strong mood of resignation. The slow rhythm is like a chant or a prayer. This airman has a fatalistic temperament. He seems completely relaxed when he says 'Those that I fight I do not hate'. In a way, he seems to have distanced himself from everything and everyone. He appears to have something of a death wish and his mood becomes very disillusioned towards the final section. For him, the past and future are a 'waste'. In general, his mood is quite resigned to death.

Examiner's Comment

This candidate focuses well on the negative moods within the poem. Apt quotes are also effectively used in reference. The paragraph might have included some mention of the contrasting euphoria of war. The language towards the end is also slightly stilted. Overall, a C-grade standard.

CLASS/HOMEWORK EXERCISES

1. Do you consider 'An Irish Airman Foresees his Death' to be an anti-war poem? Give reasons for your answer.

2. Copy the table below into your own notes and fill in critical comments about the last two quotations.

Key Quotes

I know that I shall meet my fate	The narrator, Robert Gregory, accepts that he will be killed in battle, yet his desire to take risks is more powerful.
waste of breath	The speaker's disenchantment with ordinary life is emphasised.
Nor law, nor duty bade me fight	
In balance with this life, this death	

simple language.

⑤   EASTER, 1916

I have met them at close of day
Coming with vivid faces
From counter or desk among grey
Eighteenth-century houses.
I have passed with a nod of the head   5
Or polite meaningless words,
Or have lingered awhile and said
Polite meaningless words,
And thought before I had done
Of a mocking tale or a gibe   10
To please a companion
Around the fire at the club,
Being certain that they and I
But lived where motley is worn:
All changed, changed utterly: 15
A terrible beauty is born.

refers to the sacrifice they made for the cause.

↑ refers to the bloodshed

That woman's days were spent
In ignorant good-will,
Her nights in argument
Until her voice grew shrill.   20
What voice more sweet than hers
When, young and beautiful,
She rode to harriers?
This man had kept a school
And rode our wingèd horse;   25
This other his helper and friend
Was coming into his force;
He might have won fame in the end,
So sensitive his nature seemed,
So daring and sweet his thought.   30
This other man I had dreamed
A drunken, vainglorious lout.
He had done most bitter wrong
To some who are near my heart,
Yet I number him in the song;   35
He, too, has resigned his part
In the casual comedy;

He, too, has been changed in his turn,
Transformed utterly:
A terrible beauty is born.   40

Hearts with one purpose alone
Through summer and winter seem
Enchanted to a stone
To trouble the living stream.
The horse that comes from the road,   45
The rider, the birds that range
From cloud to tumbling cloud,
Minute by minute they change;
A shadow of cloud on the stream
Changes minute by minute;   50
A horse-hoof slides on the brim,
And a horse plashes within it;
The long-legged moor-hens dive,
And hens to moor-cocks call;
Minute by minute they live: 55
The stone's in the midst of all.

Too long a sacrifice
Can make a stone of the heart.
O when may it suffice?
That is Heaven's part, our part   60
To murmur name upon name,
As a mother names her child
When sleep at last has come
On limbs that had run wild.
What is it but nightfall?   65
No, no, not night but death;
Was it needless death after all?
For England may keep faith
For all that is done and said.
We know their dream; enough   70
To know they dreamed and are dead;
And what if excess of love
Bewildered them till they died?
I write it out in a verse –
MacDonagh and MacBride   75

And Connolly and Pearse
Now and in time to be,
Wherever green is worn,
Are changed, changed utterly:
A terrible beauty is born.   80

'All changed, changed utterly'

GLOSSARY

Title: On 24 April 1916, Easter Monday, about 700 Irish Republicans took over several key buildings in Dublin. These included the Four Courts, Bolands Mills, the Royal College of Surgeons and the General Post Office. The rebellion lasted six days and was followed by the execution of its leaders. The Rising was a pivotal event in modern Irish history.

1 *them*: the rebels involved in the Rising.
14 *motley*: ridiculous clothing.
17 *That woman*: Countess Markiewicz, friend of Yeats and a committed nationalist.
24 *This man*: Padraig Pearse, poet and teacher, was shot as a leader of the Rising.
25 *wingèd horse*: Pegasus, the mythical white horse that flies across the sky, was a symbol of poetic inspiration.

26 *This other*: Thomas MacDonagh, writer and teacher, executed in 1916.
31 *This other man*: Major John MacBride was also executed for his part in the rebellion. He was the husband of Maud Gonne.
33 *most bitter wrong*: there were recurring rumours that MacBride had mistreated Maud Gonne.
67 *needless death*: Yeats asks if the Rising was a waste of life, since the British were already considering independence for Ireland.
76 *Connolly*: Trade union leader and revolutionary, executed in 1916.

EXPLORATIONS

1. Describe the atmosphere in the opening stanza of the poem. Refer closely to the text in your answer.

2. 'Easter, 1916' has many striking images. Choose two that you find particularly interesting and briefly explain their effectiveness.

3. On balance, does Yeats approve or disapprove of the Easter Rising? Refer to the text in your answer.

STUDY NOTES

Yeats, who was in London at the time of the Rising, had mixed feelings about what had happened. He was clearly fascinated but also troubled by this heroic and yet in some ways pointless sacrifice. He did not publish the poem until 1920.

In the **opening stanza**, Yeats recalls how he used to meet some of the people who were later involved in the Easter Rising. He was unimpressed by their 'vivid faces' and he remembers routinely dismissing them with 'Polite meaningless words'. His admission that he **misjudged these insignificant Republicans** as subjects for 'a mocking tale or a gibe' among his clever friends is a reminder of his derisive attitude in 'September 1913'. Before 1916, Yeats had considered Ireland a ridiculous place, a circus 'where motley is worn'. But the poet confesses that the Rising transformed everything – including his own condescending apathy. In the stanza's final lines, Yeats introduces what becomes an ambivalent refrain ending in 'A terrible beauty is born'.

This sense of shock and the need to completely re-evaluate his views is developed in **stanza two**. The poet singles out individual martyrs killed or imprisoned for their activities, among them his close friend Countess Markiewicz. He also mentions Major John MacBride, husband of Maud Gonne, who had refused Yeats's proposal of marriage. Although he had always considered MacBride as little more than a 'drunken, vainglorious lout', Yeats now acknowledges that he too has been distinguished by his bravery and heroism. The poet wonders about the usefulness of all the passion that sparked the rebels to make such a bold move, but his emphasis is on the fact that **the people as well as the whole atmosphere have changed**. Even MacBride, whom he held in utter contempt, has grown in stature.

In **stanza three**, Yeats takes powerful images from nature and uses them to explore the meaning of Irish heroism. The metaphor of the stubborn stone in the stream might represent the defiance of the revolutionaries towards all the forces around them. **The poet evokes the constant energy and dynamism of the natural world**, focusing on the changes that happen 'minute by minute'. Image after dazzling image conjures up a vivid picture of unpredictable movement and seasonal regeneration (as 'hens to moor-cocks call') and skies change 'From cloud to tumbling cloud'.

For the poet, the Rising presented many contradictions, as he weighs the success of the revolt against the shocking costs. In contrasting the inflexibility of the revolutionaries with the 'living stream', he **indicates a reluctant admiration for the rebels' dedication**. Does Yeats suggest that the rebels risked the loss of their own humanity, allowing their hearts to harden to stone? Or is he also thinking of Maud Gonne and blaming her cold-hearted rejection of him on her fanatical political views?

In the **final stanza**, the poet returns to the metaphor of the unmoving stone in a flowing stream to warn of the dangers of fanaticism. The rhetorical questions about the significance of the rebellion reveal his **continuing struggle to understand** what happened. Then he asks the single most important question about the Rising: 'Was it needless death after all', particularly as 'England may keep faith' and allow Ireland its independence, all of which would prompt a more disturbing conclusion, i.e. that the insurgents died in vain.

Yeats quickly abandons essentially unanswerable questions about the value of the Irish struggle for freedom. Instead, he simply pays tribute to the fallen patriots by naming them tenderly, 'As a mother names her child'. The final assertive lines commemorate the 1916 leaders in dramatic style. Setting aside his earlier ambivalence, Yeats acknowledges that these patriots died for their dreams. The hushed tone is reverential, almost sacred. The rebels have been transformed into martyrs who will be remembered for their selfless heroism 'Wherever green is worn'. The insistent final refrain has a stirring and increasingly disquieting quality. The poem's central paradox, 'A terrible beauty is born', concludes that **all the heroic achievements of the 1916 Rising were at the tragic expense of human life**.

ANALYSIS

Write a paragraph outlining Yeats's feelings about the Irish patriots as expressed in the final stanza of 'Easter, 1916'. Support the points you make with suitable reference or quotation.

Sample Paragraph

The final verse reveals many of Yeats's unanswered questions and confused thinking about the 1916 patriots. However, he sees that his own role is to record what he knows to be true and to 'write it out in a verse'. This allows him to pay his own tribute to the 1916 leaders whom he lists formally, almost like a graveside oration. The slow, deliberate rhythm is deeply respectful. The mood is serious, almost sombre, in keeping with the poet's newfound respect for the dead heroes. Yeats ends with the keynote comment, 'A terrible beauty is born'. This oxymoron derives its power from the obvious contrast between the terms. He believed that the Easter Rising was terrible because of all the unnecessary suffering that had occurred. Nevertheless, Yeats accepts that there was a transforming beauty that took the rebels, and perhaps many others, out of their lives of 'casual comedy' into the tragic drama of real life.

Examiner's Comment

This short paragraph is well focused and supported. The candidate touches on several interesting aspects of the poet's mixed feelings about 1916. The references to features of style contribute much to this well-written A-grade response.

Compare and contrast September 1913 + Easter Rising 1916

CLASS/HOMEWORK EXERCISES

1. Yeats emphasises change of one kind or another throughout 'Easter, 1916'. List the main changes and comment briefly on them.

2. Copy the table below into your own notes and fill in critical comments about the last two quotations.

Key Quotes

All changed, changed utterly:/A terrible beauty is born	The 1916 Rising, in all its idealism and brutality, had transformed not just Ireland, but Yeats's own attitudes.
Enchanted to a stone	The poet uses the metaphor to show both the determination of the rebels and their unswerving fanaticism.
polite meaningless words	
Being certain that they and I/But lived where motley is worn	

⑥ THE SECOND COMING

Turning and turning in the widening gyre
The falcon cannot hear the falconer;
Things fall apart; the centre cannot hold;
Mere anarchy is loosed upon the world,
The blood-dimmed tide is loosed, and everywhere   5
The ceremony of innocence is drowned;
The best lack all conviction, while the worst
Are full of passionate intensity.

Surely some revelation is at hand;
Surely the Second Coming is at hand.   10
The Second Coming! Hardly are those words out
When a vast image out of *Spiritus Mundi*
Troubles my sight: somewhere in sands of the desert
A shape with lion body and the head of a man,
A gaze blank and pitiless as the sun,   15
Is moving its slow thighs, while all about it
Reel shadows of the indignant desert birds.
The darkness drops again; but now I know
That twenty centuries of stony sleep
Were vexed to nightmare by a rocking cradle,   20
And what rough beast, its hour come round at last,
Slouches towards Bethlehem to be born?

'somewhere in sands of the desert/A shape with lion body and the head of a man'

GLOSSARY

The Second Coming: This is a reference to the Bible. It is from Matthew and speaks of Christ's return to reward the good.

1 *in the widening gyre*: Yeats regarded a cycle of history as a gyre. He visualised these cycles as interconnecting cones that moved in a circular motion, widening outwards until they could not widen any further, then a new gyre or cone formed from the centre of the circle created. This spun in the opposite direction to the original cone. The Christian era was coming to a close and a new, disturbed time was coming into view. In summary, the gyre is a symbol of constant change.

2 *falcon*: a bird of prey, trained to hunt by the aristocracy.

2 *falconer*: the trainer of the falcon. If the bird flies too far away, it cannot be directed.

4 *Mere*: nothing more than; just; only.

4 *anarchy*: lack of government or order. Yeats believed that bloodshed and a worship of bloodshed were the end of an historical era.

5 *blood-dimmed*: made dark with blood.

12 *Spiritus Mundi*: Spirit of the World, the collective soul of the world.

14 *lion body and the head of a man*: famous statue in Egypt; an enigmatic person.

17 *desert birds*: birds of prey.

19 *twenty centuries*: Yeats believed that two thousand years was the length of a period in history.

20 *vexed*: annoyed; distressed.

20 *rocking cradle*: coming of the infant Jesus.

21 *rough beast*: the Anti-Christ.

22 *Bethlehem*: birthplace of Christ. It is usually associated with peace and innocence, and it is terrifying that the beast is going to be born there. The spiral has reversed its spinning. A savage god is coming.

EXPLORATIONS

1. This poem suggests that politics are not important. Does the poet convince you? Write a paragraph in response, with reference to the text.

2. Yeats uses symbols to express some of his most profound ideas. What symbols in this poem appeal to you? Use reference to the text in your response.

3. 'Yeats is yearning for order, and fearing anarchy.' Discuss two ways in which the poem illustrates this statement. Support your answer with reference to the text.

'The Second Coming' is a terrifying, apocalyptic poem written in January 1919 against a background of the disintegration of three great European empires at the end of the First World War and against the catastrophic War of Independence in Ireland. These were bloody times. Yeats yearned for order and feared anarchy.

Sparked off by both disgust at what was happening in Europe as well as his interest in the occult, Yeats explores, in **stanza one**, what he perceives to be the failure at the heart of society: 'Things fall apart'. In his opinion, **the whole world was disintegrating** into a bloody, chaotic mess. This break-up of civilisation is described in metaphorical language. For Yeats, the 'gyre' is a symbol representing an era. He believed contrary expanding and contracting forces influence people and cultures and that the Christian era was nearing its end. Images of hunting show how the old world represented its failing – 'The falcon cannot hear the falconer'. We have lost touch with Christ, just as the falcon loses touch with the falconer as he swings into ever-increasing circles. This bird was trained to fly in circles to catch its prey. The circular imagery, with the repetitive '-ing', describes the continuous, swirling movement. Civilisation is also 'Turning and turning in the widening gyre' as it buckles and fragments.

The **tension** is reflected in a list of contrasts: 'centre' and 'fall apart', 'falcon' and 'falconer', 'lack all conviction' and 'intensity', 'innocence' and 'anarchy'. The strain is too much: 'the centre cannot hold'. The verbs also graphically describe this chaotic world: 'Turning and turning', 'loosed', 'drowned', 'fall apart'. Humans are changing amidst the chaos: 'innocence is drowned'. **Anarchy** is described in terms of a great tidal wave, 'the blood-dimmed tide', which sweeps everything before it. The compound word reinforces the overwhelming nature of the water. Yeats feels that the 'best', the leaders and thinkers, have no energy; they are indifferent and 'lack all conviction'. On the other hand, the 'worst', the cynics and fanatics, are consumed with hatred and violence, 'full of passionate intensity'.

Disillusioned, Yeats thinks **a new order has to be emerging**. He imagines a Second Coming. He repeats the word 'Surely' in a tone of both belief and fear in **stanza two**. The Second Coming is usually thought of as a time when Christ will return to reward the good, but the image Yeats presents us with is terrifying. **A blank, pitiless creature emerges.** It is straight from the Book of Revelations: 'And

I saw a beast rising out of the sea'. This was regarded as a sign that the end of the world was near. Such an unnatural hybrid of human and animal is the Anti-Christ, the opposite force of the gentle infant Jesus who signalled the end of the Greek and Roman Empires. The 'gaze blank' suggests its lack of intelligence. The phrase 'pitiless as the sun' tells us the creature has no empathy or compassion. It 'Slouches'. It is a brutish, graceless monstrosity.

The **hostile environment** is a nightmare scenario of blazing desert sun, shifting sands and circling predatory birds. The verbs suggest everything is out of focus: 'Reel', 'rocking', 'Slouches'. 'The darkness drops again' shows how disorder, disconnectedness and the 'widening gyre' have brought us to nihilism. This seems to be a prophetic statement, as fascism was to sweep the world in the mid-20th century. Then Yeats has a moment of epiphany: 'but now I know'. Other eras have been destroyed before. The baby in the 'rocking cradle' created an upheaval that resulted in the end of 'twenty centuries of stony sleep'.

Yeats believed that a **cycle of history** lasted two thousand years in a single evolution of birth, growth, decline and death. All change causes upheaval. The Christian era, with its qualities of innocence, order, maternal love and goodness, is at an end. The new era of the 'rough beast' is about to start. It is pitiless, destructive, violent and murderous. This new era has already begun: 'its hour come round at last'. It is a savage god who is coming, uninvited. The spiral has reversed its motion and is now spinning in the opposite direction. The lack of end rhyme mirrors a world of chaos. Yeats looks back over thousands of years. We are given a thrilling and terrifying prospect from a vast perspective of millennia.

ANALYSIS

Yeats declared that a poet should think like a wise man, but express himself as one of the common people. Write a paragraph in response to this view, using close reference to 'The Second Coming'.

Sample Paragraph

I feel that the themes of stability and anarchy are wisely considered by Yeats. When I look at the events of the mid to late 20th century from the perspective of the 21st century, I see a very prophetic voice warning of the dangers of the cynic, 'lack all conviction', and the fundamentalist fanatic, 'while the worst/ Are full of passionate intensity'. The rise of fascism, the Second World War, the Vietnam War, the atom bomb – none of these were known when Yeats wrote this poem in 1919. Things did 'fall apart' and 'darkness' did drop again. However, the human spirit, 'Spiritus Mundi', rose again, and I would suggest that he was wrong to be so gloomy. Out of the turmoil and chaos of the Second World War came a cry. 'Surely some revelation is at hand'. But it was not the 'rough beast' with a 'gaze blank and pitiless as the sun'. Instead we had the foundation of the European Union, which has led to a long peace and stability. So, unlike Yeats's doom-laden prophecy, I think the 'centre' did 'hold'. In my opinion, the references to the Bible, Matthew, 'The Second Coming', and the Book of Revelations, 'I saw a beast', the phrases 'widening gyre', 'Spiritus Mundi' and the image of the Sphinx are not the language of the common man. It is very interesting to discover the meaning behind these phrases, but this is not the language of everyday speech. So although I do agree that Yeats did think like a wise man, I feel he was too pessimistic about the human race. I also think that although his expressions are powerful and thought provoking, they are not the language of the common man. This is in keeping with Yeats's view that the nobles and aristocrats should rule, not the masses.

Examiner's Comment

This impressive response focused clearly on the task, which was to consider Yeats's wisdom and his ability to express himself as one of the common people. A real sense of individual engagement with the poem came across in this well-argued answer. A grade.

CLASS/HOMEWORK EXERCISES

1. This is a political poem. What kind of political vision does it convey? Illustrate your answer with reference to the text.

2. Copy the table below into your own notes and fill in critical comments about the last two quotations.

Key Quotes

Things fall apart	Yeats believed that civilisation was breaking up and a new, brutish order would be established.
The ceremony of innocence is drowned	This metaphor highlights that the rituals and celebration of goodness represented by the Christian era are swept away by anarchy.
Turning and turning in the widening gyre	
Surely the Second Coming is at hand	

7 SAILING TO BYZANTIUM

I

That is no country for old men. The young
In one another's arms, birds in the trees
– Those dying generations – at their song,
The salmon-falls, the mackerel-crowded seas,
Fish, flesh, or fowl, commend all summer long   5
Whatever is begotten, born, and dies.
Caught in that sensual music all neglect
Monuments of unageing intellect.

II

An aged man is but a paltry thing,
A tattered coat upon a stick, unless   10
Soul clap its hands and sing, and louder sing
For every tatter in its mortal dress,
Nor is there singing school but studying
Monuments of its own magnificence;
And therefore I have sailed the seas and come   15
To the holy city of Byzantium.

III

O sages standing in God's holy fire
As in the gold mosaic of a wall,
Come from the holy fire, perne in a gyre,
And be the singing-masters of my soul.   20
Consume my heart away; sick with desire
And fastened to a dying animal
It knows not what it is; and gather me
Into the artifice of eternity.

IV

Once out of nature I shall never take   25
My bodily form from any natural thing,
But such a form as Grecian goldsmiths make
Of hammered gold and gold enamelling
To keep a drowsy Emperor awake;
Or set upon a golden bough to sing   30

To lords and ladies of Byzantium
Of what is past, or passing, or to come.

he holy city of Byzantium'

GLOSSARY

Sailing to Byzantium: for Yeats, this voyage would be one taken to find perfection. This country only exists in the mind. It is an ideal. The original old city of Byzantium was famous as a centre of religion, art and architecture.

1   *That*: Ireland – all who live there are subject to ageing, decay and death.

3   *dying generations*: opposites are linked to show that in the midst of life is death.

7   *sensual music*: the young are living life to the full through their senses and are neglecting the inner spiritual life of the soul.

9   *paltry thing*: worthless, of no importance. Old age is not valued in Ireland.

10   *tattered coat*: an old man is as worthless as a scarecrow.

10-11   *unless/Soul clap its hands and sing*: man can only break free if he allows his spirit the freedom to express itself.

13-14   *Nor is there ... own magnificence*: all schools of art should study the discipline they teach, while the soul should study the immortal art of previous generations.

17   *O sages*: wise men, cleansed by the holy fire of God.

19-24   *Come ... artifice of eternity*: Yeats asks the sages to teach him the wonders of Byzantium and gather his soul into the perfection of art.

19   *perne in a gyre*: spinning; turning very fast.

22   *fastened to a dying animal*: the soul trapped in a decaying body.

32   *past, or passing, or to come*: in eternity, the golden bird sings of transience (passing time).

EXPLORATIONS

1. This poem tries to offer a form of escape from old age. Does it succeed? Write a paragraph in response, with support from the text.

2. Why are the 'Monuments of unageing intellect' of such importance to Yeats? What does this imply about contemporary Ireland?

3. The poem is defiant in its exploration of eternity. Discuss, using reference or quotation.

STUDY NOTES

'Sailing to Byzantium' confronts the universal issue of old age. There is no easy solution to this problem. Yeats found the idea of advancing age repulsive and longed to escape. Here he imagines an ideal place, Byzantium, which allowed all to enjoy eternal works of art. He celebrates what man can create and he bitterly condemns the mortality to which man is subject.

Yeats wrote, 'When Irishmen were illuminating the Book of Kells ... Byzantium was the centre of European civilization ... so I symbolise the search for the spiritual life by a journey to that city.'

The poet declares the theme in the **first stanza** as he confidently declaims that the world of the senses is not for the old – they must seek another way which is timeless, **a life of the spirit and intellect**. The word 'That' tells us he is looking back, as he has already started his journey. But he is looking back wistfully at the world of the lovers ('The young/In one another's arms') and the world of teeming nature ('The salmon-falls, the mackerel-crowded seas'). The compound words emphasise the dynamism and fertility of the life of the senses, even though he admits the flaw in this wonderful life of plenty is mortality ('Those dying generations'). The life of the senses and nature is governed by the harsh cycle of procreation, life and death.

The poet asserts in the **second stanza** that **what gives meaning to a person is the soul**, 'unless/Soul clap its hands and sing'. Otherwise an elderly man is worthless, 'a paltry thing'. We are given a chilling image of the thin, wasting frame of an old man as a scarecrow in tattered clothes. In contrast, we are shown the wonders of the intellect as the poet tells us that all schools of art study what they compose, what they produce – 'Monuments of unageing intellect'. These works of art are timeless; unlike the body, they are not subject to decay. Thus, music schools study great music and art schools study great paintings. The life of the intellect and spirit must take precedence over the life of the senses. Yeats will no longer listen to the 'sensual music' that is appropriate only for the young, but will study the carefully composed 'music' of classic art.

In Byzantium, the buildings had beautiful mosaics, pictures made with little tiles and inlaid with gold. One of these had a picture of martyrs being burned. Yeats addresses these wise men ('sages') in **stanza three**. He wants them to whirl through time ('perne in a gyre') and come to **teach his soul how to 'sing'**, how to live the life of the spirit. His soul craves this ('sick with desire'), **but it is trapped in the decaying, mortal body** ('fastened to a dying animal'). This is a horrendous image of old age. The soul has lost its identity: 'It knows not what it is'.

He pleads to be saved from this using two interesting verbs, 'Consume' and 'gather'. Both suggest a desire to be taken away. A fire consumes what is put into it and changes the form of the substance. Yeats wants a new body. He pleads to be embraced like a child coming home: 'gather me'. But where will he go? He will journey into the cold world of art, 'the artifice of eternity'. 'Artifice' refers to the skill of those who have created the greatest works of art, but it also means artificial, not real. Is the poet suggesting that eternity also has a flaw?

The **fourth stanza** starts confidently as Yeats declares that 'Once out of nature', he will be transformed into the ageless perfect work of art, the **golden bird**. This is the new body for his soul. Now he will sing to the court. But is the court listening? The word 'drowsy' suggests not. Isn't he singing about transience, the passing of time: 'what is past, or passing, or to come'? Has this any relevance in eternity? Is there a perfect solution to the dilemma of old age?

Yeats raises these questions for our consideration. He has explored this problem by contrasting the abundant life of the young with the 'tattered coat' of old age. He has shown us the golden bird of immortality in opposition to the 'dying animal' of the decaying body. The poet has lulled us with end-rhymes and half-rhymes. He has used groups of threes – 'Fish, flesh, or fowl', 'begotten, born, and dies', 'past, or passing, or to come' – to argue his case. At the end of the poem, do we feel that Yeats genuinely longs for the warm, teeming life of the senses with all its imperfections, rather than the cold, disinterested world of the 'artifice of eternity'?

ANALYSIS

'Yeats is often concerned with finding ways of escape from the sorrows and oppressions which are so much a part of life.' What evidence do you find for this statement in 'Sailing to Byzantium'?

Sample Paragraph

I believe that Yeats was preoccupied with the inescapable fact of ageing and death. This poem, 'Sailing to Byzantium', concerns a voyage to perfection. In ordinary life there is no perfection, a fact that Yeats recognises in the phrase 'dying generations'. All must die so that more can be born into the abundant, mortal world of nature. He rages against the weaknesses of old age: an old man is a 'tattered coat upon a stick', 'a paltry thing'. The body is a 'dying animal'. Terrible, grotesque imagery vividly describes the ravages of the ageing process. Yeats intends to turn his back on this and seek immortality, hence his journey to Byzantium. This city, in his opinion, is the perfect city, as it was the cradle of European civilisation and religious philosophy. He wants the figures that are in the golden mosaics to come and instruct him how to live this life of the intellect: 'gather me'. He wants to escape the sorrows and oppressions of ordinary life. Then he paints an idyllic picture of himself, now in the shape of a golden bird, singing his songs. But this world seems cold, 'artifice of eternity', lifeless and a poor contrast to the warm, heaving, teeming 'salmon-falls, mackerel-crowded seas' world of stanza one. I don't believe Yeats has found the perfect solution to the problem of ageing. Is there one?

Examiner's Comment

A close reading of the poem is evident in this response to Yeats's search for escape. Engagement is evident in the response and was well supported by quotations. The student showed confidence in the concluding remarks. A-grade standard.

▶ CLASS/HOMEWORK EXERCISES

1. Yeats often places himself at the centre of his work. Do you find this to be true in 'Sailing to Byzantium'? Give reasons for your answer.

2. Copy the table below into your own notes and fill in critical comments about the last two quotations.

Key Quotes

That is no country for old men	Yeats feels that Ireland is not a suitable place to live when old.
all neglect/Monuments of unageing intellect	Young people, because they are in the vigour of their youth, are only concerned with living life through their senses and have no time for matters of the mind or soul.
Into the artifice of eternity	
I shall never take/My bodily form from any natural thing	

8 *from* MEDITATIONS IN TIME OF CIVIL WAR: THE STARE'S NEST BY MY WINDOW

The bees build in the crevices
Of loosening masonry, and there
The mother birds bring grubs and flies.
My wall is loosening; honey-bees,
Come build in the empty house of the stare.   5

We are closed in, and the key is turned
On our uncertainty; somewhere
A man is killed, or a house burned,
Yet no clear fact to be discerned:
Come build in the empty house of the stare.   10

A barricade of stone or of wood;
Some fourteen days of civil war;
Last night they trundled down the road
That dead young soldier in his blood:
Come build in the empty house of the stare.   15

We had fed the heart on fantasies,
The heart's grown brutal from the fare;
More substance in our enmities
Than in our love; O honey-bees,
Come build in the empty house of the stare.   20

'days of civil war'

GLOSSARY

Stare is another name for the starling,
a bird with distinctive dark brown or
greenish-black feathers.
3   *grubs*: larvae of insects.
12   *civil war*: the Irish Civil War (1922–23)
between Republicans who fought for
full independence and supporters of the
Anglo-Irish Treaty.

13   *trundled*: rolled.
17   *fare*: diet (of dreams).
18   *enmities*: disputes; hatred.

EXPLORATIONS

1. Comment on how Yeats creates an atmosphere of concern and insecurity in
    stanzas two and three.

2. In your opinion, how effective is the symbol of the bees as a civilising force
    amid all the destruction of war? Support your answer with close reference
    to the poem.

3. How would you describe the dominant mood of the poem? Is it positive or
    negative? Refer closely to the text in your answer.

STUDY NOTES

*The Irish Civil War prompted Yeats to consider the brutality and insecurity caused
by conflict. It also made him reflect on his own identity as part of the Anglo-Irish
Ascendancy. The poet wrote elsewhere that he had been shocked and depressed by the
fighting during the first months of hostilities, yet he was determined not to grow bitter
or to lose sight of the beauty of nature. He wrote this poem after seeing a stare building
its nest in a hole beside his window.*

Much of the poem is dominated by the images of building and collapse. **Stanza
one** introduces this tension between creativity ('bees build') and disintegration
('loosening'). In responding to the bitter civil war, Yeats finds suitable **symbols in
the nurturing natural world** to express his own hopes. Addressing the bees, he

asks that they 'build in the empty house of the stare'. He is desperately conscious of the political vacuum being presently filled by bloodshed. His desperate cry for help seems heartfelt in tone. There is also a possibility that the poet is addressing himself – he will have to revise his own attitudes to the changing political realities caused by the war.

In **stanza two**, Yeats expresses a sense of being **threatened by the conflict** around him: 'We are closed in'. The use of the plural pronoun suggests a community under siege. He is fearful of the future: 'our uncertainty'. Is the poet reflecting on the threat to his own immediate household or to the once powerful Anglo-Irish ruling class? The constant rumours of everyday violence are highlighted in the stark descriptions: 'A man is killed, or a house burned'. Such occurrences almost seem routine in the grim reality of war.

Stanza three opens with a **haunting image**, the 'barricade of stone', an enduring symbol of division and hostility. The vehemence and inhumanity of the times is driven home by the stark report of soldiers who 'trundled down the road' and left one 'dead young soldier in his blood'. Such atrocities add greater depth to the plaintive refrain for regeneration: 'Come build in the empty house of the stare'.

In the **final stanza**, Yeats faces up to the root causes of war: 'We had fed the heart on fantasies'. Dreams of achieving independence have led to even greater hatred ('enmities') and intransigence than could have been imagined. It is a tragic irony that the Irish nation has become more divided than ever before. The poet seems despairing as he accepts the failure represented by civil conflict: 'The heart's grown brutal'. It is as though he is reprimanding himself for daring to imagine a brave new world. His **final plea for healing** and reconstruction is strengthened by an emphatic 'O' to show Yeats's depth of feeling: 'O honeybees,/ Come build in the empty house of the stare'.

ANALYSIS

'Images of ruin and renewal are in constant opposition in this poem.' Write a paragraph in response to this statement, supporting your points with reference from the text.

Sample Paragraph

'The Stare's Nest by my Window' is mainly about conflict, and particularly the Irish Civil War. It is not surprising that the poem contains many symbols and images of ruin and destruction. Yeats watches the bees building a nest in 'loosening masonry' outside his window. It's ironic. Something new is happening among the ruins. The bees are constructing. Building for the future. It is symbolic that something positive is taking place. This is a key theme in the poem. Yeats is hopeful in spite of the war. The poet's use of symbolism contrasts the two forces of ruin and renewal when he says 'build in the empty house'. There are other images of ruin e.g. the 'house burned' and the ruined life of the 'young soldier in his blood'. These images remind us of what happens in wartime. But Yeats seems to argue that we can learn from nature. He hopes that just as the birds take care of their young, Ireland will recover from war. In the future there will be renewal after all the ruin.

Examiner's Comment

There are a number of focused points made in this paragraph and the candidate makes a reasonable attempt to use supporting references. The expression is disjointed at times and the point about symbolism is repeated unnecessarily. A solid C-grade standard.

CLASS/HOMEWORK EXERCISES

1. Repetition is an important feature in this poem. Comment on its effectiveness in enhancing our understanding of the poet's themes.

2. Copy the table below into your own notes and fill in critical comments about the last two quotations.

Key Quotes

The mother birds bring grubs and flies	Details of nurturing in nature are used as a contrast to the background violence and devastation of warfare.
Yet no clear fact to be discerned	Many Irish people were confused by the Civil War and families were sometimes bitterly divided.
My wall is loosening	
The heart's grown brutal	

9 IN MEMORY OF EVA GORE-BOOTH AND CON MARKIEWICZ

The light of evening, Lissadell,
Great windows open to the south,
Two girls in silk kimonos, both
Beautiful, one a gazelle.
But a raving autumn shears
Blossom from the summer's wreath;
The older is condemned to death,
Pardoned, drags out lonely years
Conspiring among the ignorant.
I know not what the younger dreams –
Some vague Utopia – and she seems   10
When withered old and skeleton-gaunt,
An image of such politics.
Many a time I think to seek
One or the other out and speak
Of that old Georgian mansion, mix   15
Pictures of the mind, recall
That table and the talk of youth,
Two girls in silk kimonos, both
Beautiful, one a gazelle.   20

Dear shadows, now you know it all,
All the folly of a fight
With a common wrong or right.
The innocent and the beautiful
Have no enemy but time;   25
Arise and bid me strike a match
And strike another till time catch;
Should the conflagration climb,
Run till all the sages know.
We the great gazebo built,   30
They convicted us of guilt;
Bid me strike a match and blow.

'that old Georgian mansion'

GLOSSARY

1	*Lissadell*: the Gore-Booth family home in Co. Sligo.	11	*Utopia*: a perfect world.
3	*kimonos*: traditional Japanese robes.	22	*folly*: foolishness.
4	*gazelle*: graceful antelope.	28	*conflagration*: blazing inferno.
5	*shears*: cuts.	29	*sages*: philosophers.
9	*Conspiring*: plotting; scheming.	30	*gazebo*: ornamental summer house, sometimes seen as a sign of extravagance.

EXPLORATIONS

1. What mood does Yeats create in the first four lines of the poem? Explain how he achieves this mood.

2. Would you agree that this is a poem of contrasts? How does Yeats use contrasts to express his thoughts and feelings? Support your points with relevant reference.

3. What picture of Yeats himself emerges from this poem? Use close reference to the text to support the points you make.

STUDY NOTES

Yeats wrote this poem about the two Gore-Booth sisters shortly after their deaths. He was 62 at the time. Eva was a noted campaigner for women's rights and Constance was a revolutionary who took part in the 1916 Rising. She later became the first woman elected to the British House of Commons at Westminster. The poet had once been fascinated by their youthful grace and beauty, but he became increasingly opposed to their political activism. Although the poem is a memorial to the two women, it also reveals Yeats's own views about the changes that had occurred in Ireland over his lifetime.

Stanza one begins on a nostalgic note, with Yeats recalling a magical summer's evening in the company of the Gore-Booth sisters. The details he remembers suggest a **world of elegance and privilege** in the girls' family home, Lissadell

House, overlooking Sligo Bay. 'Great windows' are a reminder of the grandeur to be found in the Anglo-Irish 'Big House'. Eva and Constance are portrayed as being delicately beautiful, their elusive femininity indicated by the exotic 'silk kimonos' they wear. The poet compares one of the girls to 'a gazelle', stylishly poised and graceful.

The abrupt contrast of mood in **line 5** disrupts the tranquil scene. Yeats considers the harsh effects of time and how it changes everything. He describes autumn (personified as an overenthusiastic gardener) as 'raving' and uncontrollable. The metaphor illustrates the way **time destroys** ('shears') the simple perfection of youth ('Blossom'). Typically, Yeats chooses images from the natural world to express his own retrospective outlook.

In **lines 7–13**, the poet shows his **deep contempt** for the involvement of both the Gore-Booth sisters in revolutionary politics. As far as Yeats is concerned, their activism 'among the ignorant' was a great mistake. These beautiful young women wasted their lives for a 'vague Utopia'. The graphic image of one of the girls growing 'withered old and skeleton-gaunt' is also used to symbolise the unattractive political developments of the era. Repulsed by the idea, Yeats retreats into the more sophisticated world of Lissadell's 'old Georgian mansion'.

The **second stanza** is in marked contrast to the first. Yeats addresses the spirits ('shadows') of Eva and Constance. The tone of voice is unclear. It appears to be compassionate, but there is an undertone of weariness as well. He goes on to scold the two women for wasting their lives on 'folly'. Yeats seems angry that their innocence and beauty have been sacrificed for nothing. It is as though he feels **they have betrayed both their own femininity and their social class**. If they had only known it, their one and only enemy was time.

In the **final lines** of the poem, Yeats dramatises his feelings by turning all his **resentment against time** itself. He associates the failed lives of the women with the decay of the Anglo-Irish Ascendancy. The energetic rhythm and repetition reflect his fury as he imagines striking match after match ('And strike another till time catch') and is consumed in a great 'conflagration'. The poet imagines that the significance of this inferno will eventually be understood by those who are wise, the 'sages'. In the last sentence, Yeats considers how 'They' (the enemies of the Anglo-Irish Ascendancy) hastened the end of a grand cultural era in Ireland. The 'great gazebo' is a symbol of the fine houses and gracious living that were slowly disappearing. The poem ends on a defiant note ('Bid me strike a match and blow'), with Yeats inviting the ghosts of Eva and Constance to help him resist the devastating effects of time.

ANALYSIS

To what extent is the poem a lament for the loss of youth and beauty? Refer closely to the text in your answer.

Sample Paragraph

'In Memory of Eva Gore-Booth and Con Markiewicz' is largely focused on the effects of time as an agent of destruction. Yeats begins by describing the two sisters as 'two girls'. I think his nostalgic portrayal of the time he shared with them at Lissadell is filled with regret. He remembers the summer evenings relaxing together 'and the talk of youth'. Yeats contrasts the beautiful girls in their silk kimonos with the way they were in their later years – 'withered old and skeleton-gaunt'. The image is startling, evidence of how he views the ravages of time. It is all the more shocking when compared with the exquisite kimonos – symbols of lost beauty. I think Yeats is also regretful of his own lost youth. At the end of the poem, he shows his anger at ageing and argues that youth has 'no enemy but time'.

Examiner's Comment

Although short, this is a well-focused paragraph which directly addresses the question. The references and quotes are carefully chosen and show a clear engagement with the poem. The use of the unnecessary 'I think' weakens the expression slightly. Otherwise, a good B-grade response.

CLASS/HOMEWORK EXERCISES

1. From your reading of the poem, how would you describe Yeats's true feelings towards the two women? Support the points you make with reference and/or quotation.

2. Copy the table below into your own notes and fill in critical comments about the last two quotations.

Key Quotes

The light of evening, Lissadell,/Great windows open to the south	These beautiful opening lines recreate the leisurely lifestyle associated with the Anglo-Irish gentry, the class to which Yeats belonged.
That table and the talk of youth	This is another reminder of the potential the sophisticated Gore-Booth sisters once had.
Two girls in silk kimonos	
Arise and bid me strike a match	

10 SWIFT'S EPITAPH

Swift has sailed into his rest;
Savage indignation there
Cannot lacerate his breast.
Imitate him if you dare,
World-besotted traveller; he   5
Served human liberty.

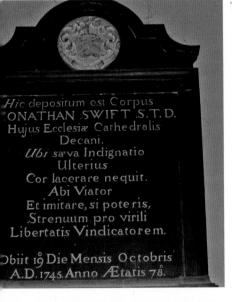

'Swift's Epitaph'

GLOSSARY

Swift: Jonathan Swift, satirist and clergyman, author of *Gulliver's Travels* and dean of St Patrick's Cathedral. The original inscription in Latin is on his memorial in the cathedral. Yeats liked to spend time there.

Epitaph: inscription for a tomb or memorial.

1   *his rest*: suggestion of afterlife; death is not an end.

2   *Savage indignation*: the driving force of Swift's satirical work. He believed in a society where wrong was punished and good rewarded.

3   *lacerate*: cut; tear.

5   *World-besotted*: obsessed with travelling or with material concerns rather than spiritual matters.

5–6   *he /Served human liberty*: Yeats believed Swift served the liberty of the intellect, not liberty for the common people. Yeats associated democracy with organised mobs of ignorant people.

EXPLORATIONS

1. How would you describe the tone of this poem?

2. Comment on the poet's use of the verb 'lacerate'. What do you think Yeats is trying to convey?

STUDY NOTES

'Swift's Epitaph' is a translation from the original Latin epitaph composed by Swift for himself. Yeats adds a new first line to the original. He regarded this epitaph as the 'greatest ... in history'.

W. B. Yeats admired Swift, who was proud and solitary and belonged to the Anglo-Irish tradition, as did Yeats himself. He regarded the Anglo-Irish as superior. He once said, 'We have created most of the modern literature of this country. We have created the best of its political intelligence.' **Yeats's additional first line** to the epitaph conveys a dignified sailing into the spiritual afterlife by the deceased Swift. The rest of the poem is a **translation** from the Latin original. Swift is now free from all the negative reactions he was subjected to when alive: 'Savage indignation there/Cannot lacerate his breast.' Swift's self-portrait conveys the impression of a man of fierce **independence and pride**. 'Imitate him if you dare' is the challenge thrown down like a gauntlet to the reader to try to be like him. 'World-besotted traveller' can be read as a man who has travelled extensively in his imagination as well as in reality. His contribution to humanity is summed up in the final sentence: 'he/Served human liberty'. **He freed the artist** from the masses so that the artist could 'make liberty visible'. The tone of this short, compressed poem is proud and defiant, like Swift.

ANALYSIS

What impression of Swift do you get from this poem by Yeats? Write a paragraph in response, supporting your views with reference to the text.

Sample Paragraph

I thought that Swift was a confident, fearless man who dared to voice his own truth. The tone of the poem, from its opening, 'Swift has sailed into his rest', suggests a man who knew what he was doing and did it with style. It suggests a spiritual man, 'into his rest'. He is embarking on an afterlife of some sort. He was a man who braved the censure of the world, 'Savage indignation there/Cannot lacerate his breast'. He dared to say what he felt he had to say. A challenge is thrown down to the reader, 'Imitate him if you dare'. Obviously, both Swift and Yeats considered that Swift would be a hard act to follow. The phrase 'world-besotted traveller' could mean that the poet considered that modern man was too obsessed with material possessions, while Swift was concerned with loftier matters such as the moral good. The final sentence, 'he/Served human liberty', states that he improved the human condition by making us all free. This is where I, as a 21st-century reader, part company with the epitaph. Swift did not fight for freedom as we understand it. It could be argued that he only believed in liberty for a select few, the Anglo-Irish Protestants. Yeats's tone is one of admiration for this courageous man, but modern man would not agree with this elitist view of freedom for a select group. Also the confident challenge to the reader to match Swift 'if you dare' comes across to me as arrogance. While I admire Swift's fearlessness, I do not admire his elitism or arrogance.

Examiner's Comment

An original A-grade response to the question. The paragraph raises interesting discussion points about both writers. There is detailed support throughout and a fluent control of language in arguing the case vigorously.

CLASS/HOMEWORK EXERCISES

1. Is Yeats's use of the sailing metaphor effective? Briefly explain your answer.

2. Copy the table below into your own notes and fill in critical comments about the last two quotations.

Key Quotes

Swift has sailed into his rest	Swift has now entered the next life. The tone reflects Yeats's admiration and respect.
Savage indignation there/ Cannot lacerate his breast	He is free from criticism now. Ironically, Swift's own savage criticism is now also at rest.
World-besotted traveller	
he/Served human liberty	

11   AN ACRE OF GRASS

Picture and book remain,
An acre of green grass
For air and exercise,
Now strength and body goes;
Midnight, an old house   5
Where nothing stirs but a mouse.

My temptation is quiet.
Here at life's end
Neither loose imagination,
Nor the mill of the mind   10
Consuming its rag and bone,
Can make the truth known.

Grant me an old man's frenzy,
Myself must I remake
Till I am Timon and Lear   15
Or that William Blake
Who beat upon the wall
Till Truth obeyed his call;

A mind Michael Angelo knew
That can pierce the clouds,   20
Or inspired by frenzy
Shake the dead in their shrouds;
Forgotten else by mankind,
An old man's eagle mind.

'An acre of green grass'

GLOSSARY

2   *acre*: the secluded garden of Yeats's home, where he spent his final years.

5   *an old house*: the house was in Rathfarnham, Co. Dublin.

9   *loose imagination*: vague, unfocused ideas.

13   *frenzy*: wildly excited state.

15   *Timon and Lear*: two of Shakespeare's elderly tragic heroes, both of whom raged against the world.

16   *William Blake*: English visionary poet and painter (1757–1827).

19   *Michael Angelo*: Michelangelo, Italian Renaissance artist (1475–1564).

22   *shrouds*: burial garments.

EXPLORATIONS

1. How does Yeats create a mood of calm and serenity in the opening stanza?

2. Briefly explain the change of tone in stanza three.

STUDY NOTES

Written in 1936 when Yeats was 71, the poet expresses his resentment towards ageing gracefully. Instead, he will dedicate himself to seeking wisdom through frenzied creativity. People sometimes take a narrow view of the elderly and consider them completely redundant. In Yeats's case, he is determined not to let old age crush his spirit.

Stanza one paints a picture of retirement as a surrender to death. Yeats's life has been reduced to suit his basic needs. 'Picture and book' might refer to the poet's memories. Physically weak, he feels like a prisoner whose enclosed garden area is for 'air and exercise'. There is an underlying **feeling of alienation and inactivity**: 'nothing stirs'.

In **stanza two**, the poet says that it would be easy to give in to the stereotypical image of placid contentment: 'My temptation is quiet', especially since old age ('life's end') has weakened his creative powers. **Yeats admits that his 'loose imagination' is not as sharp as it was when he was in his prime.** He no longer finds immediate inspiration ('truth') in everyday experiences, which he compares to life's 'rag and bone'.

The **third stanza** opens on a much more dramatic and forceful note as the poet confronts his fears: 'Grant me an old man's frenzy'. Yeats's personal prayer is totally lacking in meekness. Instead, he urges himself to focus enthusiastically on his own creative purpose – 'frenzy'. **He pledges to 'remake' himself** in the image of such heroic figures as Timon, Lear and William Blake. The passionate tone and run-on lines add to his sense of commitment to his art.

In **stanza four**, Yeats develops **his spirited pursuit of meaningful old age** by reflecting on 'A mind Michael Angelo knew'. The poet is stimulated and encouraged to follow the great artist's example and 'pierce the clouds'. The image suggests the daring power of imagination to lift the spirit in the search for truth and beauty. The final lines build to a climax as Yeats imagines the joys of 'An old man's eagle mind'. Such intense creativity can 'Shake the dead' and allow the poet to continue experiencing life to its fullest.

ANALYSIS

Based on your reading of the poem, comment on Yeats's response to old age. Refer to the text in your answer.

Sample Paragraph

Yeats takes a highly unusual approach to ageing in 'An Acre of Grass'. He seems to be happy to sit reading in his quiet 'acre of grass'. Everything seems to be very organised, a little too organised for his liking. In the first few lines, we get a picture of someone close to second childhood, with his 'picture and book'. Late at night, he is awake and feels that 'nothing stirs but a mouse'. This is like the mind of a little child and it is what Yeats rebels against. He does not want to fade away. He really wants to keep being a poet and seek truth. To him, it is 'an old man's frenzy'. This suggests that he would prefer to be thought of as mad, but to keep producing his poems rather than fade away quietly. He wants to be like King Lear, the old king in Shakespeare's play who fought to the bitter end. Yeats wants to live life to the full, not fade away quietly. He wants to write his poetry and make use of his active mind until he takes his last breath. I admire his energy even though he seems a grumpy old man. His tone is fierce and defiant throughout most of the poem. He will not fade away on his acre of grass.

Examiner's Comment

There is some very good discussion in this paragraph and a clear sense of individual engagement. The idea of Yeats rejecting second childhood is well supported. The style of writing lacks control at times and there are some awkward expressions and repetition ('fade away'). An average C grade.

CLASS/HOMEWORK EXERCISES

1. How would you describe the structure of this poem? Formal or informal? Regular or irregular? How does the poem's structure and form emphasise Yeats's message about old age?

2. Copy the table below into your own notes and fill in critical comments about the last two quotations.

Key Quotes

Midnight, an old house/ Where nothing stirs but a mouse	Yeats creates an atmosphere of stillness and emptiness associated with lonely old age.
Here at life's end	Central to the poem is Yeats's awareness of death, which makes him determined to make the most of life.
Grant me an old man's frenzy	
An old man's eagle mind	

12 ## UNDER BEN BULBEN

V

Irish poets, learn your trade,
Sing whatever is well made,
Scorn the sort now growing up
All out of shape from toe to top,
Their unremembering hearts and heads   5
Base-born products of base beds.
Sing the peasantry, and then
Hard-riding country gentlemen,
The holiness of monks, and after
Porter-drinkers' randy laughter;   10
Sing the lords and ladies gay
That were beaten into the clay
Through seven heroic centuries;
Cast your mind on other days
That we in coming days may be   15
Still the indomitable Irishry.

VI

Under bare Ben Bulben's head
In Drumcliff churchyard Yeats is laid,
An ancestor was rector there
Long years ago, a church stands near,   20
By the road an ancient cross.
No marble, no conventional phrase;
On limestone quarried near the spot
By his command these words are cut:
    Cast a cold eye   25
    On life, on death.
    Horseman, pass by!

'Under bare Ben Bulben's head'

GLOSSARY

2	*whatever is well made*: great art.
6	*base*: low; unworthy.
16	*indomitable*: invincible; unbeatable.
17	*Under bare Ben Bulben's head*: defiant symbol of the famous mountain.
19	*ancestor*: the poet's great-grandfather.
27	*Horseman*: possibly a symbolic figure from local folklore; or possibly any passer-by.

EXPLORATIONS

1. Comment on the tone used by Yeats in giving advice to other writers. Refer to the text in your answer.

2. From your reading of the poem, explain the kind of 'Irishry' that Yeats wishes to see celebrated in poetry. Support the points you make with reference or quotation.

3. Describe the mood of Drumcliff churchyard as visualised by the poet. Use close reference to the text to show how Yeats uses language to create this mood.

STUDY NOTES

This was one of Yeats's last poems. Sections V and VI of the elegy sum up his personal views on the future of Irish poetry and also include the enigmatic epitaph he composed for his own gravestone. Using art as a gateway to spiritual fulfilment is characteristic of the poet.

Section V is a hard-hitting address by Yeats to his contemporaries and all the poets who will come after him. He encourages them to set the highest 'well made' standards for their work. His uncompromisingly negative view of contemporary writing ('out of shape from toe to top') is quickly clarified. The reason why modern literature is in such a state of confusion is that the poets' 'unremembering hearts and heads' **have lost touch with tradition**. The formality and discipline of great classic poetry have been replaced by unstructured writing and free verse. The authoritative tone becomes even more scathing as Yeats castigates the inferiority of his peers as 'Base-born products'.

It is not only intellectual artistic tradition that the poet admires; he finds another valuable tradition in the legends and myths of old Ireland. Yeats urges his fellow writers to 'Sing the peasantry'. But he also advises them to **absorb other cultural traditions**. Here he includes the 'Hard-riding country gentlemen' of his own Anglo-Irish class and the 'holiness of monks' – those who seek truth through ascetic or spiritual means. Even the more sensuous 'randy laughter' of 'Porter-drinkers' can be inspirational. For Yeats, the peasant and aristocratic traditions are equally worth celebrating. Irish history is marked by a combination of joy, heroism, defeat and resilience. Yet despite (or perhaps because of) his harsh criticism of the present generation, there is little doubt about the poet's passionate desire to encourage new writing that would reflect the true greatness of 'indomitable Irishry'.

Section VI is a great deal less dogmatic. Writing in the third person, Yeats describes his final resting place in Drumcliff. The voice is **detached and dignified**. Using a series of unadorned images, he takes us to the simple churchyard at the foot of Ben Bulben. The mountain stands as a proud symbol of how our unchanging silent origins outlive human tragedy. It is to his Irish roots that the poet ultimately wants to return. His wishes are modest but curt – 'No marble'. Keen to avoid the well-worn headstone inscriptions, Yeats provides his own incisive epitaph. The three short lines are enigmatic and balance opposing views, typical of so much of his poetry. The poet's last warning ('Cast a cold eye') reminds us to live measured lives based on a realistic understanding of the cycle of life and death. The beautiful Christian setting, subdued tone and measured rhythm all contribute to the quiet dignity of Yeats's final farewell.

ANALYSIS

Some people have criticised this poem as 'a bitter old man's snobbish rant'. Write your response to this comment, supporting your views with reference to the text.

Sample Paragraph

It's easy to see why Yeats could be accused of being elitist and superior. As he nears death, he is clearly not concerned with political correctness. He knows his own worth as the leading Irish writer of his times. He gets straight to the point in advising younger poets – 'learn your trade'. If I was an unpublished writer, I would take him seriously, rather than feeling precious. Yeats does not suffer fools easily and he has no respect for shoddy work that is 'out of shape'. His tone can be harsh, even shrill on occasions, but he is stressing a basic lesson that good writing must be disciplined. Rather than seeing him as someone who is ranting, I appreciate the way Yeats shows his interest in standards. His attitude is actually inclusive. He wants young poets to learn from every source available to them – sacred texts, the Protestant and peasant Catholic traditions, and from the 'Porter-drinkers' of Ireland. I can see no bitterness here. His own funeral instructions are actually humble. He does not demand a hero's courageous tomb, just a simple plot in a country graveyard. To me, Yeats comes across as a man who is neither arrogant nor snobbish, but as a legendary writer concerned about Irish literature.

Examiner's Comment

This is a very spirited and well-sustained personal response that reflects a clear viewpoint. Points are supported robustly with apt quotations and the arguments range over the whole poem. In the main, expression is fluent and controlled. An impressive A-grade standard.

CLASS/HOMEWORK EXERCISES

1. Is Yeats's epitaph in keeping with the views he expresses throughout the rest of the poem? Explain your answer using reference to the text.

2. Copy the table below into your own notes and fill in critical comments about the last two quotations.

Key Quotes

Irish poets, learn your trade	Yeats is enthusiastic about the need for poets to return to the formal, classical tradition that will again celebrate Ireland's heroic and spiritual values.
Base-born products of base beds	The poet is contemptuous of modern poetry, much of which he believed came from inferior writers. Repetition emphasises his disdain.
By the road an ancient cross	
Cast a cold eye/On life, on death	

13   POLITICS

'In our time the destiny of man presents its meanings in political terms.'
Thomas Mann

How can I, that girl standing there,
My attention fix
On Roman or on Russian
Or on Spanish politics,
Yet here's a travelled man that knows   5
What he talks about,
And there's a politician
That has read and thought,
And maybe what they say is true
Of war and war's alarms,   10
But O that I were young again
And held her in my arms!

'But O that I were young again/And held her in my arms'

GLOSSARY

Politics: winning and using power to govern society.
Thomas Mann was a German novelist who argued that the future of man was determined by states and governments.

3-4 *On Roman or on Russian/Or on Spanish politics*: a reference to the political upheavals of Europe in the 1930s.

EXPLORATIONS

1. This poem suggests that politics are not important. Does the poet convince you? Write a paragraph in response, with reference to the text.

2. Where does the language used in the poem convey a sense of deep longing? How effective is this?

STUDY NOTES

'Politics' is a satire written in 1939, when Yeats was 73, in response to a magazine article. He said it was based on 'a moment of meditation'.

A **satire** uses ridicule to expose foolishness. A magazine article praised Yeats for his 'public' work. The poet was delighted with this word, as one of his aims had always been to 'move the common people'. However, the article went on to say that Yeats should have used this 'public' voice to address public issues such as politics. Yeats disagreed, as he had always regarded politics as dishonest and superficial. He thought professional politicians manipulated through 'false news'. This is evident from the ironic comment, 'And maybe what they say is true'. Here we see the poet's indifference to these matters.

This poem addresses **real truths**, the proper material for poems, the universal experience of **human relationships**, not the infinite abstractions that occupied politicians ('war and war's alarms'). Big public events, Yeats is suggesting, are not as important as love. The girl in the poem is more important than all the politics in the world: 'How can I ... My attention fix/On Roman or on Russian/Or on Spanish politics'? So Yeats is overthrowing the epigraph at the beginning of the poem, where the novelist Thomas Mann is stating that people should be concerned with political matters. Politics is the winning and using of power to govern the state. Yeats is adopting the persona of the distracted lover who is unable to focus on the tangled web of European politics in the 1930s. This poem was to be placed in his last poetry collection, almost like a farewell, as he states again that what he desires is youth and love.

But this poem can also give another view. Is the 'she' in the poem Ireland? Yeats has addressed public issues in poems such as 'Easter, 1916' and 'September 1913' and he was already a senator in the Irish government. As usual, he leaves us with questions as he draws us through this deceptively simple poem with its **ever-changing tones** that range from the questioning opening to mockery, doubt and finally longing. The **steady rhyme** (the second line rhymes with the fourth and so on) drives the poem forward to its emphatic **closing wish**, the cry of an old man who wishes to recapture his youth and lost love.

ANALYSIS

Do you agree with Yeats that only youth and love matter? Discuss, using reference to the poem.

Sample Paragraph

I think Yeats is expressing a deep-seated desire in all of us. We all want to be concerned with our own lives ('My attention fix'), not on the mess that the political world seems to be in, 'Roman or on Russian/Or on Spanish politics'. It is the same today. How often have we turned off the news in disgust or because we just couldn't take any more 'Of war and war's alarms'? And yet I would like to suggest another view on this. We get the governments we deserve. Democracy is fragile when good people are inattentive. So although I agree with Yeats's sentiments and can fully understand his closing wish, 'But O that I were young again/And held her in my arms', I feel that we have to sometimes safeguard the destiny of man. We are the generation that is on watch now for the protection of the environment and the safety of humanity. I think Thomas Mann has a point as he says, 'In our time the destiny of man presents its meanings in political terms'.

Examiner's Comment

The student has engaged personally with the question and has presented a considered argument using relevant quotations effectively. The answer reads well and adjectives (such as 'fragile' and 'inattentive') are well chosen. Grade A.

CLASS/HOMEWORK EXERCISES

1. Comment on the rhythm of the poem, paying particular attention to the use of run-on lines.

2. Copy the table below into your own notes and fill in critical comments about the last two quotations.

Key Quotes

How can I, that girl standing there,/My attention fix	The poet is declaring that his attention is on his personal concerns rather than public concerns such as politics.
On Roman or on Russian	The alliterative 'r' emphasises Yeats's tone of frustration.
And there's a politician/That has read and thought	
But O that I were young again/And held her in my arms	

LEAVING CERT SAMPLE ESSAY

'Yeats explores themes of disintegration and immortality in his passionately personal quest for truth.' Write a response to the poetry of W.B. Yeats in light of this statement, supporting your points with suitable reference to the poems on your course.

Marking Scheme Guidelines

Reward responses that show clear evidence of personal engagement with the poems. The key terms ('themes of disintegration and immortality' and 'passionately personal quest for truth') should be addressed (though not necessarily equally). Allow for a wide range of approaches to answering the question.

Material might be drawn from the following:

- Intensely conflicting visions of culture, history, politics, ageing
- Art and nature offer escape from overwhelming disillusionment with reality
- Wide range and depth and of the poet's views/feelings
- Tensions in the poems reveal soul-searching and yearning
- Engaging effect of dramatic language, imagery, symbolism, verbal music, etc.

Sample Essay

(Yeats explores themes of disintegration and immortality in his passionately personal quest for truth)

1. *I wholeheartedly agree that Yeats is a passionate poetic voice. Alienated, despondent, hurt and disenchanted, his poems rage as he examines the decay in his personal life and the corruption in political and business life. Yeats refused to accept the hypocritical reality. Instead, he dared to imagine the ideal which transcends time and place.*

2. *In 'The Lake Isle of Innisfree', the tranquil atmosphere is conveyed by the phrase 'and peace comes dropping slow'. The beauty of immortal nature has been conjured up by the poet. Yeats stored this hypnotic image in his mind and returned to it every time he needed escape from the sombre monotony of city life, 'while I stand on the roadway or on the pavements grey'. He heard it in 'the deep heart's core'. The poet dared to dream a dream which is universally appealing. He captured for me the immortal stillness of nature again in 'The Wild Swans at Coole': 'The trees are in their autumn beauty,/The woodland paths are dry,/Under the October twilight the water/Mirrors a still sky'. Nature embodies truth. These poems reflect his deep yearning for truth and beauty – a refuge from all the aspects of real life which he found unbearable.*

3. *I found 'September 1913' a scathing attack on modern Ireland, avaricious, selfish and materialistic. Yeats wrote this poem primarily in response to the 1913 Lockout and*

the failure to fund the Hugh Lane Gallery with its collection of wonderful modern art. The anger is evident as he graphically describes these self-centred people who are concerned with outward appearances only. The phrase 'fumble in a greasy till' shows their obsession with money. Equally depressing is their attitude to religion which does not sustain them, but 'dries the marrow from the bone'. The image illustrates the disintegration of the self-serving Irish ruling class. In contrast, the Fenian poet John O'Leary is what an Irishman should be, someone who thought of his country, not himself. The refrain 'It's with O'Leary in the grave' drives this message home, as Yeats gets angrier at the inability of people to understand the bigger picture. Bitterly he resigns himself to the fact that his contemporaries just don't understand and he warns them not to judge these heroes by their own standards, 'But let them be ... They're with O' Leary in the grave'.

4. 'Easter 1916' I particularly liked because Yeats was big enough to admit he was wrong. The people he had condemned in the previous poem were capable of great sacrifices and indeed 'A terrible beauty' was born. Even Major MacBride who had married Maud Gonne, the love of Yeats's life, 'A drunken vainglorious lout', was included in 'the song'. Yeats admires the revolutionary spirit and their dream for independence for Ireland. But his choice of 'the stone' as a symbol of this spirit warns of danger. Sacrifice can turn a heart to stone: 'O when may it suffice?' He dares to criticise political fanaticism. The poem ends with a list of holy names, of the dead, they are 'changed' and will be remembered 'wherever green is worn'. The Easter Rising changed politics. It is a force which rose from the chaos and is now immortal, an enduring and honourable part of our history.

5. In 'Sailing to Byzantium', Yeats rages against old age and death. He writes from an unusual perspective, looking back as he embarks on a journey. He realises he has to go because 'That is no country for old men.' The alliteration shows a fertile land teeming with passionate young life. 'Fish, flesh, or fowl, commend all summer long/ whatever is begotten, born and dies.' He is disenchanted at the hedonism of the young who neglect art. Pitiful images describe old age, 'A tattered coat upon a stick', something that is only used to scare birds. Again, Yeats longs to escape. He decides that he will not have a body which is natural because then it is subject to age. This fierce resistance to old age and its mortal disintegration is a central theme. The poet yearns to discard his ageing body 'consume my heart away' and become an 'artifice'. He really wishes to be with 'the young/In one another's arms'. Yeats also refers to

the devastating consequences of disintegration in 'The Second Coming' with the terrifying lines 'Things fall apart; the centre cannot hold;/Mere anarchy is loosed upon the world'.

6. Yeats evokes the chaos of sudden change in memorable similes, 'They have gone about the world like wind' and vivid visual images, 'scatter wheeling in great broken wings'. But he realises that truth is attained by educating the imagination with art. He describes this idea in the alliterative lines, 'Nor is there singing school but studying/Monuments of its own magnificence'. Truth is emotional 'A lonely impulse of delight' but it is finely tuned which is shown in the delicately constructed line, 'I balanced all, brought all to mind'. I found that Yeats's exploration of disintegration led him to find immortal truth as he created images of delight for me and so many others to enjoy. Yeats is a poet who sings to us 'Of what is past, or passing or to come'.

(approx. 860 words)

Examiner's Comment

An admirable response to a very challenging question. Overall, expression is impressive throughout. There is also clear evidence of focused personal engagement. Most points are effectively supported with a wide range of accurate quotations. However, some of the references – particularly in the final paragraph – could have been contextualised.

GRADE: A2
P = 13/15
C = 12/15
L = 13/15
M = 5/5
Total = 43/50

SAMPLE LEAVING CERT QUESTIONS ON YEATS'S POETRY

(45/50 MINUTES)

1. 'W.B. Yeats examines the relationship between nature and art through his use of symbolism and dramatic language.' Write a response to this view with reference to both the style and subject matter of Yeats's poetry. Support your points with suitable reference to the poems on your course.

2. 'Yeats is a poet who confronts old age fearlessly and with regret.' Discuss this statement, referring both to the subject matter and style of W.B. Yeats's poems. Support your views by reference to the poems on your course.

3. 'Yeats's poetry is defined by the contrast between the real world in which the poet lives and the ideal world.' Write a response to this statement, supporting your answer with close reference to the poems by Yeats on your course.

Sample Essay Plan (Q1)

'Yeats's poetry is defined by the contrast between the real world in which the poet lives and the ideal world.' Write a response to this statement, supporting your answer with close reference to the poems by Yeats on your course.

- Intro: Clear evidence of contrast is required; mention both themes and style in the response. Public and personal poems provide grounds of the conflict between reality and the ideal.

- Point 1: 'September 1913' – public poem, accusatory. Note the changing refrain, litany, rhetorical questions, bitter tone, nostalgic view of Irish history. Savage contrast between the selfish society he saw and the ideal world that no longer exists.

- Point 2: 'Easter 1916' – another public poem, an attempt to answer questions raised by the 1916 Rising. All had changed. Yeats admits he was wrong.

- Point 3: 'The Wild Swans at Coole' – autumnal retrospection as the poet realises how his life has changed over the years. Laments loss of youth, passion and love. Compares transience and old age with the immortality of the swans.

- Point 4: 'Sailing to Byzantium' – theme of ageing, use of contrast to convey theme, repetition, declamatory opening, uncertainty a sign of his humanity.

- Conclusion: Yeats – ideal past contrasted with unsatisfactory present, attitude to Irish patriotism, escape, ageing. Raises questions rather than providing answers.

Sample Essay Plan (Q1)

Develop one of the above points into a paragraph.

Sample Paragraph: Point 4

'Sailing to Byzantium' is an intriguing poem. Yeats hated the weaknesses brought on by old age: 'An aged man is but a paltry thing'. Yet with passion, he defies Time, 'Once out of nature I shall never take/My bodily form from any natural thing'.

The rhythmic phrasing conveys the natural harmony of youth and fertility: 'Fish, flesh, or fowl'. This is the world of which Yeats wants to be a part: 'The young/In one another's arms'. But that is not life. He presents us with the contrasting truth: 'That is no country for old men.' Again, the difference is shown as the beauty of 'artifice': 'the gold mosaic of a wall' is lined up against the brute reality of the soul 'fastened to a dying animal'. The poet through his clever comparisons explores the dilemma of ageing, which faces everyone, even though at eighteen, it seems very remote to me. I was also interested in Yeats's discovery of a flaw in Paradise. Now Yeats is immortal as his soul has now taken the bodily form of a golden bird, 'such a form as Grecian goldsmiths make/Of hammered gold and gold enamelling'. However, the audience for his songs and poems, the Emperor, is 'drowsy' and not paying attention. Yeats is now raising the question – is paradise, 'artifice', all that it is supposed to be? Who will listen as Yeats sings of the great truths, 'Of what is past, or passing, or to come'? Yeats is forced to raise questions about life and existence for us to consider as he highlights the clear differences between what is and what can be, if imagined.

Examiner's Comment

As part of a full essay answer, this is a competent grade-A standard that offers a personal response firmly rooted in the text of the poem. The paragraph focuses well on the use of contrast used by Yeats to explore ageing, and both style and content are examined effectively. Very well supported by a range of suitable quotes.

LAST WORDS

'All that is beautiful in art is laboured over.'

W.B. Yeats

'Yeats's poetry is simple and eloquent to the heart.'

Robert Louis Stevenson

'I have spent my life saying the same thing in different ways.'

W.B. Yeats writing to his wife

Glossary of Common Literary Terms

alliteration: the use of the same letter at the beginning of each word or stressed syllable in a line of verse, e.g. 'boilers bursting'.

assonance: the use of the same vowel sound in a group of words, e.g. 'bleared, smeared with toil'.

aubade: a celebratory morning song, sometimes lamenting the parting of lovers.

blank verse: unrhymed iambic pentameter, e.g. 'These waters, rolling from their mountain-springs'.

conceit: an elaborate image or far-fetched comparison, e.g. 'This flea is you and I, and this/Our marriage bed'.

couplet: two successive lines of verse, usually rhymed and of the same metre, e.g. 'So long as men can breathe or eyes can see,/So long lives this, and this gives life to thee'.

elegy: a mournful poem, usually for the dead, e.g. 'Sleep in a world your final sleep has woken'.

emotive language: language designed to arouse an emotional response in the reader, e.g. 'For this that all that blood was shed?'

epiphany: a moment of insight or understanding, e.g. 'Somebody loves us all'.

free verse: unrhymed and unmetred poetry, often used by modern poets, e.g. 'but the words are shadows and you cannot hear me./You walk away and I cannot follow'.

imagery: descriptive language or word-pictures, especially appealing to the senses, e.g. 'He was speckled with barnacles,/fine rosettes of lime'.

irony: when one thing is said and the opposite is meant, e.g. 'For men were born to pray and save'.

lyric: short musical poem expressing feeling.

metaphor: image that compares two things without using the words 'like' or 'as', e.g. 'I am gall, I am heartburn'.

onomatopoeia: the sound of the word imitates or echoes the sound being described, e.g. 'The murmurous haunt of flies on summer eves'.

paradox: a statement that on the surface appears self-contradictory, e.g. 'I shall have written him one/poem maybe as cold/And passionate as the dawn'.

persona: the speaker or voice in the poem. This is not always the poet, e.g. 'I know that I shall meet my fate/Somewhere among the clouds above'.

personification: where the characteristics of an animate or living being are given to something inanimate, e.g. 'The yellow fog that rubs its back upon the window panes'.

rhyme: identical sound of words, usually at the end of lines of verse, e.g. 'I get down on my knees and do what must be done/And kiss Achilles' hand, the killer of my son'.

rhythm: the beat or movement of words, the arrangement of stressed and unstressed, short and long syllables in a line of poetry, e.g. 'I will arise and go now, and go to Innisfree'.

sestina: a six-stanza, six-line poem with the same six end words occurring throughout. The final stanza contains these six words. 'Time to plant tears, says the almanac:/

The grandmother sings to the marvellous stove/and the child draws another inscrutable house'.

sibilance: the whispering, hissing 's' sound, e.g. 'Singest of summer in full-throated ease'.

sonnet: a 14-line poem. The Petrarchan or Italian sonnet is divided into eight lines (octave), which present a problem or situation. The remaining six lines (sestet) resolve the problem or present another view of the situation. The Shakespearean sonnet is divided into three quatrains and concludes with a rhyming couplet, either summing up what preceded or reversing it.

symbol: a word or phrase representing something other than itself, e.g. 'A tattered coat upon a stick'.

theme: the central idea or message in a poem.

tone: the type of voice or attitude used by the poet towards his or her subject, e.g. 'O but it is dirty'.

villanelle: a five-stanza poem of three lines each, with a concluding quatrain, using only two end rhyming words throughout, e.g. 'I am just going outside and may be some time,/At the heart of the ridiculous, the sublime'.

Acknowledgements

The authors and publisher are grateful to the following for permission to reproduce copyrighted material:

'At the Fishhouses', 'In the Waiting Room', 'Filling Station', 'First Death in Nova Scotia', 'Questions of Travel', 'Sestina', 'The Armadillo', 'The Bight', 'The Fish' and 'The Prodigal' by Elizabeth Bishop from *The Complete Poems, 1927-1979*. Copyright © 1979, 1983 by Alice Helen Methfessel. Reprinted by permission of Farrar, Straus and Giroux, LLC;

The poems by Emily Dickinson are reprinted by permission of the publishers and the Trustees of Amherst College from *The Poems of Emily Dickinson*, Thomas H. Johnson, ed., Cambridge, Mass: The Belknap Press of Harvard University Press, Copyright © 1951, 1955, 1979, 1983 by the President and Fellows of Harvard College;

'En Famille, 1979', 'Father's Day, 21 June 1992', 'Ireland 2002', 'Madman', 'Nessa', 'Parents', 'Rosie Joyce', 'Six Nuns Die in Convent Inferno', 'Sport', 'The Arnolfini Marriage', 'The Difficulty That Is Marriage', 'The Girl with the Key's to Pearse's Cottage', 'The MacBride Dynasty', 'Wife Who Smashed Television Gets Jail' and ' "Windfall", 8 Parnell Hill, Cork', by Paul Durcan from *Life is a Dream: 40 Years Reading Poems 1967–2007* (Harvill Secker, 2009). Copyright © Paul Durcan 2009. Reproduced by permission of the author c/o Rogers, Coleridge & White Ltd., 20 Powis Mews, London W11 1JN;

'A Game of Chess', 'Aunt Helen', 'East Coker IV', 'Journey of the Magi', 'The Love Song of J. Alfred Prufrock', 'Preludes', 'Rannoch by Glencoe' and 'Usk' by T.S. Eliot are reproduced by kind permission of Faber and Faber Ltd;

'Ambulances' 'An Arundel Tomb', 'At Grass', 'Church Going', 'Cut Grass', 'MCMXIV', 'The Explosion', 'The Trees', 'The Whitsun Weddings' and 'Wedding-Wind' by Philip Larkin are reproduced by kind permission of Faber and Faber Ltd;

Poems of Eiléan Ní Chuilleanáin reprinted by kind permission of the author and The Gallery Press, Loughcrew, Oldcastle, County Meath, Ireland, from *Selected Poems* (2008) and *The Sun-fish* (2009);

Collected Poems by Sylvia Plath © Sylvia Plath. Reprinted by kind permission of Faber & Faber Ltd.

The authors and publisher have made every effort to trace all copyright holders, but if any has been inadvertently overlooked we would be pleased to make the necessary arrangement at the first opportunity.

Mirror Quotes: Poem deals with self perceptions / self knowledge.

"Whatever I see I swallow immediately." = the mirror returns images goo[d?]

"I am not cruel, only truthful" It is truthful, unbiased, not affected by love/[?]

"The eye of a little god, four cornered" Metaphor, comparison to God.

"It is pink, with speckles. I have looked at it for so long I think it is part of m[y] heart, but it flickers". Describing the mirror and the mirrors heart. tender bone. Poem deals with the troubled self.

2nd Stanza:

"Now I am a lake, a woman bends over me, searching my reaches for what she i[s?] This shows plaths lost identity Metaphor, comparing the lake to a mirror The only difference between a mirror and a lake is a lake has more inner depth, it can hide things, mirrors can't.

"I am important to her, she comes and goes" shows plaths insecurity.

"In me she has drowned a young girl and in me an old woman rises day after day like a terrible fish". This is a metaphor for the aging process. Time will pass inevitably. Mortality is very evident here, time will effect us all at some stage and we will all appear to be drowned young girls in the reflection of a mirror, our youth will be drowned and gone forever.

Child - Sylvia Plath. Poem deals with theme of motherhood.

"your clear eye is the one absolutely beautiful thing. I want to fill it with colour and ducks. The zoo of the new" This sugge[sts] to me that there is not much beauty surrounding her, her child[?] to her most prized possession. I feel she wants to give her child the absolute best judging by this quote. I feel she longs to give he[r] child beautiful and colourful images which to me evokes the childlike feeling of wonder and awe.

2nd Stanza: "April snowdrops, Indian pipe" By this quote I get the idea of her comparing her child to snowdrops, I get the images of flowers and spring which evokes a real positive and hopeful feeling in me. I love the metaphor of comparing her child to April snowdr[ops]

3rd Stanza: "Stalk without wrinkle, pool in which all images should be grand and classical" From this quote I get the idea that she perceives her child to be unblemished and untouched from any feeling of turmoil in life. I feel she only